YANKEE MISSIONARIES
IN THE SOUTH

YANKEE MISSIONARIES IN THE SOUTH

The Penn School Experiment

ELIZABETH JACOWAY

Louisiana State University Press
Baton Rouge and London

Copyright © 1980 by Louisiana State University Press
All rights reserved
Manufactured in the United States of America

The photographs are from the Penn Normal, Industrial and Agricultural School Papers in the Southern Historical Collection, Library of the University of North Carolina at Chapel Hill, and are used with the permission of Penn Community Services, Frogmore, South Carolina.

The author gratefully acknowledges permission to use material originally published in "Education for Life: The Penn School Experience," *South Atlantic Urban Studies*, II (1978).

Designer: Elizabeth A. Martin
Typeface: VIP Baskerville
Composition: LSU Press
Printing: Thomson-Shore, Inc.
Binding: John H. Dekker and Sons, Inc.

LIBRARY OF CONGRESS CATALOGING IN PUBLICATION DATA

Jacoway, Elizabeth, 1944–
Yankee missionaries in the South.

Bibliography: p.
Includes index.
1. Penn School, St. Helena Island, S. C. I. Title.
T171.P45J32   373.2′46′0975799   79–21024
ISBN 0–8071–0571–6

*With grateful appreciation and deep respect
this book is dedicated to*

Edith Mitchell Dabbs

*friend to St. Helena
friend to me*

It was on these islands off the coast of South Carolina that the last of the slave ships discharged their cargo of primitive Africans, bootlegged across the Atlantic long after the outlawing of the trade. And it was here on these islands, occupied during the early years of the war by Union forces, that emancipation first reached the southern cotton lands and beginnings were made by Negro freeholders on their own small plots.

A great human responsibility developed from the freeing of these simple, carefree, dependent people, wrested from their native life and marooned in ignorance under slavery. Freed—they had to be taught how to live as free men.

—Penn School Publicity Film, 1942

CONTENTS

	Preface	xiii
1	The Industrial Education Myth	1
2	The Rebirth of Penn School	23
3	Transitions	47
4	Community Building	62
5	Crises and Opportunities	82
6	Things of the Spirit and Service	101
7	New Challenges, New Beginnings	120
8	The More Abundant Life	138
9	Old Problems, New Appeals	162
10	Spreading the Gospel	181
11	The Outside Presses In	202
12	Years of Struggle	220
13	Years of Decline	238
14	The Penn School Experiment	252

APPENDICES

A	Penn School Trustees	269
B	Calendar of the All-Year School	272
C	Contributors to the Penn Normal, Industrial, and Agricultural School	273
	Bibliography	279
	Index	297

ILLUSTRATIONS

Following page 100

Original Penn schoolhouse, 1902
Founders' Hall, 1905
Penn School's teachers, 1905
Aunt Jane's cabin
Thaddeus Watkins' home
Prophet Wyne planting corn
Mrs. Green winnowing rice
Middleton, an island fisherman
Joshua Blanton
St. Helena Island and vicinity

Following page 180

Rossa Belle Cooley and Grace Bigelow House
Dr. Hollis Burke Frissell
Old Negro Civil War soldiers
Penn School laundry
Frissell Memorial Community House, 1925
Dedication of the Frissell Memorial, 1925
Old South Pines School, 1933
New South Pines School
Bas-relief of Frissell
Ndulamo

PREFACE

Just off the coast of South Carolina, midway between Charleston and Savannah, the sleepy island of St. Helena lies unnoticed and unremarked, quietly concealing a colorful and dramatic history and a significant heritage. Home of the famed Sea Island cotton—world renowned for its fine long staple—St. Helena Island became in 1862 the center of the Port Royal Experiment, a northern abolitionist scheme which sought to prove that even the coarsest of field hands could be taught to be responsible, productive citizens. Northern missionaries poured into the area in the early years of the war, and the island churches and plantation houses soon resounded with the noises of black children and their parents learning to read. Although most of these little schools collapsed with the loss of crusading fervor at the end of the war, one of them, Penn School, managed to weather the shifting tides of fortune on the island for nearly a hundred years.

Reflecting the goals and assumptions of the larger Port Royal Experiment, the founders of Penn School hoped ultimately to prove to a skeptical public that Negroes were worthy of their freedom. For forty years the two northern missionaries at St. Helena labored at the tasks of education and uplift, but as one year followed another and more pressing concerns captured the nation's attention, northern interest in the experiment waned, and the island fell into an undisturbed serenity. In the winter of 1900 a veteran white educator made his way to St. Helena Island, and he was thrilled by the possibilities of using this isolated island and school as a "laboratory" to test his social theories. Convinced that the black character was malleable and that the Hampton-Tuskegee program of industrial education could mold it into a form more pleasing to middle-class sensibilities, this principal of Hampton Institute adopted Penn School as a protégé; attempting to put an end to the frightening "Negro Problem" by altering black values and behavior, he hoped also to allay white fears of black "depravity" by providing "proof" of black capabilities. Thirty years later a young sociologist repeated this experience, exulting in the island's isolation from other shaping influences and echoing the older man's call for proof. Today there is proof in abundance, and yet the mood of popular opinion has moved away from the desire—or the taste—for such human evidence. St. Helena Island has slipped once again into the obscurity and anonymity that the Hampton educator disrupted.

The Penn School story allows the most unusual opportunity of following day-by-day the application of an ideology. For forty years after 1900, Penn School's admirers and supporters proclaimed it to be a near-perfect embodiment of the Hampton-Tuskegee program of industrial education, and thus the Penn School experience holds promise of offering new insight into the goals and assumptions of that solution to the "Negro Problem."

The white participants in the Penn School experience—the principals, trustees, and supporters—were an unusually articulate band of men and women. Well-educated and highly literate, they expressed their ideas clearly and often; and they left behind a voluminous collection of letters and papers from which it has been possible to reconstruct their story. Because they were scattered up and down the eastern seaboard, they resorted to pen and ink with a frequency that has alternately staggered and delighted their historian; and because they were acutely conscious of themselves as participants in the unfolding drama of American democracy, they recorded and preserved with great care a great variety of information about themselves and their experiment in Negro education. From this vast collection of correspondence, annual reports, trustees' minutes, and other assorted memorabilia one can discern not only what kinds of programs Penn School fostered, but also what the white participants expected these programs to accomplish.

The Penn School experience suggests that industrial education, as formulated at Hampton Institute and as championed by its Yankee supporters, was at its core a program of moral uplift and development. Not only was it not designed to train and exploit a cheap black labor supply, it was not designed to relegate black Americans to an inferior social status. Its champions accepted an inferior status for blacks as a matter of course—and as a legitimate, if temporary, expedient—but the motivating force behind their concern for industrial education was not a desire to trap black Americans in a web of white supremacy. Instead, the Penn School experience suggests that the northern interest in industrial education was stimulated, ultimately, by a desire to liberate blacks from what was perceived to be their "depravity"; by instilling in black Americans all the prerequisites of "character," these Yankee missionaries hoped to defend American democracy from the perils of immorality and ignorance. In this sense the industrial education "experiment" in Negro education was as misguided as it was hopeful, as arrogant as it was naive.

Many people have contributed to the completion of this study. Joel Williamson suggested the topic and encouraged the first efforts at analysis, and he has been a warm friend and rigorous critic through every stage of the process. George Tindall supervised the dissertation, and his example of excellence has been a continuing inspiration and challenge. Donald G. Mathews' penetrating questions and unfailing support redirected my efforts and rekindled my enthusiasm at many a crucial juncture.

My dear friend Edith Dabbs has shared unsparingly, over the years, of her wealth of knowledge about St. Helena Island, of her voluminous Penn School manuscript collection, of her marvelous refuge at Rip Raps Plantation, and most important, of her wisdom and friendship. She has helped to make of the reconstruction process an adventure and an experience of growth.

Numerous friends and colleagues have devoted long and fruitful hours to discussions of Penn School; most important among these have been Phillip Muller, Dorothy Gay, Joseph Herzenberg, George Pozzetta, Richard Scher, and Patricia Schmidt. The staff of the Southern Historical Collection at the University of North Carolina assisted me through many months of research, and I owe a special thanks to Isaac Copeland, Carolyn Wallace, Anna Brooke Allen, Mike Martin, and Ellen Neal. My typists, Muriel Dyer, Sarah Ramirez, and Jean Williams, suffered patiently through many drafts; and the National Endowment for the Humanities provided financial assistance at a crucial stage of the process.

Several other people have read the manuscript in various

stages of completion. For their fair-minded criticisms I want to thank William W. Freehling, Paul and Mary Gaston, Ernest Lander, and James McPherson.

Finally, but certainly not least, I owe a special debt to Augustus M. Burns. Without his encouragement and support this project would never have been initiated; without his patience and understanding, it would never have been completed.

All of the people named above, and many others as well, have contributed time and energy to recapturing the Penn School experience. Whatever merits this book may possess are attributable in large measure to these friends; whatever limitations remain—whether of conception or expression—I acknowledge as my own.

*YANKEE MISSIONARIES
IN THE SOUTH*

1

The Industrial Education Myth

On a warm September day in 1895, a young black teacher rose up out of the South and offered a solution to a great national problem; with one stroke, with one masterful speech, Booker Taliaferro Washington captivated the American people and became the spokesman for his race. Speaking in Atlanta during a period of degenerating racial relations, Washington addressed himself to the primary source of white concern about the fearful "Negro Problem," the issue of social equality. "The wisest among my race," he assured his listeners, "understand that the agitation of questions of social equality is the extremest folly, and that progress in the enjoyment of all the privileges that will come to us must be the result of severe and constant struggle rather than of artificial forcing." The right to struggle—this was all that Washington asked for his people, in return for which white America could rest assured that, "In all things that are purely social we can be as separate as the fingers, yet one as the hand in all things essential to mutual progress."[1] The right to struggle—to equip themselves for economic usefulness and efficiency, to develop character and a spirit of service to the community—these were the goals that Washington sought and pleaded for in Atlanta. These were the skills and attributes that he believed would

1. Booker Taliaferro Washington, *Up From Slavery* (Rev. ed.; Garden City, N.Y., 1947), 219.

put an end to the "Negro Problem" and that he had learned at Hampton Institute could be gained through industrial education.

The industrial education idea, as developed at Hampton and later replicated at Washington's Tuskegee Institute, sought primarily to prepare young blacks for economic self-sufficiency, usefulness to the community, and intelligent and upright living. It was subject to many different interpretations, however, and thus the industrial education idea appealed to a broad range of people and for a variety of reasons. Coming into the national consciousness, as it did, at the very moment when America's industrial boom had captured the nation's imagination, industrial education seemed to many to be preeminently suited to develop a much-needed trained and efficient laboring force. Emphasizing the possibilities for the Negro in southern agriculture and supplying him with modern, intelligent farming methods, the industrial education idea seemed also to assure that the nation's blacks would remain in a subordinate, though contented, social and economic position. And perhaps most important, preaching as it always did the value of hard work in developing character, the Hampton idea promised white America that it would lift the Negro out of his supposed sloth and immorality and make of him a safe, if not an equal, neighbor. Whatever its merits or its actual intent, since 1895 the industrial education idea has been linked with the social accomodation Booker T. Washington elaborated in Atlanta, and the failures of the "compromise" have colored all evaluations of the Hampton-Tuskegee solution to America's racial dilemma.

For the last half-century and more, historians have regarded industrial education as a product of compromise—between North and South, between black and white. Following the lead of W. E. B. Dubois, historians have argued consistently that the "compromise" of 1895 was simply an extension of the compromise of 1877, and they have interpreted the Hampton-Tuskegee plan of industrial education as an accommodation to the demands of the white South; whether it was a result of callous deception or of pitiful naivete, they have concluded, industrial education assured both white supremacy and a trained labor supply. Black historian Henry Allen Bullock was one of the leading critics of what he called "the great detour" in black education. "Since the South

The Industrial Education Myth

would not accept any other kind of Negro education," he wrote, " ... leaders of the [industrial education movement] struck a compromise with the South and settled for a special kind of education that would prepare Negroes for the caste position prescribed for them by white Southerners." August Meier was similarly disenchanted with the industrial education idea. "Negroes were to be 'uplifted,'" he suggested, "to the extent that they would adopt middle-class virtues and thus be a docile and stable laboring force." Both of these historians, and many others as well, interpreted industrial education as a cynical exploitation of the black's aspirations that took his yearnings for dignity and advancement and turned them against him.[2]

The three leading interpretations of industrial education—that it was an extension of the campaign for white supremacy, that it was designed to exploit black labor, and that it was outmoded even as it was being implemented—have engendered considerable cynicism; they have also blinded historians to important and revealing perspectives on the industrial education idea. In their haste to castigate the racist past and find assurances that old errors can be transcended, modern historians have allowed major questions about the industrial education movement to remain un-

2. William Edward Burghardt Du Bois, "The Talented Tenth," in *The Negro Problem: A Series of Articles by Representative American Negroes of Today* (New York, 1903) and "Of Mr. Booker T. Washington and Others," in *Souls of Black Folk* (Chicago, 1904). Du Bois announced his opposition to industrial education in these two articles and maintained an ever-growing opposition through nearly half a century as editor of the *Crisis*, the magazine of the National Association for the Advancement of Colored People. For discussions of industrial education as an accommodation to southern racial prejudices see, among others: Claude Nolen, *The Negro's Image in the South: The Anatomy of White Supremacy* (Lexington, Ky., 1967); Horace Mann Bond, *The Education of the Negro in the American Social Order* (New York, 1934); Henry Allen Bullock, *A History of Negro Education in the South from 1619 to the Present* (Cambridge, Mass., 1967), 689; George Brown Tindall, *South Carolina Negroes: 1877–1900* (Columbia, S.C., 1952); George Brown Tindall, *The Emergence of the New South, 1913–1945* (Baton Rouge, La., 1967); C. Vann Woodward, *Origins of the New South, 1877–1913* (Baton Rouge, La., 1951); August Meier, *Negro Thought in America, 1880–1915: Racial Ideologies in the Age of Booker T. Washington* (Ann Arbor, Mich., 1963), 93; Hugh C. Bailey, *Liberalism in the New South: Social Reformers and the Progressive Movement* (Coral Gables, Fla., 1969). For discussions of industrial education as a means of exploiting black labor, see especially Meier above and Merle Curti, *Social Ideas of American Educators* (New York, 1935). For discussions of industrial education as an outmoded program see Woodward and Bond above and John Hope Franklin, *From Slavery to Freedom: A History of American Negroes* (New York, 1947). For similar criticisms see also Jack Temple Kirby, *Darkness at the Dawning: Race and Reform in the Progressive South* (Philadelphia, 1972); Idus A. Newby, *Black Carolinians: A History of Blacks in South Carolina from 1865–1968* (Columbia, S.C., 1973).

answered, even unasked. Who, for instance, were the supporters of the movement? Who provided the funds to maintain Hampton and Tuskegee and the dozens of smaller schools patterned after them throughout the South? And why were they interested? What were the motivating forces behind the concern for industrial education? Of even greater importance, what were the programs of these schools, and what were the goals being sought? Surely these questions must be answered before any meaningful analysis can be attempted of the industrial education movement.

These questions have not been answered satisfactorily for a number of reasons. The primary difficulty has been one of perspective: historians have tended to concentrate on the outcome of the industrial education movement—analyzing the product rather than the process—and often they have read history backwards from the outcome to the intent. More important, historians have not made extended studies of any of the small schools where industrial education was practiced, primarily because few of these records have been preserved. The practical problem undoubtedly stimulated the methodological one, but the result has been an unacceptable distortion of past experience.

Fortunately, the records of one of these schools—Penn School on St. Helena Island, South Carolina—have been preserved and have recently been made available to scholars, and they are unusually full. Revealing the day-to-day life of this one institution over a period of forty years, the records of this small school, which was widely acclaimed as a model of industrial education, also reveal some overlooked dimensions of the larger industrial education movement.

Of primary importance, and most surprising to those who have learned that industrial education was an extension of the southern campaign for white supremacy, the Penn School experience reveals that industrial education was developed through, and sustained by, northern energies and support. Other historians have noted the northern element in the industrial education movement, but they have argued consistently that the northern supporters simply acquiesced in what was essentially a southern solution. The Penn School experience suggests that northern patricians formulated the program and that southern needs and demands were very rarely considered. Equally important, the Penn School experience suggests that the industrial education solution to what was then called the "Negro Problem" developed in response to the needs of northern whites rather than in response to the needs of those blacks it ostensibly helped. And finally, the Penn School experience reveals that the ultimate goal of these northern supporters was the creation of morality, or what they called "character," in the black population of the South.

The modern researcher has often been led astray in his analysis of industrial education because of semantic differences between the present and the past. *Character*, for instance, and *service*—two words that are central to an understanding of the industrial education movement—no longer convey the meanings they held for an earlier time. Similarly, *industrial*, as in *industrial education*, has lost its earlier connotations. Understandably, most modern observers, as well as many in the earlier age, have assumed that industrial education was a response to the industrial revolution, and thus they have expected the Hampton program to provide preparation for life in an industrial age. This was not the case, however; as a close reading of the evidence reveals, industrial education was a moral program designed to inculcate the primary virtue of *industry*, and industry was thought to be the keystone in the arch of moral development. As Hampton's founder had explained it, "In all men, education is conditioned not alone on an enlightened head and a changed heart, but very largely on a routine of *industrious* habits, which is to *character* what the foundation is to the pyramid. It should never be forgotten that it is only upon a foundation of regular daily activities that there can be any fine and permanent upbuilding. *Morality* and *industry* generally go together" (italics added).[3]

In its original design, industrial education was much more than vocational education, which merely provides the student with a skill and prepares him to earn a living. As conceived at Hamp-

   3. As quoted in Thomas Jesse Jones (ed.), *Negro Education: A Study of the Private and Higher Schools for Colored People in the United States* (2 vols. Washington, D.C., 1917), 82.

ton Institute and practiced at Penn School, industrial education aimed to teach its students nothing less than "how to live"; it was, in other words, an "education for life." An article in Hampton's *Southern Workman* described "The Real Aim of Industrial Schools": A "very significant movement in educational thought is that which defines education as learning how to live. Not how to know nor even how to think is the all-in-all of education; how to live is now stated by progressive educators to be the true aim of all schools." Furthermore, the article continued, although many people feared that the industrial schools had been "captured by materialists to accomplish some selfish end," these people simply did not understand that the term *industrial* should not be taken to mean that "the chief end of the institution is to develop mechanical skill.... The chief end of the industrial schools, at least of those among the colored people, is the development of *character* and the squaring of the educational system with the demands of the best in life" (italics added).[4]

Thomas Jesse Jones, author of the government-sponsored study of *Negro Education* in 1916 and a proponent of the Hampton philosophy, described the program as follows: "The phrase 'industrial education' as applied to colored schools is very misleading. While the effective industrial schools are making genuine efforts to develop industrial skill, their fundamental purpose is much broader than vocational efficiency and the resulting comfort and culture." Stated differently, although Samuel Chapman Armstrong and Booker T. Washington had regarded industrial and agricultural skill and practical knowledge of household arts as "important by-products" of the school activities, their ultimate aim was always "the development of manhood and womanhood, through the common tasks of the common day, as well as through the ordinary school activities." In other words, their ultimate aim was "the character development of the colored people."[5]

This emphasis on character building can be more readily understood when one identifies the assumptions at the base of the

---

4. "The Real Aim of Industrial Schools," *Southern Workman*, XXXVII (January, 1908), 374-75.

5. Jones, *Negro Education*, 10, 81, 82.

industrial education movement; and this is where the records of the Penn School experience offer the historian their finest insights. Conscious of being engaged in a historically significant enterprise and spread up and down the eastern seaboard, the principals and trustees of Penn School carried on a voluminous correspondence, and they saved everything. From these records it has been possible to reconstruct the mind-set of the genteel northerners who supported Penn School and who were among the guiding spirits in the movement for industrial education for the southern blacks.

Foremost among the social assumptions of the Penn School hierarchy was their belief that they were the natural leaders of society and that their values and attitudes embodied the summit of man's civilization and achievement. Representative of the same genteel tradition as the nationalistic historian George Bancroft, they also believed that American democracy represented the finest expression of God's will on earth and that this creation (over which they had long presided) must at all costs be preserved. At the base of all their beliefs was the certainty that there was a moral and spiritual order in the world, a harmony and rhythm in which man found his place and expressed his faith through rendering service to both God and man. And closely related to their consciousness of order-in-the-world was their belief in progress. The watchword of the American experiment in democracy, progress had been the cardinel tenet of Hegelian idealistic philosophy, and now it had been proven by men of science to be the unquestionable outcome of the workings of the natural universe. As educated men and women who were abreast of the scientific developments of their day, these northern patricians accommodated themselves easily to Darwinian evolutionary philosophy; indeed, from their point of view, their hegemony over American life represented little more than the "survival of the fittest" in the continuing struggle for dominance.

When they attempted to solve the threatening "Negro Problem," these men and women were predisposed to perceive that problem in certain ways. Unquestionably they believed in Anglo-Saxon superiority and the unfortunate but real "fact" of black depravity, but their belief in progress precluded despair. The black man could in time be expected to develop into a responsible, civilized being; but since the evolutionary process was slow if sure, blacks should be content in the meantime to occupy a place in society that reflected their status as apprentices and their failure to contribute to the general well-being. Not only did these patricians conceive of society as being hierarchical, they also believed that all change should be gradual, so as not to rend the fabric of society. Thus if the status of the Negro in American society posed distressing ethical and political questions, plain common sense dictated that the delicate and exquisitely balanced American democratic system should not be exposed to the coarse assaults of those who had received no "preparation for citizenship."

The Negro seemed to these northerners to offer the grossest violation of traditional American values and the greatest threat to the American social and political order since he was perceived to be lazy, shiftless, slothful, improvident, and ultimately criminal. But while the majority of Americans were abandoning the Negro to an ever-worsening fate, these northern patricians adopted him as their special concern; not only did they see this as necessary for the salvation of society, they also saw it as a worthy outlet for the missionary spirit of service. And so they embarked on a venture that was clearly dictated by their assumptions and the problem as they perceived it: they undertook a program of education, assuming quite naturally that it was the black man who needed to change and not they themselves. They did not expect their education of the Negro to interfere with the workings of the evolutionary process; they did expect it to help black Americans to develop nobler conceptions of living that would dignify their lives as subordinates and that would render them a nonthreatening element of society until they had been adequately prepared to participate.

In brief, the industrial education advocates found a solution to black depravity in the old Puritan work ethic. As formulated by Samuel Chapman Armstrong—Hampton's founder and a son of Puritan New England—the argument ran as follows: hard work develops an appreciation of thrift, industry, and order; or in other words, it inculcates those virtues that are the essence of character. Under slavery, however, the black man had come to despise labor, and thus he had lost the possibility of developing those virtues that hard work instills; as a result he had sunk ever deeper into the mire of degradation. Clearly, then, the cure for black moral deficiency was an educational program that would dignify labor and that would train black men and women to appreciate its rewards. Such a program would set blacks on the high road of moral development, promising ultimately to instill those attitudes and values that would allow them to contribute to the welfare of their communities as well as to the spiritual progress of mankind. Not incidentally, the inculcation of these attitudes and values would also render southern blacks nonthreatening—politically, socially, and economically.[6]

Clearly, industrial education did not provide southern blacks with the dignity, the independence, or the economic security Booker T. Washington and Samuel Chapman Armstrong had promised. Just as clearly, as the control of black education fell increasingly into southern hands, economic exploitation and the imposition of caste distinctions became characteristic products of the program Washington had proposed. And yet, although no one could deny that industrial education was mis-education in the sense that it failed to prepare blacks for active participation in twentieth-century life, conclusions about the intent must not be drawn from distressing evidence about the outcome. This has been a persistent methodological problem in the study of indus-

---

6. As James McPherson has demonstrated, as early as 1875 even many abolitionists had come to appreciate the need for character-development among the South's blacks. According to abolitionist Michael Strieby, for thirty years secretary of the American Missionary Association, the root of the race problem was not in the Negro's "color or party, but with the man himself—with his ignorance, his degradation. . . . The remedy, then, is not to change his color or his party, but his character." Accordingly, many abolitionists began to turn their attention to black education and uplift. McPherson argues that "although the *means* of missionary education were often paternalistic, the *ends* were egalitarian." In his words, "the function of the school, as the missionary educators viewed it, was to equip its graduates with both the character and skills necessary for a useful Christian life and for upward mobility in a competitive, capitalist, democratic society." The Penn School experience does not support McPherson's claims of egalitarian goals. James M. McPherson, *The Abolitionist Legacy: From Reconstruction to the NAACP* (Princeton, N.J., 1976), 56, 201.

trial education, and yet it is the intent—not the outcome—that promises to yield the greatest understanding of white participation in the industrial education movement.

The Penn School experience suggests that, as developed at Hampton Institute, industrial education was a missionary program of "uplift," designed primarily to calm northern fears. It was not an accommodation to southern needs and demands; it grew instead out of a northern desire to eliminate the threat—political, social, and economic—that black degradation and ignorance supposedly posed to the dominant culture. Its appeal to the white North lay in its twofold promise: it would inculcate the traditional Yankee virtues of industry, thrift, and self-reliance—or in other words, "character"—in the South's black population; and it would keep blacks in the South until this "civilization" process was completed by assuring them of economic independence and dignified living in their own rural communities.

This is a far cry from the traditional explanations of southern control, economic exploitation, and social subordination. Although the Penn School experience of paternalism and self-satisfied control of black lives may seem equally unacceptable to the modern observer, and although the whole program was a response to white needs rather than black, industrial education was neither spawned in cynicism nor designed for unworthy ends.

The Penn School experiment in black uplift reveals important dimensions of the spirit and the mentality of Progressive America. As a model of industrial education, it illuminates the inner core of that solution to the "Negro Problem"; as an outpost of progressive education, it yields insight into the essential nature of that movement to reform the public schools; and as the special concern of many Progressive reformers, it allows an increased understanding of the motivation behind much Progressive reform.

The concept of character building was not original with Samuel Chapman Armstrong. Traditionally, the development of character had been a primary goal of American education, but the family and the church had always aided that developmental process; with the creation of an "uprooted multitude," however, as a result of urbanization, immigration, and black emancipation, the old supporting institutions could no longer be counted on to assist in moral development—or in other words, to instill the traditional values.[7] Thus many people began to believe that if the country were to be "saved" from losing its age-old strengths, the strengths that had lifted it to unprecedented heights in the history of civilization, some means would have to be found to assure the preservation of its virtues. Consequently the traditional guardians of America's cultural heritage—that genteel band of respectable northerners who were descended from the first families of the nation—turned increasingly to the schools to perform all the necessary functions of "preparing" young people "for life." At the core of this preparation process, of course, was the inculcation of "character," or "morality," or the traditional Yankee virtues. Industrial education was one manifestation of this call for an "education for life"; progressive education was another. As Charles W. Eliot, president emeritus of Harvard University, remarked in eulogizing Hollis Burke Frissell, Hampton Institute "led the way" in the development of progressive education.[8]

The program that Samuel Chapman Armstrong developed at Hampton Institute included all the principles of the "new education," or progressive education as it later came to be called: it involved "learning by doing," developing "the whole child," making the school a microcosm of "real life," adapting education to the needs of the pupil and the community, and ultimately "reconstructing" or "regenerating" the individual as well as society. In effect the new education was an attempt to come to grips with the changed social structure of turn-of-the century America; it was a redefinition of education in response to the needs of the present.

Progressive educators were widely celebrated for having "democratized" education—for having made it responsive to the needs and capabilities of the common man. According to the advocates of the new education, American schools had traditionally served the needs of the upper classes, and educational method

---

7. Timothy L. Smith, "Progressivism in American Education, 1880–1900." *Harvard Educational Review*, XXXI (Spring, 1961), 170.

8. Charles William Eliot, "Dr. Frissell's Influence on Popular Education," *Southern Workman*, XLVI (October, 1917), 598.

and curriculum had changed very little since the Middle Ages; democracy in the content of education, however, demanded that "the curriculum shall impart culture through knowledge and practice related to the farm, the shop, the office, and, above all, the home." In other words, education should relate directly to the lives—and the future possibilities—of its students. Thus Thomas Jesse Jones could write: "Industrial education in the comprehensive sense is the very essence of democracy in education."⁹

Most of the principles of progressive education could be found in Samuel Chapman Armstrong's early annual reports. As the general wrote at one point: "The education needed is one that touches upon the whole range of life. . . . Didactic and dogmatic work has little to do with the formation of character, which is our point. This is done by making the school a little world in itself. . . . School life should be like real life." Furthermore, Armstrong believed: "Real progress is not in increase of wealth or power, but is gained in wisdom, in self control, in guiding principles, and in Christian ideas. That is the only true reconstruction. To that Hampton's work is devoted." The elimination of black "immorality," then, was the goal Armstrong sought through his program of industrial education. As a true son of Puritan New England, he placed his faith in hard work; but "hard work" was simply the mechanism for developing morality. "Subtract hard work from life," he wrote, "and in a few months it will have all gone to pieces. Labor, next to the grace of God in the heart, is the greatest promoter of morality, the greatest power for civilization." The promotion of morality, the "civilization" of a backward people—these were Armstrong's leading goals, and this was the educational message that progressive education inherited from Hampton Institute.¹⁰

The advocates of industrial education—and progressive education—worked to accomplish two things: moral regeneration and social control. As Armstrong's successor, Hollis Burke Frissell, wrote in one of his early annual reports: "Hampton has been called upon to do a pioneer work in education. It has endeavored

9. Jones, *Negro Education*, 83.
10. *Ibid.*, 81, 82.

The Industrial Education Myth 13

to recognize and utilize industrial processes as a means of education. It has striven to lay proper emphasis upon character building and to make use of religion and the work of the hands in attaining this end. It has tried to adapt education to the needs of the type of individual to be educated." All of these principles had been worked out and employed in an effort to lead the blacks and the Indians at Hampton "to realize the responsibilities of civilized life rather than to claim its privileges" and to become self-supporting and prepared to help others to self-support. "In this way," Frissell concluded, "an attempt has been made to point out the solution to a great national problem by teaching a few representatives of the Negro and Indian races *how to adjust themselves to the life of American communities,* thus demonstrating the value of a system that, if generally adopted, will . . . accomplish this adjustment for the masses" (italics added).[11]

Industrial education and progressive education involved the same motivating forces that stimulated the movement to "Americanize" the immigrant. As Lawrence Cremin has written, "To Americanize . . . was to divest the immigrant of his ethnic character and to inculcate the dominant Anglo-Saxon morality. Americanization meant taking on the ways and beliefs of those who embodied the true historic America, the America worth preserving."[12] Americanization, industrial education, and progressive education were all designed to "adjust" the uprooted multitudes to "the life of American communities." They were designed, in other words, to preserve an older America by inculcating the old values, or the old morality, in a people who had not shared the American political and cultural traditions and whose inclusion in the society therefore posed a threat to those traditions.[13] All three

---

11. Hollis Burke Frissell, "Thirty-Seventh Annual Report of the Principal of Hampton Institute," *Southern Workman*, XXXIV (May, 1905), 291.

12. Lawrence Arthur Cremin, *The Transformation of the School: Progressivism in American Education, 1876–1957* (New York, 1961), 68.

13. James McPherson has found this impulse operating in an earlier generation. "In an 1883 speech on 'The Negro in America,'" he writes, "Henry L. Morehouse defined the goal of missionary education as 'America in the Negro,' which meant 'American ideas of citizenship, of church membership, of family life, etc., incorporated into the Negro character.' American ideas in this context were those of white native-born middle-class Protestants. Minority groups were expected to assimilate these ideas before they in

programs stressed vocational and civic training, and the ultimate goal of all three was social regeneration.

In an address before the Southern Sociological Congress in 1913, Grace Bigelow House, assistant principal of Penn School, called for a program to meet the needs of a rapidly changing world. "We are living," she began, "in a stirring age.... We feel the restless change, and are beginning to realize that old traditions, old methods of education, old habits of thought and action are inadequate to grapple with the new problems." Especially inadequate was the old educational system "which is proving unequal to the great task of preparing the youth of our country for efficient and helpful citizenship in our modern America. The solution of the immigration problem, the race problem, the economic and industrial problems depends largely on what kind of citizens our schools are turning out." Shiftlessness, crime, and pauperism, Miss House claimed, could be blamed on a "lack of definite training," and yet the schools were doing very little to prevent these evils. "What is our race problem," she asked, "but the problem of fitting a backward people to lead useful, industrious, and moral lives in the communities where they live? Are our schools giving the kind of training that leads to industry, skill, and strong moral character?"[14]

Miss House claimed that the value of industrial education could be seen in the "efficient service" that the graduates of industrial schools had given to their communities; as proof of this she cited the following facts: "Not a single graduate of the Hampton Institute nor of the Tuskegee Institute can be found today in any jail or State penitentiary.... The records of the South show that 90 per cent of the colored people in prisons are without knowledge of trades, and 61 per cent are illiterate."[15] Industrial

---

turn could become assimilated as full-fledged Americans." In an apt turn of phrase, McPherson concludes that the "principal purpose" of the missionary educators in the South "remained the transformation of the freedmen into ebony Puritans." McPherson, *Abolitionist Legacy*, 184.

14. Grace Bigelow House, "The Need and Purpose of Industrial Education," In James E. McCulloch (ed.), *The Human Way: Addresses on Race Problems at the Southern Sociological Congress, Atlanta, 1913* (Nashville, Tenn., 1913), 89, 90, 91.

15. *Ibid.*, 92.

education, then, was a bulwark against crime and immorality and a creator of happy, useful citizens.

The Penn School program reflected at every point the goals and methods of progressive education. The emphasis on the whole child—his head, his hand, and his heart; the adaptation of the school to the perceived needs of the child; the conception of the school as a social dynamo that must regenerate the life of the community—all were reflected in a simple diagram that Penn's principal, Rossa Belle Cooley, included in an article in the journal entitled *Progressive Education*. Picturing a child in the center of a series of concentric circles, the drawing depicted ever-widening spheres of education opening out from the child through his school to his parents, his farm, his home, and his community.[16] Here was a simple but eloquent statement of the goals of progressive education: education could uplift a whole people, a community at a time.

As originally conceived, industrial education and progressive education were one and the same thing. Contrary to popular belief, the one did not aim to exploit; the other did not aim to liberate. Both were essentially conservative; both were explicitly moral. Designed to control the forces of change in a rapidly changing world, both were products of fear.

The fear that pervaded the respectable North welled up from a single source; but just as the ocean rises by stages over a sandy beach, northern fears were registered and expressed at a number of different levels. On the level most easily perceived, because most often documented, the genteel northerner feared the rise to power of a new breed of men: crude newly rich magnates—railroad, oil, and steel—who abused and threatened free enterprise; callous and corrupt politicians who traded on the immigrant vote; grim-faced financiers and bankers who scoffed at standards and ethics.[17] Threatening not only the social, political, economic, and cultural preeminence of the nation's traditional leaders, the rise

---

16. Rossa Belle Cooley, "Education in the Soil," *Progressive Education*, X (December, 1933), 448–55.
17. See especially George E. Mowry, *The California Progressives* (Berkeley, Calif. 1951); Richard C. Hofstadter, *The Age of Reform: From Bryan to F.D.R.* (New York, 1955).

to power of these men seemed also to assure that traditional American virtues would be swept away in the scramble for power and place. What was at stake was not only the status, but also the values, of the elite.

On a second level, therefore, perceiving themselves to be guardians of the nation's cultural heritage, these respectable northerners believed that their loss of preeminence in society heralded the loss of American virtue. Arrogant, self-satisfied, innocent almost beyond modern comprehension, these patricians equated their values with morality; industry, thrift, frugality, temperance, self-reliance, cleanliness, order—all these and more, they believed, were simply the outward expressions of an inner morality, or character, and without them morality was impossible. Unlettered blacks and immigrants, who had had no opportunity to share in the American cultural and moral tradition, threatened only to augment the forces of plutocracy, socialism, and anarchy that were displacing the values of the elite. Morality itself, therefore, was what the social dislocations of the late nineteenth century were threatening to destroy.

On a third and even deeper level this "loss of morality" seemed an exceptionally frightening prospect to the genteel northerner of the late nineteenth and early twentieth centuries, for he believed morality to be the essence of man's spiritual nature. What had lifted man above the beasts, he believed, was his capacity to order his life in harmony with God's plan and will; and he earnestly believed that his own moral tradition was man's best effort toward the fulfillment of God's will on earth. An inheritor of the Transcendentalist and Evangelical traditions, he believed that Christian progress would come through moral choices; the rise of the Social Gospel reinforced this belief, making "social service" the means of working toward perfection, or of bringing the Kingdom of Heaven on Earth.[18] "Morality," therefore, was essential to the patrician's conception of himself and his conception of the world around him. Without it, he believed, he would

---

18. See especially Timothy L. Smith, *Revivalism and Social Reform in Mid-Nineteenth Century America* (New York, 1957); Daniel Aaron, *Men of Good Hope: A Story of American Progressives* (New York, 1951).

be lost in a spiritual void; and on the very deepest level, this was the source of his fear.

The fear of the loss of spirituality was augmented by the rise of industrialism, which threatened to impede—if not destroy—man's spiritual progress by placing the demands of the machine above the needs of the human spirit. Subordinating humanitarian to mechanical considerations, industrialism promised to cripple the individual will, leaving little room in an amoral system for moral choices and judgments.

The northern patrician dealt with his fears in a completely rational manner, given his perception of the problem. Perceiving "morality" to be essential to man's continued advancement or progress, he devised a series of programs designed to inculcate morality wherever it was lacking—programs that would stand as a bulwark against the potential dehumanization and spiritual stagnation of turn-of-the-century life. The goals to be attained were quite clear: the development of *character*—that mystical blend of the ethical and the moral—which lifted man above the beasts, and the development of a spirit of *service*—an outward sign of grace—through which those values, that morality, could be spread into the world.

The outgrowth of northern fears, what emerged in late nineteenth-century America was essentially a missionary mentality—a disposition not simply to expect deference from the disadvantaged masses, but to crusade with evangelical zeal, and with unexamined arrogance, for "backward" peoples to abandon their threatening differences and assimilate the traditional values. Inextricably intertwined with these patricians' conception of religion, *uplift* became a form of social service that was believed to be as essential to the health of the nation and to the continued advancement of mankind as to the welfare of those being uplifted. The inculcation of morality, therefore, became a means not only of rendering service, but also of increasing God's dominion and precluding dehumanization, as well as of preserving American virtues and reestablishing the leadership of the genteel elite.

The many dimensions of this mentality can be discerned in a Founder's Day speech that Francis Greenwood Peabody, the quintessential northern patrician, delivered at Tuskegee Institute. Harvard professor of ethics and dean of the Divinity School, long-time trustee of Hampton Institute and advocate of the "new education," Social Gospeler and early Progressive, Peabody entitled his speech "Education for Life."[19]

Calling essentially for an education that would lift blacks up to a new level of religious and spiritual understanding, Peabody's speech reflected his fears of black degradation and his eagerness to apply the principles of industrial education and progressive education to the problem of black deficiencies. Praising Booker T. Washington as "the symbol of racial progress up from slavery into a self-sustaining and efficient citizenship," Peabody claimed that Tuskegee's founder had been "called of God to establish peace between two races on whose cooperation the *stability* of this nation depends" (italics added). Furthermore, Peabody claimed, all thoughtful Americans had recently become aware that "the *stability* of our institutions depends on the education of its people. . . . On one thing we are all agreed: that universal education is the cornerstone of democracy" (italics added).[20] But what should be the content of that education. Peabody asked; "what kind of education prepares one for life?"

According to Peabody, education could be approached in either of two ways: from the point of view of the teacher or from the point of view of the pupil, "as a communication of knowledge or as an awakening of life." The first view of education had prevailed for hundreds of years, but within the past generation an educational revolution had occurred that involved a complete change of method. Its purpose was to "draw out the mind of the pupil into self-development and self-control. . . .What we call the higher education is thus determined," Peabody explained, "not by the subjects taught but by the effect of the subjects taught on the half-awakened mind of the pupil. . . . A human mind, that is to say, is not wax to be molded into a predetermined form but a sensitive and responsive life, which has in it the capacity to grow

---

19. Francis Greenwood Peabody, "Education for Life," *Southern Workman*, LV (June, 1926), 248–56.
20. *Ibid.*

and must grow in its own way." In the name of flexibility, therefore, and of being responsive to "the needs, experiences and capacities of the pupil," the "new education" had come to reflect, and perpetuate, the hierarchical view of society that its patrician advocates believed to be elemental in proper social relations.

Peabody explained that the new education involved three principles that made it an education for life. First was the principle of *individualization*, or the belief that since "each life is made for something," education should aim "not to make all lives alike but to make of each what it was meant to be." Peabody did not explain who should determine what each life "was meant to be," but clearly he had no difficulty accepting different kinds of education for different kinds of people.

The second principle—*unification*—recognized the fact that "the pupil's life is not made of separate elements but is a composite unit, of body, mind, and soul, and that to train one part alone is to make life a fragment rather than a unit." Here Peabody claimed to find "the deeper meaning of industrial education" with its "effect . . . upon character and its product in precision, thoroughness, and intellectual integrity." Industrial education had made possible a combination of the three areas of education "to make a whole life," and this was "the great educational discovery of the present age." Industrial education, in other words, had discovered a way to perform all the functions of character building that the church, the family, and the school had performed in an earlier age.

Finally, the new education involved the principle of *spiritualization*. "After all," Peabody claimed, "there is but one thing that distinguishes the life of a human from that of a beast of the field. It is the mysterious fact that while a beast seems governed by animal desires . . . a human being can outgrow the life of the animal and enter into the life of the spirit with its hopes and thoughts, its ideals and dreams." To outgrow the beast "is what humanizes animals and gives a new hunger, not of the stomach but of the mind, the imagination, and the heart." And that is what Peabody believed blacks needed—to be lifted from their animal state into the higher life of the spirit. Peabody continued, "This is what should be called the higher education . . . the drawing out from among the desires of physical life new desires of thought, of will, of faith. This is the aim of industrial education: To lift manual work out of mechanism into a science or an art. . . . In so far as one attains this vision one becomes educated; small tasks become great, and plain things beautiful, and material things spiritual." And that, Peabody claimed, "is where the work of education touches the work of religion. For what is religion but drawing out from within the undiscovered self of the capacity for consecration?"

In the final analysis, Peabody believed religion also was an education for life. "It asks of one, not that fragment of life which we call the soul but the whole of life and the whole at its best. Holiness is but another name for wholeness. . . . To this the education which is offered to you here opens the way," Peabody informed his black audience, "and in this the religion you need is to be found." Concluding on this note, Peabody asked: "Could there be any better way for us to celebrate Founder's Day than to dedicate ourselves, in the spirit of the Founder, to an education which is not for learning only but for the enrichment and consecration and fulfillment of life?"[21]

Here was a complete formula for the resolution of patrician fears: instill the morality, and the conception of religion, which will eliminate the threat to the nation's stability of backward conceptions of life. What Peabody spelled out here was clearly a missionary venture—as condescending and arrogant as such ventures ever are—and the ultimate concern was for the welfare of the dominant group. It involved, however, much more than a simple desire for regained control by a displaced elite; these fearful northern patricians, with Peabody at the fore, believed that the

21. James McPherson quotes Henry L. Morehouse, secretary of the Baptist Home Mission Society, in this vein. According to Morehouse, "It would be 'a narrow conception of missionary effort . . . to suppose that it consists merely of inducing men to accept Christ.'" Jesus and his disciples were teachers; like them the missionary teachers must "mold character and sharpen the intellectual powers of students, that they may more clearly apprehend and more forcibly declare the great truths of the Christian system." McPherson, *Abolitionist Legacy*, 150.

nation needed a restoration of the traditional values not only to meet their own status needs, but also to assure the continued advancement of mankind. This is not to say that they were merely clinging to the past, or attempting to return the nation to a half-remembered, half-imagined golden age; on the contrary, they faced manfully into the future, but they hoped to reduce the threat of that future by working to preserve the time-honored virtues of the past. Thus the "search for order," which Robert Wiebe has suggested was the underlying theme of the Progressive Era, also involved a search for the means of preserving a threatened spiritual order.[22] The solution that the Progressives found was a moral one, and one that attempted to preserve the certainties of the past by reasserting the traditional values.

The industrial education movement can easily be—and has been—misinterpreted by allowing present assumptions and categories to illuminate the shadowy path into the past. Cynicism, exploitation, racism—all of these may seem to the unwary observer to have been the hallmarks of the Hampton-Tuskegee tradition. To draw such conclusions, however, would be unfair—to the present as well as to the past—because they deny the integrity of past experience and thus diminish the value of history as an explicator of human behavior.

A complete understanding of the industrial education movement must rest first of all on a correct identification and assessment of the assumptions underlying the experience, and persons in a secular and pragmatic age have difficulty appreciating the moral imperatives of an age that was dominated by a belief in "'the sovereignty of God, the kingship of Christ . . . the coming kingdom,' the transformation of life and the promise of salvation."[23] The twentieth century has lost the ethical dimension of the nineteenth, and the moral and religious context of America has changed dramatically in the last three-quarters of a century; but

---

22. Robert H. Wiebe, *The Search for Order, 1877–1920* (New York, 1967).
23. H. Richard Niebuhr, *The Kingdom of God in America* (1937), as quoted in Will Herberg, *Protestant, Catholic, Jew: An Essay in American Religious Sociology* (1st. rev. ed.: Garden City, N.Y., 1955), 123.

the historian can approach an understanding of a vastly different age by focusing attention on process rather than product and by remaining sensitive to the myths of the past.

Myths, as Henry Nash Smith has used the term, are "images which simultaneously express collective desires and impose coherence on the infinitely numerous and infinitely varied data of experience."[24] These "large, controlling image[s] . . . which [give] philosophical meaning to the facts of ordinary life" reveal as much, if not more, about human behavior than the objective reality they are an attempt to describe; as "perceived reality" they provide the connecting link between a man's assumptions about a problem and his choice of solution to the problem he perceives.[25] The "industrial education myth," therefore, opens a path into the minds of the northern white patricians who allowed it to control their experience, and it reveals them to have been motivated by fear and determined to preserve their world. Although the passage of time has proven the industrial education solution to the "Negro Problem" to have been misguided and naive, an examination of its development at one small outpost in the South nonetheless reveals important dimensions of the American mind at the dawn of the industrial age.

---

24. Henry Nash Smith, *Virgin Land: The American West as Symbol and Myth* (Cambridge, Mass., 1950), ix.

25. Mark Schorer, "The Necessity of Myth," in Henry A. Murray (ed.), *Myth and Mythmaking* (New York, 1960), 355; for an engaging and perceptive discussion of the concept of myth, see George B. Tindall, "Mythology: A New Frontier in Southern History," in Frank E. Vandiver (ed.), *The Idea of the South: Pursuit of a Central Theme* (Chicago: University of Chicago Press, 1964), 1–15.

2

The Rebirth of Penn School

As gentle tides crept in and out of the marshes around Frogmore Plantation, long autumn shadows stretched into the room where Laura Towne lay dying. From her upstairs bedroom in the old clapboard house, Miss Towne could hear the sounds of life in the marshes below—wild ducks skittering across the surface of the water before winging their way seaward, marsh hens darting among the reeds in pursuit of their evening meal, sea gulls and mockingbirds filling the air with their imperious cries. As she lay before the log fire, waiting through the hours, she must have pondered what she knew to be true: that she would never again see her island dressed in its wintry garb—bright pearls of mistletoe nestling in the branches of the majestic live oaks, splashes of southern smilax and scarlet cassino berries delighting the eye along the roadside, lonely palmettoes nodding gracefully along the shoreline and down to the sea. And as she pondered all these things, she must also have turned her thoughts to the last forty years of her life—years that had set her down at the end of the earth, in a strange and difficult environment, surrounded by primitive and sometimes hostile people, and caused her to love it as her own.

The day of "gun shoot at Bay Point" had marked the end of

an era for the South Carolina Sea Islands.[1] On that clear November day in 1861, Commodore Samuel Francis DuPont, United States Navy, had captured the whole Port Royal area for the Union, and the Sea Island blacks at last could cry:

"Oh none in all the world before
    Were ever glad as we!
We're free on Carolina's shore
    We're all at home and free."[2]

The whites of the area found no cause for rejoicing. From their front-row seats on the veranda of the Tom B. Chaplin plantation house on St. Helena Island, the small band of Confederate wives and daughters who had gathered to watch the Battle of Port Royal had visited nervously, awaiting amid feelings of anxiety and confidence the moment when their boys would put the Yankees to rout. How surprised and frightened they must have been when they saw the two Confederate forts on the bay lower their flags in defeat. Sending a messenger to the Episcopal Chapel of Ease, where the rest of the white families had gathered to pray for a Confederate victory, these ladies lost no time in following their menfolk's prior instructions. They gathered up only their children and the barest necessities, casting many a wistful glance around their elegant and beloved plantations, and then fled to the mainland, many of them never to return.[3]

With the departure of their white masters, the blacks confronted a situation for which they were totally unprepared; although they had long dreamed of this Day of Jubilee, they now found their lives thrown into chaos. Freed now from their joyless toil, able at last to sing "No more driver call for me . . . No more hundred lash for me," the St. Helena blacks also found to their

---

1. Willie Lee Rose, *Rehearsal for Reconstruction: The Port Royal Experiment* (New York, 1964), 17.
2. John Greenleaf Whittier, "The St. Helena Hymn," as quoted in Jackson E. Davis, "A Unique People's School," reprinted from *Southern Workman*, XLII (April, 1914), 4, in Penn School Papers, Southern Historical Collection, University of North Carolina (hereinafter cited as PSP).
3. The information in this paragraph comes from a series of interviews with Mrs. James McBride Dabbs (who is preparing a history of St. Helena Island) in March, 1972, Mayesville, S.C.

consternation that there was "No more peck of corn for me," and they began to experience some unanticipated dimensions of freedom.[4]

When Union soldiers reported that the Port Royal area had fallen into a state of anarchy and confusion, Treasury Secretary Salmon P. Chase assumed responsibility for guiding the several thousand blacks through the oncoming winter. As concerned as he was about the welfare of the people, however, Secretary Chase was equally concerned about salvaging the partially gathered cotton crop; he knew that the famed Sea Island cotton—renowned for its fine long fiber—would command a generous price on the open market and would pour much-needed revenue into the Union war chest. He lost little time, therefore, in appointing Edward L. Pierce, a young lawyer from Milton, Massachusetts, as a special government agent to aid the blacks and oversee the cotton production for that year. Thus began the Port Royal Experiment, the first phase in what was to be almost a century of testing white social theories.[5]

Conservative theorists both North and South had long contended that blacks would not work if left to their own devices; liberal economists had been waiting for an opportunity, such as the one presented at Port Royal, to disprove this theory and to prove "the superior productivity of free labor." Furthermore, as Willie Lee Rose has suggested: "The Sea Island conditions seemed ready and waiting for a real transplanting of Northern values"; not only were the Sea Island blacks expected to prove "the fundamental precept of classical economics, progress through enlightened self-interest," they were also expected to justify the abolitionists' faith that they would be found worthy of their freedom. The abolitionists who flocked to the Sea Islands hoped to demonstrate to a

4. Rose, *Rehearsal for Reconstruction*, 20–22. See also Rupert Sargent Holland (ed.), *Letters and Diary of Laura M. Towne: Written from the Sea Islands of South Carolina, 1862–1884* (Cambridge, Mass. 1912); Elizabeth Ware Pearson, *Letters from Port Royal* (Boston: W. B. Clarke, 1906); J. Miller McKim, "The Freedmen of South Carolina: An Address Delivered by J. Miller McKim in Sansom Hall, July 9, 1862 . . ." (Philadelphia, 1862), 13, as quoted in Edwin D. Hoffman, "From Slavery to Self-Reliance," *Journal of Negro History*, XXI (January, 1956), 15–16.
5. Rose, *Rehearsal for Reconstruction*, 17–20.

skeptical public that the former slaves could develop a capacity for self-reliance and responsible citizenship.[6]

Before many weeks had passed in 1862, the citizens of several northern cities had formed organizations to support the Port Royal Experiment, and soon scores of missionaries—whether as school teachers or plantation managers—had departed for the Sea Islands. The decision to go required no small measure of courage and idealism, for "the islands were known to be very unhealthy, smallpox was a frequent visitor, the Confederate army had retreated only a short distance on the mainland and might return at any time. They were setting out for a region where, since the flight of the white masters, there were few besides Negroes, a race then practically unknown to them, who were likely to view their coming with suspicion." But this venture into the exotic and unknown South also promised to be rich in romance and historic significance, and despite the obstacles, the young missionaries took up the challenge determined to build "a new New England, replete with Yankee institutions."[7]

Using the schoolroom to sermonize on proper civilized behavior, the northern teachers infused the Yankee virtues of order, industry, and thrift with a spiritual meaning, insisting always that moral behavior was an outward sign of grace. They little intended, however, that their transmission of culture should extend so far as to encompass social equality, as Rose has made clear. Challenging the traditional characterization of these missionaries as being "inspired by a . . . faith in human freedom and equality," Rose defines more closely the parameters of Yankee idealism. "The limited goal of a free peasantry," she writes, "was . . . the

6. *Ibid.*, 38; Hoffman, "From Slavery to Self-Reliance," 8, 9. As Rufus Saxton, military commander at Port Royal, conceived his mission, he was conducting "a critical experiment of the capabilities of the Negro for freedom and self-support and self-improvement, to determine whether he is specifically distinct from and inferior to the white race, and normally a slave or dependent, or only inferior by accident of position and circumstance." *War of the Rebellion: A Compilation of the Official Records of the Union and Confederate Armies* (130 vols.; Washington, D.C., 1880–1901), Ser. III, Vol. IV, p. 1029.

7. Primary among these cities were New York, Philadelphia, and Boston. Rossa Belle Cooley, *School Acres: An Adventure in Rural Education* (New Haven, Conn., 1930), 10; Rose, *Rehearsal for Reconstruction*, 229.

most common ideal among the missionaries. . . . The pattern sought after was that of industrious and self-reliant families working the cotton through the week and enjoying their Sunday holiday in clean clothes, with happy, shining faces."[8]

For many of the freedmen, education and freedom were synonymous; no matter how inappropriate a classical education may have been to their circumstances, "they demanded the same schooling that white southerners had received before the war as both a badge and a guarantee of their freedom." The freedmen's desires corresponded with the northern teachers' own educational backgrounds, and so their schools commonly emphasized such subjects as reading, penmanship, history, and arithmetic. Since the object was "civilization," and since the endeavor was admittedly experimental, the northern teachers actually cared very little what subjects their pupils attempted to master. As Carter Woodson has suggested, the missionaries' teaching "was more of an effort toward social uplift than actual education. Their aim was to transform the Negroes, not to develop them."[9]

Second only to education, the Sea Island blacks wanted land; for in their minds freedom meant farming their own ground. When in 1864 the government finally instituted a tax sale on St. Helena Island, offering twenty-acre lots to "heads of families of the African race" at a preferred rate of $1.25 per acre, many former slaves seized the moment and established themselves as sturdy yeoman farmers. By 1890 blacks owned 75 percent of the land in Beaufort County; this landownership set them apart from other southern blacks and would evoke much interest in later years.[10]

---

8. Willie Lee Rose suggests that northerners feared a black inundation of the North and that the evangels were constantly trying to reassure northerners that blacks did not want to leave the South. Rose, *Rehearsal for Reconstruction*, 235, 238. See also George M. Frederickson, *The Black Image in the White Mind: The Debate on Afro-American Character and Destiny, 1817–1914* (New York, 1971), 134–35, for a similar fear in the Midwest. E. Franklin Frazier, *The Negro in the United States* (Rev. ed; New York, 1957), 421.

9. Rush Welter, *Popular Education and Democratic Thought in America* (New York, 1962), 145. As Welter suggests (145n), it is highly likely that "southern white resistance to education of the freedman, and especially to academic education of the freedman, helped to confirm the Negroes' commitment to it." Carter Godwin Woodson, *The Mis-Education of the Negro* (Washington, D.C., 1933), 17.

10. Rose, *Rehearsal for Reconstruction*, 272–397. See also Hoffman, "From Slavery

Despite the fervent efforts of the northern missionaries, despite the conviction that to "make another Massachusetts of South Carolina it is only necessary to give her freedom and education," the slave culture of the Sea Islands would be slow to yield to "the newly imported culture of freedom and free enterprise." Before long the strain of the experiment began to tell on many of the missionaries. As the war drew to a close and the need for active commitment seemed to subside, as northern support for the endeavor waned and new issues arose, and as the entrenched slave culture refused to transform itself into a model of New England piety, a great many of the northern teachers and managers lost heart and gave up in despair.[11]

Not all, however, lost the vision so easily; among those who remained to carry on the struggle was a young woman named Laura Towne. Born and raised in Salem, Massachusetts, Laura Towne was the daughter of a prosperous merchant. She was a bright and idealistic girl; and when the family moved to Philadelphia in 1840, Laura came under the spell of the old Philadelphia abolitionist, Dr. William Furness. Dr. Furness taught her to loathe both the slave system and the men who used it to their advantage, and with each passing day her abhorrence of the slavocracy intensified until her dedication to the struggle for freedom became the consuming passion of her life. Unlike many of her abolitionist compatriots, however, Laura Towne understood that the slave in the South needed much more than emancipation. To her the Negro was a man, not a moral abstraction; and when the opportunity arose to help him prove his worth, she accepted the challenge with commitment and zeal.[12]

---

to Self-Reliance," for a full discussion of the Negroes' desire to own land on St. Helena Island.

11. James Thompson, Beaufort *Free South*, January 2, 1864, as quoted in Rose, *Rehearsal for Reconstruction*, xvii, 385.

12. Laura Towne's brother was John Henry Towne, a distinguished engineer, manufacturer, and philanthropist, who bequeathed a major portion of his estate to the University of Pennsylvania and for whom the Towne Scientific School was named. See *Who Was Who in America, 1607–1896*, p. 535. John Henry Towne's son (Laura's nephew), Henry Robinson Towne, entered into a partnership with the locksmith-inventor Linus Yale to form the Yale and Towne Manufacturing Company, of which he was president, 1868–1915, and then chairman of the board until his death in 1924. *Who Was Who in America, 1897–1942, p. 1248; Frederick T. Towne Memorial Volume* (n.p., 1906), in the pos-

Laura Towne arrived on St. Helena Island on April 15, 1862. She worked initially as an aide to the government officers, "collecting data, arranging papers, answering inquiries from Washington, being interviewed on the state of the Negroes, their fitness for soldiers, their ability to learn." She soon tired of the petty bureaucracy, however, and so she developed her own program, one that helped the islanders improve their standard of living. As Miss Towne's Canadian companion, Ellen Murray, recalled years later: "The condition of things was appalling. . . . The field hands had been reduced to a state but little above the animals. Family ties were made and severed at the owner's will. I did not find a girl over sixteen that was not a mother." Apparently many of the blacks had been recent arrivals from Africa, smuggled in at high tide along the secluded tidal rivers; Miss Murray described a woman "who still prayed as her mother had taught her, pouring out water in worship to the full moon," and a tattooed man who told of his wife and children left on "the other side of the great water." Not only were there African survivals in abundance, but the heritage of slavery had been a pitifully low standard of living. Under the slave system, a peck of corn was the weekly ration, and "the slaves ground it themselves on Saturday night, taking turns until daylight. Their homes were of rough boards and had small windows without glass. The floors were of sand and lime. Long oyster shells served for spoons, and they did not know the use of a knife and fork." Clearly, Miss Towne and Miss Murray had much work to do if they were to bring this island culture in line with dominant American norms and values.[13]

Laura Towne had had a little medical training, and she spent most of her time in the first few years ministering to the needs of the sick. She battled a smallpox epidemic and the persistent yellow fever; every day she visited different plantations, dispensing advice and comforts to the best of her knowledge and ability. She was a true child of New England, however, and before long she

---

session of Mrs. James McBride Dabbs, Rip Raps Plantation, Mayesville, S.C. (hereinafter cited as JMD). Rose, *Rehearsal for Reconstruction*, 375.

13. Ellen Murray, "Annual Report of the Principal," June, 1901, p. 16, in PSP; Cooley, *School Acres*, 12; Jackson Davis, "A Unique People's School," 5.

and Miss Murray began to turn their thoughts to education. Determined to prove that even the lowly field hand could learn through books rather than through force, the two ladies opened a little school in the living room of "The Oaks" plantation.[14]

On opening day they had nine pupils, all adults. Within a month they had eighty "scholars," and their growing enrollment forced the ladies to move their school into Brick Church, which had been built for the whites prior to the war. Miss Towne described her first pupils as an awesome challenge to the proper New England schoolteacher:

> They had no idea of sitting still, of giving attention, of ceasing to talk aloud. They lay down and went to sleep; they scuffled and struck each other. They got up by the dozen and made their curtsies, and walked off to the neighboring fields for blackberries, coming back to their seats with a curtsy when they were ready. They evidently did not understand me, and I could not understand them, and after two hours and a half I was thoroughly exhausted.[15]

Named Penn School in honor of William Penn, Miss Towne's school seemed a fulfillment of an old slave dream, expressed in the island spiritual:

> I would like to read,
> Like to read,
> Like to read dat sweet story ob ole,
> I would like to read.

Fittingly, Laura Towne presented her new school with a fine brass bell patterned after the one in Independence Hall, which bore the inscription "Proclaim Liberty." In 1863 the Pennsylvania Freedmen's Association sent down by boat a three-room frame building, ready-built, which was "the first school house in the South constructed for the use of the freedmen."[16]

14. Rossa Belle Cooley, *Homes of the Freed* (New York, 1926), 4, 48; Cooley, *School Acres*, 13; Murray, "Annual Report," June, 1901, p. 17, in PSP.
15. Rossa Belle Cooley, "History of Penn School," 1944, in PSP; Laura Matilda Towne, "Pioneer Work on the Sea Islands," reprinted from *Southern Workman*, XXX (July, 1901), 7, in PSP.
16. Cooley, *School Acres*, 5,11; "Annual Report of the Penn Normal, Industrial and Agricultural School," June, 1901, p. 18, 1917, p. 11, both in PSP; Edith Mitchell Dabbs, *Walking Tall* (Frogmore, S.C. 1964), 6.

The early years were full of activity and promise, but with the passage of time popular attention in the North turned to other matters. As the various relief societies disbanded one by one, Laura Towne had to fight to maintain her school. Eventually she had to pay her teachers out of her own and her family's money, but she remained unshaken in her conviction that the freedman could prove his worth and that her efforts in his behalf would bear impressive fruit.[17]

For forty years Miss Towne and Miss Murray remained at their labors. Unfortunately for those who would wish to know of their accomplishments, they kept no records of their school. But Miss Towne did keep a diary, and it is obvious from her entries that these women exerted a powerful influence on the lives and mores of the people they had come to call their own ("We have got to calling them *our* people and loving them really"). Patiently over the years they encouraged the islanders to shed their "primitive superstition" and to develop a spirit of community. They sponsored such programs as a mothers' homemaking class, a Sunday School, and a strong temperance society, all designed to inculcate the values the two ladies thought desirable. Under this guidance, the blacks abandoned much of their African heritage; they also learned the importance of saving a portion of their earnings and cultivated more careful habits of crop husbandry. As Miss Murray described the influence of Penn School:

> The majority of our pupils after graduation settle down as farmers, either inheriting their fathers' farms or buying land of their own. They are now putting up four and six-roomed houses instead of the old time huts. Some of our graduates have become trusted clerks and employees in the Island stores, or the pastors, deacons and spiritual leaders of the churches. Others have passed the County school examinations, and all over the County and in the country places between Beaufort and Charleston teachers from the Penn School easily find employment. Ten of the public schools on the Island are taught by our graduates.

Despite these encouraging results, the Penn School influence

17. Towne, "Pioneer Work on the Sea Islands," 7.

touched only a small proportion of the total population, and the great majority of the island blacks remained beyond the reach of the two northern ladies.[18]

Early in 1900, when Laura Towne began to fear that the work of her little school would languish after her death, she summoned the man who was thought to be America's leading authority on black education and asked him to assume responsibility for the continued operation of Penn School. Hollis Burke Frissell, principal of Hampton Institute, responded to Miss Towne's call and traveled to her bedside at Frogmore Plantation, for he thought St. Helena Island to be an ideal laboratory for testing his theories and demonstrating the effectiveness of his methods. Here, he felt, was "an opportunity to work out a plan for industrial education that would help the rural South."[19]

A small man with rounded shoulders and stooping posture, Hollis Burke Frissell peered out at the world from under a prominent and shaggy brow. His pale gray eyes lacked the fire of a more vital spirit, but they were quick to show compassion and understanding for the objects of his interest, and they revealed no weakness of purpose or resolve. His carefully manicured moustache and goatee, his shiny bald head, and his high cheekbones gave him a rather startling resemblance to another of the world's ideologues—Nikolai Lenin—but he really resembled nothing so much as a painting by one of the great Renaissance artists, Giotto de Bondone. Frissell could have stepped right down from one of Giotto's frescoes, with their flat lines, their pale tones, and their saintly characters; indeed, he was often described by his admirers as "Christ-like." As William Howard Taft said at his death: "Frissell had more christ-like qualities than almost anybody in my personal acquaintance." And yet the Hampton educator exhibited none of the saint's rigidity or ruthlessness; he was always gentle in his dealings with others, though he held firmly to the positions he believed to be right.[20]

18. Holland, *Letters and Diary of Laura M. Towne*, 7; Dabbs, *Walking Tall*, 1, 7; "Annual Report," 1904, p. 10, in PSP.
19. Cooley, *School Acres*, 13; Rossa Belle Cooley, "Service to Penn School," *Southern Workman*, XLVI (October, 1917), 605.
20. William Howard Taft, *Southern Workman*, XLVI (October, 1917), 569; Jerome D. Greene, "An Apostle of Good Will," *Southern Workman*, XLVI (October, 1917), 615.

Frissell's unlimited patience and his unquestionable sincerity inspired men's confidence and stimulated their best impulses. As one of his admirers described him: "He was a type of man whom to know was to love. The more one saw him and heard him speak, the more deeply one appreciated his lofty ideals and noble character." The source of Frissell's strength was his unswerving faith in moral progress and "the eventual salvation of humanity." To him the fatherhood of God and the brotherhood of man were attainable goals, and he dedicated himself to bringing the Kingdom of Heaven on Earth. He had a "vivid consciousness of the Divine Purpose that rules the Universe" and an "unwavering optimism that peace and goodwill among men will ultimately conquer all prejudice and hatred." Thus he could march undaunted into the future, always looking forward and upward, because he believed that he was God's servant and that he was building a better world.[21]

Frissell often referred to Hampton's work as an "experiment" in racial adjustment. "It seems incumbent upon schools like Hampton," he wrote, "to help people realize that under proper conditions, the Negro can be fitted for Christian citizenship." Frissell conceived of Hampton as a laboratory that sought to prove to white America that the Negro could become a useful and non-threatening element in American society, and he assumed that such a demonstration was both laudable and necessary. He believed that the Hampton experiment had provided answers to a number of disturbing questions about America's racial situation, and he proudly offered the Hampton experience as proof that the Negro race was capable of producing "good mechanics, good farmers, and a high grade of teachers and academic students, and of enjoying the best kind of domestic life" and that "negro youth can be so trained as to develop strong character and purity of life." Such proof seemed to be a vindication of Hampton's rather presumptuous aim of teaching people "how to live," and it also buttressed Frissell's belief that the Negro's task should be to adjust himself to American society rather than to challenge it. As he reminded the Hampton graduates shortly before his death in

21. Leo M. Favrot, *Southern Workman*, XLVI (October, 1917), 572; Oswald Garrison Villard, "A True Patriot," *Southern Workman*, XLVI (October, 1917), 632; Thomas Jesse Jones, "Frissell of Hampton," *Southern Workman*, LX (January, 1931), 11, 15.

1917: "[The] colored man is going to secure recognition, not by demanding his rights, but by deserving them."[22]

As he was rowed across the Beaufort River from the South Carolina mainland, Frissell reflected on the isolation of St. Helena Island and the benefits of that isolation for the island blacks. Though just a mile across the river from aristocratic old Beaufort, with its double-galleried mansions and quiet walled gardens, St. Helena had been considered too unhealthy and malarial for habitation by whites. And though the Port Royal area had been the focus of intense interest and concern in the early Reconstruction years, in the thirty years since, it had faded from the public eye into almost total obscurity. No bridge connected the island to the mainland, and few white men had reason to go there; consequently, the Sea Island blacks had been spared the horrors and brutality of late nineteenth-century race relations. Isolated as they were from white culture, these blacks comprised a nearly "unspoiled" group, they were of "pure African stock," as Frissell would often say. Here, then, was an unparalleled opportunity for an experiment to see what the blacks could do "when led to develop themselves under favorable circumstances." In the idiom of the day, this was to be an "object lesson"—to the blacks of St. Helena Island, to the South, and to the nation.[23]

The largest of the chain known as "Sea Islands," St. Helena had a long and picturesque history, filled with the mystery and romance of Indian, Spanish, French, English, and African traditions. Everything about the place had an exotic flavor. The island could be reached only by way of a primitive rowboat, or bateau (a reminder of the days of French control). Owing to the continuous, moisture-laden sea breezes, the mild climate, and the early arrival of spring, the island sustained a varied animal population and a lush vegetation, with the wild iris and wisteria, the

22. Hollis Burke Frissell, "Forty-Seventh Annual Report of the Principal," *Southern Workman*, XLIV (May, 1915), 300; "Forty-Fourth Annual Report of the Principal," *Southern Workman*, XLI (May, 1912), 296; "Forty-First Annual Report of the Principal," *Southern Workman*, XXXVIII (May, 1909), 305; "To Hampton Graduates," *Southern Workman*, XLVI (May, 1917), 261.
23. Cooley, *School Acres*, 23; "Annual Report," 1902, pp. 7, 8, Penn School publicity brochure, 1902, both in PSP.

cherokee roses, the yellow jessamine, and red cassino berries assuring a virtual riot of color at all seasons of the year. On all sides the eye encountered unaccustomed sights: the graceful, nodding palmettoes that lined the water's edge; the gnarled, brooding live oaks with their hoary fringes of Spanish moss; the white oyster-shell roads traversed by primitive, two-wheeled oxcarts; the golden-brown marshes through which ran ribbons of tidal rivers, shining like satin in the sunlight.[24]

Even more arresting were the people—as black as any on this side of the world. Occasionally the visitor would encounter a turbaned woman or a girl balancing a bucket on her head. More frequently one might spy a woman on the road with a hoe over her shoulder and a basket on her head, her skirts tied below the hips with a stout cord—"to give her strength" as she would tell you. In encounters with whites there was none of the embarrassment or reserve that the constant reminder of the color line had fostered elsewhere.[25]

Perhaps the strongest manifestation of these people's difference was their manner of speaking—*Gullah*, as their dialect is often called. A creolized language drawn largely from African sources, the Gullah dialect is characterized by "rapidly spoken phrases ... staccato accents,—and ... rising and falling intonations." In the Gullah dialect, the same word can stand for both singular and plural, masculine, feminine, or neuter; verb forms do not change for singular or plural nouns; and nouns have the same form in all cases. "E shum," for example, can mean "He sees her," "She saw him," or "It has seen them"! All combined to give the place an other-wordly quality, lovely, eerie, and serene.[26]

24. St. Helena Island covered an area of fifty-six square miles. A good secondary account of St. Helena's picturesque history is Paul Quattlebaum, *The Land Called Chicora* (Gainesville, Fla., 1956).
25. Cooley, *Homes of the Freed*, 70; Thomas Jackson Woofter, *Black Yeomanry: Life on St. Helena Island* (New York, 1930), 7; "The Week," *Outlook*, CXI (December 8, 1915), 826.
26. Lorenzo Dow Turner, *Africanisms in the Gullah Dialect* (Chicago, 1949); Guy Benton Johnson, *Folk Culture on St. Helena Island, South Carolina* (Chapel Hill, N.C., 1930), 5, 12–13; Hermes Nye, "Animal Tales Told in the Gullah Dialect," n.d., clipping, in PSP. The following tale reveals not only the dialect, but also the folk wisdom of the people: "Buh Lion bin a hunt, an eh (he) spy Buh Goat duh leddown (lie down) topper

The island's sheer physical beauty overwhelmed most of its visitors—its soft, lanquid qualities offering such striking contrast to the frenzied pace of a booming America. As a future Penn School principal would describe it years later:

> Great live-oaks stretch friendly arms across the road, and the soft, trailing gray moss catches the golden glint of the sunshine sifting through the archway of dark green leaves. Beyond, where the avenue ends, is the gleam of the open sky, beckoning to new beauties of the roadside—the broad level marshes, with their wide horizons, and the silver of the tide-river winding its devious way out to the open sea. And there at the margin of the river, against the yellow background of the marshes a great white heron stands, etched like a print of old Japan.

Perhaps it is not to be wondered that the northern visitors who came to the island in later years were enchanted, lost their perspective, and surrendered to the spell of the place. One enthralled northern visitor described his visit to St. Helena as being similar to "going to a foreign country, into a new language, a new economic life, a new mental attitude and a new folk-lore." Another visitor, from Pennsylvania, left this ode in the Penn School guest book:

> Oh sweet delight once more to feel
> The chorus of Dixie over me steal
> To breathe thy pure and _____ air
> To revel in thy beauties rare
> To hear the mocking bird's glad bay
> Pour forth throughout the live long day.
> To feel life's troubles melt away
> In this your happy home.[27]

---

er big rock duh wuk eh mout an der chaw. Eh creep up fuh ketch um. Wen eh git close ter um eh notus um good. Buh Goat keep on chaw. Buh Lion try fuh fine out wuh Buh Goat duh eat. Eh Yent (ain't) see nutte (nothing) nigh um Buh Goat. Buh Goat keep on chaw, an chaw an chaw. Buh Lion cnat mek de ting out, an eh come close, an eh say: 'Hay! Buh Goat, wuh you duh eat?' But Goat skade (scared) weh Buh Lion rise up befo um, but eh keep er bole hart, an eh mek ansur: 'Me dun chaw dis rock, an ef you don leff, wen me done long um me guine eat you.' Dis wud sabe Buh Goat. Bole man git out diffikelty way (where) coward man lose eh life." Charles Colcock Jones, Jr., *Negro Myths from the Georgia Coast Told in the Vernacular* (New York, 1888), 38.

27. Grace Bigelow House, "Roads of Learning on St. Helena Island," reprinted

The Rebirth of Penn School 37

As Dr. Frissell rode the six miles from the water's edge to Miss Towne's bedside, he must have been thrilled by the possibilities of his new venture. He, and Hampton, had sponsored many small black schools across the South—next to Tuskegee the most notable was Miss Charlotte Thorne's Calhoun Colored School. Indeed it was Miss Thorne's niece, Mrs. William Furness Jenks of Philadelphia, who had contacted Frissell about Penn School, for Mrs. Jenks was also the niece of Laura Towne. But none of Hampton's other "step-children" had captured Frissell's imagination as Penn was to do. None of them had the unique combination of isolation, pure blood, and landownership; nowhere else was there such an opportunity to prove the wisdom and merit of the Hampton solution to the "Negro Problem."[28]

After meeting with Miss Towne and discussing Penn School's history and future, Frissell returned to Hampton and wrote to Mrs. Jenks: "I know of no place which presents such excellent opportunities for a certain sort of experiment station work among the negroes, as does this island." Frissell felt, of course, that the school was "far behind the times"; but with great tact and appreciation of the old order, he began to unfold his vision of the school's future possibilities. Following the pattern established at Tuskegee and at the Calhoun School, he suggested the formation of a board of trustees, and he suggested that the school be incorporated; then the real work of breathing new life into Penn School could begin. Primarily the trustees should search for "a good colored man to go down there, look into the work, and if possible introduce some new methods." This man, and Frissell said he knew of two or three suitable Hampton graduates, should concentrate his efforts on improving both the island's agricultural practices and its public schools. This was a far cry from the academic emphasis

---

from *Progressive Education*, XIV (April, 1937), 246–55, in Howard Anderson Kester Papers, Black Mountain, N.C. (hereinafter cited as HKP); Hebert E. Mills to Rossa Belle Cooley, April 5, 1916, in PSP; Joseph Elkinton, Moylan, Pa. in Hampton House guest book, March, 1912, in JMD.

28. Cooley, *School Acres*, 22; Helen Carnan Jenks to Hollis Burke Frissell, April, 1900, in Hollis Burke Frissell Papers, Presidents' Archives, Hampton Institute (hereinafter cited as HBF).

of the old Penn School, but Miss Towne had assured Frissell that she would accept anything her niece approved. Thus St. Helena became, almost overnight, an outpost of Hampton Institute.[29]

For the next few months Mrs. Jenks devoted herself to establishing Penn School on a permanent basis. After a careful search she found several men and women, most of them from Philadelphia, to join the new board of trustees. Her son drew up a charter incorporating the "Penn Normal, Industrial and Agricultural School" under South Carolina state law, and on the eve of the new year an earnest and hopeful band gathered at Frogmore Plantation to ring in an exciting new adventure in Negro education.[30]

The new Penn School trustees comprised a distinguished and colorful band. Foremost among them, of course, was Frissell, who sat as chairman of the board for sixteen years. Miss Towne and Miss Murray, who stayed on nominally as "principals" until their deaths a few years later, also sat on the board; but their influence was negligible, if not negative, in the new development of the school. Mrs. Jenks headed the list of active trustees, and she had been notably successful in enlisting the support of several prominent Philadelphians. As the daughter of a distinguished manufacturer-philanthropist, the wife of a prominent physician, and a niece by marriage of the fiery old abolitionist William Furness, Helen Carnan Towne Jenks needed no entree into old-line Philadelphia society. She had not only the credentials, but also the interests and tastes of the elite: she was a Unitarian and a Republican; she devoted herself for years to charitable work for the Philadelphia Visiting Nurse Society; and in the summers she took her family away from the heat and grime of the city to secluded Camden, Maine, just down the coast from fashionable Bar Harbor.[31]

29. Cooley, "Service to Penn School," 605; H. B. Frissell to H. C. Jenks, May 23, 1900, H B. Frissell to H. C. Jenks, May 23, 1900, H. C. Jenks to H. B. Frissell, June 29, 1900, all in HBF; Francis Reeve Cope, Jr., "Service to Penn School," *Southern Workman*, XLVI (October, 1917), 604.

30. H. C. Jenks to H. B. Frissell, June 14, 1900, in HBF; *Robert D. Jenks, 1875–1917: A Memorial and a Tribute from His Friends* (Philadelphia, 1917), in JMD.

31. Frederick A. Virkus (ed), *The Abridged Compendium of American Genealogy: First*

Among the distinguished citizens who responded to Mrs. Jenks's appeal was Isaac Sharpless, president of Haverford College. As Mrs. Jenks described him to Frissell, he was "a good clear-headed man, active not only in the work of his own college . . . but also a public spirited citizen of Bryn-Mawr, where he lives. I think he is Chairman of the local party for Good Government, and he has in many ways a decided interest in the welfare of the community."[32]

Sharpless must have seen in this new program for black development much that he could affirm. In his inaugural address at Haverford, Sharpless had told his listeners that he hoped to extend the objectives of the college "so as to include not merely intellectual development, but also the development of character and morals" for he believed that "character is more important than intellect." Surely he must have greeted Frissell's disquisitions on character building with enthusiasm. Moreover, as "a good orthodox Friend," Sharpless believed that "life is no mercenary pursuit of comfort or gain but an opportunity to help in making the world a better place in which to live" and that the man who "builds quietly for the future is the greatest benefactor." All of these attitudes and assumptions must have disposed him to view the Penn School venture as an exceptionally worthwhile outlet for his energies and talents.[33]

Mrs. Jenks also succeeded in enlisting the efforts of William Channing Russell, who, as his name indicates, was a descendant of the old abolitionist families of Massachusetts. As Mrs. Jenks described him: "He is a quiet man but decidedly interested for the better part in political and social life." Perhaps even more important, he wrote for the Philadelphia *Record*, and he would be in a position to keep the Penn School venture in the public eye.[34]

Mrs. Jenks's own son, Robert Darrah Jenks, also joined the

Families of America (Chicago, 1925), I, 616, 861; Philadelphia *Evening Bulletin*, January 23, 1917, p. 56; *Robert D. Jenks: A Memorial;* H. C. Jenks to H. B. Frissell, June 29, 1900, in HBF.

32. H. C. Jenks to H. B. Frissell, April 9, 1901, in HBF.

33. Edward Evans, "Isaac Sharpless," in *Quaker Biographies* (Philadelphia, n.d.), Series II, 93, 193–94. H. C. Jenks to H. B. Frissell, n.d., in HBF.

34. H. C. Jenks to H. B. Frissell, March 19, April 9, 1901, in HBF.

Penn board, assuming the real direction of the enterprise as chairman of the executive committee. A Harvard graduate and a lawyer, Jenks was an expert on railroad rates and interstate commerce law. His friends described him as having "a great interest in regulating public utilities" and as being "an expert who opposed the corporations." He was a committed worker in the Civil Service Reform League, and he excited the admiration of his colleagues because his professional ideals were "untainted by commercialism." The years at Harvard had reinforced the lessons he had learned from his family, and he returned to Philadelphia imbued with "the duty and need for service."[35]

While at Harvard, Robert Jenks had become a close friend of a young Bostonian, Henry Wilder Foote. Now a Unitarian minister, Foote was a nephew of Harvard president Charles W. Eliot and a close relative of Cambridge's leading Social Gospeler, Francis Greenwood Peabody. His grandfather had served with the Union army at Port Royal, and his father had been a trustee of Hampton Institute under Samuel Chapman Armstrong, so Foote was no stranger to social concern, industrial education, or St. Helena Island. At Frissell's suggestion he and his sister joined the Penn board, and they were soon joined by one of Foote's close Harvard friends, Francis Cope.[36]

Francis Reeve Cope, Jr., was a Philadelphia Quaker of independent means. His grandfather, an abolitionist, had been a good friend of Miss Towne's and a strong supporter of her school. Cope epitomized the Quaker ideal of "service," which is the Quaker equivalent of missionary activity. Believing that evil in the world is destroyed by "concern," Quakers everywhere "have a concern"— to eliminate war, to work for righteousness in economic and political life, to treat all humans as equals, to stimulate education. Education and black uplift were Francis Cope's leading concerns, and he dedicated a major portion of his life and means to these

---

35. *Robert Darrah Jenks: 1875–1917* (N.p., n.d.), in HBF; *Robert D. Jenks: A Memorial*.
36. Ralph Luker, "The Northern Social Gospel Prophets and the Negro: 1890–1917" (M.A. thesis, Univerity of North Carolina, 1969), 64; *Robert D. Jenks: A Memorial*; E. W. Hooper to Henry Wilder Foote, February 23, 1863, in JMD; H. B. Frissell to George Foster Peabody, April 10, 1901, in HBF.

two fields of endeavor. After Robert Jenks stepped down from the Penn School chair, Cope assumed the leadership of the executive committee, eventually becoming chairman of the board itself. He was a major actor in the unfolding Penn School drama, and he consistently couched his concern in terms of service to his fellow man.[37]

Another Philadelphia Quaker who joined the Penn School trustees out of a desire to render service was Alfred Collins Maule. For years he was in charge of Penn's publicity, and one of his typical letters to potential contributors would read as follows: "The Penn School is the one civilizing influence in a community of about forty white people and seven thousand negroes.... The children must be taught and the fathers and mothers must be reached if we are to raise this pathetically ignorant people to intelligent service for others and for their country." Service, then, was a characteristic of civilized living, and it was to be instilled as well as rendered.[38]

A transplanted Quaker in New York, L. Hollingsworth Wood, joined the Penn board in 1908. A lawyer, he was a founder and long-time president of the National Urban League, an organization that came into being to assist the masses of blacks then migrating to northern urban centers. Under Wood's leadership the league was a moderate, cooperative effort, dependent on white philanthropy, which accepted certain types of discrimination and injustice as "inevitable in the present situation." A handsome man with a charming sense of humor, Wood and his talents were in great demand, and he engaged in a wide variety of activities relating to education and black development. He and his family lived at fashionable Mt. Kiscoe, New York.[39]

Frissell had also been successful in enlisting trustees for the Penn effort. Arthur Curtiss James, a Hampton trustee, was the

37. Rose, *Rehearsal for Reconstruction*, 403–404; Mrs. Francis Reeve Cope, Jr., to author, June 2, 1972; Richmond P. Miller, "What Is a Quaker?" in Leo Rosten (ed.), *A Guide to the Religions of America* (New York, 1955), 128, 133.
38. Alfred Collins Maule to Penn School contributors, March, 1909, in JMD.
39. Gunnar Myrdal, *An American Dilemma: The Negro Problem and Modern Democracy* (2 vols.; New York, 1944) II, 837; Paul Ernest Baker, *Negro-White Adjustment: An Investigation and Analysis of Methods in the Interracial Movement in the United States* (New York, 1934), 22; *New York Times*, July 23, 1956, clipping, in JMD.

son of exceptionally wealthy parents, who had been devoted friends of General Armstrong. As a Penn trustee he could always be counted on in times of expansion or crisis. Whether the need was a new building, a bull for the farm, a car, a country home, or a trip abroad, James's generosity never flagged.[40]

Although James never took an active interest in the day-to-day developments on St. Helena, another Hampton trustee, George Foster Peabody, threw himself with enthusiasm into the new enterprise. A Georgian by birth, Peabody had moved to New York as a young man, where he had been inordinately successful in the banking and securities business. He was imbued with a keen sense of responsibility, and he had an almost mystical faith in democracy. His papers at the Library of Congress reflect a staggering amount of activities and commitments, with southern education and Negro development ranking high on his list of priorities. His name on the letterhead was an invaluable asset to the Penn School endeavor, and his affection and generosity toward the work at St. Helena carried the school through many a critical period.[41]

Interest in Penn School centered primarily in Philadelphia, New York, and Boston; but there were always a few southern trustees to help with pressing local issues. One of these, James Ross Macdonald, a northerner by birth, had settled on St. Helena Island in the 1870s. He opened a dry-goods store at the little settlement of Frogmore, just down the road from Penn School; and he became a valuable friend to Miss Towne and Miss Murray. Though he was a participant in the vicious crop-lien system—he bought the blacks' cotton and sold them their provisions—he always worked with the school in "combatting the liquor traffic and refusing to take morgages [sic] on the people's land." He was a fair and faithful friend to the islanders, and his firm, Macdonald, Wilkins & Co., gave this isolated community its primary contact with the outside world.[42]

This is but a sampling of the early board of trustees. Many

40. Frissell to H. C. Jenks, March 16, 1901, H. B. Frissell to Peabody, April 10, 1901, both in HBF; *Southern Workman*, XLV (June, 1910, 331–32.

41. Louise Ware, *George Foster Peabody: Banker, Philanthropist, Publicist* (Athens, Ga., 1951), Chap. 1.

42. Albert Bushnell Hart, "Through the Heart of the South," Boston Evening

others served; and many, such as Mrs. Henry L. Stimson, were asked to serve, primarily for the credibility their endorsement would lend to the enterprise among the representatives of northern wealth. Others, such as William Knox Tate, were invited in the hope of lending legitimacy to the enterprise among southerners. Most, however, would have felt themselves fairly represented by Ethel Paine Moors, descendant of Robert Treat Paine and wife of a partner in Boston's Moors and Cabot law firm. She was an active and dedicated trustee for many years, and clearly she was one of America's "Best People."[43]

All of the northern trustees were wellborn, well educated, refined, and moderate; and in their dealings with blacks they shared a set of assumptions that made them a congenial band. Reflecting the Social Darwinism of their day, they believed in the inevitability of progress as surely as they accepted the natural superiority of the Anglo-Saxon race. The "Negro Problem," they believed, was therefore soluble. It was simply a matter of giving blacks the time and the opportunity to develop their capacities, and those capacities could best be developed through education.

These men and women responded to the Penn School endeavor for a variety of reasons. Many shared Frissell's conception of the centrality of industrial training in the development of character; all shared Frissell's eagerness to conduct an educational "experiment" to see what effect industrial training would have upon blacks. All seemed to agree that the new venture would be "a rare opportunity to test the capability of the race in self-development under suitable guidance" and that St. Helena would be a "model community" and an "object lesson" to all who doubted the capacities of the Negro. Most of the new trustees also shared Frissell's conception of their work at St. Helena as a missionary enterprise and an opportunity to render service to their fellow man.[44]

Transcript, February 19, 1908, p. 16, clipping, Cooley to South Carolina secretary of state, Octber 25, 1907, both in JMD.

43. Mrs. Henry L. Stimson was the wife of the future secretary of state under Franklin D. Roosevelt; William Knox Tate was a General-Education-Board-sponsored supervisor of rural education in South Carolina and later professor of rural education at George Peabody College; Robert Treat Paine was a signer of the Declaration of Independence.

44. Henry Wilder Foote, "The Penn School on St. Helena Island," *Southern Workman*, XXXI (May, 1902), 270; "Annual Report of the Principal," 1903 p. 8, in PSP.

Some among the trustees may have shared the sense of guilt that James E. Gregg, a future Hampton president and Penn trustee, expressed in the Hampton newspaper, the *Southern Workman*: "For New England rum again and again went to the coast of Africa to buy Negro captives to be brought to the West Indies and the Carolinas. And in later years New England mills were glad enough to spin and weave slave-grown cotton from the Southern States. All of us who are descendants of those who profited, directly or indirectly, from slavery are indisputably under an obligation of honor to . . . the descendants of the slaves."[45]

Some of the trustees may have responded to the portrayal of Penn School, in the Progressive jargon of the day, as "a social settlement." Others must have affirmed its similarity to the Country Life Movement; Penn's most oft-repeated goal was to teach the blacks "to support themselves on their farms, and to constantly improve the conditions under which they live." Certainly part of this emphasis stemmed from Theodore Roosevelt's and Liberty Hyde Bailey's efforts to "regenerate" country life and institutions. The leading force in this regeneration was to be the rural school, which Bailey insisted must be "oriented to rural needs, concerned with rural problems, seeking at every juncture to cultivate a love of agriculture and the land." Furthermore, thought Bailey, "Working closely with church, library, fair, and farmers' institute, it must tie the community together and make it a better place to live in." Here was nothing less than a blueprint for the type of education Frissell sought to foster at St. Helena, and the sanction of the United States government could only have strengthened the trustees' commitment.[46]

Above all other factors motivating the Penn School trustees, however, loomed one great fact: southern blacks were drifting to the northern slums, "where they form a menace to our civic life." Whether the trustees and supporters were concerned for them-

---

45. James Edgar Gregg, "Facts: Not Feelings," *Southern Workman*, LVI (February, 1927), 60.
46. Letter to Penn School contributors, October 11, 1911, in JMD; "Annual Report of the Principal," 1904 p. 10, in PSP. Liberty Hyde Bailey was dean of Cornell's Agricultural School and a leader in the Country Life Movement. See Cremin, *The Transformation of the School*, 75–78.

selves or for the blacks' welfare is not always clear, but it is clear that they intended to keep blacks out of the North by teaching them to be satisfied with the farming life of the rural South. "It has been and will continue to be the aim of the Penn School to counteract this tendency," stated the Annual Report of Penn Normal, Industrial and Agricultural School in 1909, by teaching the people

> to realize how much better off they are on their native islands, and to help them make the most of their small farms. The importance of keeping the Negro in the community in which he has been brought up, and of teaching him to be of practical help to his neighbors, cannot be over-estimated, for particularly in the isolated country districts of the Sea Islands he is kept away from the temptations which exist in any of our larger cities.

"It is the intention of the Trustees," wrote one of that body, "to furnish a training to fit these negroes primarily for the peasant life which more than nine-tenths of them lead."[47]

And here was the nub of the matter: these cultivated and refined northern leaders, the standard-bearers of American culture, tradition, and ideals, upon reaping for the first time the rewards of their abolitionist grandfathers, recoiled in horror from the degradation of the Negro. Fearful now of the pollution and corruption of their cherished democracy, they worked to resign the darker segment of American society to the "farming class" or even a "peasant" status until the blacks had "proved" themselves capable and worthy of full partnership in the American political and social system, or in other words, until they had developed character.[48]

For Frissell and the Penn School principals, the impulse behind this new experiment was both Christian and democratic:

---

47. Lucy Davis to Francis T. Sully Darley, April 27, 1904, in JMD. Frissell explained to Miss Cooley the impact this Negro migration had had on the racial attitudes of one Penn School trustee, Thomas Cope: "His attempts to improve civic conditions in Philadelphia have thrown him up against the 25,000 purchaseable [sic] negro votes in the city, and have had the effect of creating a certain discouragement concerning the whole race." Frissell to Cooley, December 24, 1910, in HBF; "Annual Report of the Penn Normal, Industrial and Agricultural School," 1909, p. 10, in PSP.

48. "Annual Report," 1903, p. 19, in PSP.

they would seek to restore the health of the body politic by nurturing the soul; they would "uplift" black Americans and thereby contribute to creating the Kingdom of Heaven on earth. For the new Penn trustees the impulse was not nearly so lofty or inspired: however varied or diverse the elements might have been that attracted them to the Penn endeavor, their fear of black "degradation" and their desire for proof of black worth loomed large above all the others. And so it was that a little-known and little-traveled byway of American culture became at the turn of this century an outpost of the Progressive spirit of morality and order; for forty years Penn School on St. Helena Island would remain a curious manifestation of upper class hopes and fears at a moment of crisis in the American experiment in democracy.

3

Transitions

In April of 1901 the new Penn School trustees held their first real business meeting at Hampton, Virginia, where they interviewed a promising candidate for the job at St. Helena. A Hampton graduate and a special protégé of George Foster Peabody, P. W. Dawkins was currently the vice-president of Kittrell College, a small school for blacks in North Carolina. As a young man Dawkins had absorbed the Hampton message of uplift and service, and he shared Booker T. Washington's faith in black initiative and self-help as the most promising means of black advancement. Wallace Buttrick described him as one of the most intelligent and capable Negroes he had ever met; the Penn trustees felt that Dawkins was their man, and they offered him a position as Superintendent of Industries at Penn School. By the end of the week, Dawkins had written his acceptance to Frissell, rejoicing in this new challenge and opportunity "in the work of elevating my people."[1]

Dawkins soon visited the island and reported his findings to Frissell: "Trades are needed badly. All are very anxious for this industrial feature to be added to the school, and beged [*sic*] for

---

1. Trustees' minutes, April 15, 1901, in PSP; Frissell to Peabody, April 10, 1901, P. W. Dawkins to Frissell, April 19, 20, 1901, Frederick A. Eustis to Robert Darrah Jenks, September 2, 1904, all in HBF; Wallace Buttrick to Peabody, June 15, 1903, in JMD.

me to return again soon to begin it." Dawkins found that the islanders were victims of the one-crop system—planting all their land in cotton and buying all their food supplies at "the store." The Marsh tackies, or island horses, were very small and weak, and most plowing was done with the primitive ox or the hoe. Though cows were present on the island, the blacks made no use of milk or butter, and their diet was in many other ways woefully deficient. Here were the clearly identifiable problems that Dawkins' Hampton training had prepared him to surmount, but their solution called for drastic changes at Penn School.[2]

The school itself had no farm, and only one horse, a few tools, and a single shelter. Although the school was located picturesquely in a grove of live oaks, the quaint old building, sent down from Philadelphia in 1863, only masked a yawning inadequacy. The eight teachers were all Penn graduates (Penn School only had seven grades), and these eight souls were entrusted with the care of 300 lively children. "I wish our friends could look in upon us," wrote Miss Murray, describing the schoolhouse, "during one of our frequent rain storms."

> The recitation rooms, flooded, are abandoned, and books are hurried into desks. The oldest pupils slide into the driest seats, and the girls exclaim as the water drips on some cherished finery. One teacher, subject to rheumatic attacks, holds her umbrella over her as she teaches. In another class the giggling pupils are all perched, like chickens at roost, on top of the desks, the floor below them being a pool. One energetic teacher thinks it a good time to scour, and has her boys with brooms sweeping out wet and dirt together. Unless slates or boards are carefully laid over them, book closets are soaked and books spoiled.[3]

Such conditions were clearly intolerable. To make matters worse, Miss Murray and her assistant Miss Lathrop (Miss Towne had died in the winter of 1901) were elderly and poorly trained. Although they had sweet dispositions and undoubtedly exercised

---

   2. Dawkins to Frissell, May 20, 1901, in HBF: Penn School publicity brochure, n.d., in JMD.
   3. "Annual Report of the Penn Normal, Industrial and Agricultural School," 1902, pp. 9, 13, in PSP.

a beneficial influence on their pupils, their teaching methods left much to be desired. They had the students memorize their lessons instead of understanding the underlying principles. As an official of the General Education Board described them in 1903, "They remind me, and the flavor of the institution confirms the resemblance, of two dear maiden ladies who taught me how to read and sew in an old-time 'Dame School' in 1860."[4]

Miss Murray was also pathetically naive in her understanding of the islanders' social and intellectual development. "We think that ... the danger to the negro race lies in the choice of amusement," she wrote with real self-satisfaction in 1903. "And therefore to prevent the temptations of the bar room and gambling table, I teach note reading and part songs and Miss Lathrop teaches harmless games, the 'Twenty Questions,' 'Spelling Backward,' 'Bean Bags,' 'Conundrums,' 'Charades,' and we have the pleasure of knowing that the young peoples' parties are wonderfully improved in quality and decorum."[5]

In the fall of 1901 the old Penn School gave way to something new when P. W. Dawkins and his family moved to St. Helena. Dawkins began immediately to organize the islanders into farmers' conferences, modeled after the Tuskegee Farmers Conference Booker T. Washington had initiated. These conferences epitomized the Washington emphasis on self-help and self-improvement. Stating their objective to be promotion of the moral, material, and educational progress of the entire community, the St. Helena farmers' conference adopted a constitution, including the following articles:

    1. To abolish and do away with the mortgage system just as rapidly as possible.

    2. To raise our food supplies, such as corn, potatoes, syrup, peas, hogs, chickens, etc., at home rather than go into debt for them at the store.

    3. To stop throwing our time and money away on Saturday by standing around towns, drinking and disgracing ourselves in many other ways.

    4. Confidential to Francis Reeve Cope, Jr., January 21, 1903, Buttrick to Peabody, June 15, 1903, both in JMD.
    5. "Fortieth Report of the Principal of Penn School," June 20, 1903, in PSP.

4. To oppose at all times the Excursion and Campmeeting, and try earnestly to secure better schools, better teachers and better preachers.

5. To try to buy homes, to urge upon all negroes the necessity of owning farms and homes, and not only to own them, but to beautify and improve them.[6]

The St. Helena conference judiciously eschewed all interest in politics, declaring that it was not a political organization and that politics would not be permitted to enter into any discussions.[7] Clearly, Dawkins was following the Washington formula as conscientiously as possible.

A good indication of the kinds of abuses that Dawkins confronted and combatted can be gained from reading a pamphlet that he published and distributed to all members of the farmers' conferences. Entitled "St. Helena Island Don'ts," this pamphlet reads in part as follows:

A very common fault among the people is that of standing at the end of the completion of hoeing a row and talking by the hour about nothing. So our first don't is, "Don't stand at the end of the row too long." Too often Saturday is lost by the people in going to the cross-road store, or to town, when it might be avoided, therefore, the second don't is, "Don't leave Saturday out of the Commandment, which says: 'Six days shalt thou labor.'" Our third don't shows one of the ways to increase wages and insure a job. "Don't fail to give as good service for fifty cents a day as you would for a dollar." ... "Don't fail to have money in your pocket when you go home; don't let merchants and agents talk you into buying what you don't need, for you may need what you can't buy; don't fail to have something to sell, for the farmer who buys and doesn't sell, will pretty soon sell what he can't buy; don't make debts you don't mean to pay." ... "Don't try to eat all you raise, but try to raise all you eat." "Don't expect to drink milk and honey over yonder and not try to make an honest living here." "Don't forget to pay your honest debts, taxes included." "Don't spend more money for cologne on Sunday than you do for soap in the week; don't keep your children out of school." Now when you listen to beautiful discourses about the golden streets, don't come out and dodge the road men; don't fail to love virtue and protect

6. "Annual Report," 1903, p. 15, in PSP.
7. *Ibid.*

your family, and when you pray, "Watch over me through the night," don't go out and stay all night; don't talk about leaders and then not follow.

The farmers' conferences also stressed the importance of buying land and of staying away from the cities. All this was elementary, if colorful, advice to men who found themselves trapped in a bondage of ignorance. The men of St. Helena eagerly welcomed Dawkins' lessons on soil preparation, seeding, and cultivation; and several even agreed to try a small portion of their farms according to his instructions. As one of their number wrote to Francis Cope, "We Hail Bro. P. W. Dawkins as our Booker T. Washington of St. Helena and intend to stay by him as the tick stay on the cow back."[8]

By 1902 the trustees had purchased some rather poor land for a school farm, a mule, and some basic farming equipment. Dawkins now began to divide his time between clearing and planting the land and teaching in the classroom. He gave all of the advanced classes, both boys' and girls', instructions in agriculture. Every few days he sent two or three boys out into the fields for some practical instruction, and he expected all his students to work on their parents' farms before and after school.[9]

Within two years the new superintendent had increased dramatically the crop yields on the school farm—and this on land that all the islanders knew was inferior. The boys and girls in the agricultural classes began to exhibit genuine interest in their agricultural work, and many even tried to persuade their parents to adopt the new methods. Dawkins believed that through the agricultural classes, school farm, and farmers' conferences, the school was reaching not only the younger generation, but also the older people who owned most of the land on the island.[10] Dawkins consistently urged the use of horses and the cultivation of vegetables and food crops, and he pleaded fervently for an end to debt making. In encouraging and fostering self-sufficiency and self-reli-

8. "Annual Report," 1904, pp. 16–19, in PSP; Dawkins, "Report to the Trustees," June, 1903, in HBF: J. C. P. Miller to Cope, July 21, 1902, in JMD.
9. Trustees' minutes, January 22, 1902, in PSP; Foote to Frissell, January 28, 1902, Dawkins "Report," June, 1903, Dawkins to Frissell, October 21, 1902, all in HBF.
10. "Annual Report," 1904, p. 9, in PSP.

ance, Dawkins was bringing the best that Hampton had to offer to St. Helena Island.

The Hampton influence insinuated itself in other ways, also. Mrs. Dawkins, a Hampton graduate, shouldered a major part of the burden in teaching cooking and sewing to the Penn School girls. Preparation of vegetables had been virtually unknown on the island, and Mrs. Dawkins must have initiated many a culinary adventure as she led her students beyond their traditional reliance on the sweet potato. She also welcomed the older island women into her care, establishing community classes for these women who knew so little of modern household arts. Two other Hampton graduates, a Mr. and Mrs. Stephens, also joined the Penn School staff in these early years. A carpenter and a trained nurse, the Stephenses brought desperately needed skills to this isolated island culture.[11]

While continuing his educational and agricultural programs, Dawkins also developed an active interest in the public school system of the county. In 1903 he accepted an appointment to the St. Helena District School Board, and he became president of the Teachers' Institute of Beaufort County. He also cooperated with Senator Niels Christensen, Jr., state legislator from Beaufort County, to prepare an agricultural program for the county's public schools. In all these ways and more, P. W. Dawkins touched the life of this island community. Through farmers' conferences, teachers' institutes, community classes, and a score of other activities, he spread the message that he was "trying to put something new . . . into an old business and a poor system" and that Penn School was to have a new meaning for these people of the South Carolina Sea Islands.[12]

While Dawkins was getting the work in hand on St. Helena, his trustees had appealed to the General Education Board for assistance in their new venture. In 1903 one of that foundation's representatives, Wallace Buttrick, traveled to St. Helena to survey

11. Trustees' minutes (Executive Committee), August 14, 1901, "Annual Report," 1904, p. 9, Trustees' minutes, January 22, 1902, all in PSP; Dawkins, "Report," June, 1903, in HBF.

12. "Annual Report," 1904, p. 19, Trustees' minutes, January 20, 1903, both in PSP; Dawkins, "Report," June, 1903, in HBF.

the work there and evaluate its merits. Buttrick felt that the situation was demoralizing from the standpoint of both educational value and moral progress and recommended that the management of the school be taken from Miss Murray. Cataloging the ills of the school, Buttrick referred to the school farm and the poor quality of the land; the old school building, which was dilapidated and unfit for occupancy; the small industrial shop; and the inferior equipment, teachers, and instruction. Most distressing of all, however, was the failure of Miss Murray and Miss Lathrop to appreciate the purpose and substance of industrial education. To them it meant only how to sew and mend, saw and hammer, sow and reap; they did not understand that industrial education could lead to moral development and uplift, or that it could build character.[13]

Recommending the removal of Miss Murray, Buttrick suggested that the trustees "use anesthetics freely, if possible, but do not fail to perform the operation if you would save the school." He also recommended a thorough reorganization of the work, assuring the trustees that he believed Dawkins would be equal to the task.[14]

Buttrick's analysis and recommendations threw the trustees into a frenzy of correspondence and concern. Robert Jenks and Francis Cope suggested retaining Dawkins as head of the school, but Frissell disagreed. Not only did he fear that a race antagonism might be created on the island, he also did not believe that any Negro could make a success out of the plan. Frissell favored white control, for as he explained confidentially to Robert Jenks, "Even at Tuskegee under Mr. Washington himself the defects of negro control are very apparent."[15]

Frissell proposed that two white women who were teachers at Hampton should direct the work at Penn School. One, Rossa Belle Cooley, had taught for two years at Miss Round's School in

13. Trustees' minutes, October 21, 1902, in PSP; Buttrick to Peabody, June 15, 1903, in JMD.
14. Buttrick to Peabody, June 15, 1903, in JMD.
15. R. D. Jenks to Cope, July 6, 8, 1903, in JMD; James McPherson, "White Liberals and Black Power in Negro Education, 1865–1915," *American Historical Review*, LXXV (June, 1970), 1363–64.

Brooklyn and for six years at Hampton. Though Frissell looked upon her as one of his best teachers, he was willing to let her go to Penn. The other was Miss Frances Cora Butler, described by Robert Jenks as a typical New England school teacher, with not as much ability or cleverness as Miss Cooley. Both were thoroughly imbued with the missionary spirit, devoted to Frissell, and convinced of the moral and intellectual rewards of industrial education.[16]

Frissell's will prevailed, and the trustees began to reorganize the school. Miss Murray retained nominal control, but Miss Cooley understood that although she would be the practical head of the school, she would obey all orders issued by Miss Murray. She and Miss Butler would assume as many classroom duties as Miss Murray would let them, and the rest of the time they would spend working among the people in their homes. Miss Cooley, furthermore, would take charge of the industrial program and be responsible for the work done by Dawkins, Stephens, and their wives. The trustees realized that Dawkins would probably feel temporarily dissatisfied, but they thought he would become a useful assistant to Miss Cooley.[17]

At Frissell's suggestion, the board decided to wait another year before hiring Miss Cooley to reorganize the school. They hoped to be able to lay the groundwork for the reorganization they felt was necessary by preparing Miss Murray for the changes to take place. They feared that Miss Murray and Miss Lathrop might possibly be jealous and antagonistic if the new programs were carelessly or hastily presented, so Miss Cooley and Miss Butler remained at Hampton for another year, preparing themselves for the work they were to undertake.[18]

Some among the trustees understood that if Miss Cooley accepted the position they had offered her, her choice would be a manifestation of the true missionary spirit, for she fully realized

16. R. D. Jenks to Cope, July 6, August 25, in JMD; Cooley, *School Acres*, 34; Cooley, *Homes of the Freed*, 19.
17. R. D. Jenks to Cope, July 6, 8, 1903, in JMD.
18. Trustees' minutes, July 24, 1903, in PSP; R. D. Jenks to Cooley, July 25, 1903, in JMD.

the loneliness of the life on St. Helena and the obstacles in the way of carrying out any progressive plans in the immediate future. As the trustees were soon to discover, however, Rossa Belle Cooley was not one to be cowed by obstacles. On January 19, 1904, the Penn School trustees met in Robert Jenks's office and officially hired Miss Cooley and Miss Butler as assistant principal and teacher at salaries of $1,000 and $900 per year.[19]

Already Miss Cooley had established the pattern of suggesting her ideas to Frissell and asking him to present them to the board as his own. She did this avowedly in the name of harmony, but the effect of it was to allow her the fullest latitude in her planning and activities. Frissell had assured her that she would know best the needs of her school and that she must, therefore, direct its development. He advised her to educate the trustees into her beliefs, and she began immediately to assume this control. In the years ahead the trustees would become less and less significant in the direction of Penn School, providing only the authorization and the funds for the projects she initiated. But Miss Cooley had learned well from Frissell, and she would foster the illusion among the trustees that they were in control.[20]

At the autumn meeting of the trustees, Frissell remarked on the poor intellectual character of the two students sent to Hampton from St. Helena Island, suggesting that the school had formerly attempted too much and that it should now give a few students good training. Someone reported this evaluation to Miss Murray, upsetting her considerably and leading her to feel that her dedication and efforts had not been appreciated. Miss Lathrop also felt displaced. As Dawkins described it to Frissell, Miss Lathrop's influence had been against the forward movement, and she had prejudiced the minds of the people against Miss Cooley and Miss Butler. As a result, the island people did not look forward to the arrival of these two ladies. Subsequently, Miss Lath-

19. R. D. Jenks to Cope, July 6, 1903, in JMD; Trustees minutes, January 19, 1904, in PSP.
20. Cooley to H. B. Frissell, August 29, 1903, H. B. Frissell to Cooley, November 18, 1904, both in HBF.

rop applied for a position at Hampton, explaining that the coming of Miss Cooley had made her position somewhat difficult. Frissell, needless to say, was unmoved.[21]

Despite the resistance of the two older ladies, the board at its next meeting fulfilled one of Miss Cooley's first requests, authorizing the hiring of two new black teachers at $25 per month. Robert Jenks, as chairman of the executive committee, was largely responsible for the financial end of the Penn School venture, and he had opposed the hiring of these teachers; he feared increasing expenses too suddenly until they had made a trial of their new plans. Frissell, however, supported Miss Cooley, reminding Jenks that she would feel very strongly the need for more help; and the more help she could get, the more work she could do. For this and other reasons, Robert Jenks soon resigned as chairman of the executive committee, claiming that he wanted to devote more time to Civil Service reform work and that he did not think the chairmanship should remain in the hands of one person for more than a year or two at a time. In his place he recommended the election of Francis Cope, noting that a number of charitable organizations were endeavoring to enlist Cope's energies and support and that the Penn board should secure his active interest before it was too late. "I think that he will gladly give this," wrote Jenks, "not only because of his great interest in the negro question from an abstract point of view, but also because of the large amount of money invested by his family in the fortunes of the Penn School." Frissell offered Cope the job, and Cope accepted. With this acceptance, Francis Cope and Rossa Belle Cooley embarked on a forty-year quest, dedicating themselves to a hopeful and challenging new enterpise.[22]

As Miss Cooley later recalled, it was hot that first October.

21. H. B. Frissell to Cooley, November 18, 1904, H. B. Frissell to R. D. Jenks, February 20, July 16, 1904, R. D. Jenks to H. B. Frissell, April 8, 1904, all in HBF.

22. Trustees' minutes, June 24, 1904. This was comparable to public school wages throughout the South. See Louis R. Harlan, *Separate and Unequal: Public School Campaigns and Racism in the Southern Seaboard States, 1901–1915* (Chapel Hill, N.C., 1958), 31; Bullock, *A History of Negro Education*, 181. It is interesting to note that at their trustees' meeting on September 18, 1906, the Penn School trustees authorized a salary of $50 per month for a white financial secretary who was to make appeals and raise money for both Penn School and the Visiting Nurse Society. Trustees' minutes, September 28,

The two northern ladies had to learn how to live in a totally new environment. What with settling an unfinished home, unpacking furniture, and opening the new schoolhouse, "we found our days too full, and our enthusiasm ran away with our strength." For three busy, happy weeks the two young women rejoiced that they were to bring Hampton to the islands. They talked of plans for industrial training, agriculture, housekeeping for girls, and trades to help a rural community hold its boys. Everything seemed possible and probable. But then malaria struck Frances Butler, and Rossa Cooley realized for the first time the extent of her isolation. The ladies had not had time to make the aquaintance of the few white people who lived on the island, most of whom had left for the summer and autumn to avoid the fearful heat and sickness. It was a nine-mile drive through heavy sand to Fort Fremont, but sending to Beaufort meant driving six miles and then crossing the river in an irregular and undependable rowboat. Miss Cooley sent for the army doctor. He arrived at two in the morning and sent immediately to Savannah for a trained nurse. All the medicine and sickroom accessories were in Beaufort; and although the necessary supplies were sent for it was to no avail. On the night of November 1, 1904, Frances Butler died, a long way from home.[23]

Frances Eliot Foote, a Penn trustee, in eulogizing Miss Butler in the Boston *Transcript*, called her a pioneer in the New South and applauded her for going to her duty in the American missionary field. "Must we not . . . feel a thrill of pride," Miss Foote asked her New England readers, "that the spirit which triumphed in the early settler days of our country remains still a force which counts, strong and vital, to do and to dare?" At their next meeting, the Penn School trustees also lauded "the enthusiasm which she shared with those who give their lives in the missionary field."[24]

Dr. Frissell journeyed to St. Helena immediately and traveled with Miss Cooley back down the oyster-shell road, across the

---

1906, in PSP; R. D. Jenks to H. B. Frissell, June 4, September 24, 1904, H. B. Frissell to R. D. Jenks, June 6, 1904, both in HBF.

23. Cooley, *Homes of the Freed*, 17–23.

24. Frances Eliot Foote, "A Pioneer in the New South," Boston Evening *Transcript*, November 12, 1904; Trustees' minutes, January 10, 1905, in PSP.

river, through Beaufort, all the way to Boston, and out to the home in Arlington. The trustees feared that Rossa Cooley would lay down the work she had barely begun, but their fears were groundless. Although greatly shaken by her dear friend's death, Miss Cooley was now more determined than ever to go to St. Helena and help the people out of their bondage. The trustees realized that she would need a new coworker in order to resume her duties, and before the year was out Frissell had convinced another of his Hampton staff to take up the work at St. Helena.[25]

Grace Bigelow House, Miss Cooley's new assistant, was a shy, sweet-tempered woman with very impressive credentials. Her great-grandfather Bigelow knew the Marquis de Lafayette of France and had participated in welcoming him to America. Her great-uncle, John Bigelow, was minister to France during the Lincoln administration and editor of the New York *Evening Post*. Her father was John House, a missionary to the Balkans and the founder of the American Farm School in Salonica, Greece. Grace House acquired this missionary commitment from her father, and it shaped her life. After growing up in Turkey, Grace attended the fashionable Miss Dana's school in Morristown, New Jersey; and in 1896 she entered Teachers College, Columbia University, which was emerging at that time as a leader in reformist, progressive education.[26]

While at Columbia, Grace House absorbed the educational theories that have since come to be known as progressive education, and she worked in an environment that was receptive to the teachings of a young educational innovator who would soon go to Columbia himself. As John Dewey wrote in 1897, expressing a pedagogic creed that surely moved Miss House, "The teacher is engaged, not simply in the training of individuals, but in the for-

---

25. Cooley, *Homes of the Freed*, 23; R. D. Jenks to H. B. Frissell, November 7, 1904, in HBF.

26. Linnie Lumpkins Blanton, "Reminiscenses of a Friend and a Great Teacher," 1965, Anne and Ruth House, "Biography of Grace Bigelow House," January 28, 1965, both in JMD; Clipping from New York *Times*, January 4, 1946, in PSP; Joice M. Nankivell, *A Life for the Balkans* (London, 1939); "Resolutions Re Services of Dr. House," *Southern Workman*, LXVI (January, 1937), 25–26; Cremin, *The Transformation of the School*, 170–75.

mation of the proper social life," and "in this way the teacher always is the prophet of the true God and the usherer in of the true kingdom of God."[27]

As Lawrence Cremin has explained, progressive education began as progressivism in education: a many-sided effort to use the schools to improve the lives of individuals. Abandoning the old elitist conceptions of the nature and functions of education, the Progressives believed that education should be a democratizing force and influence and thus a fundamental lever of social and political regeneration. In other words, the school should be a primary instrument in fulfilling the promise of American life. The Progressives redirected the curriculum to encompass a concern for health, vocation, and the quality of family and community life; they also began to tailor their instruction to the different kinds and classes of children who were being brought within the purview of the school. Cremin has suggested that if everyone was to attend school, not only the methods but the meaning of education would have to change.[28]

Teachers College, Columbia, under the leadership of President James Earl Russell, had been founded in the 1890s explicitly to spread the new educational gospel, especially into the northern slums, but also to the benighted South. President Russell cooperated with the General Education Board in selecting young men and women to be trained at Teachers College, and more than once he joined Robert Ogden in his visits to schools and colleges throughout the South. Thus, Grace House was acting in the best Teachers College spirit when she joined Rossa Cooley on St. Helena Island. She brought to the new enterprise the patrician's

27. John Dewey, *School Journal*, LIV (1897), 77–80, as quoted in Cremin, *The Transformation of the School*, 100.
28. Cremin, *The Transformation of the School*, viii–lx, 88, 345. Arthur Bestor penned a stinging critique of progressive education in a book entitled *Educational Wastelands* in 1953. According to Cremin, Bestor argued that "democratic education differs from aristocratic education only in the number of persons with whom it deals, not in the values it seeks to impart. To convert the education of the common man into something other than systematic intellectual training is to rob him of his birthright; it is to vulgarize culture under the guise of democratizing it. By training all in the ability to think, the schools distribute intellectual power widely among the people. This and this alone is their distinctive way of contributing to social progress."

spirit of service and the Hamptonian's understanding of moral rejuvenation, as well as the missionary's millenial convictions and the Progressive's commitment to rebuilding the community; she embodied all the themes that were to characterize Penn School's development for the next forty years.[29]

One of the islanders described Miss House as quiet and modest in her manner, lacking racial or personal prejudice. All who knew her responded to her warmth and sweet sincerity, and she had many devoted followers. Miss House kept a diary and a log of her own poetry, both of which revealed her to have been romantic, timid, naive, and serious; her girlish self-doubt often spilled over into much deeper self-reproach, sadness, and regret. She was almost monastic in her devotion to the missionary life, as her most often repeated prayer reveals: "Forgetting those things which are behind, and reaching forth unto those things which are before, I press toward the mark for the prize of the high calling of God in Christ Jesus. This is my text for the new year. God help me to press forward without flinching for Jesus Christ's sake."[30]

With great trepidation and doubt, Grace House agreed to accompany Rossa Cooley on her return to St. Helena in the spring. Originally she planned to stay for only a year—later to join her parents at their school in Greece. But such overseas work seemed not to be the will of God, and Miss House spent the rest of her life ministering to the needs of the people of St. Helena.

At last all was in readiness for the new enterprise to begin: new principals, new teachers, a new schoolhouse, and a new message. Here were hundreds of acres and hundreds of homes. And here were hundreds of children getting book learning but not getting their roots down into the soil, the very basis of life. Could the old Liberty Bell help ring in a new freedom—help wake up the island boys and girls to see "that the responsibility for holding what their grandfathers and grandmothers had handed down to them rested on their own shoulders? Would it be possible for

---

29. Smith, "Progressivism in American Education," 184; Cremin, *The Transformation of the School*, 175.

30. Blanton, "Reminiscences," Grace Bigelow House, "Diary and Log," December 31, 1899, both in JMD.

Penn School to help develop a rural life rich enough to hold the generations that had not won the acres by their own labor?" These were the questions that held Rossa Cooley in their grasp, and that led her to build on St. Helena a model of community education.[31]

31. Cooley, *School Acres*, 29–30.

4

Community Building

On her first trips to the island, Miss Cooley had noted Penn School's lamentably inadequate facilities. As she described the early classrooms: "Spaces painted black served as blackboards; a few old maps; a globe in Miss Murray's room; rough desks made to seat two but often holding four; some book cupboards; and that was all!" Bad as they were, these conditions could be rectified fairly simply. One of the first improvements of the new regime was the erection of a modern new two-story school building, Founder's Hall. Not so easily changed were the methods employed inside the classrooms, for the lessons learned at Penn School had come to be a mark of freedom and a badge of honor to the islanders.[1]

Inside these classrooms Miss Cooley had witnessed incredible feats of memory. Pages of history were recited with hardly a word changed; long lines of presidents and dynasties were given, dates included, without hesitation. The blackboards reflected many an hour spent over algebra, Latin prose, and physics. In the geography class pupils identified the wiggly lines on the map as water courses but could not associate these with the blue tide rivers that some of them crossed on their way to school. States and their capitals had been as carefully memorized as kings and queens and

1. Cooley, *School Acres*, 35.

had as little relation to the lives of the children who learned them. To one so steeped in the Hampton philosophy of education, the lessons being learned at Penn School were both sterile and meaningless. Miss Cooley saw immediately that her primary tasks would be to close the gap between the working life of the people and the book learning of the schools and to make Penn School a more vital force in the day-to-day life of the community.[2]

Miss Cooley criticized the older methods of education for teaching "isolated facts learned not because they fitted into life but because they fitted into the examinations." She felt that this kind of education was merely "plastered on," regardless of the life and the needs of the people, and that true education should prepare its students "for the life they must fit into." Miss Cooley's educational philosophy was in some ways reminiscent of the writings of the evolutionist Herbert Spencer. Spencer believed that the aim of education was the preparation for life. Since he believed that mental development follows evolutionary processes that work themselves out over long periods of time, according to laws independent of immediate human acts, education could never be an important factor in social progress. The best teachers could do, therefore, was to provide the knowledge that would enable people to adapt more readily to the circumstances that surrounded them. Although Miss Cooley did not believe that the school could rush evolution, she did believe that the school could provide training for better living. The first step in reorganizing Penn School, therefore, was to get out into the community and discover what the needs and conditions were.[3]

Though neither of them had ever ridden before, Miss Cooley and Miss House boldly mounted the school horses and began "slashin' about de' island." These two women must have cut impressive figures—young and energetic, their chestnut brown hair smooth and clasped at the neck, their belted shirtwaists crisp, and long skirts flowing. Miss Cooley was a handsome woman, very erect and self-assured, and her strong face and forthright manner almost obscured the slight limp caused by one short leg. Miss

2. *Ibid.*, 4, 36.
3. *Ibid.*, 20, 21, 36; Cremin, *The Transformation of the School*, 93–94.

House, too, was a striking woman, though her beauty sprang more from within; and she preferred to let the more forceful Rossa capture the spotlight. Together they made a winning team, and before long the islanders came to accept them.[4]

As the two ladies traveled about the island, cataloging the pitiful conditions on the farms and in the homes, they became more convinced than ever of the need for linking these to the school; but they knew that their educational revolution would encounter resistance. One of the first plans for the new school involved raising the students' fees from one dollar to five dollars, thus impressing on the people that education was a costly business. Most of the islanders accepted this change without much hesitation, although one mother did remark that it was a "very expensionate school." One parent decided however, that Ezekiel was "wut de five dollars, but Benola's haid too t'ick," and it looked as if the new program would foster an unequal division of opportunity. Miss Cooley seized the moment to introduce a radical innovation. She told the parents that Benola could pay half of her fees in cash and work out the other half at the school, and this soon became the custom for all the students. "This step made it easier," reminisced Miss Cooley, "to weave in industrial education as part of the regular schedule a little later."[5]

The object of the new school was to bring the island life itself into the classroom. Since all such major changes are difficult, this one required some getting used to. "Mine was a very stiff class that marched out to the woodpile one morning," recalled Miss Cooley, "to measure a cord instead of learning about it on a page in the arithmetic." And it was a very surprised class that paced off an acre in a nearby field, rather than sitting at their desks and working a problem from their schoolbooks. But children are blessedly flexible, and before long they began to like the change from books and memory to the world about them.[6]

Symbolic of the change from old to new was Miss Cooley's

4. Cooley, *School Acres*, 37; interview with Bessie Banks Middleton, March 20, 1972, St. Helena Island, S.C.
5. Cooley, *School Acres*, 39, 40, 41; "Annual Report of the Penn Normal, Industrial and Agricultural School," 1908, p. 19, Trustees' minutes, April 13, 1906, in PSP.
6. Cooley, *School Acres*, 45.

ingenious use of the old schoolhouse. On one of her trips around the island she had come across old Aunt Jane, living in a house so "ractified" that it had to be propped up by poles. As she worried about Aunt Jane and worried also about what to do with the quaint old schoolhouse, she realized that the two could complement each other in a manner most pleasing to the Hampton way of thinking. Some of the boys had formed a Boy's Mission Club, and responding to Miss Cooley's encouragement they volunteered to give their time after school and on holidays to convert the old schoolhouse into a home for Aunt Jane. There, in a nutshell, was the epitome of the new school revolution Penn School had embarked upon. The school was to serve the community, and the boys and girls were to learn, through industrial education, the valuable lessons of cooperation and service.[7]

Despite the successes, however, this transition period was not without its difficulties. Almost as soon as they arrived on the island, the two ladies encountered, with some alarm, the moral standards of their new charges. The celebrated Mr. Stephens, the Hampton-trained carpenter, and the Reverend Mr. Simmons, an island preacher, apparently had developed for themselves an enviable relationship with Mrs. Maria Chaplin and her daughter Viola, both of them employees of Penn School. Mrs. Chaplin had graciously consented to open her home to the two young teachers from Hampton, and Miss Cooley lost no time in finding her new teachers more suitable accommodations. Stephens was summarily banished from the island, and the ladies Chaplin were excused from their duties at Penn School. All this was very unpleasant, upsetting, and a rather shocking introduction to the culture these northern ladies had chosen to refine.[8]

Even more difficult and unpleasant was the relationship with Miss Murray and Miss Lathrop. Ever since Wallace Buttrick had suggested a "surgical operation" to remove Miss Murray, the trustees had struggled to convince the elderly principal that they appreciated and needed her services and that the proposed

7. *Ibid.*, 27, 28; "Annual Report," 1905, p. 10, in PSP.
8. Cope to H. B. Frissell, April 6, 15, 1905, H. B. Frissell to Cope, May 3, 1905, all in HBF; Trustees' minutes, July 9, 1905, in PSP.

changes did not diminish her control. Their efforts failed to "anesthetize" Miss Murray, however, and she grew increasingly dissatisfied.⁹

In the spring of 1905, just a year after she had applied for a position at Hampton, Miss Lathrop asked the trustees for permission and funds to start a new school at Frogmore. Originally Miss Murray opposed this move because of the loss involved for Penn School, but by the spring of 1906, Miss Lathrop had worn down Miss Murray's resistance. The trustees also saw the logic and the advantage for themselves of Miss Lathrop's proposal, and they agreed to renovate the Frogmore schoolhouse for the two ladies' use. Miss Murray was to remain the nominal principal of Penn, but she was to be relieved of all duties and powers in connection with that position except that she would preside at least once a week at the opening exercises of the school. Miss Cooley thereupon assumed all the duties of the principal, though she had no jurisdiction over the Frogmore school. Clearly, Miss Murray had assisted in her own execution, and before long she gave vent to her frustrations. At Penn School's closing ceremonies in the spring, she made a pathetic address to the students, saying that she had been driven out of the work by the rich board of trustees. But it was too late for her now. Penn School had moved far beyond her grasp; and before much more time had passed, Miss Murray laid down her work of forty years and died quietly in her sleep.¹⁰

One of Miss Murray's old students stood dejectedly by her grave and paid her this parting tribute: "What we *is*, what we *have*, what we *done*, all, all is done by her." She had aided these people in their rise from slavery to self-respecting living. She had watched and helped as they bought and held their farms, educated their children, and lifted themselves to respectability. She had held out a standard and a vision, and she had stayed at the work through sickness, loneliness, opposition, and personal misfortune. As she remarked in 1904, no one could appreciate the

9. Buttrick to Peabody, June 15, 1903, R. D. Jenks to Cope, July 6, 1903, both in JMD.
10. H. B. Frissell to Cooley, April 7, 1905, H. B. Frissell to Cope, April 10, June 2, 1906, Cope to H. B. Frissell, January 15, 1908, all in HBF; Trustees' minutes, April 13, 1906, in PSP.

improvement more than she, for no one else had seen the degradation of forty years ago and could contrast it with the present. Although her mood and style were out of step with the latest ideas on black education, it is a shame nonetheless that the movement of time and men should have left her, at the end, cast aside.[11]

But Penn School was on the move, and the missionary's righteousness and zeal rarely leave room for appeasing the ill-favored. Miss Lathrop now found herself recalled to the North, and Miss Cooley became the undisputed ruler of the tiny island kingdom. At her request, Dr. Frissell traveled to St. Helena to explain to the people that the present administration was merely a continuation of the past and the loyalty that they had shown to Miss Murray and Miss Towne should be extended to their successors. The people responded favorably, and the two new principals now hoped to give substance to their vision for St. Helena.[12]

One final obstacle, however, impeded their forward movement. P. W. Dawkins had become increasingly dissatisfied with his position at Penn School. Even before Miss Cooley arrived, he had begun to chafe under limitations Miss Murray placed on his activities. She did not consider the agricultural work to be as important as the students' academic studies, for she felt that all such knowledge could be gleaned from farm journals; and she was very erratic in granting permission for boys to attend the carpentry or agriculture classes. Dawkins had also complained of the inadequate teaching at Penn School. Although the native teachers did the best they could, their dialect mixed with bad grammar and their inability to govern made him feel that he was sacrificing his children; and he asked for permission to send them away to school. Robert Jenks had responded that even though the education given in the academic department of Penn School was not up to modern standards, it was good enough for the education of Mr. Dawkins' children.[13]

When the trustees announced the plans for Miss Cooley's ar-

11. Maule to J. S. Bigelow, February 11, 1908, in JMD; "Forty-First Report of the Penn Normal, Industrial and Agricultural School," July, 1904, in PSP.
12. Cope to H. B. Frissell, January 10, 1908, H. B. Frissell to Cope, April 9, 1908, both in HBF; Trustees' minutes, January 24, 1908, in PSP.
13. R. D. Jenks to Cope, July 8, 1903, confidential to Cope, January 21, 1903, But-

rival, Dawkins learned that she would now take charge of the industrial work. The trustees assured him that this did not mean a diminution of his authority, but he must have known that the trustees had passed him by and that he would now be subordinate to a second white woman. By the summer of 1906 he had had his fill. He resigned from his post at Penn School and returned to Kittrell College, much to the relief of all concerned. In later years, Dawkins was forgotten at St. Helena, and Miss Cooley took the credit for much that he had done. But it was Dawkins who had started the school farm, the farmers' conferences, the teachers' institutes, and the community classes; and it was he who introduced the idea of demonstration farming. A true son of Hampton Institute, he represented the best that that program had to offer.[14]

By the time Dawkins departed in 1906, Frissell had already replaced him with another young Hampton graduate. Joshua Enoch Blanton, half-brother of Robert Russa Moton, took St. Helena by storm. A jovial and appealing man whom everybody liked, Blanton had a style in his dealings with whites that assured him a place in the affections of his trustees. A light-skinned and very handsome man, Blanton also stole the heart of Penn's most beloved young teacher, Linnie Lumpkins. "Sugar Lump," as the children called her, had been the first Hampton teacher to answer the Penn School call. Theirs was the first Penn School wedding. As Miss Cooley recalled, "We used the great yucca blossoms for decorations—beautiful ivory white wedding bells growing on tall stalks, that would make many a city bride envious!"[15]

---

trick to Peabody, June 15, 1903, all in JMD; Dawkins to H. B. Frissell, Ocotober 21, 1902, R. D. Jenks to H. B. Frissell, October 27, 1902, both in HBF.

14. Dawkins to Frissell, October 21, 1902, September 16, 1903, R. D. Jenks to Eustis, September 10, 1904, H. B. Frissell to Cope, June 2, 1906, all in HBF; Grace Bigelow House, "The Penn School and the Farmers' Conference," *Southern Workman*, XXXVI (January, 1907), 60.

15. Moton followed Booker T. Washington as principal at Tuskegee. H. B. Frissell to Cope, June 2, 1906, in HBF; Joshua Enoch Blanton to Cope, October 21, 1911, in PSP; interview with Mr. and Mrs. Benjamin Boyd, March 20, 1972, St. Helena Island, S.C. Cooley, *School Acres*, 25.

Blanton immediately tackled the school farm—an old abandoned cotton field without roads, fences, or fertile soil—and through sheer determination made it produce. "It was the first time," he later recalled, "I had ever seen anyone try to farm a bank of sand.... This was the kind of land given to me with which to dignify agriculture and inspire Penn School boys to love the farm!" It was discouraging work for a year or two; but with the addition of better land and the growing interest of the students, Blanton succeeded in producing impressive crop yields.[16]

Initially the students had resisted the introduction of agriculture into the school routine. Their fathers and grandfathers had equated manual labor with slavery; and the younger generation also felt that Latin, algebra, and physics were the proper concerns of the scholar. Miss Cooley's first agriculture class had broken and lost some of their tools, thinking that if the tools disappeared, agriculture would leave the school. The agricultural instruction consisted of such things as feeding and caring for the stock, chopping corn, raking trash for manure, plowing, and hoeing, all of which the students felt they could learn at home. But their opposition was to no avail, for the decision had been made. "In a community where less than one percent of the total population does any work other than farming," wrote one of the trustees in a typical annual report, "the fundamental teaching of the school should be practical agriculture."[17]

Originally the school was under suspicion not only because it was eliminating some of the higher subjects like Latin, but also because it was taking a questionable stand in agriculture, the one area in which the islanders felt they had some expertise. From the start the school opposed the one-crop system of dependence on cotton, encouraging the islanders to plant such food crops as corn and other vegetables and helping them to discover such cash crops as peanuts. The school also fostered the principle of crop rotation, dramatizing it through a one-acre miniature farm. All

16. Cooley, *School Acres*, 25; Joshua Enoch Blanton, "One Man's Life Story," *Southern Workman*, LII (September, 1923), 406.
17. Cooley, *School Acres*, 48, 50; "Annual Report," 1908, p. 10, in PSP.

of these innovations were met at first with skepticism, but the sheer logic of success eventually won the doubters for the Penn School methods. One could hardly argue with a corn yield of thirty-five bushels per acre on the Penn School farm, when the St. Helena Island average was a puny sixteen bushels per acre. Mr. Blanton was able to use the Penn farm not only to show the island farmers how to increase their crops, but also to improve their stock and poultry, to develop truck farming and winter vegetables, and with a fine Guernsey bull that Arthur Curtiss James sent down, to develop dairying. The school had acquired a fine and highly prized mowing machine, and Miss Cooley allowed selected islanders to use this on their own acres; the school also possessed a molasses mill, which many people used to grind their sugarcane into syrup. In such ways, then, Penn School began to win the confidence of the islanders, as well as community acceptance of the school's leadership.[18]

In 1905 Penn School held its first Farmers' Fair in connection with the Farmers' Conference, and the variety and quantity of products on exhibition surprised all who attended. Among the farm products were sweet and white potatoes, pumpkins, corn, sugarcane, pecans, peanuts, benne, rice, and bananas. And supplementing the exhibits of livestock and farm products, there were also baskets, quilts, corn-shuck mats, rag rugs, canned fruit, and needlework. The farmers themselves were as astonished as any, and they examined each others' exhibits with keen eagerness and growing determination to beat the record the next year. The day ended with a festive barbeque at sunset. The people had rasied the money for this themselves, and it was a delighted crowd that gathered in an open field and feasted on rice and vegetables and a whole cow, talking over the events of the day and laying plans to win the next year's prizes. The day had captured the people's imagination and enthusiasm, and the fair had come to stay.[19]

Following the fair, constant rains in the summer of 1905

18. Cooley, *School Acres*, 47, 50; Davis, "A Unique People's School," 7, 9; Trustees' minutes, January 20, 1916, Arthur Curtiss James to Blanton, May 31, 1916, Cooley, "Report to Trustees," January 14, 1913, all in PSP.

19. House, "The Penn School and the Farmers' Conference," 58; Cooley, *School Acres*, 106.

caused much damage to the crops, but the second fair in 1906 proved an inspiration nonetheless. As one of the farmers exclaimed: "I came here last year and 'lowed if things go on like-adat, I git a colored millionaire, but dis year kind of taken things out of my hands. But I see better corn, accordin' to my eyesight, dis year dan last and dis conference must go on!"[20]

The farmers' conferences became a natural vehicle for spreading the Penn School gospel, and agriculture was not the only topic Miss Cooley wanted these farmers to discuss. At one of the farmers' conferences, the special topic for discussion was how to keep the young people away from the cities. Moses Dudley, a Penn School graduate, had made a survey of a number of plantations, and he gave a report on the young people who had left the island. His report was brief and to the point: "I might say one third are still in the North; one third come back damaged; one third come back in their coffins, no good to anybody." This was one of the problems that distressed Miss Cooley most.[21]

Many of the young people had left the island, and Miss Cooley could well understand their wanting to go; farm life to them had meant only drudgery, and rarely did their back-breaking labor provide them with sufficient cash to carry them through the following year. Furthermore, to these provincial and unsophisticated blacks, the city offered dazzling opportunities and entertainments. Increasingly, Miss Cooley understood this as she sought to build a viable community on St. Helena. One day when old Uncle Jim came over from Dathaw Island for some "drinkin' medicine," he was thunderstruck at the sight of Hampton House, the principals' new home. "Jes' one step from Heaven," he declared, as he marveled at all the finery and conveniences. As he started off, he murmured to himself, "I sure been to de city." As Miss Cooley thought of his half-hour's trip in a leaky bateau through tidal river and marsh grass to a tiny island where a handful of blacks lived in homes even more primitive than those on St. Helena, she could understand why St. Helena could seem like the city to him and why Savannah, Charleston, Atlanta, and the

20. House, "The Penn School and the Farmers' Conference," 58.
21. "Annual Report," 1908, 13, in PSP; Cooley, *School Acres*, 20.

cities of the North seemed so appealing to the young people of the Sea Islands.[22]

And there were other explanations. In the 1880s the phosphate industry, which had been a major employer, had broken down and decayed. Then in 1893 the islands had fallen beneath an immense tidal wave driven forward by a devastating hurricane and followed by torrential rains and flooding. All had been lost, and many had left in preference to rebuilding their shattered lives on the island. These forces, added to the nationwide cityward migration, had started a trend that increasing numbers had followed of leaving the drudgery and isolation of St. Helena for the glamor of the city. This was the trend that Penn School sought to reverse.[23]

Penn School had other goals as well. Miss Cooley had a special empathy for the women of the Sea Islands. She saw their weakness and vulnerability, and she understood the sociological forces at work that conspired to keep them down. From her writings it is clear that she felt a great bond with these women and a great determination to help them improve their lives. She understood that they had had very little opportunity for home life, either in slavery or since: "From before 'dayclean' [sunrise]," she wrote "til the tasks in the field were done, they carried their share of the work along with the men." As a result, the women had never had a chance to learn to make comfortable, attractive homes. [24]

Her encounter with Aunt Binah, amusing though it was, reminded Miss Cooley how primitive this island culture was and how little its women knew of the necessities and comforts of modern life. When she and Miss House had first gone to St. Helena, they had carried their water from the well down by the roadside. Then came the well driven nearer their own kitchen and the convenient pump. Finally the trustees installed a water tower and system for Hampton House, and the islanders exhibited an enormous amount of interest and approval. Aunt Binah remained unimpressed, however, as she informed Miss Cooley one morning, pointing to the new water tank: "W'at de good o'him? I ben watch

22. Cooley, *Homes of the Freed*, 131.
23. Cooley, *School Acres*, 17.
24. Cooley, *Homes of the Freed*, 80, 108, 110.

him ebery day. He ain't do a ting yet." Miss Cooley took Aunt Binah to the corners of the house and showed her the big spigots for the fire hose, explaining how the system would work. Then she took the old woman into the kitchen and turned on the water for her to see. Incredulous, Aunt Binah fell to her knees and with arms upraised exclaimed, "Tank God, I lib to see dis day."[25]

Miss Cooley fervently believed that home life is at the center of civilized living, and she wanted to help these women build the comfortable, healthy homes that would bring self-respect. This, she believed, would also help to hold the young people on the island. Miss Cooley was determined that these women of the southern countryside were not to become mere housemaids for city dwellers; instead, she hoped to help them become homemakers, mothers, cultural leaders, and farm women for their own communities.[26] Thus, following the Hampton pattern once again, Miss Cooley introduced domestic training as a part of the regular curriculum at Penn School. Under Mrs. Dawkins the girls had had lessons in sewing and cooking; now they were to master all aspects of the domestic arts, from housecleaning and cooking to decorating and laundering and child care.

Very early Miss Cooley began to lobby for a small boarding department at the school. She wanted all the older students to board for awhile before they graduated, hoping in this way to refine their tastes and sensibilities. Frissell heartily endorsed this plan, considering a boarding department of great importance as a means for teaching the islanders a proper standard of living; and by Miss Cooley's second year this plan had become a reality. Before long there were nineteen boarders, all gaining special training in housekeeping and proper living. Miss Rosetta Mason, much beloved on the island, presided over the boarding department. In keeping with the Hampton spirit she placed great stress on the formation of habits of industry, orderliness, punctuality, and cleanliness.[27]

Miss Cooley realized from the start that St. Helena's isolation

25. *Ibid.*, 119–120. The money for this system had come from the estate of Ruth Ann Cope, one of Francis Cope's aunts. Trustees' minutes, February 5, 1909, in PSP.
26. Cooley, *Homes of the Freed*, 12.
27. Trustees' minutes, March 2, 1908, "Annual Report," 1908, p. 17, both in PSP.

gave Penn a unique opportunity to influence the life of the entire island community. From the beginning, therefore, she pursued the goal of community education—of reaching the fathers and mothers as well as the children, and of molding the lives of the people in as many ways as possible. As soon as they arrived on the island, Miss Cooley and Miss House had set about the task of getting to know the people and of visiting them in their homes. This home visitation became a regular feature of the Penn School program, with every teacher visiting the students' homes at least twice a year. Miss Cooley believed that teachers must be as interested in the family as in the child and that the larger community interests were as important as the classrooms.[28]

Penn reached out to the community in a variety of ways. Even under Miss Towne and Miss Murray, Penn had played an active part in the life of the little public schools on the island, especially by providing and preparing the teachers. Under Frissell's influence, Miss Cooley continued and extended this emphasis. Now when the public school children came once a month to Penn School to observe Temperance Monday, a custom Miss Towne had initiated in keeping with her abhorrence of strong drink, Miss Cooley invited the teachers to spend the mornings visiting Penn School classrooms; and she arranged the work in such a way as to give them practical hints. Eventually she initiated a Teachers' Institute, a two-week session for the island teachers, with speakers from Hampton and elsewhere to instruct the teachers in such areas as hygiene, Bible history, and school management. In this way she hoped to extend the Penn School influence to those homes that had no children at Penn.[29]

Penn also reached out to the older folk on the island. "We wants to come to de college" was a plea Miss Cooley found irresistible. In the early years of the transition Mrs. Dawkins had organized a community class of fifty or so older women who would meet periodically at the school for special instruction in sewing or cooking, or just for visiting. When the new schoolhouse went up in 1904, most of the islanders had never seen such an impressive

28. Trustees' minutes, November 30, 1910, in PSP; Cooley, *School Acres*, 37.
29. "Annual Report," 1906 p. 20, 1910 p. 26, both in PSP.

structure; and they were intrigued by all the goings-on at Penn. These women wanted to be a part of the new developments, and Miss Cooley realized that this was another opportunity for Penn to reach out into the community and touch the lives of its members. The community class, or "We Class" as its members affectionately called it, became an institution in the Penn School curriculum and a prime agent for transmitting Penn School news and ideas. The class met at the school every Wednesday, tackling a variety of projects before Miss Cooley finally struck the right combination. Her course in hygiene and home emergency nursing was an instant success and remained the course of study for years to come. After their lessons were completed, the women would sit at the school for hours, sewing quilts for the needy and singing spirituals.[30]

Penn performed a major service to the community when it employed a practical nurse. The arrival of a Penn School nurse in 1908 was the fulfillment of a dream, first formulated on the night of Miss Cooley's tragic introduction to the health problems of the island. Ever since Frances Butler's death, Miss Cooley had been deeply concerned about improving the island's health standards; but there were many obstacles in the way. Many of the blacks were only three or four generations removed from the African village, and they had had little contact with whites. Consequently, on St. Helena the old ideas continued and the old superstitions prevailed. Where superstition had given way to more modern remedies, the alluring titles and promises of the patent medicine bottles had become almost as great an enemy to the introduction of improved health practices. Miss Cooley reported the case of one old lady who had "drunk nine dollars and fifty cents wut ob medecine" before she died, and this, apparently, was not unusual. This was an economy, moreover, in which there was very little cash; and even if there had been a doctor on the island, few could have afforded him. Miss Cooley cared for many of the sick as best she could, both at Hampton House and in the island homes, but her knowledge was very limited; when some northern

---

30. Cooley, *Homes of the Freed*, 82, 84, 87; "Annual Report," 1904, p. 9, in PSP.

friends of the school volunteered to provide a trained nurse for the island, Rossa Cooley felt that her prayers had been answered.[31]

"Doctor Nurse" initiated first aid lessons for the boys and girls at Penn and for the mothers and grandmothers in the community class. She also carried her health instruction out to the county schools, and she instructed a class of midwives in principles of health care and cleanliness. The school began providing hot lunches for the students, gradually modifying their dietary habits; and at last Miss Cooley felt that the school was making progress in health education on the island. With the arrival of Dr. York Bailey, a Penn School graduate who had gone on to Howard University to study medicine, Miss Cooley could see real hope for the health standards of the island.[32]

Another important tie between school and community was the Sales House. In 1904 when the two northern ladies first went to the island, they had to decide how to handle all the barrels of clothing that had begun to flow in from the North. They adopted a little building on the edge of the school grounds near the road, where they sold the contents of the barrels to the people. Often the islanders were able to buy here the things that made it possible for them to go to church or send their children to school. And here they could use eggs, chickens, or sweet potatoes as well as money in exchange, thereby saving their self-respect and preserving a measure of independence. Mrs. Juno Washington, a remarkable woman in many ways, took charge of the Sales House. Born a slave, she had attended Penn School in its early days, taught there herself, married, and reared a family. Unlike many of the older islanders, she regarded the new Penn School without suspicion or distrust, and Miss Cooley thought of her as a bridge between the old and the new—one who could lead the old to understand and smooth the way for the new. When Mrs. Washington prayed at one of the school services, "Darlin' Jesus, please to bind us all together with a bandage of love," she turned a phrase

---

31. Cooley, *Homes of the Freed*, 24, 26, 45, 46; Davis to R. D. Jenks, November 25, 1903, in HBF; Trustees' minutes, September 28, 1906, "Annual Report," 1908, p. 25, both in PSP.

32. Cooley, *Homes of the Freed*, 49, 50, 57, 65.

that touched Miss Cooley deeply and expressed much of what the new principal had been feeling. For the young principal knew that any who work to build up a community and uplift a people make many blunders and can often feel a discouragement that needs the "bandage of love."[33]

Despite the helpful cooperation in all these areas of life, the bond between school and community that had the most far-reaching significance for the inhabitants of St. Helena Island was Penn's designation, in 1909, as a United States Department of Agriculture demonstration farm. Although there was very little chance of starvation on St. Helena Island, with oysters and crabs and all manner of seafood in abundance at every turn, Miss Cooley saw that the island economy was not holding the oncoming generation; and she realized that the farms would have to produce if they were to hold their young. One of the key problems the school had to face, however, was the farmers' deep-rooted conservatism and independence. Though their methods were primitive and their soil exhausted, farming was the area they felt was their own, and they resented the efforts of a "mere boy" (Blanton) to get them to change their ways. And though an island leader might proclaim with enthusiasm at one of the Farmers' Fairs, "De bes' way to strike down de liar who say de negro ain't wuk, is to show him de wuk," more than work was needed to combat "worn-out soil and outworn methods."[34]

Far in advance of its actaul appearance, Miss Cooley realized that the boll weevil was on its way to the Atlantic coast. In vain she tried to arouse the people, telling them in their churches and on their farms that they must diversify their crops and raise their food, for cotton was doomed. But they were not impressed. "I ain't fearful," proclaimed one old stalwart, "I stan' ober my fiel' and shoot him down jes luk a chicken hawk!"[35] So Penn School acknowledged that other methods of persuasion would have to be found.

Fortunately Dr. Frissell had the answer. Through his associa-

33. *Ibid.*, 102–105, 113, 114.
34. Cooley, *School Acres*, 106, 111, 114.
35. *Ibid.*, 108.

tion with Wallace Buttrick, now head of the General Education Board, he had become familiar with the work of Seaman Knapp, the father of the demonstration idea. Knapp had long been a proponent of scientific farming as the answer to rural economic distress, and in 1903 he discovered that the one sure way to get local farmers to adopt scientific methods was to have one of their neighbors demonstrate the superiority of these methods on his own farm under Department of Agriculture tutelage. After studying Dr. Knapp's methods and successes, Wallace Buttrick induced the General Education Board to sponsor his work throughout the South, largely in an effort to generate the capital for a southern public school system.[36]

In 1909 Frissell took Knapp to St. Helena to attend the annual Farmers' Fair. Observing the desperate condition of most of the island farmers, Knapp agreed to use the Penn School farm as a demonstration station to carry out various agricultural experiments. At first Miss Cooley and Mr. Cope resisted this arrangement, for they feared that Blanton would resent the intrusion into his territory. Penn had had crop failures the year before; and since the time for planting had already arrived, Miss Cooley and Cope also feared that further delay would cause a reduction of their credibility. Frissell insisted, however, and eventually all agreed that the regular agricultural work should continue on the school farm, with Blanton becoming a United States demonstration agent. Blanton then would go out among the people and encourage them to try the new methods on their own farms.[37]

Buttrick and Frissell felt a keen urgency that this work should go forward. In spite of all that the school had done, Frissell felt that in the last thirty years the islanders had declined instead of improving; and he thought this condition would continue as long as the storekeepers continued to squeeze them. (The store-

36. Joseph Cannon Bailey, *Seaman A. Knapp: Schoolmaster of American Agriculture* (New York, 1945); Cremin, *The Transformation of the School*, 80; Charles William Dabney, *Universal Education in the South* (2 vols; Chapel Hill, N.C., 1936), II, 164; Raymond Blaine Fosdick, *Adventure in Giving: The Story of the General Education Board* (New York, 1962), 61.

37. Trustees' minutes, February 5, 1909, "Annual Report," 1909, p. 15, Seaman Knapp to Cooley, May 25, 1909, H. B. Frissell to Cooley, May 28, 1909, all in PSP; Cope to H. B. Frissell, February 18, 1910, H. B. Frissell to Cope, March 10, 1910, both in HBF.

keepers, apparently, had endeavored consistently to persuade the people to raise long-staple cotton, for which there was no fixed market price. As a result, the farmers probably did not get as much for their cotton as it was worth, and they constantly stayed in debt to the store.) As one of the old islanders described the never-ending cycle of borrowing, planting, paying, and then borrowing for the next crop, "We owed it before we growed it"; and Frissell was adamant that this situation must be changed. He even went so far as to inform Miss Cooley that unless she made some changes, unless the islanders were able to "get out from the grip" of the storekeepers, there seemed to be very little future for Penn School.[38]

At length Blanton and Knapp began to cooperate in the efforts to improve St. Helena farming and to induce the island farmers to diversify their crops. First they would try to secure the best cultivation of cotton and corn possible so there would be an increase in those crops. Then they would concentrate on other cash crops, preferably sugarcane and peanuts, all with an eye to improving the soil as quickly as possible. To begin the work, Knapp directed Blanton to secure six or seven men who would work their farms under Blanton's direction, and this number would gradually be increased each year until he could reach the whole island.[39]

Originally the islanders opposed the new methods; they greatly resented Blanton's efforts in not only helping them to plan their farm crops but actually helping some of them figure up their accounts. Many of them resented his trips into the fields, where he would take the plow himself and show what he meant by close cultivation, or they resented his suggestions that they plant their corn two feet nearer together than their fathers and grandfathers had taught them to do. Six of their number, however, agreed to sign on as demonstrators and to plant a half acre of their farms according to Department of Agriculture directions.[40]

38. S. Knapp to Cooley May 25, 1909, Trustees' minutes, April 19, 1910, both in PSP; H. B. Frissell to Cooley, May 21, 1908, March 18, 1909, in HBF; Cooley, *School Acres*, 117.
39. S. Knapp to Blanton, March 16, 1910, in PSP.
40. Blanton to Bradford Knapp, December, 1913, in PSP; Cooley, *School Acres*, 109, 111; Fosdick, *Adventure in Giving*, 48–49.

The island farmers had long been getting fifteen bushels of corn an acre, and they watched the demonstrators with great skepticism that first year. To their surprise and Joshua Blanton's delight, every demonstration came through successfully, with the Reverend D. C. Washington producing fifty-four bushels on his tiny plot! The demonstrators all received, and wore with great pride, prize buttons sent from Washington. This recognition and their indisputable success won many converts to the movement, and within three years there were sixty-seven demonstrators—all of them planting from three to six acres by the new methods—producing an average yield of thirty-four bushels an acre. Ultimately the St. Helena demonstration agent was able to lead his people in a number of significant agricultural revolutions, but first a handful of daring demonstrators had to prove that the movement had substance and that this "mere boy" merited their attention and respect.[41]

Blanton also organized the Penn School boys and girls into a Corn Club, another Knapp innovation. One of the most pernicious aspects of the one-crop system of cotton cultivation lay in the tendency of the boys and men to leave the community between crops in search of winter work. This was the largest barrier to the development of any feeling or spirit of community. Knapp had envisioned the corn clubs as a way to get rural boys to plant corn on their fathers' farms; Penn School extended this function, placing emphasis on the winter work so necessary on any good farm and so entirely neglected on most of the home farms from which the Penn School boys and girls came. Some white friends on the island offered a first prize of $10, a veritable fortune, to any who could raise forty bushels of corn to the acre, and the competition was keen. The prize-winners had front seats at the Farmers' Fair, and each member wore on his sleeve a wide band of the Penn School red, clearly marked "Corn Club." Such distinction could hardly fail to inspire these isolated rural children, and the Corn Club was a booming success.[42]

41. Cooley, *School Acres*, 110; Cooley, "Report to Trustees," January 14, 1913, "Annual Report," 1914, p. 21, both in PSP.

42. Fosdick, *Adventure in Giving*, 51–52; Bailey, *Seaman A. Knapp*, 213–30; "Annual Report," 1916, p. 11, in PSP.

As Mr. Blanton explained his goals to Bradford Knapp, who succeeded his father after the older man's death: "Our chance here runs as much to home improvement as it does to actual farm products increase. We are therefore trying to increase all sides of the farmer's life and at the same time make the farm the center of the work." The farm demonstration idea, where the school farmer visited the home farms and gave instruction in the field with the farmer's own equipment, seemed naturally to suggest extension work in the homes, so the Penn School cooking teacher began to go into the homes and teach the women in their own kitchens. She also organized a series of homemakers clubs on the island and taught the women much about balanced diets, canning, preserving, and pickling, as well as how to improve the kitchen. These lessons virtually revolutionized the diet of the island families. Eventually the women learned about proper ventilation, renewing shabby furniture, dressmaking, the care of babies, and a multitude of other ways to make their homes more healthy and attractive. The school nurse and the home demonstration agent worked in cooperation, and ultimately they had an enormous impact on the health and living standards of these island families.[43]

Eventually both farm demonstration and home demonstration became special concerns of the United States government, since the passage of the Smith-Lever Act in 1914 and the Smith-Hughes Act in 1917 put an end to the cooperation between government and philanthropy in this area. Ultimately these were also institutionalized in the Penn School curriculum when in 1917 Penn became an "All-Year School," using the children's home acres and home farms as a part of the school equipment. Together these two forms of the demonstration idea reached into the island homes and out onto the farms in a way that brought the island blacks in touch with the latest developments in the outside world.

---

43. Blanton to B. Knapp, November 30, 1912, in PSP; Cooley, *School Acres*, 96.

5

Crises and Opportunities

In 1893 a hurricane had ravaged the Sea Islands, destroying homes and stores, uprooting trees, sweeping livestock and people into the ocean, and burying the crops in the mud. For years after this, "the great storm" replaced "gun shoot" as the point from which all time was measured, and the islanders trembled to think that one day the storm might return. Late in the summer of 1911, their worst fears were realized. A hurricane struck the islands for three nightmarish days, and for many of the people, all but life itself was lost. Miss Cooley returned to the island at once. (She usually remained in the North soliciting funds until the end of September.) She found that houses had been wrecked, crops that had promised to surpass the record of several years were destroyed, and the exposure during the storm had meant suffering and death to the people and the livestock. Miss Cooley sent out an urgent appeal, and by mid-October three thousand dollars had poured into a Relief Fund set up at the school. In an effort to avoid charity and save self-respect, Miss Cooley urged the people to bring in their old grindstones and trade them for lumber, or nails, or food, or whatever they needed to get them through the winter. These grindstones went far back into the lives of the people; on the old plantations they had been used for grinding the weekly peck of corn into grits. They were the only stones on sandy St. Helena, so they did represent a kind of wealth to the people, and in this crisis they became "great rough coins of island credit." For many years these great round stones formed the walkway to the door of Hampton House, and Miss Cooley liked to think of them as symbolizing the struggle of the people in securing the necessities of life.[1]

Whenever possible, the people exchanged their stones for lumber or provisions. Rarely did Miss Cooley simply give away relief, and never did she completely repair or reconstruct a home without any assistance from the family. Construing this as an opportunity to build self-reliance, she insisted that the recipients of her assistance do as much as they could for themselves. "I find ... that the people are very grateful," she wrote to her trustees, "and I find also that they are very loath to ask for more even if they need it badly, which proves that the policy has not tended to make beggars of them."[2]

But, of course, many of the people did need help urgently. Some of them were trying to live in their corn houses, "so small sometimes that they cannot lie straight"; others flew about "like de birds w'en he rain," for many of the shaky little homes bore generous proof of the storm's visit. To make matters worse, an unusually severe and wet winter followed the storm, and there was much suffering. Many of the men and boys went into Savannah and Charleston to look for work, but many others were unable to leave their families; Penn School provided work for some and weekly rations for others, and the barrels that came to the Sales House from all parts of the country clothed many a needy family.[3]

With characteristic optimism Miss Cooley looked upon this crisis as a blessing in disguise. As she explained to her trustees, the storm gave the school a great opportunity to come into closer touch with the people, for many of the neighbors came in to the school for the first time, and they were most interested in all they saw there. Even more important, however, the crisis hastened the

1. Cooley, *School Acres*, 17, 114–15; Cope to H. B. Frissell, September 27, 1911, Cooley to H. B. Frissell, October 12, 1911, both in HBF, "Annual Report of the Penn Normal, Industrial and Agricultural School," 1912, p. 13, in PSP.
2. Cooley, "Report to Trustees," January 14, 1913, in PSP.
3. Cooley, *School Acres*, 115; "Annual Report," 1912, 14–15, in PSP.

introduction of a cooperative banking plan that the trustees had designed to end the islanders' dependence on the storekeepers. Ever since Frissell and Seaman Knapp had visited the island, the trustees had been searching for a solution to the islanders' economic problems. At length they had developed the idea of a cooperative loan association that would be managed and financed by the islanders themselves and that would foster both economic independence and scientific farming among St. Helena's blacks. As Mr. Cope wrote to Frissell, the cooperative scheme would enable the trustees to advance small loans to the farmers, who would otherwise have been dependent for their credit during the next year upon the storekeepers.[4]

The development of a cooperative spirit among blacks was a key Hampton goal. According to Miss Cooley, black gatherings and meetings had been discouraged under the slave system because the owners and overseers feared a development of leadership among the slaves. As a consequence, except for the churches, there had been no tradition of teamwork among the island people; and the conservative, doggedly independent farmers stubbornly held on to their old ways, even at a cost of economic bondage to the cotton merchants.[5]

Frissell had early become aware of the work of an Irishman, Sir Horace Plunkett, in ameliorating the abuses of the Irish tenant and landlord system. Plunkett had helped the Irish farmer to help himself by teaching him to work cooperatively and by giving him the means to make small farming profitable. Frissell believed that Plunkett's ideas could be applied directly to the problems of the southern black, and he and Wallace Buttrick began to champion the cooperative solution to the evils of the crop lien system.[6]

By February of 1912, the Penn trustees had worked out their cooperative scheme for the islanders, and the plan went into operation one evening at Mr. Blanton's house. Nine men came together that night and formed the St. Helena Cooperative Society,

    4. Cooley, "Report to Trustees," January 14, 1913, Trustees' minutes, January 10, 1912, both in PSP; Cope to H. B. Frissell, September 27, 1911, in HBF.
    5. Cooley, *School Acres*, 116.
    6. "Hampton Incidents: Horace Plunkett," *Southern Workman*, XXXII (February, 1903), 118.

accepting with enthusiasm and gratitude the $2,000 loan (at 4 percent interest) from the trustees of Penn School. Miss Cooley was there, and she reported proudly that Blanton read and explained the rules like a general. Adapted from some of Sir Horace Plunkett's suggestions, the rules stipulated that all loans were to be strictly agricultural; also, no one could negotiate a loan who had more than $50 debt at the time; no loans would be given to anyone who owed more than two firms, including the society (this was clearly directed at the storekeepers); and every borrower would be required to work his crop according to the following set of instructions:

> No. 1. Each borrower is expected to rotate his crops.
> No. 2. Every borrower is expected to plant corn for a good home supply, one acre for each member of his family and three acres for each horse.
> No. 3. Every borrower is expected to plant peas and potatoes for good home supply.
> No. 4. Every borrower is expected to plant his corn in 4½ ft. rows and 2 ft. on the bed, one stalk to the hill.

Every member also accepted the total liability clause making the society liable for the debts of all the members. Here in one stroke the Penn School trustees used a great and urgent crisis to further the goals they had been seeking all along—an end to the one-crop system of agriculture, economic independence for the blacks, and the adoption of scientific methods of agriculture.[7]

The 9 founders of the St. Helena Cooperative Society went out from their first meeting determined to recruit new members, and that first year they increased their number to 111. They made sixty-three loans, the average loan being $24.07, and they bought ninety sacks of fertilizer and sold them to the members. It was a good crop year, and "the little society sailed through smooth waters with flags flying." Successful as the Cooperative Society was in changing agricultural practices on the island, however, ultimately it was the boll weevil that forced diversification by putting an end to the possibility of a one-crop system of agriculture.[8]

7. Cooley, *School Acres*, 115; Cooley to H. B. Frissell, February 6, 1912, in HBF; "Annual Report," 1917, p. 29, in PSP; Davis, "A Unique People's School," 10.
8. Cooley, *School Acres*, 108, 119.

Reflecting the Penn School emphasis on service, the members of the Cooperative Society also volunteered to do some important work for the community. The hurricane had left the main road in terrible condition; and though the county had hauled in a great pile of oyster shells for the repair, these had remained by the side of the road for over a year. The members of the society saw this as a chance for usefulness. When the farm work was slack, they brought out their oxen, ponies, and carts, and spread the shells along the road. In time these were broken down by wear, and the islanders once again had a good road after a short time of discomfort.[9]

The St. Helena Cooperative Society enjoyed a growing success in its first few years, becoming an object of continuing pride to the Penn School establishment. Although initially it met opposition from William Keyserling, the new head of Macdonald, Wilkins, and Co., Miss Cooley was characteristically successful in bringing the storekeeper around to her point of view. This support was of the first importance to the Penn School principals, for they believed that the combined efforts of the society, the demonstration work, and the school would lead to the construction of a new pattern of life in the Sea Islands.[10]

On April 14, 1912, a wizened little band of soldiers marched into Darrah Hall on St. Helena Island to celebrate the fiftieth anniversary of Penn School. They were the First South Carolina Volunteers, known later as the Thirty-third United States Colored Infantry, for after the fall of Port Royal they had been the first regiment of Negro soldiers to serve in the United States Army. Behind them on this memorable day marched hundreds of Penn School students, past and present, until the building, which seated a thousand, overflowed. After singing John Greenleaf Whittier's "The St. Helena Hymn," they settled back for a day of reminiscences and exhortations, all of which Miss Cooley had designed to show the black people's incredible progress over fifty years.[11]

9. *Ibid.*, 119.
10. Cope to H. B. Frissell, March 25, 1912, in HBF; *The Anniversary Year* (N.p., April 13, 1912), 17, in PSP.
11. Grace Bigelow House, "The Fiftieth Anniversary of Penn School," *Southern Workman*, XLI (May, 1912), 318; "Annual Report," 1912, p. 35, in PSP.

One of the heroes of the Civil War, Captain Robert Smalls of Beaufort, addressed the audience briefly. He was the South Carolina slave who coolly captured the Confederate steamer, the *Planter*, and delivered it to waiting Union gunboats off Charleston harbor. In return he had been made captain of the *Planter*, and he recalled for the audience the gallantry and excitement of those days.[12]

Dr. Samuel Chiles Mitchell, president of the University of South Carolina, gave a stirring appeal for black self-improvement, which the audience heartily applauded. (Apparently the day made as big an impression on Dr. Mitchell as he did upon the occasion, for he soon wrote to Miss Cooley that he would not take anything for those enriching experiences. "You have occupied a strategic place in the South, unlike any other place known to me. I shall be constantly strengthened in my work by the thought of what you are doing for all of that region.")[13]

Because of unexpected rains, a most dramatic part of the celebration had to be omitted. Miss Cooley and Miss House had planned to lead the assemblage out into the school grove, where they would repeat the scene of fifty years before when the Emancipation Proclamation had been read to the expectant islanders. Mothers had brought their babies to hear that historic reading, fearing that any who failed to hear would be left in the bonds of slavery. The soldiers and the people had gathered around the platform to hear the proclamation. As the white South Carolinian who had read the document turned to present a flag to the black regiment, symbolic of their people's patriation, a man's voice near the platform broke forth with "My Country 'Tis of Thee," and the people spontaneously took up the refrain. "I never saw anything so electric," Colonel Thomas Wentworth Higginson wrote in his diary. "It made all other words cheap, it seemed like the choked voice of a race at last unloosed. . . . Art could not have dreamed of a tribute to the Day of Jubilee that should be so affecting, history will not believe it, and when I came to speak of it after it was ended, tears were everywhere."[14]

12. House, "The Fiftieth Anniversary," 319.
13. *Ibid.*; Samuel Chiles Mitchell to Cooley, April 18, 1912, in PSP.
14. Pearson, *Letters from Port Royal*, 128–32; House, "The Fiftieth Anniversary,"

Although the rehearsal in the grove had to be foregone, Mr. J. R. Macdonald presented two flags to the school and regiment, gifts from Mr. Cope. In accepting the flag for the school, Lorenzo Hall spoke of the opportunities that had come to his race along with the flag. "It is with a feeling of pride and solemnity," he said, "that we accept this emblem of our great nation. Along with this flag we also accept the duties and responsibilities that good citizenship involves." And on this note, the crowd rose in a body and sang "My Country 'Tis of Thee." This ceremony reflected Miss House's love of the dramatic and was reported by her with a great deal of pride and emotion.[15]

The highlight of the day was the dedication of a new industrial building—the Cope Shops—that the islanders had built entirely by themselves. The gray, one-story Spanish-looking building with red-tiled roof impressed Dr. Frissell as the islanders' proudest achievement, a monument to the Negroes of St. Helena after fifty years of freedom.[16]

Dr. Frissell and Miss Cooley had long desired a well-equipped industrial building for the island. An interest in trades had never developed on St. Helena, and the people took all their repair work into Beaufort. Miss Cooley saw this as a waste, as well as a blow to self-sufficiency, and she began very early to dream of a full program of industrial instruction. Carpentry had been a part of the school program from the beginning, but the shop was woefully inadequate, and the training consisted only of repair work and painting on the school buildings. By 1910 the school had added a cobbling department, but even this work could not be taught adequately without classrooms and workspace designed for the purpose.[17]

The school also taught basketmaking. Miss Cooley doubtless thought it a fine way to foster industry, precision, and persistence—the celebrated raionale for Hampton's industrial training—but primarily she thought it a way to provide the baskets

---

318; Thomas Wentworth Higginson, *Army Life in a Black Regiment* (Boston, 1890; reprinted, 1962), 41.

15. House, "The Fiftieth Anniversary," 319.
16. Davis, "A Unique People's School," 4; House, "The Fiftieth Anniversary," 320.
17. Cooley, *School Acres*, 51–52; "Annual Report," 1910, p. 14, in PSP.

needed in every home while preserving a valuable African heritage. Moreover, there was a commercial demand for these native island baskets, for they were often exquisitely beautiful. Made of rushes that grew in the tidal rivers, and sewn with strips of palmetto, these baskets found their way into many a northern home during the years of Penn School ascendancy.[18]

By 1910 Miss Cooley had sold the trustees her dream of an industrial building, and they had embarked on a program to raise $50,000 to be used for the industrial development of the Sea Island Negroes. Arthur Curtiss James gave $5,000, and the General Education Board gave another $5,000 (the trustees had asked them for $15,000). The remainder came from the estate of Miss Clementine Cope, an aunt of Francis Cope, who had willed $50,000 in 1903 for the promotion of Negro education on the island of St. Helena.[19]

Mr. Blanton had been in charge of the building's construction. Two other Hampton graduates, John F. Burrell and Anthony D. Watson, had directed the masonry work and the carpentry, and ninety-four men had worked on the construction at a dollar a day. Using oyster shells and sand from nearby rivers and oyster factories, the men constructed a beautiful and durable structure out of oyster shells, sand, and concrete, a substance known as *tabby* along the South Atlantic coast. The building housed blacksmith, wheelwright, carpentry, and paint shops, as well as cobbling and basketry. Here horses could be shod, and wagons, furniture, and tools made and repaired; from these shops island boys could go out into the community to paint, build, or repair churches and houses. "We building" as the islanders called it, was to become a major link with the community, one that would provide countless services for the homes and farms and one that would make the school an even more important factor in the lives of the people.[20]

18. "Annual Report," 1910, pp. 15, 54, in PSP.
19. Trustees' minutes, July 24, 1903, April 19, 1910, January 14, 1913, Penn School appeal letter, January 20, 1911, all in PSP; W. W. Carman to Cooley, December 6, 1910, in HBF; Cope to Foote, February 1, 1955, in JMD.
20. Trustees' minutes (Executive Committee), June 5, 1911, Trustees' minutes, January 10, 1912, both in PSP; Davis, "A Unique People's School," 10; Cooley, *School Acres*, 53.

The dedication of the new Cope Industrial Building followed the fiftieth anniversary ceremonies in Darrah Hall. Dr. Frissell presented the building to the school and island on behalf of the board of trustees. Standing between the two columns on the front porch, he congratulated the little band of workmen immediately before him; and with his arm upraised in a characteristic pose, he exhorted the larger crowd to continue in their struggle for improvement. Tom Fields, an island farmer, received this building for the people, and J. E. Blanton made the response for the school. As Miss House later recalled, "He voiced the gratitude of the people for all that the Penn School had meant to them in the past, as well as their appreciation of what this new development must mean for the future." It was a full and exciting day; and as the islanders turned homeward that evening, they must have carried a new understanding of Penn School's centrality in their lives.

The islanders were not the only ones who had been impressed. A number of white visitors had shared in the ceremonies, both from Beaufort and from the North, and the response of Miss Marian Homans of Boston doubtless typified that of many visitors. "I shall never forget my days on St. Helena," she wrote Miss Cooley, "for I don't think anything could make more impression on my mind than those exercises on Sunday . . . and above all the faces of those kindly, patient, courteous people, among whom you live."[21]

This was the response Penn School wanted. The whole celebration had been conceived as a great advertisement, a chance to put Penn School before a larger northern audience. "We must educate the North," Frissell urged continually, for they "are not in touch with the Southern situation," and they had to be made aware of the condition and needs of the blacks. The trustees had

21. House, "The Fiftieth Anniversary," 319-20. "Struggle" was a characteristic Frissell theme. A typical address is the one that follows: "I am glad that we have problems to face. Some of your race think that life is not worth living because there are so many; but I believe that the members of this conference think that life is not worth living without them." "Report of the Third Annual Negro Conference," *Southern Workman*, XXVIII (September, 1899), 326; Cooley to H. B. Frissell, February 27, 1912, in HBF; House, "The Fiftieth Anniversary," 320; "50th Anniversary Celebrated at Penn School Last Saturday and Sunday," Beaufort *Gazette*, April 19, 1912, clipping, Marian Homans to Cooley, April 19, 1912, both in PSP.

sent numerous invitations to the anniversary celebration, and the regrets from Beacon Street and Germantown and Fifth Avenue all bore the marks of sophistication, formality, and wealth. Even some favored journalists received invitations, doubtless as a way to their audiences. As Ray Stannard Baker replied, "I have long wished to visit this school and to know more of the work being done there." Apparently, the hope of attracting national attention was not without foundation.[22]

After the anniversary celebration, the school settled down to its regular hectic routine, and Miss Cooley pushed forward her work on all fronts: supervising the academic and industrial work at the school, overseeing the Cooperative Society and the extension work, visiting in the homes and envisioning the needs of the future, writing appeals for the school, and traveling in the North to raise funds. Somehow she even found time to make friends and extend her contacts in South Carolina, serving as secretary of the South Carolina Federation of Women's Clubs, which she described as taking the place of college work with many of the South's women. Miss Cooley and Miss House also belonged to Beaufort's exclusive Clover Club, a literary society of twelve white women, including Beaufort's leading ladies (most of them descendants of the northerners who had moved to Beaufort after the Civil War).[23]

In the summer of 1914 a typhoid epidemic broke out on the island, striking twenty-two and killing five. Miss Cooley had already left for the summer, but she telegraphed the South Carolina State Board of Health, urgently requesting an investigation and innoculation where necessary. Two months later, the secretary of the state board responded to Miss Cooley's wire. This was precisely the kind of negligence the trustees had foreseen and attempted to forestall when they asked William Knox Tate, the agent of the General Education Board for rural schools in South Carolina, to join their board. Tate had by this time become a member

22. Trustees' minutes, April 19, 1920, February 6, 1914, Ray Stannard Baker to Cope, March 25, 1912, all in PSP.
23. Cooley to H. B. Frissell, May 19, 1913, in HBF; Cooley, "Report to Trustees," January 14, 1913, in PSP.

of the faculty of Peabody College, but he still had enough clout in South Carolina to inspire the State Board of Health. Within a week of Tate's writing to them, the state board had swung into action on the situation at St. Helena, and by Christmas both typhoid and hookworm had been brought under control on the island.[24]

Before Miss Cooley returned to the island in the fall, two representatives of the Rockefeller Sanitary Commission had visited St. Helena and begun a preliminary investigation of the typhoid and hookworm problems. Because of a breakdown in communications, however, neither Dr. Bailey nor Blanton had cooperated in the doctors' efforts to gather specimens. The gentlemen from the Sanitary Commission had returned to Columbia in disgust, writing Miss Cooley that they would have to abandon the project.[25]

Miss Cooley was not cowed by the pique of these southern white men. Instead she merely exhibited her own superior public relations and advertising skills, initiating upon her return a rousing sanitary campaign on the island. She chose Corner Plantation as her model sanitary district, embarking on a program to convince every family on the plantation to erect a sanitary privy, dig a twenty-foot well, and receive the typhoid innoculation. She drew an enormous map of the plantation, showing every road and home, and posted it in a conspicuous place. Brightly colored pins marked the participation of each family—red for the innoculation, yellow for the privy, and blue for the well—and the goal of a perfectly decorated map was hard to resist. Dr. F. M. Routh of the State Board of Health spent two weeks on the island, visiting every home on Corner Plantation, checking for hookworm, in-

---

24. "Annual Report," 1915, p. 17, Cooley to South Carolina State Board of Health, June 25, 1914, James H. Hayne to Cooley, August 15, 1914, Trustees' minutes, June 24, 1912, all in PSP; Dabney, *Universal Education in the South*, II, 224. Tate was a leader in the fight for improved rural schools. P. P. Claxton, United States commissioner of education from Tennessee, described Tate as the foremost worker in this field, concluding that "the improved rural school, with its longer term, its better housing and equipment, its readjusted course of study, its more adequately trained teachers, and its firmer grasp on the higher life of the community, is his most appropriate monument." Dabney, *Universal Education in the South*, II, 228–29; J. La Bruce Ward to Tate, August 29, 1914, in PSP.

25. Ward to Cooley, September 9, 14, 15, 18, 1914, in PSP.

noculating against typhoid, and instructing the people in ways to prevent soil pollution. He discovered a 25 percent incidence of hookworm, which he treated; and the school shop constructed wooden privies for all the families. Despite the success on Corner Plantation, however, the "health epidemic" did not catch on among the islanders, and Penn School was unable to eradicate the hookworm scourge completely. The school nurse did, however, carry the sanitary gospel wherever she went, and Miss Cooley convinced the St. Helena District Board of Trustees to provide privies for all the public schools, so Penn School continued in these ways to fight for improved health conditions on the island.[26]

In 1915 the island suffered the worst crop year it had had since Miss Cooley took up her work there. The previous year had been a poor one with the prices for cotton very low, and the unceasing rains in 1915 made the crops very short and left the people practically bankrupt. In the crisis the merchants, who felt very keenly the people's diminished buying power, set themselves the task of discovering the causes of the crop failures. Their study led them to realize that the failure stemmed largely from poor drainage.[27]

Under the old plantation system, ditching had been a regular part of the year's work. The cotton crop had depended on the ditches being kept open, and there were always adequate hands to do the work. But with the division of the plantations into smaller holdings after the war, there no longer existed an organization to direct the effort, and the drainage canals fell into disrepair, became clogged, and served as breeding places for mosquitoes.[28]

Ditching had been much discussed at the early Farmers' Fairs, but Miss Cooley did not understand the principle of it and many people opposed the strenuous work. Since many of the men went off to the cities to hunt jobs during the winter, they were not available in the off-season to help with this kind of project; and ditch-

26. Cooley, *Homes of the Freed*, 51, 52; Ward to Cooley, October 30, 1914, "Annual Report," 1916, p. 13, Cooley to St. Helena District Board of Trustees, November 13, 1914, all in PSP.
27. "Annual Report," 1916, p. 8, in PSP; Cooley to H. B. Frissell, December 3, 1915, George Waterhouse to H. B. Frissell, December 1, 1915, both in HBF.
28. Cooley, *School Acres*, 120.

ing depended on community effort, if it was to be done at all. Miss Cooley later explained that if a man dug the ditch on his own farm it did little good if his neighbor did not dig his, so the ditches had not remained open. When the merchants became aroused in 1915, however, they convinced Miss Cooley and Frissell of the necessity for reinstituting the old practice. Dr. Frissell saw this as a prime opportunity to develop cooperation. He felt that if the men would dig ditches together, they would do other things together too. Miss Cooley doubtless shared this concern, but her more immediate interest was in finding a solution to the islanders' critical financial difficulties.[29]

Eventually the Cooperative Society came to the fore as the champion of the ditching effort. Under Blanton's leadership, the society organized the farmers into corps of workers, and by early spring they had cleared fourteen miles of ditches. Keyserling convinced the county commissioners to levy a one-mill tax for ditching purposes, and within another year's time, the men had opened twenty-eight miles of ditches on twenty-five plantations. Immediately the crops improved dramatically, malaria subsided, and Miss Cooley lamented that she had not known enough to tackle the matter her first year on the island.[30]

At the fair that fall, one of the older farmers told of his successes that year. He had been able to pay his debt of $200 on his house, $90 at the store, $30 at the school where he had his buggy repaired, and then put some money in the bank. He had been one of the men most opposed to helping in the ditching outside his own land. Now as he walked down the aisle, someone in the audience called out, "What about those ditches?" After a moment he said, with a twinkle in his eye, "Dem ditches ain't do one bit of harm to my lan'." Slowly the Penn School successes were wearing down islander resistance.[31]

By now Penn School had become a central element in the islanders' lives. Clearly its methods and suggestions had benefited

---

29. *Ibid.*; H. B. Frissell to Cooley, December 17, 1915, in HBF.
30. "Annual Report," 1916 p. 15, in PSP; Cooley, *School Acres*, 120–21; Cooley to H. B. Frissell, December 3, 1915, in HBF.
31. Cooley, *School Acres*, 121.

those who adopted them, and the school seemed to have the power to solve whatever problems and crises might arise. To the isolated islanders, Penn had become the source of all things good, whether that be clothes at the Sales House, repairs at the shops, new ideas in the clubs, or help in the Cooperative Society. Unfortunately, it had also begun to foster a growing dependency among the people. As Alfred Collins Maule wrote to a contributor, "To the two white women at the head, parents as well as pupils come with touching confidence asking for advice in settling disputes, in straightening out difficulties, in tiding over emergencies." In other words, Penn had become far more than a school. In Miss Cooley's assessment it had become a bureau of information and practical help for all the people. Despite the pernicious effects of paternalism, Penn School seemed to be well on its way toward its goal of reshaping the lives of the people.[32]

In the autumn of 1917, Penn suffered a great loss in the death of Hollis Burke Frissell. Frissell had been the moving force in the Penn School endeavor. He had seen its possibilities and masterminded its reorganization, and his counsel and advice had been forthcoming at every stage of the school's new development. He had in a real sense been a father figure for the whole enterprise. As one of the trustees wrote in requiem, "Penn School which had so large a place in his affections mourns the loss of a father who was always confident and optimistic about the development and future usefulness of this outgrowth of the Hampton spirit." And as Miss Cooley wrote of Frissell several years later, "His marvelous grasp of details gave him the power of becoming as a father to his own students and also to that larger group who turned to him constantly as if they were a very part of Hampton." Again and again Frissell's admirers referred to his confidence and optimism, his unending kindness, and the sense of calm he brought when all about him read crisis. Problems seemed to vanish under his consideration: "Instead of difficulties they became interesting problems to tackle, and instead of weariness in the struggle, there came inspiration and determination." Miss Cooley would remem-

32. Maule to Penn School contributosrs, March, 1909, in JMD; Cooley to United States Department of Agriculture, July 14, 1913, in PSP.

ber him with his hand upraised, "his great message of 'struggle' on his lips, with his keen sense of humor, which so often set things in their right proportion; with that quiet force—so quiet that you often wondered just where the force lay." The father figure was dead, and Penn's second great era had come to a close; but the Frissell ideas and influence would remain central. As Francis Cope wrote of him, "Just as the Hampton of today, built so well on the foundations laid by General Armstrong, is a monument to Dr. Frissell, so the new Penn School bears living testimony through its teachers and workers to his ideals and influence."[33]

Rossa Belle Cooley would miss Dr. Frissell. She had worked through him for years, and now she would have to direct the school, and her trustees, out of her own strength. She had been endlessly inspired by Frissell's vision of the coming Kingdom of God, and she had always been calmed by his confidence and sense of proportion. Above all she had loved and admired him as a great and noble figure, and she felt a keen sense of loss at his death. She must also have felt a measure of fear for her school, for Frissell had been the influential name whose approval virtually guaranteed acceptance and success. He had been the link with Wallace Buttrick and James Hardy Dillard and Thomas Jesse Jones and Anson Phelps Stokes—the men who controlled the large foundations and whose approval determined the fate of many a school for blacks. This was a realistic fear, and Francis Cope was impelled to call upon Frissell's admirers to redouble their efforts so that the cause for which he labored would not suffer. But fears for Penn School were unnecessary. By the time of Frissell's death, Penn's reputation and acceptability had been established in the North; and even if it had not, Rossa Cooley's determination and force would have kept the school alive.[34]

Penn School had a wide appeal. One of the school's strongest assets was the sheer physical beauty of its setting, and visitors to the island invariably succumbed to the exotic charm of the place.

---

33. L. Hollingsworth Wood for trustees, September 25, 1917, in PSP; Cooley, *School Acres*, 24; Cooley, "Service to Penn School," Cope, "Service to Penn School," 604–605.

34. Cope, "Service to Penn School," 605.

"I should like to settle down for a week," wrote a typically captivated visitor, "and be down-right lazy, and just drink in the Southern beauty, and the stillness, and the melody of darky voices and the peace of your helpful services." "I wish I knew how to tell you," wrote another, "the feeling that St. Helena stirs up in me: the high, single aim, the joyful, prayerful service—it is a refreshment and inspiration to mind and soul just to think of these. Everything seems in harmony—the leaders, the people, and nature."[35]

Penn School appealed strongly to missionaries, who responded to the Christian aims of service and helpfulness and who found inspiration in such practical solutions to the problems of a "backward" race. "The work you are doing was indeed a revelation to me," wrote an officer of the Presbyterian Home Missions. "It is beyond anything I had ever hoped to see." "My visit to Penn," wrote another, "was the most wonderful and helpful experience I had in the United States."[36]

A primary reason for Penn School's popularity was the proof of black capabilities it promised to produce. The fear of a black "reversion to barbarism" was widespread among southerners at the turn of the century, and many northerners also shared this fear. Harvard historian Albert Bushnell Hart reported after a trip through South Carolina that there were dark hints that voodooism had reasserted itself and that pagan worship was taking the place of Christianity. Even worse, there were dire predictions that, left alone, the blacks of the Sea Islands would be practicing cannibalism within ten years. Penn seemed to be clear proof of the nonsense of this theory, and Frissell had been eager to make of the island a model Negro community so that this fear could be buried once and for all.[37]

Rather than reveal the Negro as beast, Penn School prom-

35. Margaret Norton to Cooley, April 4, 1914, Cornelia P. Lowell to Cooley, May 3–5, 1914, both in PSP.
36. Homer McMillan to Cooley, December 13, 1915, Charles Templeman Loram to Cooley, October 30, 1915?, both in PSP.
37. Frederickson, *The Black Image in the White Mind*, Chapter 9; Albert Bushnell Hart, "Through the Heart of the South," Boston Evening *Transcript*, February 19, 1908, p. 16, clipping, in JMD; E. L. Parks to Cooley, April 2, 1912, in PSP; Frissell to Cooley, November 2, 1915, in HBF.

ised to lead the way in showing the virtues and possibilities of country living. Penn seemed to be a model of the ideal rural school: it was a community center, it emphasized agriculture and domestic science, and its primary objective was the revival of country life. One of the leaders of the Country Life Movement, Professor Mabel Carney, affirmed Penn in the strongest terms, eventually using it as a training school for her courses at Teachers College, Columbia.[38]

Penn also appealed to a number of southern racial liberals, men who were seeking a Christian solution to the problems of race in the South. Samuel Chiles Mitchell, president of the University of South Carolina, told his audience at Penn's fiftieth anniversary celebration that he had made up his mind that "my heart cannot grow on hatred, neither can yours." He became an ardent supporter of the Penn School effort, writing to Miss Cooley in 1913 that her influence had affected his own life. Willis Duke Weatherford, southern secretary of the Young Men's Christian Association, applauded Penn's efforts to educate blacks and regarded Miss Cooley as one of the South's leading social workers. Jackson Davis, the Virginia gentleman who had discovered Virginia Randolph and instituted the Jeanes supervising teachers and who later became president of the General Education Board, admired Penn's efforts to help the Negroes. Despite the approval of these southerners, however, Penn was far from popular in the South. Any education for blacks still met opposition in some quarters, and the state and county politicians still regarded Penn with considerable suspicion. Most southerners, however, remained oblivious to Penn's existence, since the real targets of the school's publicity were in the North.[39]

By 1917, the Slater Fund, the Phelps-Stokes Fund, the Gen-

---

38. For an elaboration of the goals and philosophy of the Country Life Movement see Mabel Carney, *Country Life and the Country School: A Study of the Country Community* (Chicago, 1912).

39. *The Anniversary Year*; S. C. Mitchell to Cooley, May 22, 1913, Trustees' minutes, April 19, 1915, Ila O'Steele to Cooley, February 2, 1917, Willis Duke Weatherford to Cooley, September 15, 1912, all in PSP; Davis, "A Unique People's School," 5; Cooley to H. B. Frissell, May 18, 1916, Cooley to James Hardy Dillard, June 12, 1916, both in HBF.

eral Education Board, and Julius Rosenwald had all discovered Penn School and contributed to its development. This resulted largely from Frissell's connections with these boards, but it also reflected these philanthropists' affirmation of Penn's emphasis on industrial education and its unique program of community education. The interlocking directorate of philanthropy had by this time committed itself quite firmly to the industrial education movement, and Penn promised to be a most hopeful demonstration of the wisdom of that idea.

In 1917 the United States government in conjunction with the Phelps-Stokes Fund published a two-volume survey of Negro education. The author of the report, Thomas Jesse Jones, was the director of the Phelps-Stokes Fund, a graduate of Union Theological Seminary, and a former teacher at Hampton Institute. His report, which was largely a bid for southern cooperation in the movement to educate black people, cataloged the ills of contemporary black education and made a strong plea for widespread acceptance of industrial education. Jones had served at Hampton under Frissell, and he had learned his lessons well. In criticizing the literary or academic emphasis in Negro education, Jones suggested that, although the literary institutions had stressed thrift, cleanliness, honesty, perseverance, and the simple but fundamental virtues, these influences had failed in the character development of the Negroes because they were unfortunately regarded as incidental benefits. Among his conclusions and recommendations for the further development of black education, Jones placed the following high in his priorities: "That all education shall stress, first, the development of character, including the simple but fundamental virtues of cleanliness, order, perserverance, and the qualities essential to the home, and second, adaptation to the needs of the pupil and the community."[40]

Jones had visited Penn on a number of occasions with Dr. Frissell, and he shared the older man's enthusiasm for the Penn School endeavor. In his report, he described Penn as an excellent community school that provided industrial and agricultural train-

40. Jones, *Negro Education*, 18, 82.

ing adapted to the needs of the island. He noted that Penn stressed health and character development, and he concluded with the recommendation that more ample funds be provided to carry on the important work of this institution. Here was a clear endorsement of Penn as a character builder and an exemplar of the Hampton ideals. With such support Penn could hardly fail, and in the next few years it went on to become one of the favored projects of northern philanthropy.[41]

41. *Ibid.*, 483, 485.

Original Penn schoolhouse, sent from Philadelphia in 1863.
Photographed by Helen Jenks, 1902

Founders' Hall, the new schoolhouse built in 1905. Hampton House, the principals' new home directly across the road, was of similar architecture.

Penn School's new Hampton-trained teachers, 1905. Standing, left to right: Joshua E. Blanton, Mary Alice Person, Mabel Hickman, Linnie Lumpkins. Seated, left to right: Helena McGavitt, Antoinette Norwell.

Aunt Jane, whose cabin had to be propped up with poles. Penn School boys used the old schoolhouse to build Aunt Jane a new home.

Thaddeus Watkins at home.

Prophet Wyne and his family planting corn on the family farm.

Mrs. Green winnowing her rice.
Photograph by Leigh Richmond Minor

"Big Dick" Middleton, an island fisherman.
Photograph by Leigh Richmond Minor

Joshua Blanton, Penn School farmer and U.S. demonstration agent, giving lessons on the students' home acres on Dathaw Island, 1915.

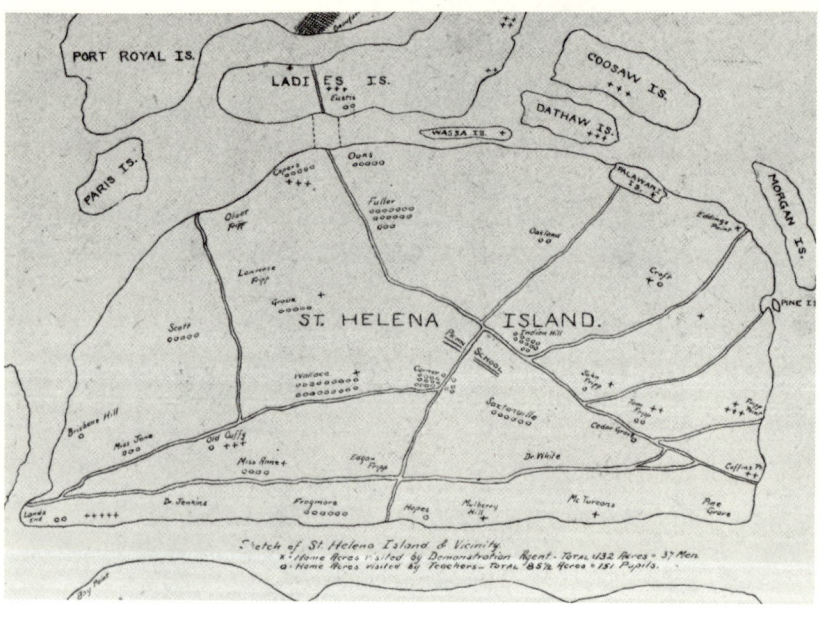

St. Helena Island and vicinity, showing island plantations and homes of Penn School students.

6

Things of the Spirit and Service

"To one brought up on the Bible," wrote Miss Cooley, describing her impressions of St. Helena Island, "there are everywhere suggestions of life and labor in Judea." The cotton pickers bending in their rows, the oxen pulling their ancient two-wheeled carts, the fishermen coming in on the tide after dark—all bore strong resemblances to scenes from the Old and New Testaments. And the resemblance was more than physical. To Miss Cooley's perceptive eye, a religious imagery seemed to overlay fields and roads and tidal rivers. Abraham and the prophets were more real to the islanders than their recently departed white masters, and the ancient Bible heroes lived in their imaginations. The minister who prayed for Penn School as "de bridge over de Red Sea into de Promised Land fo' we people, de pillar of cloud by day and de pillar of fire by night" was using an imagery clearly understood by his listeners.[1]

And yet Miss Cooley perceived her islanders' religion to be disturbingly primitive, filled with superstition and expressed with emotion. "The big wind seems to many of them as the direct Breath of God," she wrote, "the thunder as God's voice." Many of the older people kept a door open in the daytime "to guard against shutting out the Good Spirit," and many kept both doors shut at night so that "the old hag" would not come and draw out any of

---

1. Cooley, *School Acres*, 135–36.

the occupants. A widespread practice on the island was the giving of "basket-names" to the newborn child—names that usually reflected the child's significance or the weather conditions under which he was born. Thus Miss Cooley found Precious, Treasure, Stormy, Freezie, Husky, Worky, Handsome, Better Days, and the twins Peas and Beans! When she asked a mother the reason for this custom, the mother replied, "So the evil one can't know the real name."[2]

However colorful they may have been, these practices disturbed Miss Cooley, for she believed superstition to be the crudest expression of the religious feeling in all races. From the start, then, she endeavored to uplift the religious life of these people, for her religious message was central to the message she was seeking to bring to St. Helena. From the start she sought to lead the island people from superstition toward enlightened religion and to direct them toward useful, moral, and mind-elevating endeavors. Believing that the highest expression of Christianity was the spirit of service, she followed her Puritan forebears in thinking that inner grace revealed itself through works and through virtue; defining herself as a Christian missionary, she had little tolerance for these remnants of the African heritage.[3]

The original band of Yankee missionaries on St. Helena Island, Miss Towne included, had been appalled by the blacks' religious practices. The New Englanders among their number had

---

2. *Ibid.*, 136, 156; Cooley, *Homes of the Freed*, 72. Miss House suggested a different origin for these "basket-names." Miss House wrote a number of touching stories about island life, all of them taken from her own experiences. One of these, entitled "The Promise of Better Days," tells the story of the child named Better Days, who had been born in slavery. "In dem days we ain't ben had no trimmin's onto our names," recalled Better Days. "White folks just called him (her father) ole Benjamin Day's nigger, Hosea, but de colored folks day calls him Prophet Hosea. Well, when I done borned, he been tink he pint a moral wid me, so he name me Freedom, very secret like so de white folks cyan't hear 'bout it. Den he say, 'we don't dast call dat chile Freedom, for de white folks ain't ben like dat, but when freedom come,' he say, 'den will come better days for we po' Etiopian people, so we gwine call him Better Days an de white folks ain't neber gwine ter know dats jes anoder name for freedom.' 'I low dey allus kine tink I been name for my young missus, Miss Betty,' she ended, with a sudden gleam of amusement in her eyes." Grace Bigelow House, "The Promise of Better Days," reprinted from the *Southern Workman*, XXXVII (October, 1908), 6, in PSP.

3. Cooley, *School Acres*, 156; script for Penn School movie, "To Live as Free Men," August 20, 1942, in PSP.

begun immediately to spread the gospel of enlighten Christianity; the New Yorkers, however, became the most popular preachers because their brand of religion was evangelistic. As Willie Lee Rose has explained, among the unlettered blacks, "moral discourses on duty, truth, cleanliness, and so on were apt to pale in interest beside the stirring message of the crucified Christ." Most of the young missionaries eventually left the island in despair or disgust, and Miss Towne and Miss Murray apparently made little headway in substituting their civilized ethics for the emotional fervor of the blacks' religion.[4]

Miss Cooley was more successful. She was wise enough to discern the centrality of religion in the islanders' lives, and she found much in their religious expression that she approved of and wanted to preserve. She understood also that the islanders found her mode of worship pale and sterile, for as one of the oldsters had told her, "De white folks has got de knowin' of de hows and de whys of religion but they ain't never got de feel of it yet!" And so she moved with caution around this important subject. With a subtlety that few could approach, however, she modified the religious life of the island, or at least that considerable part of the island that fell under Penn School's influence. Her economic program was but the means of achieving these more fundamental goals. As she explained these priorities, the Hampton education aimed toward "the flowering out of cultural things once the soil of livelihood had been harrowed." Thus the revolution she would work to bring on St. Helena Island was primarily a spiritual one.[5]

As Miss Cooley wrote in an early annual report, "The Religious work of the school is the foundation of our aims." Better farms, better homes, better characters all would combine to make better lives, more civilized lives, lives that were open and receptive to the messages of enlightened Christianity. Penn School would work to bring "the more abundant life" to St. Helena by improving the standard of living and by building a recognition of

4. Rose *Rehearsal for Reconstruction*, 73, 92–93.
5. Cooley, *School Acres*, 22, 137; this incident was later reported in a partially fictionalized account, Grace Bigelow House, "The Long Look," *Christian Endeavor World*, December 31, 1944, pp. 246–55.

the spiritual forces that contribute to the building of character, home, and community. Although the island people were intensely religious, they did not always associate religion with everyday life. Penn School would help them make that association. It would lead them to believe that cleanliness, temperance, industry, and thrift all carried a religious imperative. It would make of them good Yankees.[6]

At the center of island religious life was the *praise house*, an inheritance from the days of slavery. The old plantations, about forty of them, still gave geographic definition to the island, and on each of these was located a little tumble-down building with rude benches, where the islanders gathered three nights a week for simple, informal, spontaneous worship. As one observer described a praise house service, "In the prayers and songs the emotional experience of the Islanders . . . takes on a vividness and depth which is hardly to be entered into by a member of another race." Here the old-time spirituals, sung in a minor key with many variations of tone and rhythm, remained unchanged.

> I look all around me
> It looks so shine,
> I ask muh Lord
> Ef all were mine.
> Oh, ebery time I feels de sperit
> Movin' in-a muh heart
> I will pray.

Here also were found the prayers, full of poetic imagery, powerful in their simplicity. "Pray on de knees ob yo' heart," the leader directed, and an old woman would pray, "May de bird ob love be in muh heart an' de Lam ob Christ in muh bosom, an' oh, God, who tuk up de sun in de palm ob yo' han' an' t'rowed her out into de sky to be Queen ob de day, Listen to we." All through her prayer the murmurs of response could be heard, slowly building into a rhythm and finally breaking forth in the gentle singing of a spiritual. Soon the song would blend with the prayer; and as the singing grew in power, the prayer would fade out and the spir-

---

6. "Annual Report of the Penn Normal, Industrial and Agricultural School," 1910, p. 17, 1929, p. 7, both in PSP.

itual go on. Soon another prayer would rise, and the congregation would join in again: "Now as we bend our hearts equal to our knees, Lord Jesus, wilt Thou climb up on dat milk-white steed called 'Victory,' and' ride ober de mountains and t'rough de valleys of our sins an' backslidin's." The images were vivid, and there can be little doubt that they were real to these simple folk for whom the Bible gave the only suggestions of life beyond their island. As the meeting broke up, someone would strike up another of the spirituals, and the worshipers would go from one to another shaking hands in rhythm with the singing before wandering home in the moonlight down the little plantation paths.[7]

The praise house was essentially a community institution, where neighbors gathered not only to worship but also to socialize and to promote community solidarity. The praise house was the unit on which the church was built. It was also the central information agency, since the island had no newspapers. Whenever the school wanted to spread word of its activities, it went to the praise leaders. Here the school initiated its campaigns against disease, the boll weevil, and a hundred other evils. Here the school sent home the word that tax payments were due. Here as well as in the fields, the demonstration agent made his pleas for deeper plowing and diversified crops. In short, as a sociologist described the praise house in the 1920s: "Here the community in simplest form initiates its business and promotes law and order."[8]

The plantation was a larger extension of several families that had intermarried, and thus it was a neighborhood where relationships were complicated but well recognized. This organization and family relationship gave the plantation a remarkable solidarity and unity of action that enabled the church to exercise efficient control over disputes. All minor offenses were settled in a church or praise house trial, and the county court in Beaufort rarely heard of problems on the island. The islanders dreaded civil law for its discrimination and injustices as well as its expense, and they thought of it as the unjust law as contrasted with the just

7. For a fictional account of a typical praise house service, see House, "The Long Look"; Woofter, *Black Yeomanry*, 225; Cooley, *School Acres*, 140, 150, 159.
8. Woofter, *Black Yeomanry*, 238.

law of the churches. Penn School proudly proclaimed that no sheriff had ever been stationed on the island; no sheriff was needed because the church machinery took care of all his business.[9]

Occasionally the praise house meeting ended with a *Shout*, a vigorous semireligious form of entertainment. Undoubtedly an African survival modified to encompass Christianity, the Shout was one of the few forms of entertainment the slaves had been allowed to enjoy. After the benediction of the worship service, benches would be moved back and singers would form a loose circle in the center of the floor. The group would never be mixed—it was always either all men or all women. Someone would begin a spiritual with a lively rhythm, and those outside the ring would clap to emphasize the beat. Gradually the ring would begin to revolve, slowly at first, but with increasing vigor; and the participants would shuffle along, losing themselves in the rhythm. (Although the step closely resembled the "Charleston," the watchful leader allowed no one to "cross de foot," for that savored too much of the worldly dance.) As the performance became more lively, elbows, shoulders, and hips came into play, requiring great energy; and there was constant dropping out and returning to the ring. This would go on for hours, sometime until dawn, until all were near exhaustion, and the little praise houses fairly rocked with the rhythm. In later years, as more secular entertainments found their way into island life, the Shouts became less and less frequent; but they had been a valuable link between home and church, for they gave young people as well as old some excitement to anticipate in the dreary sameness of their lives.[10]

Another religious expression, unique to the islands, was the *House Blessing*. On St. Helena no new house was complete until the House Blessing had taken place. All the family, the neighbors, and the men who had worked on the house gathered together to

9. *Ibid.*, 213; Clyde Vernon Kiser, *Sea Island to City: A Study of St. Helena Islanders in Harlem and Other Urban Centers* (New York, 1932), 79–80; George A. Kuyper, "The Powerful Influence of a Notable School," *Southern Workman*. LX (January, 1931), 31.

10. Cooley, *School Acres*, 156; Rose, *Rehearsal for Reconstruction*, 96. The description of the Shout is taken from Cooley, *School Acres*, 150–51, and from Woofter, *Black Yeomanry*, 219–20.

sing spirituals and read a few passages of scripture. One of their number, perhaps a workman in overalls, would offer a prayer of dedication and consecration, after which more spirituals would fill the rooms with their poignant melodies.

> We ask thy blessing upon this home with all its newness and charm. . . . Be Thou the first occupant; may Thy presence be in every nook and corner and let Thy spirit hover over and in each and every room; May the windows let in the light of happiness and may welcome be the hinges of each and every door; May the atmosphere of the home be most congenial, and may peace ever abide herein. Bless all those who have had a hand in its construction; those who have come to help dedicate it; and especially those who shall dwell herein. So fill them with happiness, that the stranger passing by and the friend dropping in may truly feel that this is a house by the side of the road.

A charming and moving custom, the House Blessing was but another expression of the centrality of religion in the islanders' lives.[11]

Superimposed on the praise house structure were the churches, seven of them across the island. Six of them were Baptist, and the seventh was Methodist—a remnant of some upcountry followers of Sherman's army. Miss Cooley understood the importance of these churches for a people who had had little experience in business enterprise and who had no part in the political life of the region, and she made no effort to weaken or displace their influence. Indeed, she had learned very early that the islanders had little regard for her staid and pious brand of religion when she had tried to give the Community Class a course in Bible lessons. It had seemed a reasonable thing to do. They loved the Bible, as did she. She had taught Bible at Hampton for several years, and it had been a favorite subject with teachers and students. But with the old grandmothers of the Community Class, Miss Cooley fell flat. She finally defined the problem when one of the old women declared, "I yeddy [reckon] yo' ben a Presbylocian"; and she knew that she would have to find another way to communicate her conception of religion. In the meantime she

11. Cooley, *Homes of the Freed*, 149–50; "House Blessing" (N.p., n.d.), in James P. King Papers, JMD.

sought to work through the existing church structures, and this was a strategy that she never abandoned. She adopted the policy of airing any new plan through the churches and deciding no important issue without considering the minister's point of view. The ministers served on the various Penn-sponsored committees, and they always kept their pulpits open to the school. For a while they even sponsored Penn School Sundays, when Miss Cooley and Miss House would speak in the churches and bring the school before the people.[12]

Although she reached out to the older people and developed rapport with them through the churches, Miss Cooley placed her real hope in the young people at her school. Every morning she and Miss House held a morning prayer service at Hampton House, and any visitors who arrived during the service were invited to join in. Everyday at noon there were chapel services at the school, and on Wednesday a "Big Chapel," with a speaker and a lesson to which the whole community was invited. Sometimes these services brought Miss House to the stand to report and interpret current news happenings throughout the world; usually, however, through story and lecture the speakers explained the rewards of the virtuous life and the spirit of service. There were daily Bible lessons in the classrooms and weekly prayer meetings for the students and the teachers. Every evening brought chapel services for the boarders in the Butler Memorial Room, and every Sunday brought them a special Sunday School.[13]

The *pièce de résistance* in the school's religious campaign was the Christmas mystery play, a semiannual spectacle that profoundly moved the community. Written and directed by Miss House, this play became a cherished and much-anticipated part of the Christmas season. As Miss Cooley suggested, "Even a cold night and the dark of the moon do not keep the people in their homes, for it has become a tradition and each year makes it dearer

12. Cooley, *School Acres*, 155, 156; Cooley, *Homes of the Freed*, 86; "Annual Report," 1917, p. 32, Cooley, "Report to the Trustees," January 14, 1913, both in PSP.

13. James P. King, "A Tribute to Miss Cooley," (N.p., n.d.), in James P. King Papers, Linnie Lumpkins Blanton, "Reminiscences of a Friend and Great Teacher," both in JMD; "Two Women on an Atlantic Island," 1932, p. 4, "Annual Report," 1909, p. 25, 1910, p. 17, 1917, p. 32, all in PSP.

to the hearts of the island folk." Miss Cooley could think of nothing that had a stronger influence on the spiritual life of the school. The play must have been quite effective, for even years later one of the early Penn teachers—who was well educated and knowledgeable on such matters—described the mystery play as a beautiful Biblical interpretation of music and art.[14]

The first year it was given was something of a disappointment, however. The ladies had not sufficiently prepared their naive and unsophisticated audience; and when children and teachers appeared on the stage dressed in so strange a fashion, there were giggles all over the hall. "When the angels came on the stage," recalled Miss Cooley, "that was too much! Nervousness and general excitement prevailed and rather spoiled the effect!"[15]

In later years the principals gave plenty of explanation: the audience was to remember that they were far away in Bethlehem and that they were seeing the pictures of the Christ Child's birth; they were to forget their children and teachers and think only of the story. The solemnity of the occasion came through to the islanders, and no giggles ever again destroyed the mood of the evening. Every year the staging and costuming grew more elaborate, though all was the creation of island minds and hands. The vigilant committee on costumes rifled the barrels of second-hand goods sent down from the North and came up with many a treasure, such as the old piano cover that was quickly pressed into service on the back of the tallest king! Mary and Joseph and the innkeeper, Gabriel and the shepherds, the kings and the angels—all lost their everyday personalities for one glorious evening. The blending of the lovely old spirituals with English Christmas carols, the crude stage of Darrah Hall with its great rafters and rough finish, the palmettoes and Spanish moss used in the staging and the use of Biblical language and simple conversation—all went together to fit the mystery into the native imagination of players and people. It was a triumph of both worship and communica-

14. Cooley, *School Acres*, 144; Cooley to trustees, December 2, 1920, in George Foster Peabody Papers, Library of Congress (hereinafter cited as GFP); Blanton, "Reminiscences," in JMD.
15. Cooley, *School Acres*, 144.

tion, for it placed Penn School in the minds of the people as an institution that shared their faith and loyalties.[16]

Penn probably also captured the loyalty of the people simply because two white women were at its head. Willie Lee Rose has suggested that in the pandemonium after the capture of Port Royal, "white ladies" brought reassurance to the Negroes.[17] Very few white people had ever been seen on the island in the days before the Civil War, and after the collapse of the Port Royal experiment whites had little reason at all to go to St. Helena. Undoubtedly, white womanhood had a mystique about it that Miss Towne and Miss Murray had preserved and Miss Cooley and Miss House had inherited. This, as well as the fact that the ladies spoke in the same religious idiom as the blacks, must have given their leadership added authority.

Their religious message, however, was a strange and difficult one for a people who yearned for the Promised Land, and who turned their eyes toward Heaven rather than earth. It was hard for them to grasp Miss Cooley's vision, which held that the truest happiness and development are found in a life of service. She labored mightily, however, to bring this message home to them, organizing numerous activities whereby her students could learn the rewards of service. The school organized a YMCA and a YWCA to give opportunities to the students to begin home missionary service, and Christmas at the school was always a time of missionary activity. At Christmas every student brought in a gift for the poorer families—from a few pennies to a box of matches to a large bag of grits or potatoes— and laid them on the benches below the school Chirstmas tree before they received their own presents. The school Santa Claus then gave each child some candy and an orange, but none were so thrilled as the old grandmothers of the Community Class who made their curtsies and murmured, "T'ank yo', Sir!" as they passed in solemn procession.[18]

Miss Cooley's proudest creation was the Public Service Committee, a group of twelve students from the higher grades who

16. Ibid., 144, 147, 148.
17. Rose, *Rehearsal for Reconstruction*, 85.
18. "Annual Report," 1917, p. 32, 1929, p. 7, in PSP; Cooley, *School Acres*, 142, 143.

were responsible for the school morale. Their motto was "Honor, duty, service," and to be a member of this committee was the highest honor in the school. The committee was essentially Miss House's idea, and she envisioned it as the first step in self-government among the students. The members settled playground disputes and took responsibility for the cleanliness of the school grounds. They handled numerous school questions and helped the principals create public opinion in favor of changes and improvements the ladies desired. When, for instance, the Penn principals wanted to put an end to the practice of fastening clothes with pins instead of buttons, they enlisted the aid of Ophelia Fields, chairman of the Girls Committee. "Down the line of girls she and her committee marched every morning and the pins became conspicuous to the whole group and fairly pricked their owners!" Within six months, the pin problem had been beaten.[19]

The Public Service Committee also chose a word for the school to consider each month, and they gave a talk to the school on the word they had chosen. They posted these words in each classroom—honesty, reverence, self-control, self-respect, faithfulness, thrift, courtesy, gratitude—and in this way kept before the students the lofty ideals that Penn School sought to instill.[20]

Miss Cooley and Miss House had a vision of transforming sterile knowledge "through the Spirit of Service—the Spirit of Christ, into fertile fields, happy homes and noble ideals of life and living." For a while the two ladies had few indications that their lessons were taking hold, but one Easter they realized that some of the islanders had begun to understand the connection between improved standards of living and worthier lives. As one of the young mothers said to Miss Cooley, "I had the yard clean up very nice and in the house very nice to meet the great Easter morning." This, wrote Miss Cooley with pride, was one of the fundamental realities that the school was trying to pass on to its people.[21]

19. "Annual Report," 1927, p. 24, in PSP; Woofter, *Black Yeomanry*, 289; Cooley, *Homes of the Freed*, 180.
20. Cooley, *Homes of the Freed*, 180.
21. *Historical Handbook of Penn School and St. Helena Island, South Carolina*, (N.p., n.d.), 3, in HKP; Cooley, *Homes of the Freed*, 165.

Miss Cooley and Miss House believed that their people's salvation—spiritual as well as economic—lay in agriculture. Consistently they admonished their students to remain in the country where they could be independent and self-sufficient, where they could be free from white domination and the evils of the city ghettos, and where they could develop those traits of personality and character so essential to civilized living. The heart of the ladies' message, however, was that in the country, on his own home acres, the black student could be of more service to himself and his race than anywhere else. The students at Penn School learned that the greatest service they could render was to carry on the ideals taught at the school by serving their own race in their own communities, thus improving the standard of living and helping to build character. The school therefore cast the decision of what to do with one's life in missionary terms, and many Penn graduates remained on the island as farmers or teachers, foregoing the larger wages and cultural opportunities to be had elsewhere because they had chosen to spread the Penn School gospel as missionaries to their own race.[22]

The ladies' cultivation of this spirit of service contributed to one of Penn School's finest achievements—the corps of inspired and dedicated teachers that assembled on St. Helena Island. Replacing the old teachers had been the most difficult and painful aspect of building a new Penn School, for these teachers, all Penn School graduates, had stood by the school for forty years. But Miss Cooley knew that her teachers were the pivot around which her program would swing and that success would depend on the extent to which they understood and shared her zeal for the Hampton educational doctrine. So the old teachers were replaced as quickly as possible with finer stuff.[23]

In the very early years of the new regime, all of the new teachers were Virginia born and Hampton trained, and they were thoroughly inoculated with the Hampton spirit. They went to Penn School and worked for much less pay than their Hampton degrees could have earned them elsewhere, for their training had

22. "Annual Report," 1919, p. 11, "Penn School Facts," 1931, both in PSP.
23. Cooley, *School Acres*, 39.

Things of the Spirit and Service 113

instilled the self-sacrificing devotion of the missionary. As Miss Cooley wrote of them, their strength lay in the fact that they had made the journey up themselves: "They are of the race and know their own strengths and needs and weaknesses." Though the black teacher had inherited much less than the white teacher "of those things that are of greatest value," she could offer her people much nonetheless because she could "keep head and shoulders above her class and be a leader they love to follow for she inspires them to be like her."[24]

At first, of course, there had been no dormitories, and the teachers had had to live in the community and walk to school just as the children did. Later the trustees sent down some portable houses, which leaked and to which water had to be carried from a pump in the field; but all was endured with quiet patience and resolution and even joy, if one would believe Miss Cooley. Among these early workers were Linnie Lumpkins (later Mrs. Joshua Blanton); Rosetta Mason, matron of the boarding department; James P. King, bookkeeper and later superintendent of industries; and Nurse King. All of them had come to stay, and they committed themselves totally to uplifting their people on St. Helena Island. Every teacher shared the responsibility for bringing the more abundant life to the Sea Islands. They had given their lives for a cause, and they worked for nothing less than the re-creation and regeneration of all of life on St. Helena.[25]

Miss Cooley expected much of these workers. (All teachers were called workers at Penn, for their responsibilities involved far more than simply teaching in the classroom.) All of them were expected to lead exemplary lives, setting high standards for the community to emulate. Their clothing, their personal habits and behavior, and especially their homes were to serve as a constant model and inspiration to students and community. In short, they were to lead St. Helena away from "century-old habits of makeshift living" by holding out a vision of a broader and worthier life.[26]

24. *Ibid.*, 24; Cooley, *Homes of the Freed*, 189–90.
25. Cooley, *School Acres*, 24, 26.
26. Cooley, *Homes of the Freed*, 149, 166, 185; Julius Rosenwald Fund, "Penn School on St. Helena Island: Journal of the Rural School Exploration, Number 7" (Chicago, July, 1936), 15, in HKP.

Miss Cooley expected all of her teachers to understand farm problems so well that they could win the respect of the parents. "It means a great love for the land, and for the handicapped rural child," Miss Cooley wrote, as well as "a determination to remove these handicaps as far as possible and to be a power in developing a satisfying rural life."[27]

Miss Cooley expected Penn School workers to involve themselves completely in the life of the community. She felt that no one should apply for rural work who had mental reservations about his or her time and personal interests. A worker's whole life had to enter the community life. So every Penn School worker had to be associated with some church on the island, and in the early years the workers divided into squads and attended every church according to plan. Most of them volunteered their time as Sunday School teachers and club leaders, and in these ways they built up contacts and injected the Penn School influence into the life of the community.[28]

They also served on the Community Council. This was probably the most effective device the school ever created for directing and influencing community policy. Under Miss Cooley's direction and leadership, the teachers from Penn School and the public schools, the farm and home demonstration agents, the nurse, the preachers, the doctor, and representatives from each of the lodges and societies met together once a month to plan and discuss the activities of the community. The members all served on the various council committees, including Health and Sanitation, Home Improvement, Farm Improvement, Recreation, Education and Religious Life, and Leadership; and they drew up Five Year Plans for community development. Their "vision " as Miss House described it years later, was "the creation of a country community of home owners living in simple, attractive cottages . . . where the poultry yards, barns, and well-ordered farm fields speak of industry and thrift; where schools, churches, and all

27. "Annual Report," 1919, p. 15, in PSP.
28. Rossa Belle Cooley, "Education in the Soil," *Progressive Education*, X (December, 1933), 4; King, "Tribute to Miss Cooley," in JMD; Davis, "A Unique People's School," 12.

Things of the Spirit and Service

public buildings and recreation centers point to a progressive, public-spirited people who have learned to cooperate."[29]

In the 1920s a European visitor to Penn School marveled at the Community Council in action, suggesting that the islanders had, in fact, learned to cooperate. She wrote to her sponsors that she had never seen a better public spirit and a more devoted service to all municipal needs. She was stunned that such a high public spirit should have been achieved amongst a people so recently released from slavery. "Through this spirit," she wrote approvingly, "the population of the island . . . has achieved a joy in life and an outlook on life which in all its modesty is a high form of civilization."[30] She perhaps claimed too much for the efforts of the Community Council, and she may not have realized that that body was far from representative of the island population as a whole. But she was not mistaken in her perception of a high degree of initiative, self-direction, and community spirit; and these were the contributions of the Penn School workers.

By 1920 Miss Cooley had gathered around her a remarkable group of teachers and community workers, most of whom dedicated the better part of their mature adult lives to the Penn School endeavor. Though there was some movement and shifting around the periphery of the group, the important nucleus of Penn School workers remained constant from the early 1920s until the closing of the school in 1948. Benjamin and Grace Barnwell, Benjamin and Catherine Boyd, Fred and Salome Fripp, Maurice and Louise Wildy, William and C. B. Flynt, Miss Lottye Wright, Mrs. Ethel Bailey, Miss Mable Price, George Brown, Aurelius Brown, and Benjamin H. Washington, and, of course, Mr. and Mrs. King and Miss Rosetta Mason formed a band of dedicated and self-respecting workers who committed themselves tirelessly and unselfishly to building a better life for their people. Most of them were graduates of Penn School. Most of them had been to Hampton. All of them believed that agriculture was the great hope for their

---

29. Woofter, *Black Yeomanry*, 196; House, "Roads of Learning on St. Helena Island," 5, 6.
30. Mrs. Anna Wicksell, "Some Colored Schools in the U.S.," 1927, in PSP.

people and that the Penn School ideals offered a finer and nobler existence.[31]

The Penn School workers understood very clearly what the school was trying to accomplish, and they either supported those goals or they left. As Mr. Wildy described the aims of the school: Penn sought to teach its students to be self-respecting and self-supporting; it sought to create a desire for a quiet, fruitful rural life; and it sought to develop the whole community to be loyal citizens of the island. Catherine Gregory (later Boyd) explained that Penn was trying to raise the pupils and their homes to the same level so that the pupils would want to stay on the island and help the school to do the building. And Mrs. Bailey believed that the aim of Penn School was to stamp out prejudice, superstition, and ignorance and to replace those with belief in the brotherhood of man, belief in God, belief in prayer, and belief in the home as the family altar. One of the teachers who remained on the island but a few short years sounded a discordant note. "Are the results commensurate to the amount of money and labor being invested?" he queried. "There can be no doubt as to the purity of our motives or the highness of our aim; the question is, are we hitting the mark?" This lack of conviction and commitment would hardly sustain a Penn worker, and this name disappeared from the register fairly quickly.[32]

Isolated as they were from others of similar education and outlook, the Penn workers developed a camaraderie and a loyalty to the school rarely to be duplicated in educational endeavor. They liked to think of themselves as the Penn School family, a suggestion of the extent to which their relationships to each other and to the school transcended the purely professional. Dr. Robert Russa Moton of Tuskegee, a frequent guest to the island, reported an incident that illustrates this relationship. One evening as he sat on Dr. Bailey's porch, enjoying the moonlight and the fresh spring air and chatting with a group of Penn School teachers, he announced his intention of contributing $50 to the fund Miss Cooley was raising. "It would have done your heart good,"

31. "Teachers' Term of Service," October, 1939, in PSP.
32. "The Aims of Penn School," 1926, in PSP.

Things of the Spirit and Service

he wrote to Miss Cooley, "to see how they applauded. It made me very happy to see this fine expression of the loyalty of the staff to you and the work." He had meant to pledge his $50 to Miss Cooley when he saw her that day, but there were some strangers present and he did not think it would sound modest. "Of course, it was all right with the family," he explained, "because we are all mutually interested and appreciative of the work which grows more unique and more effective with the years."[33]

As J. P. King reminded an island audience many years after Penn School had closed, Miss Cooley and Miss House had formulated and directed the program and received the applause in the Penn School endeavor, but it was the teachers who gave substance to the principals' vision. King had been looking over a list of those who had been associated through the years with Penn School, and he said it reminded him of the eleventh chapter of Hebrews, sometimes called the roll call of the faithful. "I thought of those who had carried on at Penn for the advancement of God and humanity," he said, revealing his understanding of the work Penn had tried to do; and he went on to quote a line from General Eisenhower, upon his return from the Second World War. "I accept this ovation not for myself as the head of the army," Eisenhower had said, "but for the men in the ranks that carried out the orders. It was they who won the war." As Mr. King realized, it was the Penn School workers who waged the battle on St. Helena Island against poverty and ignorance and limited vision; and their cooperation and persistence, as well as their example, were the keys to Penn's success in becoming a model of community education.[34]

As its core, Penn School was a missionary venture. Designed to inculcate the values and the conceptions of living that would lead to the more abundant life, Penn School battled against economic and cultural obstacles in an effort to reach the things of the spirit. Its central message of service—so difficult to explain, so difficult to comprehend—seemed to its white heralds to carry with it the promise of true liberation. To the Hampton mentality,

33. Robert Russa Moton to Cooley, May 26, 1933, in PSP.
34. King, "Tribute to Miss Cooley," in JMD.

an understanding of the need for service was the distinguishing mark of the truly civilized life. The message to St. Helena's blacks, though never quite explicit, seemed to be that an understanding of the mysteries of service would be the surest way up for their people; and those blacks who "caught the spirit" were a constant reassurance to the white ladies and became the prizes of the Penn School experiment.

As missionaries above all other things, the two white ladies at Penn School had no difficulty accepting a hierarchical pattern of thought. The essence of life, they believed, was to be found in struggle—always upward, always toward the Cross. As Miss House expressed it when she wrote "The Penn School Song":

> Oh Island blest, God's hand is laid upon thee,
> Oh dear Penn School, God guide thy upward way,
> And on that "rough and rugged road" to heaven,
> May we all help bring in the glad and brighter day!

Thus Miss Cooley and Miss House were able to accept what they perceived to be black inferiority as a logical consequence of the degradation of slavery; and there is very little evidence that they expected—or believed themselves to be working toward—social or political equality. They did believe, however—and this belief was at the core of all their thought and action—that they could lead black people into lives not only of dignity but also of heightened ethical understanding. In this way the two ladies believed they were validating their own religion through lives of Christian service and that they were thereby contributing to the coming of the Kingdom of Heaven on Earth. Miss House made this belief explicit in a letter to Miss Cooley in 1925, in which she described a board of trustees meeting: "I spoke up and said that Dr. Frissell had a very clear vision for St. Helena which I thought you and I, and some of the Trustees had caught, and that we were working toward a very definite goal—to bring the Kingdom of Heaven on Earth at St. Helena."[35]

The two white ladies' conception of religion, growing as it did

---

35. Grace B. House, "Penn School Song," 1935, in York W. Bailey Museum, Penn Community Services, St. Helena Island, S.C.; House to Cooley, 1925, Trustees' minutes, September 21, 1925, both in PSP.

Things of the Spirit and Service 119

from the central idea of service (with Jesus Christ as the divine manifestation), clearly involved the notion that social responsibility was essential to mankind's ethical progress. Miss House expressed her understanding of the catalytic effects of lives properly spent in a song she wrote to memorialize the founders of Penn School:

> Oh their courage and hope were great,
> Their lives were strong and true;
> May we who live on this fair Isle,
> Through them our strength renew.[36]

There was no lack of dedication or noble purpose on St. Helena Island. The two white ladies at Penn School gave their lives for an idea they affirmed, and their courage and persistence in the face of overwhelming obstacles entitle them to no small measure of respect and admiration. Ultimately, however, despite forty years of effort, their program ran aground on the rough shoals of economic distress; and they never had to face the reality that the goals and assumptions of the missionary were woefully inadequate—even inappropriate—to deal with the problems of race in America.

36. Grace House and Rossa Belle Cooley, "Founders' Hymn," in York W. Bailey Museum, St. Helena Island, S.C.

7

New Challenges, New Beginnings

All through his long and useful life, George Foster Peabody loved the wife of his best friend and business partner, Spencer Trask. Trask and Peabody had vied for Katrina's hand when they were very young, and Spencer had won. But Katrina was one of those remarkable women who can sustain complex relationships, and the three of them remained warm friends, and increasingly frequent companions, throughout their lives. Several years after Spencer Trask's untimely death in a railroad accident, when Katrina was sixty-eight and Peabody was sixty-nine, the two of them were wed. Katrina was ill, and she spent most of their brief marriage in a darkened room, finally dying only a few months after the wedding. Nearly twenty years later when Peabody died he made eternal the triangle they had shared, directing that his remains be laid beside Spencer and Katrina.[1]

Like Peabody, Spencer Trask had made a fortune in the banking and securities business, and he provided Katrina (who brought wealth of her own to the marriage) with the style of life of the sophisticated New York socialite. "In the fashion of wealthy young matrons of her day," wrote Peabody's biographer, "Kate directed a household staff. She arranged the flowers, wrote letters, read and received her friends. Her husband, a busy Wall Street banker, perhaps stopped in at an art gallery or at his club

---

1. Ware, *George Foster Peabody*.

on the way home. They entertained at dinner." The Trasks spent much of their time at Yaddo, their Saratoga Springs estate, and Peabody was a frequent visitor. Here Katrina escaped from the pain of losing two children by creating a world of medieval romance and fantasy, with gardens, fountains, and rooms upon rooms of valuable art treasures, all of which gave vivid expression to her visionary longings for a better world. Here also she played the gracious hostess and patroness of the arts. As one description has it: "At the psychological moment Katrina would appear on the landing of the great staircase dressed in a trailing gown and wearing gleaming jewels about her neck. Though short in stature, she appeared tall as she descended the stairs to join her faithful courtiers." And then all would come alive with the lavish hospitality and sumptuous delights of food, music, and spiritous drink.[2]

In the long afternoons at her New York mansion, or at Yaddo, Katrina frequently devoted herself to writing medieval plays, in which she strove to capture eternal themes of good and evil. Her efforts were childish and simplistic, but they appealed to Peabody, for she often cast him in the virtuous and conquering role of the white knight. An unusually tall man with a flowing mane of white hair, Peabody looked the part—and he relished the role of conquering hero, standing always for the right. According to Peabody's biographer, Katrina was the central figure of his life and the chief source of his inspiration, and her conception of him as a knight with deeds to perform undoubtedly inspired this naive and idealistic soul to ever greater feats of generosity and concern for his fellow man.[3]

Peabody was ever the idealist. As a young man he had worked for good government and civil service reform, writing a constitution for the Young Men's Democratic Club that prohibited the members from holding political office. Obviously, he believed with the Mugwumps that politics was no business for proper young men.[4]

His political philosophy grew progressively more radical as

2. Ibid., 15, 42, 254.
3. Ibid., 254.
4. Ibid., 30.

he moved from the advocacy of gold, free trade, and tariff reform to a championship of the single tax and government ownership of the railroads. At the center of his often confused political musings lay one great abstraction—democracy—which he believed could best be realized through education. All of his energies and beneficences were aimed toward the achievement of that central idea, and he served generously and untiringly on the boards of many educational institutions, including Penn School, Hampton and Tuskegee, the University of Georgia, and Colorado College for Women. Concerned especially about black education, he helped to organize and finance the Southern Education Board, and he served for many years as treasurer of the General Education Board.[5]

Dedicated as he was to the creation of an enlightened electorate and a responsible citizenry, Peabody also felt to an unusual degree the responsibilities of wealth. Believing that wealth was a trust given by God to be used for the benefit of mankind, he retired from business at the age of fifty-four to distribute his fortune.[6]

A lifelong Democrat and an intense pacifist, Peabody looked upon Woodrow Wilson as a kind of God who would bring peace on earth; and he valued highly his friendship with the president. Although he supported the League to Enforce Peace, he said he wanted peace without force. Even more interesting, especially in light of his considerable political influence with such men as Woodrow Wilson and Newton Baker, are the sentiments he expressed in 1917:

> War is the wrong way to settle any great question, it being inhuman of necessity, and alas it is inherently and necessarily undemocratic.... I have believed that if England and France had had the grace to be truly democratic, and disarmed, and thus emphasized to the German people their lack of animosity and their confidence in the true basis of human brotherhood, that the German people would have restrained and finally overthrown Prussian militaristic dynastic power. I personally still believe that if France and Belgium had had the *grace not to*

5. *Ibid.*, viii, 30, 149.
6. *Ibid.*, 106, 134, 144, 224.

resist Germany but allow the German devastators to march over them without resistance it would have been but a few weeks before, and with an expenditure of only a hundred thousand lives that the German soldiers thoroughly trained as they are to obey would have revolted, and instead of millions of lives and no results we should have had permanent peace because of the awakening of the German conscience, and the dethronement of Hohenzollerns from within the Empire.[7]

Had he been less rich, Peabody would doubtless have been dismissed as a crackpot; but his money made the difference, and the connections it brought gave him authority and influence in the councils of government and with the public at large. In 1896, for example, Peabody and Spencer Trask helped reorganize and refinance the *New York Times*, bringing Adolph Ochs from Chattanooga to serve as publisher. Thereafter, the newspaper respected Peabody's opinions; and though his writing was ungrammatical, tortured, and totally lacking in style, the *Times* often printed his letters on its editorial page. An inveterate writer—he often dictated his letters far into the night ("an average of about fifty a day, many of them two and three pages, single spaced")—he participated vigorously in a wide range of activities, seeking always the creation of an enlightened democracy.[8]

As a man of wealth and influence who was dedicated to the principles of industrial education for blacks, Peabody had seemed to be a natural for the Penn School board in 1900. From the beginning he gave generously of his means as a board member, although initially he did not have the time to concern himself with the day-to-day operations of the school. When Frissell died in 1917, however, Peabody consented to serve as chairman of the board, and he relished the role of patriarch over such a well-established and increasingly noteworthy enterprise. Given his mystical bent, he must also have responded to the romantic and otherworldly qualities of St. Helena Island, much in the same way he responded to the medieval fantasies of Katrina Trask and Yaddo.

Among Peabody's close friends was Natalie Curtis-Burlin, sister of civil service reformer George William Curtis and heir to the

7. *Ibid.*, 178, 180–81.
8. *Ibid.*, 56, 156.

Curtis publishing fortune. A musician, Mrs. Burlin had long been a friend of Hampton Institute; in the teens she had also spent some time on St. Helena Island studying the old plantation melodies, or spirituals. The white directors of black education had encouraged the preservation of these spirituals as a treasured heritage and as an interpretation of the sorrow and tragedy of a race in bondage. Mrs. Burlin concluded, however, that the spirituals had a much broader significance than previously realized, and she convinced George Foster Peabody that they were the blacks' first real contribution to American culture. "The artistic utterance of the Negro," wrote Mrs. Burlin, "which has so important a place in the music of America, might help build a bridge of understanding between the races, spanning the chasm of prejudice." This was all the challenge that Peabody needed. Proclaiming now the musical and dramatic talent and power and the innate art instinct of black people, Peabody began to champion the spiritual for its potential service to the attainment of democracy. Perhaps even more important was the effect the cultivation of the spiritual supposedly would have on black people. "Through hardship and slavery," wrote one who shared Peabody's sympathies, "song has borne the Negro, and through prejudice and unhappiness; and it is the people of faith who saw that it would also bring him to the heights of ethical understanding." Clearly, much was to be expected from the singing of spirituals.[9]

In the mid-1920s, Peabody sponsored another research project on St. Helena Island, this time by an African musician, Nicholas Julius Ballanta (known in America as G. L. Taylor) of Sierra Leone. Ballanta collected and arranged the old island spirituals in an attempt to prove their African origin. His studies on St. Helena confirmed his discoveries in Africa respecting the African use of seventeen notes or tones in the octave instead of the twelve of the classical scale, and he concluded that the spirituals

---

9. *Ibid.*, 149; Natalie Curtis Burlin, *Negro Folk Songs* (New York & Boston, 1918–19); Grace Bigelow House, "The Little Foe of All the World," *Southern Workman*, XXXV (November, 1906), 609; Frances R. Grant, "Negro Patriotism and Negro Music," *Outlook*, February 26, 1919, p. 345; Peabody to Dr. Sara W. Brown, September 12, 1923, E. R. Ames to Peabody, September 13, 1923, both in PSP.

were not the result of slavery's hardships but were instead an African survival. As Peabody explained to Henry Morgenthau, "This promises to be of notable importance in the musical world perhaps as well as with reference to the part the Negro ten percent of our population should and may play in a right development of art in this country." Despite Peabody's enthusiasm, the noted sociologist Guy B. Johnson concluded in a later study that an equally plausible thesis might suggest that the Negroes took their religious folk songs from the folk productions of the English and Scotch-Irish. Nonetheless, Peabody expected music to teach Americans an appreciation for black contributions to the national life, and he lauded it as the blacks' contribution to the growth and practice of democracy in this country.[10]

All of this fervor from the new chairman of the board had a profound effect on Miss Cooley and Miss House. The ladies embraced Peabody's formulations, declaring in their publicity literature that the blacks must have some contribution to make to American life; and the spirituals, which showed their love of rhythm and their dramatic ability, were this contribution. In short, the black American could potentially be a national asset rather than a burden, and schools such as Penn could prove his ability to develop as a valuable citizen if given an education adapted to his needs.[11]

As a part of the national effort to develop patriotism during World War I, Penn School began to sponsor Community Sings once a month. These would bring the people together to sing the old-time spirituals, which the Sea Island people sang in minor key, following a leader who would limn (pronounced *line*) out the verses. The Penn principals also instituted a Week of Song, which sought to foster an appreciation of music. The week began with sermons in the island churches on the value of singing, followed during the week with a short concert at the school. Penn School

---

10. Peabody to Henry Morgenthau, August 12, 1926, in PSP; Guy Benton Johnson, *Folk Culture on St. Helena Island, South Carolina* (Chapel Hill, N.C., 1930), 101; Peabody to Blanton, May 14, 1919, in GFP.

11. Rossa Belle Cooley, "The Negro in His Own Environment," *Vassar Quarterly*, (May, 1920), 178, 179, in PSP; Rossa Belle Cooley, "America's Sea Islands," *Outlook*, April 30, 1919, p. 741.

also formed a quartet that occasionally traveled to the North seeking funds, and quartet contests became a leading pastime on the island. In one shining moment of triumph the Penn School Quartette even performed at Carnegie Hall, thanks to Peabody's connections, and the four men must have returned to St. Helena with many tales of another world. All of this interest in music can be traced to Peabody's influence and his fervent championship of music as the way out for the black American.[12]

World War I, with its goals of self-determination and democracy, seemed to Peabody to be a grand opportunity for blacks to prove their patriotism and usefulness. Many rural blacks, however, did not understand the war and its great issues, as Peabody realized when he received a letter from Grace House describing a meeting on St. Helena. Several of the island men had been drafted; and the night before they were to leave, a meeting was held in one of the little society halls to explain why they had been called upon to fight for freedom. Miss House described the dimly lighted hall, gay with flags, with its rows of anxious, troubled faces listening so patiently to get an understanding of what their "call" meant. And in a partially fictionalized account she recounted the speech of a Penn and Hampton graduate, the new school farmer, Benjamin Barnwell.[13]

> Friends, we have been found worthy to serve our country and our flag in a great cause. We are Soldiers of Freedom! . . . Our President has called us to go overseas to help put an end forever to war, so that never again will man be called upon to lift his hand against his fellow man! . . . We Negro soldiers are proud to have a share in this great work. . . . To no people on earth does the word freedom mean so much as it does to us, to whom it is still a new and sacred treasure. Our fathers remember the day when freedom was more to be desired than life itself. The longing for freedom is in our blood—our inheritance! . . . We go to do our share . . . with . . . a deep rooted living hope that when we have proved ourselves men, worthy to work

---

12. The Community Sing became an institution on St. Helena Island, continued to this day, thus preserving the beautiful and unusual spirituals so foreign to modern ears. Cooley, "America's Sea Islands," 741; Announcement of quartet's performance, October 3, 1928, Trustees' minutes, September 20, 1928, E. R. Ames, September 13, 1923, all in PSP.

13. House to Peabody, July 18, 1919, in GFP.

and fight and die for our country, a grateful nation may gladly give us the recognition of real men, and the rights and privileges of true and loyal citizens of these United States.[14]

Miss House reported with pride that "The Hymn of Freedom," which Natalie Curtis-Burlin had composed, had been launched that evening on St. Helena Island. Mrs. Burlin's vision of a singing army involved interpreting the war to blacks in the army camps through the use of spirituals. "The idea of a conquering power of righteousness riding on through the world," wrote Mrs. Burlin, "and the triumphant ring of the music, with its clarion call, seemed to me to offer an inspiring theme on which to build an American battle song embodying the ideals for which America entered the war."

> O march on, Freedom,
> March on, Freedom
> March on, conquering hosts,
>   Liberty is calling.
>
> To martyred Belgium
>   Freedom!
> To wounded France,
>   Freedom!
> 'Tis God who summons our advance,
>   Liberty is calling.
>
> O blow on, bugles,
>   Blow on, bugles,
>   Blow on, bugles of hope,
>   Liberty is calling.
>
> To struggling Russia,
>   Freedom!
> To the starving Pole,
>   Freedom!
> The trumpet sounds within my soul,
>   Liberty is calling.[15]

Miss House assured Peabody that the singing of the hymn

---

14. House, "Soldiers of Freedom,'" n.d., 6–8, in PSP. This speech was a reproduction of one Robert Russa Moton gave in Beaufort in 1917—a speech that a local white, though sympathetic to the Negro, described as "the most radical address he had ever heard." House to Peabody, July 18, 1918, in GFP.

15. House to Peabody, July 18, 1918, in GFP; Grant, "Negro Patriotism and Negro Music," 343. The "Hymn of Freedom" was set to the music of the spiritual "Ride On, Jesus."

had eased the minds of the troubled men on St. Helena, and her description moved him to write in the margin of her letter, "Is not this fine, it delights my heart, which however, cannot get away from the pathos of it all." Before long Peabody had convinced Secretary of War Newton Baker to allow the YMCA to send Penn's Mr. Blanton to Europe, where he would go from camp to camp leading the men in the singing of the spirituals and using his influence to sustain their morale. Francis Cope opposed the idea of sending Blanton to Europe because several of Penn's workers had been drafted and the school was already suffering from the burdens of the war situation; but Peabody insisted, and Mr. Blanton embarked for Europe with a great deal of enthusiasm. He visited numerous camps throughout France and reported that he was finding many chances to help men who had the wrong viewpoint on the war. Blanton was no Uncle Tom, however. He wrote candidly and forthrightly to Peabody of his belief that the quickest way to democracy in the South lay through politics; and though he hastened to declare himself no agitator, he complained bitterly that no American blacks had marched in the victory parade in Paris.[16]

World War I exacted a toll on St. Helena Island and on Penn School; it also introduced many of the island men to the wider world off the island. Miss Cooley had early hoped to keep the war from St. Helena's shores by arguing the need for farmers. As she wrote to the U.S. Navy recruiter, "In view of the President's and Governor's messages urging the farmers to produce food, it seems at this time a solemn duty for members of an agricultural school and community to respond to that call and serve as farmers." Her point of view prevailed for a time, but ultimately several of the island men were called to serve on the seas and behind the lines rather than on the farms. Penn School exhorted those who remained at home to "Raise Your Food" and "Plant an Extra Acre," and patriotism on St. Helena took many forms.[17]

16. Ware, *George Foster Peabody*, 183; Grant, "Negro Patriotism and Negro Music," 344; Cope to Peabody, August 5, 1918, Peabody to Cope, August 8, 1918, Peabody to House, November 21, 1918, Blanton to Peabody, June 11, 1919, September 13, 1919, all in GFP.

17. Cooley to O. F. Cooper, April 23, 1917, "Annual Report of the Penn Normal, Industrial and Agricultural School," 1917, p. 27, both in PSP.

Miss Cooley and Miss House were ardent admirers of Wilson and supporters of the war effort, but their primary concern was for the welfare of their school and the island's men. Through irregularities in the mail on St. Helena, many men did not receive the card informing them that they had been drafted. Consequently, early in 1918 several St. Helena men had been arrested as deserters and fined $50. Two of the men were arrested in their fields and were not allowed to go to their homes to get their clothes. Benjamin Boyd, a graduate of Penn and Hampton, was arrested on his way to take a position in the carpentry department at Penn School. Strong resentment spread across St. Helena as the islanders began to suspect that they were being exploited for the sake of the fine. Miss Cooley wrote anxiously to the Beaufort Draft Board and to the commanding officer at Camp Jackson, imploring them to conduct an investigation and explaining that at that particular time when the Negroes were striving to meet the call, it was important that they should be made to feel that the government meant to give them a fair chance. The fact that the matter was not ignored but that white people were willing to go to some trouble to see that the blacks received fair play, dispelled the bitterness and resentment that might have caused trouble at some future time.[18]

Penn School used its influence with the local and federal authorities to exempt most of its teachers from the draft. Francis Cope was the first to realize the threat, and he wrote to Mr. Peabody his belief that as a war measure alone, as well as a protection for the furure, the government could not afford to cripple Penn's educational and agricultural resources. Peabody fervently agreed, and he informed the Beaufort Draft Exemption Board that it was his view that educational work should not be allowed to suffer because of the draft. Peabody's connections failed to impress the Beaufort Draft Board, however, and within a week the new school farmer, Benjamin Barnwell, had been drafted. Penn had already lost Mr. Boyd, the new carpenter, and before long it also lost the new bookkeeper and assistant superintendant of industries, Mr.

18. Cooley to Peabody, December 7, 1918, House to Peabody, July 18, 1918, both in GFP; Cooley to Beaufort Draft Board, June 10, 1918, in PSP.

King. With Mr. Blanton soon to go to France, Penn School was becoming increasingly crippled in its work, and in the fall of 1918 Miss Cooley and Miss House traveled to Washington to seek exemptions for the men who remained. With the aid of Thomas Jesse Jones they discovered that a new ruling had been made authorizing local boards to grant deferred classifications to teachers. Armed with this information, they managed to fend off further attacks on their manpower from the Beaufort Draft Board.[19]

Despite Miss Cooley's efforts to preserve her teaching staff, Penn School supported the war effort in a number of ways. Fifty-five ex-students and fourteen Penn graduates and teachers served in the armed forces. Whenever their families' allotments failed to arrive, these people turned to the school for help and advice. Penn School became a branch of the Beaufort Red Cross chapter; and the students in the sewing classes made sweaters, socks, and comfort bags to send to the men in camp. Penn also sponsored a Circle of Negro War Relief, "Victory Boys and Girls" Clubs, and a War Savings Society, all of which encouraged the purchase of Liberty Loans and War Savings and Thrift stamps.[20]

The spirit of patriotism was equally evident on the home farms. The members of the Corn Club struggled through a dreadful drought and raised fifteen hundred bushels of corn to help win the war. Miss Cooley set no small goals for her students, and in the year of the armistice she described their renewed efforts: "The drought was discouraging and the comparatively small crop was discouraging, but the children were not discouraged and they are planting again this year with enthusiasm 'to help feed the world.'" Miss Cooley used the war to teach the islanders lessons of conservation, planning, and thrift; and she reported with satisfaction that St. Helena Island had learned from the war and Penn School to do for the country what it had never done for itself. Soon the islanders would have an even more compelling reason to follow the Penn School lessons and adopt the more modern agricultural practices.[21]

19. Cope to Peabody, August 5, 1918, Cooley to trustees, October 31, 1918, both in GFP; Peabody to Beaufort Draft Exemption Board, August 26, 1918, Benjamin Barnwell to Cooley, September 8, 1918, both in PSP.
20. Cooley, "Patriotism at Penn," 1919, in PSP.
21. *Ibid.*

The Penn School men were enthusiastic soldiers, and they learned much from their venture out into the world. Perhaps most important, they realized what a difference Penn School had made in their lives and how it had set them apart from others of their race. "I am . . . thankful that I am connected with the great host that are looking for the greater things in human life," wrote a former Penn School student, expressing his renewed conviction to return to Penn School and "render service to . . . my people of the Island." After observing several days of army intelligence testing, Benjamin Barnwell wrote to Miss House of his elevation through the ranks and his conviction that the need of education for blacks was greater than ever before. Corporal Clarence Jones now saw clearly that "all I know and what I am today I got it at dear old Penn," and this seemed to be the prevailing sentiment among all the Penn School soldiers.[22]

All of the men seemed to see themselves as Soldiers of Freedom, and they exulted in the high mission they were serving. "I thank God for liveing [sic] in such an age," wrote Aurelius J. Brown. And though he was thrilled with the armistice, Clarence Jones wrote with some regret that he did not have a chance "to get a whack at the huns."[23]

Letter after letter poured into the Frogmore Post Office carrying the same message: "If there be any vacancies at Penn, that you think I could fill, I shall be more than glad to help what little I can." Penn School had successfully instilled in her students the spirit of service, and the soldiers returned to Penn with a broadened understanding of the work it was trying to do.[24]

Soon they would see that work expanded in new directions. Before the war in 1917, Miss Cooley had initiated her second revolution at Penn School. In 1904 she had brought the farms into the classrooms; now she was to make classrooms out of the farms. Her goal always had been to enrich and influence the life of the entire community in such a way that rural living would be-

22. Aurelius J. Brown to House, December 18, 1918, Barnwell to House, December 12 1918, Barnwell to Cooley, September 8, 1918, Clarence Jones to Cooley, September 24, 1918, all in PSP.
23. A. J. Brown to House, December 18, 1918, C. Jones to House, November 11, 1918, both in PSP.
24. Benjamin Boyd to Cooley, January 16, 1919, in PSP.

come sufficiently appealing to hold the young people on the island. In time she had realized that her school was out of step with the agricultural life of the island: "The crop often called the children to the fields at the same time our old Liberty Bell called them to the classroom; and we had that paradox—an agricultural school seemingly in conflict with the farming community it served." As soon as she realized that Penn's program—the holidays and school days—coincided with the routine of city life, she began to seek a way to adapt her school to the peculiar needs of the island farmer and to make Penn a rural school.[25]

Miss House's father had started an agricultural school in Salonica, Greece, and Miss Cooley borrowed from him the plan of an all-year school that was geared to the special needs of the agricultural community. She believed that in a community of farmers the school should be based on agriculture. Such an idea was in the best progressive education tradition, reflecting as it did John Dewey's conception of the school as an embryonic community life. "When the school introduces and trains each child of society into membership within such a little community," Dewey had written, "saturating him with the spirit of service, and providing him with the instruments of self-direction, we shall have the deepest and best guarantee of a larger society which is worthy, lovely, and harmonious."[26]

In adapting John Dewey's ideas to the situation and conditions of St. Helena Island, Miss Cooley and Miss House demonstrated the essential similarity between the ideas of Samuel Chapman Armstrong and those of the progressive educator. Though one aimed to regenerate the individual and the other sought social regeneration, both relied on the daily round and the common task to work their educational magic. And both rode quite comfortably—overlapping but causing no friction—in the front of the educational revolution the two white ladies were bringing to Penn School. "For the country child," Miss House

---

25. "Annual Report," 1917, p. 13, PSP; Cooley, *School Acres*, 68.
26. Cooley, *School Acres*, xiii; "Annual Report," 1917, p. 12, in PSP; John Dewey, *School and Society* (Rev. ed.; Chicago, 1915), 43–44, as quoted in Cremin, *The Transformation of the School*, 118.

would later write, "the processes of living are problems to be worked out—not in theory but in practice." One can hardly tell whether Armstrong or Dewey was uppermost in her mind when she continued: "The water supply, sanitary system, roads, making a crop and marketing it, are not merely studies in civics, economics, engineering, or agriuclture, but are part of the very fabric of his life." Clearly, at Penn School industrial education and progressive education were a part and parcel of the same thing. As Miss Cooley expressed it in one of her annual reports: "Industrial education is easily misunderstood. It can become a term expressing an education that is material only. It should be used in a broad sense to include an education that fits the needs of life as they must be met by the young people leaving school. In that sense we use it at Penn School, and in that sense the whole of life is considered."[27]

John Dewey was concerned primarily to preserve American democracy in the face of urbanization and industrialization. According to Dewey industrialization had so modified American social life that the school would now have to assume all the educative aspects of traditional agrarian life. Of course, St. Helena Island had in no way suffered from the ill effects of the nation's industrialization process, but the two ladies nonetheless echoed Dewey's formulations in such statements as, "When we remember what modern industry has done to the children, we should be more willing to give them, through their schools, at least a part of their lost birthright." Of course, this statement was directed to a northern audience, and perhaps it was designed to appeal to their educational sympathies. The important point here is that Penn School was consciously attempting to broaden its scope to make the school become a miniature community and, in a real sense, to make the community become the school.[28]

27. House, "Roads of Learning on St. Helena Island," 12. As Lawrence Cremin suggests in his study of progressive education: "The phrase *progressive education* was in fairly common use during the decade before World War I, most frequently referring to industrial education of one sort or another and to the movement to transform the school into a social center." Cremin, *The Transformation of the School*, 88n; "Annual Report," 1930, p. 32, in PSP.

28. Cremin, *The Transformation of the School*, 117; "Annual Report," 1935, p. 10, in PSP.

With a series of grants of from $5,000 to $10,000 from the General Education Board, Miss Cooley reorganized her school and put the new plan into operation in the spring of 1917. She divided the school year into four terms and arranged the work of each term to correspond to the work on the farms.[29]

The spring term began with a parade of the Corn Club. The Penn School band led a merry procession of students, wearing green and yellow banners and carrying spades and hoes over their shoulders, down the school road to the corner store and then back again, unobserved by any save the ancient, embracing oaks and the empty cotton fields. "Many of the boys could not achieve blue overalls," recalled Miss Cooley, "as they had to wear out their old suits, so it was a motley parade, all sizes, all colors, but all enthusiasm." Planting Week then took the place of the old spring holiday; and during this week the Penn School teachers visited all of their students on their home acres, encouraging the parents to give their children an acre to work according to school agriculture. After Planting Week school opened, and all students above the primary grades reported for classroom work on Monday, Wednesday, and Friday, remaining at home the other four days to oversee their crops and help their parents on the farm. The teachers also visited the home acres on these days, thus building a bridge between home and school by gaining a better understanding of the children's home conditions.[30]

When the crop was set, the older students again came to school every day for the summer term. This sunrise school started at six-thirty every morning and lasted until noon. The children all walked to school, some of them as far as eight or nine miles each way; and the sunrise school was an effort to spare them from the debilitating summer heat. "I likes this school," said one of the boys, "for it comes at the waking up of the brains," and so the Penn School students ate breakfast instead of lunch at school and found themselves at home again in the early afternoon. This added term allowed the students to progress through the grades

29. Cooley, *School Acres*, 88–89; "Annual Report," 1917, p. 13, in PSP.
30. "Annual Report," 1917, pp. 17, 18 in PSP; Cooley, *School Acres*, 77.

much faster than formerly and prevented many of them from dropping out in sheer discouragement as the older students had often done. The summer term ended with a festive watermelon picnic. "Then is the time to see our school," wrote Miss Cooley. "The big wagon comes in from the fields loaded with the lucious melons. The children have 'thrown up' five cents apiece and can eat all the melon they want.... Shining dark eyes, and shining white teeth cutting through the delicious pink of the melons, are a sight to remember!" A stereotyped image, perhaps, but a vivid and mouth-watering one at that![31]

The highlight of the autumn term was the Farmer's Fair and then the Junior Farmer's Fair, when the islanders came to the school for a day of exhibits, prizes, speeches, and games, followed by a mammoth barbeque. In the autumn, beginning in October, the students came to school every day for three weeks, and then the school released them for two weeks—known on the island as Potato Week—while they helped their parents harvest the sweet potato crop. Once again, while school was closed, the teachers went out to the homes to observe and instruct their students, working primarily to enlist the parents' support in the home acre work to be carried through the winter and helping the students to select their acres.[32]

The winter term was a primary feature of Miss Cooley's new plan. The long-established pattern of going "off island" to seek work after the fall harvest had meant that in the winter months few gave any thought to the farms. Under the new system, daily classroom lessons in agriculture and reports from the home acres kept the interest centered on the land. In every classroom a large chart showed when each child had selected a home acre, when the compost pile was prepared, and when the fall and spring plowing was done. The teachers posted the record of each child's yield in a central hallway of the classroom building where everyone was sure to see it, and the record remained posted until the

31. "Annual Report," 1917, p. 18, 1919, p. 12, in PSP; Cooley, "America's Sea Islands," 740; Cooley, *School Acres*, 83.
32. "Annual Report," 1917, p. 14, 1920, p. 13, in PSP; Cooley, *School Acres*, 69–70.

following year. Penn School was now a genuine all-year school, using the homes as one large dormitory system and the farms as an extended agricultural experiment.[33]

At first some of the parents refused to cooperate with the new plan, giving their children very poor land to work, or no land at all. But the increased crop yields and the full corn houses convinced most of the doubters, and soon many of the best acres on the home farms were given for the school acre. Food crops began to vie with the cotton crop, and gardens became a recognized feature of the spring plan. So the lessons of crop rotation and diversification went home with the children, and the principles of farm demonstration became institutionalized in the Penn School curriculum. The Penn School farm now confined itself to two functions: to serve as a laboratory for the students to learn agriculture adapted to Sea Island conditions and as a productive agency to support the school family of teachers and boarding students.[34]

In a real sense Penn could now claim that it was an all-island school, an all-the-year school, merging school and community into a common adventure. Penn captured this realization in its new proclamation, "The Island Is The School." The teachers now aimed to consider the entire background of their students and use all of the equipment at their disposal to reach into that background and better it. "Thus," wrote Miss Cooley in terms that would have delighted John Dewey, "the home, the home farm, the church, the store, the school, the playground, should be educational forces in the child's life." Equally important, she continued, "the merchant, the doctor, and the minister should be called upon to help in working out and carrying forward, not merely school policies, but what should be more properly called community policies." Here was community education writ large, the kind of all-pervasive influence that educators often dreamed of finding, impossible to secure in a more complex and sophisticated environment. Here also was education shaped by the needs of

33. "Annual Report," 1917, p. 16, 1923, p. 5, Margaret McCulloch, "Home Acre Work," April 19, 1927, all in PSP. See Appendix B for a calendar of the All-Year School.
34. McCulloch, "Home Acre Work", "Annual Report," 1918, p. 12, 1919, pp. 12–13, all in PSP.

those it served, although the determination of what those needs were was not left to the participants themselves. "I have never seen a more sensible program," wrote an officer of the Massachusetts Board of Education, "than that which you have adopted in your efforts to make your institution meet exactly the conditions of the community you are serving." Penn had now embarked on a genuinely creative venture, one that was to win it much acclaim in the years to come.[35]

35. Cooley, *School Acres*, 5; "Annual Report," 1920, p. 10, Rufus Stimson to Cooley, November 20, 1938, both in PSP.

8

The More Abundant Life

Back of all the work Penn School tried to do lay the fact of land-ownership. Only their land could make these islanders self-reliant, could give them the independence and dignity of the sturdy yeoman farmer. Without their land they would be at the mercy of the same economic forces that held other southern blacks in bondage. Without their land the Penn School experiment in community education would be all for naught, for the struggle for survival would preoccupy the blacks, keeping them apart, keeping them down. Miss Cooley understood these facts with crystal clarity, and she had worked from the beginning to help the people hold on to their inheritance.

All along Miss Cooley had known that some day the boll weevil would appear on the Atlantic coast; this pest had traveled eastward from Texas for a quarter of a century, slowly but relentlessly eating the South's tender cotton buds and undermining its shaky economy. Miss Cooley had long preached the gospel of diversification because she knew that the one-crop economy was as doomed as it was improvident. The emphasis on cotton, she believed, had resulted in poor land, poor people, and illiteracy; and she was eager to teach the people to grow their own food and to release them from the grasp of the storekeepers. Thus she greeted the boll weevil's arrival with mixed emotions: it would force the people to adopt the more modern agricultural practices, but it struck with such force the first year that the islanders were left dazed and in danger of losing their land.

In the winter of 1918–1919, the boll weevil destroyed 75 percent of the Sea Island cotton crop, thereby initiating an unprecedented agricultural depression on St. Helena. Interestingly, very little migration followed the weevil infestation, for as Miss Cooley explained, by this time the Penn School counter movement had made headway. Heavy migration away from the island had been the rule when Miss Cooley first arrived in 1904. From 1900 to 1910, the island lost 25 percent of its population; and from 1910 to 1920, another 10 percent departed. These migrations were probably a delayed reaction to a number of earlier catastrophes, such as the collapse of the phosphate industry, the hurricane of 1893, and the continuing poor crop years of 1903–1904, 1905–1908, 1910–1912, and 1915–1917.[1]

Nonetheless, farming had traditionally spelled a tedious and unrewarding life of drudgery on St. Helena Island, and disaster only quickened the desire of these rural blacks for the exciting life of the cities. Often in the early days Miss Cooley and Miss House would stop a young fellow driving an oxcart and ask him what he had been doing since he left school. "Usually the answer would be 'nuttin', and with a few more questions we would find that he was busy on the home farm." Through the years, they had sought to change that negative "nuttin'" into a positive something by showing the people how to increase their yields and enrich their lives in the country. Apparently, they were succeeding because even the boll weevil crisis did not drive the islanders off their land. Instead, with the advent of the boll weevil Penn School's community program matured and offset the weevil's disorganizing effects. Only 7 percent of the population left the island between 1920 and 1928.[2]

1. Trustees' minutes, February 26, 1921, "Annual Report of the Penn Normal, Industrial and Agricultural School," 1920, p. 13, Thomas Jackson Woofter, "Preliminary Confidential Report for the Trustees of Penn School: The Study of St. Helena Island," n.d., 3, 4, all in PSP; Cooley, *School Acres*, 112; Kiser, *Sea Island to City*, 104, 106, 197.

2. Cooley, *School Acres*, 125; Woofter, "Preliminary Report," 4, in PSP; Woofter, *Black Yeomanry*, 33.

The famed long staple Sea Island cotton, whose fine long fibers had made up into the world's most beautiful cotton cloth, was now gone forever. It had required a long maturation period, and the extra month in the fields had been all that the boll weevil had needed. Now some varieties of short staple cotton could be grown, but certainly not enough to be the main cash crop, and the Sea Island farmers once again looked to Penn School to lead them through the crisis. "With the loss of the cotton and the boll weevil," Miss Cooley wrote to a contributor, "the people must depend upon their school to help them tide over the present crisis. . . . Unless the crisis can be met, the land will most surely be lost to the Negro farmers." The initial Penn School reaction was to encourage the people to grow peanuts, but the bottom dropped out of the market that first year, and the peanuts that all had expected to bring two dollars a bushel brought only sixty cents. At Penn's suggestion a number of farmers tried a variety of crops, from velvet beans, cow peas, and soybeans to white potatoes, sweet potatoes, and lettuce. Eventually most settled down to peanuts and fertilizers, but nothing appeared to take the place of cotton.[3]

As a result of the agricultural depression, many of the farmers failed to pay the taxes on their land. By the spring of 1923, Miss Cooley was thoroughly aroused to the danger of the situation, and she bent all her efforts to keep the lands from being forfeited. The threats to the island landholders seemed to be increasing daily. Not only had the boll weevil destroyed their equilibrium, but now many of the white farmers in Beaufort had begun to covet the St. Helena lands. As long as cotton was the main crop, the little plots on St. Helena were too small to be of use to the large cotton farmers. But now that cotton was gone, large-scale mechanized truck farming had appeared to take its place on the mainland; and land on the island looked increasingly attractive to the Beaufort farmers. In an economy where cash was all too scarce, the sums being offered for their land seemed astro-

---

3. Cooley, *School Acres*, 122; Woofter, *Black Yeomanry*, 115; Cooley to Ida (Zala?) Tourtellot, Phelps-Stokes Fund, October 8, 1920, "Annual Report," 1923, p. 11, all in PSP; McDavid Horton, *St. Helena Island: A Negro Community* (Columbia, S.C., 1924), 8, in PSP.

nomical to the island farmers, and all too often they relinquished the old deeds without fully understanding that they were sacrificing their capital. Miss Cooley frantically appealed to the Cooperative Society to sound the alarm, exhorting them to lead the way in informing the people when their taxes were due and encouraging them to pay.[4]

But these were not the only threats to the community Miss Cooley was endeavoring to create on St. Helena. For years developers on the mainland had eyed St. Helena's beautiful sandy beaches and those of the outlying islands, realizing that they could well be fashioned into a lucrative white playground, much as neighboring Hilton Head has become. A connection with these beaches by way of a modern highway would also increase Beaufort's attractiveness as a tourist center. In fact, the South Carolina General Assembly had voted as early as 1911 to build a bridge from the town of Beaufort to Ladies Island, which was separated from St. Helena by a small tidal river, across which there was already a bridge. Although the township of St. Helena voted against the bond issue, the combined vote with Beaufort Township showed a majority in favor of the bonds, and in due time the bridge pushed its way across the river. The taxpayers on St. Helena had to pay a share of the cost of the Beaufort–St. Helena bridge on the principle of special benefit, despite the fact that they voted against the project; but this discrimination was not Miss Cooley's primary worry. "If automobiles and the pleasure of tourists are the main objects to be considered," she wrote, "this Negro community can only grit its teeth and make the best possible struggle to show it can hold on till it is taxed so far beyond the limit of its earning power, that the holding on is no longer in the strength of its own hands." Apparently many whites in Beaufort County shared the views of one of their prominent citizens: "The Yankees took the land from the Southern owners for taxes, and turned it over to the Negroes, and the Southerners would, therefore, be justified by taking it back by the same process." This attitude manifested

---

4. Cooley, *School Acres*, 127, 128; Cooley to St. Helena Cooperative Society, January 11, March 5, 1923, in PSP.

itself in the high taxes charged against St. Helena Township. The islanders paid far more money into the county treasury than they received back in their meager appropriations for roads and public schools.[5]

Miss Cooley feared the bridge primarily because she knew it would alter the experiment she was conducting on St. Helena Island. She had often written of the advantages of Penn's isolation. "It may be a bit of His Providence," she wrote in the Vassar alumnae magazine, "that this particular school should be in so isolated a community, and that its particular work should be among the almost unmixed negroes, and perhaps it will be able to prove certain facts that could not be so well proved on the main land."[6] She knew that the bridge would open the island to all the evils of the outside world; it would lure the blacks into Savannah and Charleston, and it would entice the fast-talking white developers onto the island. If she could have had her way, Miss Cooley would have kept the culture of her island laboratory pure, hoping in that way to convince a skeptical public of the black's capacity for advancement.

Francis Cope took a broader view of the bridge situation. He believed that the bridge was inevitable and necessary for proper economic development, and that instead of resisting the future, Miss Cooley should do everything in her power to prepare the people for its coming. "The Negro must be taught to hold his own in competition with the white man," he admonished her, "and I believe that with the help of Penn School and our Co-operative Society he can do so, especially on St. Helena where traditions are so much in his favor." Here was the good common sense that characterized all of Mr. Cope's suggestions and that made him, as chairman of the executive committee, the primary stabilizing force among the trustees.[7]

Characteristically, Rossa Belle Cooley saw the land crisis as a

5. Woofter, *Black Yeomanry*, 173, 174, 177, 246; Cooley, *School Acres*, 127.
6. Cooley, "The Negro in His Own Environment," 181.
7. Cope to Cooley, June 1, 1923, Trustees' minutes, June 9, 1927, both in PSP. The bridge finally opened in the summer of 1927, in the best lily-white tradition, with one day set aside for a celebration for the whites and another for the blacks.

challenge and as an opportunity for greater service, but she realized that a solution would have to be found quickly if she were to save her island experiment. Her trustees formed a committee to look into the matter, one of them writing to inquire "whether Penn School has any investment fund which it would be justified in loaning the peasants on mortgage under the circumstances." An old friend of the school, Paul Underwood Kellogg, editor of *Survey-Graphic*, had a better suggestion: that Penn lead in the development of cooperative marketing with the Negro farmers of St. Helena so they could compete successfully with the large truck farms. In other words, the organized development of agricultural method should be paralleled with an organized development of marketing and business method. Unfortunately, however, the Cooperative Society had engaged in minor cooperative buying schemes in the past and had even sold peanuts cooperatively the previous year, but these ventures had never been either widespread or successful.[8]

Finally Miss Cooley wrote to her trustees in desperation: "The Crisis is here. The Bridge is in sight. White people doubtless are counting on the lands on St. Helena for truck farming. The whole demonstration in rural Negro education will be crippled if the Negroes must lose their lands on this Island." A tax sale had been announced for the following week, and the Cooperative Society had discovered that at least six of the parcels of land would have to be forfeited. Miss Cooley asked her trustees for permission to allow the Cooperative Society to use all available funds to advance these six landowners the money for their taxes; the society would take a twelve months' mortgage on the land at 7 percent interest. Furthermore, Miss Cooley asked the trustees to authorize a $2,000 loan so the Cooperative Society could meet the tax sales that were to follow. The society would advise the owners on farm projects and help them cover the loans; and if the owners did not redeem the land, the society would sell it to blacks, giving

8. Trustees' minutes, April 26, 1923, Henry Van Sinderen to House, May 14, 1923, Paul Underwood Kellogg to House, May 15, 1923, Cooley to St. Helena Cooperative Society, January 11, 1923, all in PSP.

first opportunity to Penn School boys. The trustees unreservedly supported Miss Cooley's plan, and the immediate crisis passed.[9]

Miss Cooley understood, however, that the island would need a long-range program to surmount the tax problem and the boll weevil crisis. To this end she invited Dr. W. H. Mills of Clemson College, an extension specialist in agricultural economics, to help the Cooperative Society develop a five-year program of cooperative buying and selling. Dr. Mills had advised the society for several years, and he was thoroughly familiar with the situation on the island. Late in 1923 he visited St. Helena and advised the Cooperative Society to make peanuts its main money crop. He also encouraged the production of cane syrup and the growing of turkeys for marketing purposes, all operations to be carried on cooperatively. He discouraged mortgaging of land for any purpose and recommended the development of a savings branch, or credit union.[10]

The islanders took Dr. Mills's suggestions to heart, and in 1924 they formed the St. Helena Credit Union, which was really an outgrowth of the Cooperative Society, since the "Co-ops" voted to move into the new society as a body. Each member bought a five-dollar share in the Credit Union, making it possible for the members to save through their society, although a bank failure in Beaufort fairly destroyed any interest in such as banks. This was the first credit union in South Carolina, which became a matter of some pride. Perhaps more significant, this was a great step forward for Miss Cooley's goals of teamwork and cooperation, for the Cooperative Society and the Credit Union represented a set of ideas entirely foreign to the fiercely independent island farmers.[11]

At their first meeting, the Credit Union members, somewhat ironically, sang the old spiritual, "When I Lay My Burden Down." Miss Cooley was of no mind, however, to let this new project languish, as she revealed in her list of written objectives for 1925:

9. Cooley to trustees May 28, 1923?, in PSP.
10. Horton, *St. Helena Island*, 8, 9; St. Helena Cooperative Society minutes, December 3, 1923, in PSP.
11. Cooley, *School Acres*, 123, 124–25; Woofter, *Black Yeomanry*, 151.

"to help develop mutual credit, cooperative buying, cooperative marketing and other resources which will put the islanders on a new footing as a producing center." The dynamic leader of the Cooperative Society, Joshua Blanton, had left St. Helena in 1923 to take a position as principal of Voorhees Industrial School in Denmark, South Carolina, but his place was ably filled by the new demonstration agent, Benjamin Barnwell. Barnwell and James Plato King, the new superintendent of industries at Penn, guided the Credit Union through its early years, cautiously and conscientiously leading the members in a number of cooperative ventures.[12]

Despite their caution, however, and some early successes with peanuts, the Credit Union made a tragic mistake in 1928 when it went into the growing of white potatoes. The year before, white planters on the mainland had made enormous profits growing white potatoes, and in 1928 nearly everyone in the county went into the business. The Credit Union stood behind its members and made larger loans than usual to make the new crop possible. Ominously, Mr. King reported as the loans were being made that the size of the loans and the time they were made limited the amount of capital on hand for the spring operations, which was the time when most of the farmers would need it. And as fate would have it, the market failed just as the crop was ready to ship; the Florida crop, which had been delayed by a storm, reached the northern market just ahead of the South Carolina potatoes. The whole district suffered, and King reported sadly that at the beginning of the new year most of the capital of the Credit Union was out on extended loans. "This has curtailed operations for the present year," he noted; "new borrowers are being encouraged to plant peanuts."[13]

Mr. Barnwell was more optimistic. He reported from Frogmore that the men were not discouraged and that the potato crop

12. St. Helena Cooperative-Credit Union minutes, February 12, 1926, Unsigned "Memorandum," 1925, "Annual Report," 1923, p. 16, Trustees' minutes, September 20, 1922, all in PSP.
13. Cooley, *School Acres*. 124; "Superintendent's Report," 1928, p. 3, 1929, p. 3, in PSP.

had not been grown at the expense of the other crops on the school farm. The men had grown excellent crops of cotton, sweet potatoes, corn, watermelon, peas, tomatoes, and okra; and though money was not floating about neither was there any great suffering. Miss Cooley took the long look and concluded with some satisfaction that experience in team play led to increased group loyalty. Though there might be crop failures and market fluctuations, the larger lessons were taking hold; and the islanders were learning the importance of working together to solve common difficulties.[14]

Although economic stability on the island was clearly essential to the success of the Penn School venture, Miss Cooley's preoccupation with economic matters never obscured the importance of the larger goals, which were to develop individual intelligence, to build up the island household, and to improve the island farm. Miss Cooley understood that the island home was at the center of the cultural revolution she was trying to foment, and her industrial work for the girls centered squarely on that home— its beauty, its suitability, and its health. Despite the agricultural depression and the land crisis that preoccupied St. Helena in the 1920s, Penn School maintained its equilibrium and continued to expand its program, especially its program for the girls. The carpentry classes built a typical five-room house on the school grounds, and the girls used it as their homemaking classroom. Here they received thorough instruction in cooking and sewing, as well as practical experience in caring for the home. In the cooking classes the girls learned practical lessons in canning as well as in the planning and preparation of meals; in the sewing classes they made costumes for the school plays, their own graduation dresses, and a baby's layette. The older girls in the boarding department cooked all the meals for the school family (the boarders, teachers, and principals), as well as the daily school lunches, and cleaned the two small dormitories. They used the simple equipment in the Penn School kitchen and laundry, equipment that Miss Cooley purposely kept simple, "for new appli-

14. Barnwell to Cooley, August 4, 1928, in PSP; Cooley, *School Acres*, 131.

ances should be brought in slowly in rural industrial schools, or homes will be left behind." This training prepared the girls for an important community service, for they would take their new habits home with them, and they would go out from Penn School to serve as cultural leaders in their own communities.[15]

In the wake of the boll weevil crisis, the women's homemaking clubs became ever more important as the shift to food crops necessitated broader knowledge of cooking and canning. The clubs now concentrated on how to improve the corn, okra, bean, and tomato plots; and some of them even purchased their own canning equipment. At first they had used the school's canner, bringing their produce in an oxcart and learning in the school grove all that the school cooking teacher could tell them about canning. "They were at it from day clean till dark," Miss Cooley later recalled, "a jolly crowd, sitting under the great pines chatting and singing, and passing on all the Island news." At noontime a few of them would prepare lunch in the school kitchen, using the big range and all the equipment, and in the evening they returned home carrying the bright shining cans, quite naturally the apostles of the new diet. The clubs did not confine themselves to culinary questions, however. More often than not the program would center around improved homemaking techniques, the women considering such topics as, "How often should the beds be dusted, why should we dust our beds, how often should the mattress be turned, why is it necessary to turn our mattress, how many sheets should we use when making a bed, how should the second sheet be put on, how often should the bed covering be aired?" These seem like simple and elementary considerations; but to women who had had no training in domestic technique, Miss Cooley had opened a baffling new world of intriguing practices.[16]

The homes Miss Towne had found in 1862 were primitive in the extreme. The tiny clapboarded frame houses had had small shuttered windows, mud-and-stick chimneys, and dirt floors

15. Unsigned "Memorandum," 1925, "Annual Report," 1923, pp. 20–21, 1924, p. 52, all in PSP; Woofter, *Black Yeomanry*, 197–98; Cooley, *Homes of the Freed*, 167.
16. Cooley, *School Acres*, 95; Cooley, *Homes of the Freed*, 137–38, 139; Woofter, *Black Yeomanry*, 130.

beaten hard and worn in hollows. At one side was the open hearth, before which the children slept on heaps of filthy rags. The household utensils consisted of one pot and occasionally a frying pan. "The elders first helped themselves from the hominy pot, then it was given to the children, who finished all that could be easily scraped out. Then the dogs worked at it for hours and left it clean for the next meal!" Discomfort and misery were on all sides, and Miss Towne devoted much of her energy to improving these home conditions. By the time Miss Cooley arrived, white washed houses had become the rule, and they were gaily trimmed with splashes of blue, green, and purple. The one-room home had given way to three or four rooms—usually a living room, one bedroom, and a small lean-to kitchen. The father and mother slept in a double bed, rather than the old-time bunks, but the children still bundled themselves up and slept on the floor in front of the fireplace.[17]

Under Miss Cooley's persistent guidance, the *jump-up* eventually replaced the older homes. These were story-and-a-half houses, often with glass windows and brick chimneys. The bedroom and living room were separated by a hall running through the house, with the dining room and kitchen built on at the rear, sometimes a combination, sometimes divided. Up a little flight of stairs would be found two or three bedrooms for the children; if the family had not outgrown its home, there could be privacy. All too often, however, rooms were not added as the children grew in number and in size: "And so big brothers and sisters grow weary of crowded quarters, and go to the cities for money and excitement." This was the trend that Miss Cooley worked untiringly to reverse, for her experience told her that only ill could arise from the migration of black people to the city.[18]

In 1922 Miss Cooley discovered a dramatic way to carry the demonstration principle into the homes. The National Better Homes Campaign sent down a letter from Washington, asking St. Helena to participate. The letter included suggestions for all kinds

17. Towne, "Pioneer Work on the Sea Islands," 5, 6; Cooley, *Homes of the Freed*, 129.
18. Woofter, *Black Yeomanry*, 215; Cooley, *Homes of the Freed*, 130, 131.

of committees—publicity, home surroundings, home equipment, home furnishings and decorating, home budget, the reception of visitors, and program of events. A General Committee of Eight, with Miss House at the head, swung into action, using one of the teacher's homes as their first demonstration. They borrowed all the furnishings from the homes and stores; and they worked out a budget so that everyone would know the cost of the house, the furnishings, and the expenses of the imaginary family who lived in the house. The poster committee worked night and day, covering the island with signs that read: "Follow the arrow to Jessamine Cottage." Then came the red arrows, all pointing to Penn School and to the Demonstration House; and for a week the little cottage stood open for visitors. A program each afternoon opened with the school band playing "Home, Sweet, Home" and focused attention on costs, sanitation, the arrangement of flowers and pictures, books in the homes, and play. It was a delightful, exciting week, and for a time "a better home" was the subject of conversation in hundreds of island homes.[19]

Then came a letter that filled the whole island with pride and rejoicing. "It gives me real pleasure to inform you that St. Helena has won the third prize, $50.00, for having one of the best demonstration houses in the 1922 Better Homes in America Campaign." There were 961 communities that had observed Better Homes Week that first year, and St. Helena won one of the prizes! And the letter was signed by Secretary of Commerce Herbert Hoover himself! It was almost too much to take in, and the islanders began immediately to plan for the next year.[20]

The second year they took a small tumbledown cottage, an average island home, and repaired, whitewashed, and painted until the little cottage was a real model home. The boys and girls made almost all the furnishings themselves; and when they won second prize, their enthusiasm soared! The third year they built a completely new house and won a special first prize. By now a "Better Home" had become a common goal and a part of every-

19. Cooley, *School Acres*, 99; "Annual Report," 1924, p. 153, in PSP; Cooley, *Homes of the Freed*, 154, 155.
20. Cooley, *School Acres*, 99, 100.

one's vocabulary. In 1924 three island families built "Better Homes" according to Penn's suggestions, and in many other ways the campaigns had put their stamp on the island.[21]

Throughout the twenties, St. Helena won prizes every year in the Better Homes contests, and Better Homes Week became more of a production each year. Beginning on Sunday when the preachers would preach on the subject, there would be daily demonstrations on different aspects of homemaking. A successful poultry raiser might give a program in her poultry yard. Others might lead discussions of gardening, or cooking, or quilting. One year the carpenters from Penn built a smaller version of the demonstration house, half the size of the original, that showed how a small house could be planned for $600. The Penn School truck hauled the house back and forth across the island, thus making it possible for many who could not get to the demonstration to see it en route.[22]

In the autumn of 1929 Miss Cooley and Miss House paid a visit to Mrs. Herbert Hoover and told her about the Better Homes campaigns. Mrs. Hoover sent a message to the islanders, telling them she would like to visit St. Helena. When Miss Cooley announced this in church, the people were most impressed. Reverend D. C. Washington rose and explained to his flock, "You all know the President's wife is the First Lady of the Land, and if she comes to see us, she'd be the First Lady of the Island, and the First Lady of the Church too!" Miss House wrote to Mrs. Hoover, telling her of this vote of thanks, and Mrs. Hoover responded by thanking the people for conferring the titles upon her. When Miss Cooley read this letter at the Community Sing, the White House seemed close to the island indeed![23]

Penn School also carried forward its work in sanitation and public health, with the school nurse going out to the homes and the islanders bringing their health problems in to the school. In

21. "Annual Report," 1924, p. 53, Cooley to Rosenwald Fund, May 5, 1924, both in PSP; Woofter, *Black Yeomanry*, 284; Cooley, *School Acres*, 101.
22. Cooley to contributors, May 8, 1930, in PSP.
23. Cooley to trustees, November 20, 1929, in GFP; Cooley, *School Acres*, 101.

1926 Dr. James Hardy Dillard of the Jeanes and Slater Funds described Penn's health program as a model, including the development and aid of native Negroes and the cooperation of the state department. The Community Class had long been instructed in hygiene and health matters, and the Penn School students regularly received health inspections and information. But a unique feature of Penn's health program was the training of the midwives. Under slavery, the midwives had held an honored place on the plantations, some of them being sent to Charleston for lessons; and the knowledge had been passed on from one generation to the next. After slavery there was no longer any supervision, and increasingly, new life was brought into the world surrounded by superstition. As late as 1928 a team of investigators discovered many old rituals and superstitions, perhaps African survivals, persistent despite the efforts of Penn School. Sometimes, for instance, the midwives would put a hoe or a plow point or an ax under the bed to cut the afterpains attending childbirth. Gizzard tea, or tea made from the nest of the mud dauber, were also thought to reduce the afterpains. Even more extreme, one practice involved standing the woman in childbirth up in a corner and assisting the process by having several robust women beat, punch, and shake her. Often the midwife would tie a piece of the umbilical cord around the mother's toe for relief after birth, and some women thought it dangerous to bathe the baby before it was nine days old.[24]

The Penn School nurse worked untiringly to dispel these old practices, but the greatest advance came when the school organized a regular program for the midwives. The first Tuesday in each month these women would come to the school, where the nurse would give a course of lessons prescribed by the state. The women received the lessons enthusiastically, proud that their calling had now become a profession. They equipped themselves with sanitary obstetrical packages through the school nurse's of-

24. Cooley, *Homes of the Freed*, xiii; Cooley, *School Acres*, 97; Johnson, *Folk Culture on St. Helena Island*, 171; Woofter, *Black Yeomanry*, 111.

fice, and public opinion began to grow concerning the necessity of caps and aprons. Cotton, gauze, and disinfectants began to replace superstition and carelessness due to ignorance.[25]

At length the school concluded that the monthly meeting was not enough, and they decided to give intensive training to one of the midwives, Nurse Brisbane, for a three-month period. Miss Cooley met Nurse Brisbane the day she entered training and reported with feeling and pride the island woman's greeting. "Dis is de greates' day I eber seen on St. Helena," she said, "de greates' day! I walk an' walk dis day, an' yet I ain't tire. I see my limbs get lighter and lighter fo' I see de Greater Day a'comin'!" And Miss Cooley believed it *was* coming.[26]

The training of the "midders" was one important factor in the drastic reduction of infant mortality on St. Helena Island, but the annual Baby Day was equally important. Again the demonstration idea prevailed. Baby Day was a celebration as well as an educational day, and from all over the island mothers brought their babies to Penn School to be weighed, measured, and compared. All about the meeting hall posters from the State Health Bureau and the Child Welfare Bureau in Washington let the people know that this was a national movement and not just a scheme cooked up by Miss Cooley. Exhibits designed to give the mothers ideas filled the hall: a full set of baby clothes, made in the sewing classes; a table set for the baby's bath; another set with a proper meal for a one-year-old child; a baby crib, made by placing a wood basket between two kitchen chairs and covering all with mosquito netting; and a properly dressed doll, which made the children look more closely than their mothers. Mothers and babies had lunch under the live oaks in the school grove and then the weighing and measuring began. When the height and weight were up to the standard of the Federal Child Welfare Bureau, that baby won a blue ribbon, and the nearly perfect babies won

25. Woofter, *Black Yeomanry*, 287; Cooley, *Homes of the Freed*, 61; "Annual Report," 1923, p. 17, in PSP.
26. Cooley, *School Acres*, 98. When Thomas Jackson Woofter conducted a survey of St. Helena in 1927–1928, he found that "long and effective efforts of the island nurse, had borne astounding fruits in raising the general health level." Woofter, *Black Yeomanry*, 106.

red ribbons. "While the idea still prevails among some of our people," reported Miss Cooley after that first Baby Day, "that babies must die as well as grown-up people, and that it is flying in the face of Providence to try to prevent it, we feel sure that progress has been made."[27]

Initially, the island women had opposed the idea of a Baby Day, for they feared injury to the babies, thinking that there must be an element of danger lurking somewhere in so new an idea. Others opposed the idea the first year because an influential island woman had spread the rumor that Miss Cooley wanted all the babies brought to the school just to take their pictures and send them North. The graduates brought their babies that year, anyway, and Miss Cooley took not one picture. The next year, however, she spread the word that she would be there with her camera to take pictures if the mothers wanted it, and the mother could buy the picture for ten cents and have prints made to send to relatives. Baby Day that year was a huge success, and every mother wanted the picture. "I took snapshots that hot May Day," Miss Cooley recalled, "till I was exhausted!"[28]

Penn School had now established itself as a vital community center, second only to the churches perhaps in the influence it had with the people. Originally Penn School had focused its efforts on individual problems; but increasingly with the years, the emphasis shifted to group action, cooperation, and community upbuilding. This was as Frissell had hoped it would be; and it was fitting that when the trustees decided to build a community hall, a center for group meetings and entertainments, they named it the Frissell Memorial Community House.[29]

When St. Helena's young men marched away to war in 1918, Miss Cooley realized that they would return with greater needs and expectations. She proposed to her trustees, therefore, that they begin to plan for a YMCA building or a community house, to be named Frissell Hall. By the fall of 1919, the trustees had agreed

27. Woofter, *Black Yeomanry*, 106; Cooley, *Homes of the Freed*, 193–95, 197; Cooley to contributors, May 8, 1930, "Annual Report," 1921, p. 32, in PSP.
28. Cooley, *Homes of the Freed*, 197, 198.
29. Unsigned "Memorandum," 1925, in PSP.

to back a fund of $50,000 for this community building, and Penn School sent out an appeal to Frissell's friends for contributions. "We should have a building which will properly house our various community interests," Miss Cooley wrote in her annual report in 1919; "this has become a necessity if we are to hold the young people." Holding the young people was still the focus of Miss Cooley's efforts and the source of much of her appeal. "As entertainment is demanded by every normal person," she continued the next year, "unless a rural community can have more fun of the right sort, the young farmers will continue to drift to the cities." She realized that she had not emphasized this enough in the past and that what was really needed to make the rural life more attractive was more fun.[30]

By July of 1923 Miss Cooley wrote to George Foster Peabody that they were within $200 of their goal of $50,000 for the Frissell Memorial Community House and that they would soon complete the fund. In the autumn of that year, construction on the house began under the supervision of the school carpenter, Benjamin F. Boyd, assisted by W. Harris Burwell, both graduates of Penn and Hampton. A huge pile of oyster shells, the "pile of faith," had stood by the roadside for two years, and now the long wait was over as the new building took shape on the site of the old schoolhouse.[31]

The day that the work began, Miss Cooley passed by about noontime: "The men had just knocked off and were sitting in the shade of the live oaks. I heard them singing. And they were singing spirituals." In the middle of the huge hole they had dug that morning, one worker had stuck a long pole, topped with a makeshift flag. "Here seemed to be a group of laborers," thought Miss Cooley, "fired with the thought that they were starting no ordinary building, and the improvised flag as well as the spirituals told passers-by something of the meaning that underlay the building of the house."[32]

30. Trustees' minutes, January 30, 1919, September 27, 1919, February 26, 1921, "Annual Report," 1919, p. 30, all in PSP.
31. Cooley to Peabody, July 14, 1923, "Annual Report," 1924, p. 67, 1925, p. 5, Trustees' minutes, January 28, 1920, all in PSP.
32. Cooley, *School Acres*, 102.

The building had a large community room that would serve as a general meeting hall. At one end were three library rooms containing the Laura M. Towne Memorial Library; at the other was a dining room and kitchen where the daily lunches would be cooked and served. All would be used by the churches and societies of the island, and no longer would the children have to relinquish their classrooms when the grown-ups came to school.[33]

The island received the building at a formal dedication on April 17, 1925. Present among the guests were Sidney Frissell, brother of Hollis Burke Frissell, and Robert Russa Moton of Tuskegee Institute. Miss Cooley recalled Frissell's inspiration and his love for the island, and she felt that there could not be a more fitting memorial for this man who had meant so much to both races. "Here on the Sea Islands," she wrote, "we try to keep always before us the great Hampton Idea of education, 'that combination of the ideal and the practical,' the aim of struggle and service, which Frissell constantly kept before his workers and students." She hoped that the new community building would commemorate the spirit of struggle and service of Hollis Burke Frissell and serve to increase that spirit among the people of St. Helena.[34]

In 1928 George Foster Peabody presented a bas relief of Frissell to Hampton, Tuskegee, and Penn that depicted the old leader with upraised fist, exhorting his students to struggle, and surrounded in the background by Booker T. Washington, an unnamed Indian, and an island workman. The inscription below read, "The more abundant life prevails." The plaque was hung on the outside wall of the building facing the road, where it can still be seen.[35]

Clearly, any typical day for the principals of Penn School included a staggering number of activities. Aside from the weighty responsibilities involved in planning, coordinating, and running the school, there were committee meetings to attend, home visits to make, money to raise, and visitors to entertain. Increasingly,

33. "Annual Report," 1924, p. 57, in PSP.
34. Cooley, *School Acres*, 103; "Annual Report," 1923, pp. 6, 31, in PSP.
35. Trustees' minutes, September 20, 1928, September 16, 1930, in PSP. The plaque was designed and created by Evelyn Longmans Batchelder.

visitors found their way to St. Helena Island in the twenties—missionaries who had heard of Penn's remarkable program of uplift, educators who were seeking solutions to the problems of rural education, northern patricians who simply enjoyed the idyllic peace and quiet of St. Helena. And no day was complete without its hours of correspondence—writing appeals, thanking contributors, arranging new programs, arousing trustees. As Miss Cooley described herself to a Yale educator in 1932, shortly before he was to arrive on St. Helena with a large group of students: "When you speak . . . of breaking in 'upon the even tenor of your way' you make us laugh, for there is nothing 'even' here on this Island. Every day we live seems to be full of surprise, and I believe that is a peculiarity of a school of this type."[36] At any time Miss Cooley might be called from her office to quell an argument on the playground or to soothe a complaining parent or to perform any one of a hundred administrative tasks. The wonder is that she was able to plan as carefully and creatively as she did and that her program and actions retained a consistency that no crisis could alter.

Despite the vitality and color and purpose of their lives, however, Miss Cooley and Miss House on occasion felt very keenly their isolation from others of their kind. Few in Beaufort approved the work they were doing; and though they were not ostracized as the earlier missionaries had been, there was nonetheless a great social gulf between these two northern ladies and the ones who might have befriended them. And of course, the opportunities for social exchanges were severely restricted on the island, with its white population of less than fifty families. One gloomy night Miss Cooley wrote to her mother, "I feel as lonely as though I were alone in the world." Sequestered away on an Atlantic island, hours, even days, from familiar and friendly white faces, Miss Cooley must have gazed out over the moonlit marshes many a night and longed for the comforts of home. But there were deep satisfactions in her work, and her depressions never lasted for long. Unlike Katrina Trask, she had little time for longings and

36. Cooley to Loram, March 15, 1932, in PSP.

fantasies of another world; she had chosen this world, and she was determined to make it better through acting, not dreaming. Buoyant, enthusiastic, assertive, and charming—she was a strong woman, and one determined to make her mark.[37]

Grace House was more of a visionary—sweet, unassuming, self-effacing—and her loneliness on St. Helena sometimes engulfed her for days. Apparently there was unrequited love in her girlhood, for her diaries and poems are full of allusions to some lost lover, some missed opportunity. As she wrote upon arising one April morning:

>God keep thee safe, my Love,
> All through the day,
>May thorns to flowers change,
> Along thy way.
>My thoughts of thee are prayers
> Which daily rise,
>That God may send thee gifts
> Thy heart shall prize,
>And guide thee on the way
> Where Honor lies![38]

Sweet Miss House had written as a girl that "God my father knows all.... My life belongs to Him.... How I wish it were a better, stronger, and finer life I had to use for Him." She had longed to "put strong beautiful thoughts before the world in a beautiful way." There can be no doubt of the intensity of her loneliness on St. Helena:

>"To live in all this gay and crowded
> world as one of many,
>To hear the friendly greeting and to
> feel the whine of life ...
> and yet to know
>That in this crowded world of men you
> stood alone throughout your life!
>Hostile and friendly eyes may crowd around
>The busy, rushing human world may push
> and press
>And touch the human hands of you—

---

37. Cooley, *Homes of the Freed*, 31.
38. Grace Bigelow House, "Diary and Log," April 18, 1912, in JMD.

>   but you, my soul,
> Can only feel and know and see
>   the human touch—but stand alone.
> Alone! in all this lonesome, crowded
>   world of loneliness!

And this fearsome loneliness drove her ever closer to her God and to her "Isle of Dreams," her "happy refuge ... Whene'er life's toil and shadows press upon the wearied soul too heavily."[39]

One of the sources of comfort for Miss Cooley and Miss House came from the attentions of George Foster Peabody. He began by sending the ladies to his Lake George cottage in the summers, where they relaxed and unwound and were refreshed in the New York countryside. Eventually, Mr. Peabody gave his Lake George place to Miss Cooley and Miss House, and he probably also sponsored their trips to Europe in 1925, 1927, and 1931. Peabody also provided the funds for numerous smaller projects, such as improvements for the farm, a Ford car, and the like. And Peabody persuaded his fellow trustee Aruthr Curtis James to split with him the cost of a parcel of land and the old Tom Fripp plantation house, which they repaired and remodeled into a comfortable weekend home for the ladies at the edge of the island. It was a beautiful two-story house with porches all around, which faced the marsh and a sparkling tidal river. Here the ladies spent many a weekend, and here the teachers also played and relaxed. Miss Cooley named it Ndulamo (pronounced *Dulamo*), which is an African word meaning "A Place of Abounding Joy." Miss House's descriptions of Ndulamo leave little doubt that it was a delightful refuge:

> As we walked the wooden road, soft with the fallen pine needles of many seasons, a faint, elusive fragrance reminded us that the straying bits of sunshine, scattered here there along our way, were the falling bells of some aspiring jasmine that had climbed to reach the sun, beyond the sheltering branches above us. . . .
>   As we stepped out into the open once more, we saw a white-winged sail-boat move slowly around the bend of the river

---

39. *Ibid.*, December 28, 31, 1902, "The Chistmas Gift (Alone)," December 4, 1910, "The Island of Dreams," January 26, 1912, all in JMD.

into the pathway of gold that the setting sun had painted on creek and shimmering marshes. . . . We sat on the doorstep at Ndulamo, and watched the boat pass on and out to sea, while the purpling shadows of the night were changing the silver and gold of the waters to iridescent rose and green and violet hues.[40]

Thus taken care of and restored, Miss Cooley and Miss House poured themselves into the work they had chosen to do at St. Helena. Somehow amid all the activity, Miss Cooley found time to write two books and a half-dozen articles, telling the world about the unique work being done at Penn School. She wrote with great style and force, and her stories conveyed charm and vitality. Her images were clear, and it was hard to resist the delightful island characters she placed before her readers. As she described an episode in the Penn School library:

> There are only about ten books in the library that they can read, and when twenty or thirty come in at one time I am simply swamped. Yesterday all the little girls and all the little boys of Grade 2 came in and they were dead set on getting a book. One little girl threw herself at the book-shelves with passionate zeal, crying, "I gwine git me a book dis day!" And the things she did to my neatly arranged books were a caution.[41]

As might be expected, children's books soon flowed into the Penn School library, and Penn even sent a library box out to the small public schools.

All of Miss Cooley's writing was designed as publicity, and quite naturally she dwelt on the positive aspects of the work she was doing. But she also made strong pleas for consideration of her philosophy and her solution to the "Negro Problem." Throughout her writing she emphasized the importance of keeping the blacks on the farms and of regenerating rural life, and she argued for education adapted to the needs of the student.

Miss Cooley endorsed the views expressed by Robert Russa Moton, who said that the Negro asked for four fundamental

---

40. Ware, *George Foster Peabody*, 137; Cooley to Peabody, May 12, 1920, in GFP; Peabody to Lucas and Loeb, Savannah, Georgia, March 30, 1929, Trustees' minutes, September 25, 1920, February 1, 1922, both in PSP; Edith Dabbs to author, January, 1975; House, "Guardian Angels," n.d., in JMD.

41. Cooley, "America's Sea Islands," 741.

rights: protection of life and property, a chance to live amid decent surroundings, a chance to educate his children, and a chance to train his leaders thoroughly. Nothing about politics, nothing about equality. Here was a point of view Miss Cooley could affirm, and this was about the limit of her expectations for the black American. Dr. Moton continued, "I believe that God is using America as a great laboratory in which he will demonstrate to the rest of the world that different races can live and work together, each working for the good of the other, and all working toward the higher development of mankind." This was the image that Miss Cooley liked best, for she believed that St. Helena Island was a most significant corner of God's laboratory, and she felt that she had the answer to the problem of two races living together.[42]

The answer, quite simply, was one of "race adjustment," which meant little more than black accommodation to the standards and values of the dominant culture. In practice this meant preparing blacks for self-sufficient, self-respecting life in the country until they merited inclusion in the larger society, or until they had become "civilized." Again and again, Miss Cooley spoke of Penn's goal as being not only the building up of a contented rural population, but also a demonstration of race adjustment. Occasionally, Miss Cooley made a bow in the direction of good citizenship, but more consistently she defined her objectives to be to bring self-reliance and mutual self-help to the point where island life would be wholly self-dependent, and the achievement of this people and the service of this school would become the torchlight for communities everywhere. Sometimes, when Miss Cooley was off the island, Miss House would slip in an annual report declaring Penn's mission to be to bring the Kingdom of God on Earth to St. Helena; but the more consistent goal was to bring a self-reliant, dignified yeomanry to St. Helena. As Miss Cooley would write, "Education is a civilizing process and, in spite of the speed that has gripped this century, civilization is the slowest thing in the world."[43]

42. Cooley, "The Negro in His Own Environment," 178.
43. "Annual Report," 1918, p. 31, 1922, p. 29, 1923, p. 19, 1928, p. 3, Unsigned "Memorandum," 1925, all in PSP; Cooley, "America's Sea Islands," 741; Cooley, *School Acres*, 158.

"Putting money into this Island community is like putting money into a national bank," Miss Cooley informed her readers in 1924, "if the depositor will look for his interest in characters and homes which will show what a Negro people can be and do when given a fair chance." Unfortunately the "Negro Problem" had not been resolved by 1924, and white America still feared the degradation and the threat of pollution of its black neighbors. Segregation had so isolated the two races that many whites knew nothing at all of the accomplishments, or the potential for achievement, of blacks. Thus Penn continued to appeal for support on the grounds of building up a community that would prove what the Negro could accomplish, given landownership and a practical education.[44]

Samuel Chapman Armstrong had written many years before of his belief that "the temporal salvation of Negroes for some time to come is to be won out of the ground," and Miss Cooley had no quarrel with the general. She wholeheartedly believed that her islanders could best develop character and an understanding of service by remaining right where they were—where Penn School could carry out the program of using all of life to build the character and enlarge the vision of its children.[45]

It is doubtful that Miss Cooley could have achieved her objectives even if she had been able to preserve her island utopia in isolation. But before long the outside would begin to press in. Eventually the impulse to provide proof of black capacities would lose its force, and the experiment in black uplift on St. Helena would become a curious remnant of a bygone age.

---

44. "Annual Report," 1924, p. 68, Penn School appeal, 1921, both in PSP.
45. "Annual Report," 1924, p. 15, 1926, p. 3, both in PSP.

9

Old Problems, New Appeals

"This year the necessities for our School life cost from 100% to 300% more than they did three years ago, so that the income which was then adequate to maintain our work no longer suffices." Thus read a Penn School appeal letter in 1918, and it concluded ominously that the rise in the cost of supplies and labor had burdened the school with a debt of some $10,000.[1]

Financial crisis was no stranger to Penn School. When Miss Cooley went to St. Helena in 1904, the school had an annual income of $4,000; by 1914 she had expanded the work in all directions, and Penn School had a *deficit* of almost $4,000. The treasurer reported deficits nearly every year from 1904 to 1917, and Dr. Frissell neatly captured the problem when he wrote to the Penn trustees that although public interest in Penn School had been aroused, no great amount of financial support had resulted.[2]

When Frissell died in 1917, the trustees decided that although they faced a deficit of $5,000 they should continue the work so ably begun; and they embarked on a campaign to raise the necessary funds. The demands of the war and of the new All-

1. Penn School appeal letter, 1918, in PSP.
2. Cooley, "Report to Trustees," January 14, 1913, Trustees' minutes, March 2, 1908, January 10, 1912, January 24, September 25, 1917, in PSP; Cope to H. B. Frissell, December 23, 1907, December 15, 1909, January 7, 1914, H. B. Frissell to trustees, March 13, 1917, all in HBF.

Year School, however, sent their costs soaring, and by 1918 the debt had reached $10,000. "At the same time," continued the appeal sent out in 1918, "the cotton boll weevil has swept away the crop which furnishes cash to the Sea Island people, and they turn more and more to the School for advice and aid in their many difficulties, so that Penn School is in a position to lead the way toward a new system of agriculture and a greater prosperity." And as all Penn School appeals concluded, "This is an opportunity for service which must be grasped."[3]

The rising costs of the wartime economy, the extra burden of the All-Year School, and the salary raises so necessary to secure good teachers all combined to create a crisis just as the arrival of the boll weevil made the work of the school most imperative. Having dipped into her principal funds to cover the shortage in contributions, Miss Cooley reported a deficit in 1920 of over $14,000, and by 1921 that figure had risen to $21,000. Miss Cooley redoubled her already considerable efforts to raise funds, even resorting at last to asking Arthur Curtiss James to increase his annual contribution of $4,000. In her charming way, she tried to admonish Mr. Peabody, the new chairman of the board: "I don't know just how to work out the problem of the money getting when all of us workers are needed to keep our hands on the plow, literally. I wish we could find the dollars in this sandy soil, but that wouldn't be Dr. Frissell's idea of helping the white people!"[4]

Aside from the dreary fact that six of the staunch supporters who had annually contributed $1,000 apiece had died, Penn School's continuing financial difficulties owed much to two persistent problems: poor financial administration and lack of trustee commitment. As Francis Cope wrote to Peabody in 1919, "Mr. Howell advises me that our Penn School Treasury is empty, with supply bills amounting to nearly $1000 unpaid and pay roll due Oct. 27th." Alarmed, Cope asked Peabody if the latter could se-

3. Trustees' minutes, September 25, 1918, Penn School appeal letter, 1918, both in PSP.
4. Cope to Peabody, August 5, 1918, Peabody to Cope, August 8, 1918, Cooley to Peabody, May 12, 1920, all in GFP; Trustees' minutes, November 28, 1920, June 17, 1921, Cooley to James, May 5, 1920, all in PSP.

cure additional funds in New York, and he tried to explain the reasons for the deficit. He felt that part of it was due to a general falling off in current subscriptions, part to the heavy increase in expense—particularly the increased salary budget—and part to the fact that most of the $2,500 to pay for new forest land had to be taken largely from current funds. Apparently it was far easier to authorize expenditures over a gracious luncheon in New York than it was to give substance to those authorizations by raising the money.[5]

"Who is to deal with the situation?" wrote the new chairman of the board, as he succinctly described the problem at hand. "The Trustees are, of course, a body corporate and it is a business institution, the Trustees of which are the only responsible agency in the premises; yet, when we look at the body, we do not find it so constituted as to deal with this situation." The school was a going concern, however, and it could not shut down.[6]

The trustees sent Mr. Barnwell out with the Hampton campaign for funds, and Mr. Blanton made a fund-raising tour through Ohio and Illinois. The trustees also sought to develop a connection between Penn School and Tuskegee, while Miss Cooley wrote endless letters and spent long months off the island campaigning in the North speaking to women's clubs and calling on prominent matrons. Slowly the contributions began to rise as the expenses leveled off, and by 1924 the deficit stood at only $15,000 (the trustees had borrowed $20,000 for current expenses from the Frissell Memorial fund, and construction had been halted on that building for almost a year).[7]

The General Education Board was still giving $10,000 a year toward the work of the All-Year School; but their philosophy of giving required equal participation from the recipient, and they had no intention of artificially supporting a program that could not stand on its own. Unofficially, the General Education Board

5. Isabella Curtis to contributors, n.d., Cope to Peabody, October 31, 1919, both in PSP.
6. Peabody to Cope, May 28, 192?, in GFP.
7. Cooley to Peabody, March 20, 1920, Cooley to trustees, December 2, 1920, both in GFP; Moton to Eustis, March 10, 1921, Trustees' minutes, February 26, June 17, 1921, February 1, September 20, 1922, February 5, 1924, all in PSP.

suggested they might donate $100,000 if the trustees would raise a similar amount in order to establish an endowment fund; and though Mr Cope, as chairman of the executive committee, urgently felt the need for this endowment, Mr. Peabody and Miss Cooley opposed such a move.[8]

Peabody probably shared Dr. Frissell's aversion to endowments because they reduced the necessity of appealing for funds, thereby leaving the North uneducated about the "Negro Problem"; he also held the conviction that large giving had the effect of discouraging the small givers from doing their part. Even more visionary, he opposed the endowment as being unchristian in that it implied that God's interest in the matter was so uncertain that the future of the school would have to be mortgaged for the present. Miss Cooley was concerned that her school might be brought under the control of the state of South Carolina and that Penn's endowment would then fall prey to the hostile and prejudiced politicians in the state. And so, though the missionary era was fast receding, Penn chose to base its existence on the continued interest and goodwill of wealthy individuals (mostly northern), counting every new contributor as a convert to the cause. In essence, then, Penn accepted responsibility for raising racial sensibilities in the North as well as for educating the children, regenerating the farms, and reshaping the culture of the St. Helena community. Consequently, Penn remained unendowed, and the pursuit of funds continued at the old relentless pace.[9]

Peabody wrote to Cope again in 1924, complaining of the trustees' failure to secure adequate funds and expressing his desire to resign from the chairmanship. Although Peabody gave generously of his own means in many a Penn School crisis, he displayed no leadership ability in his role as chairman of the board. By May of 1926 he was writing to Cope that Penn's finances were again critical. He seized on Negro music as the solution, con-

8. Wood to Cooley, February 29, 1924, Trustees' minutes, June 18, 1924, April 15, 1930, September 16, 1930, all in PSP; Peabody to Cope, April 14, 1924, Cope to Peabody, February 20, 1930, both in GFP.

9. J. Howard Melish, "George Foster Peabody," *Religion in Life* (Winter, 1938), 92; Peabody to Cooley, July 26, 1928, in GFP; Trustees' minutes (Executive and Finance Committees), September 16, 1930, in PSP.

vinced that such proof of talent would surely arouse sustained commitment and interest.[10]

Throughout the summer of 1926 the Penn School Quartette entertained the fashionable North; however, it followed on the heels of the Hampton Quartette and raised but a pittance for the Penn School till. Hampton and Tuskegee had been waging a ferocious two-year campaign to raise $8 million together, and their campaign had undoubtedly sapped much of the support that might have been forthcoming for Penn School. Nevertheless, Peabody alerted his friends in Bar Harbor and Lenox, telling them of the twenty years of devotion of Miss Cooley and Miss House and expecting the "dirt farmers' quartette" to charm completely their patrician listeners. Apparently, Peabody had designed the whole quartet venture to capture the attention of John D. Rockefeller and Henry Ford, which it failed completely to do. Even the planning and the publicity had been poor, and the tour netted the school a total of $382.98. (Peabody paid all the expenses.)[11]

In the meantime, Peabody continued to seek answers to Penn's continuing difficulties. "Successful business men find that it pays to advertise," he wrote to one of the trustees, "and Penn's difficulty is that it has not had the business direction it should have had for its appeal to the people of this country who are willing to help the Negro."[12] He was one of the most successful businessmen in the country, and yet he expected quartets and spirituals to sustain the life of the school, complaining in the meantime about inadequate "business direction." Funds for such an enterprise were definitely to be had, for Hampton and Tuskegee were flourishing in those years; but Penn School's inept management and possible misappropriation of funds kept it ever close to the edge, despite prodigious efforts.

In the autumn of 1926 Peabody wrote an alarming letter to L. Hollingsworth Wood, the chairman of the finance committee,

10. Peabody to Cope, April 14, 1924, May 28, 1926, in GFP.
11. Ware, *George Foster Peabody*, 215; Van Sinderen to Cooley, August 9, 1926, "Boston to Hear Penn School Singers," Boston *Evening Transcript*, August 21, 1926, clipping, Peabody to Mrs. Frances Barlow, July 24, 1926, Foote to Cooley, August 26, 1926, John D. Rockefeller to Foote, August 18, 1926, Trustees' minutes, October 22, 1926, all in PSP.
12. Peabody to Foote, August 4, 1926, in PSP.

charging the Penn School treasurer with negligence, if not worse. "It seems clear that there was lack of proper analysis on the part of the Treasurer . . . and seemingly of the auditor in not having the Board informed as to just what the situation was." Apparently, some of the funds appropriated by the General Education Board had not been collected, and the auditor had included capital investment with operating expenses in his financial statement. At any rate, Peabody thought it "evident that when the effort had been made to raise the deficit $14,000, someone was gravely negligent in not informing those making the effort that the true deficit was nearly $27,000." Disgusted with the whole unyielding mess, Peabody resigned from the board altogether at the next meeting of the trustees. Eventually he agreed to serve as honorary chairman, but Francis Cope took over the effective leadership and management of the board.[13]

The Penn School treasurer also resigned from the board, and the trustees learned that the school's overall deficit now rested at $28,481.93. Mr. Wood assured the trustees that there had been no rascality involved, that no money had been stolen, and that those involved were perfectly honest but the school had been living off capital for the last few years.[14]

As chairman of the finance committee, Hollingsworth Wood expended considerable energy in behalf of Penn School—largely in trying to enlist foundation support for the venture, in which he was mildly successful. He was a charming man, well-connected, who should have been able to save Penn from much of its financial misery. He took great pride and comfort in the work being done on St. Helena, and he admired profoundly the two white "saints" who were doing it. "We trustees never come away from our meetings with you without new confidence and enthusiasm," he wrote them, "and you may rest assured that whether you do any good to the 'darks' on the Island you certainly do a lot to reform your white friends in the North."[15]

13. Peabody to Wood, September 11, 1926, Trustees' minutes, October 22, 1926, both in PSP.
14. Trustees' minutes, October 22, 1926, Wood to Cooley, October 22, 1926, both in PSP.
15. Wood to "Ladies of St. Helena," October 2, 19??, Wood to Cooley, January 11, 1924, both in PSP.

Such inspiration would have given comfort to Dr. Frissell, but it hardly put money in the treasury; and Wood's sunny disposition often led him into some rather flip posturing and misplaced optimism about Penn School finances. He did worry about Penn's financial difficulties, however, realizing that a great part of the problem was distance. "We must make it a rule," he wrote to the ladies, "that every trustee must visit the school at least once in two years. . . . It is a different thing planning for a school when its beauty and life and gaity [sic] and pathos are fresh in one's mind." Another trustee wrote after a visit to the island, "I always come away wishing I had time and strength and means to do so much more for Penn than seems possible, but rejoicing that these . . . visits give me so much of renewed confidence and faith." Wood's suggestion of trustee visits was doubtless a good one, for such visits would have provided powerful mental images as well as firsthand knowledge of the school's difficulties and achievements; one trustee, for instance, who had been very active in Penn's early years, visited the island for the first time in twenty-five years and was staggered by the "unbelievable" improvement. But somehow the urgency and concern seemed to fade in the bustle of Philadelphia and New York and Boston as other needs and interests competed for attention, and the two ladies remained without adequate finances for their school.[16]

The problem seems to have been one of leadership. Peabody felt that he was really just an honorary chairman, chosen for the endorsement his name would lend to the enterprise; Cope felt that he had to defer to Peabody; and Wood felt that he was just the third man down the line. The infrequent and democratic trustees' meetings (two or three a year) increasingly became luncheon meetings at some gracious New York club, where the trustees gathered for fellowship and inspiration more than for active decision making. No one felt impelled, or empowered, to exert real leadership or initiative, and all expected Miss Cooley to direct their efforts.

16. Wood to Cooley and House, April 30, 1924, Foote to Cooley, May 1, 1928, Trustees' minutes, September 16, 1930, all in PSP.

Old Problems, New Appeals 169

The trustees were spread out across the northeast, which made sustained effort difficult and often caused gaps and overlaps in the work. Ideally, each trustee was supposed to serve as the nucleus of a group of contributors; but without clear guidance and responsibility, many of them simply considered Penn as an interesting and very worthwhile concern that brought them together two or three times a year with a group of interesting and worthwhile people. Occasionally, they would get on the bandwagon when the board decided to undertake a campaign, or when Miss Cooley passed through town, but they were trying to finance an increasingly sophisticated institution with woefully inadequate techniques and commitment.

As a school that sought to serve the community, Penn became increasingly expensive, for the needs of the community seemed always to expand; and as the school reached out into the community, the community began to demand more of the school. With the widespread use of the automobile, Miss Cooley and Mr. Cope felt that Penn needed an auto repair shop, and this meant training the blacksmith and buying the equipment. With the rise in educational standards across the South, Penn felt compelled to add to the school's offerings, so by 1929 Penn School had twelve grades. Such growth was a sign of health and vigor, and much to be desired, but inadequate finances impeded that growth and consumed Miss Cooley's valuable energy. As Dr. Frissell had written in 1917: "It seems too bad that Miss Cooley and Miss House should be hampered by a deficit and worry over financial matters when they are doing so much for the Negroes and for the country."[17]

One trustee who did commit herself to the work was Miss Isabella Curtis. A tiny woman, red-haired and explosive, Miss Curtis had no lack of connections, funds, or time; and she set fire to the publicity and finance committees with her energy. She had a beautiful home in Boston and a summer "cottage" at Sharks-

17. "Superintendent's Report," 1926, Trustees' minutes, September 19, 1924, March 4, 1926, H. J. DeYarmett to James P. King, April 16, 1926, "Annual Report of the Penn Normal, Industrial and Agricultural School," 1926, p. 17, all in PSP; H. B. Frissell to trustees, March 13, 1917, in HBF.

mouth, Manchester-By-The-Sea; and even in the days when such was not done she smoked monogrammed, multicolored cigarettes. She was a woman to be reckoned with; and from the twenties on she handled all the contributions to Penn School, using her influence to encourage or intimidate contributors. She kept the vast contributor's files up to date (at one point there were 3,500 names in the files), she sent out reminders when friends were remiss, and she wrote thank-you notes for even the tiniest offering. But in spite of all her efforts, the expenditures at Penn School continued to outrun the income.[18]

At length, Penn discovered the appeal that promised to endear it to the real source of money in the education business, the large foundations. For years, Penn had received yearly contributions of $500 to $1,000 from the Slater Board and the Phelps-Stokes Fund and had turned frequently to the General Education Board for aid in specific projects. Penn's early appeals as a solution to the "Negro Problem," and then as a scheme of rural education and racial adjustment, had begun to lose their ring, however. Penn needed a new approach for the foundations.

Thomas Jesse Jones, director of the Phelps-Stokes Fund, was an old friend of Penn School and a devoted supporter of its brand of education. Under his direction the Phelps-Stokes Fund had increasingly turned its attention to Africa, supporting African education as a means of "civilizing" the natives. Jones heartily endorsed the activities and views of a native South African, Charles Templeman Loram, who had dedicated himself to uplifting the people among whom he lived and who became the representative of the Phelps-Stokes Fund in Africa. Loram had earned a Ph.D. in education at Teachers College, Columbia. In his dissertation he had laid out a plan for African education that called for industrial and agricultural training of the natives—an education designed to develop intelligence and character and also to promote industriousness so that the Africans might become a benefit, and not a hindrance, to their country. For a native white South African, this was a progressive point of view.[19]

18. Author's interview with Howard Kester, July, 1971, Black Mountain, N.C. Lardner Howell to Peabody, September 24, 1918, in GFP.
19. Richard D. Heyman, "C. T. Loram: A South African Liberal in Race Rela-

Under the leadership of men who shared Jones's and Loram's convictions, the League of Nations' Permanent Mandates Commission in 1924 resolved its position on educational policy to be as follows: "By making character-training and discipline, the teaching of agriculture, animal husbandry, arts and crafts, and elementary hygiene the keynote of educational policy, the gradual civilization of the native populations as well as the economic development of the countries will be furthered in the best possible manner." Furthermore, the British Royal Advisory Committee on Native Education stated its belief in 1925 that the aim of education "should be to render the individual more efficient in his or her condition of life, whatever it may be, and to promote the advancement of the community as a whole through the improvement of agriculture, the development of native industries and the improvement of health."[20]

Jones became convinced that Penn's program of health training, agricultural instruction, handicrafts and trades, and uplift was wholly applicable to African education; and he launched a vigorous campaign to spread Penn School's message and techniques across Africa, using Phelps-Stokes money to send scores of missionaries to observe firsthand the Penn School experiment in community education. As Mabel Carney, who was making a survey of the African situation for Teachers College, Columbia, wrote Miss House, "Everywhere I go up the length and breadth of the whole continent of Africa, *everyone* knows of you and Miss Cooley and Penn School."[21]

Jones believed that Penn provided a perfect example of the kind of effective education that was adapted to the needs of the people it served. As the introduction to one of Miss Cooley's books read, "Dr. Thomas Jesse Jones, who had headed commissions sent by the Phelps-Stokes Fund . . . has spread the story of these islands among those who would recast missionary enterprise in

---

tions," *International Journal of African Historical Studies*, V (January, 1972), 41, 44; Charles Templeman Loram, *Education of the South African Native* (London, 1917; reprinted, New York, 1969), 155–61, 234–38, 412–25.

20. Anna Wicksell to Permanent Mandates Commission, 1927, in PSP.

21. Trustees' minutes, February 1, 1922, Mabel Carney to House, May 10, 1926, Peabody to Mrs. Maurice Hooper, July 22, 1926, all in PSP.

modern terms." Jones greeted Miss Cooley's book, *School Acres*, with the greatest enthusiasm, declaring it to be an extraordinary achievement in the field of educational method and educational objectives.[22]

At Jones's insistence, C. T. Loram went to St. Helena in the autumn of 1926 hoping to find creative solutions to the problems he faced in Africa. He was not disappointed. "At Penn School, South Carolina," he informed a Phelps-Stokes gathering, "I believe I have found the ideal school and model for African education." And he wrote in the Hampton House guest book, "I believe I've found what I came to America to get, a community center with its head in God's heaven but with its feet firmly planted in the good and the bad of this earth.... With a thousand Penns we could transform Africa." He remained a devoted admirer of Penn School, often sending students and natives to study Penn's methods.[23]

Other visitors shared Loram's enthusiasm: "I count Penn as my most valuable experience of Negro education in the U.S." "Your work amongst a backward community, full of ignorance and superstitious beliefs, unprogressive, is what is the most similar to our work in Central Africa. The new methods ... you are so successfully putting into practice, will be most helpful to us." All agreed that the work at Penn was "the ideal for uplifting a primative [sic] community and at the same time keeping them at home." "I wish I could take all St. Helena Island and move it over to Cameroons or Togoland, just to show what can be done in the way of making the people happy and useful citizens in their own home place." Many of the visitors noted the self-respecting dignity of St. Helena's blacks. "May the inspiration of Penn School," wrote one of them, "lead to the realization of self-sufficient and self-controlled African communities."[24]

22. Typescript press release, August 21, 1926, Thomas Jesse Jones to Curtis, May 24, 1926, T. J. Jones to Kellogg, November 15, 1930, all in PSP; Paul Underwood Kellogg, Introduction to Cooley, *School Acres*, xi.
23. C. T. Loram, Speech at Phelps-Stokes dinner, October 25, 1926, in PSP; Loram in Hampton House guest book, October 13, 14, 1926, in JMD.
24. Wicksell to Cooley, May 12, 1927, G. Sawyer to Cooley, June 2, 1928, George Schwab to Cooley, August 1, 1928, all in PSP; S. G. Butler, Hampton House guest book, October 29, 1928, in JMD.

With so much fervent praise, it was hard for the ladies not to get just a little giddy, but they kept their perspective intact and their focus on St. Helena. The African map at the school, however, filled up with pins marking visitors' homelands, and by 1928 eighty-six pins dotted the map.[25]

Responding to all this enthusiasm, and with a stroke of advertising genius, Miss Isabella Curtis produced an appeal entitled "How Penn School Serves Africa," in which she showed how far-reaching the influence of Penn School was by quoting the tributes of visiting missionaries. "We hope that you will contribute to it," concluded the wily Miss Curtis, "and have the satisfaction of knowing that your dollars do double service."[26]

The appeal hit its mark. Thomas Jesse Jones was completely captivated, writing to Miss Curtis his appraisal of the leaflet as being one of the most appealing statements of educational service that he had ever read. Following this lead, Miss Cooley and her trustees began immediately to develop a new financial appeal, which they submitted to the Phelps-Stokes Fund and to the General Education Board.[27]

The General Education Board had reduced its annual contribution for the All-Year School, explaining that it disapproved of contributions for current expenses and that the All-Year School should now be able to stand on its own. Miss Cooley apparently did not understand the board's philosophy of giving and wrote petulantly to Mr. Cope that she had thought the extension work and much of the work that ran twelve months of the year was just the sort of educational work the General Education Board would help continuously. She had learned a valuable lesson about the limits of her work, however, and she determined that the time had come to work intensively on the plans as they were outlined and to add nothing to increase the present budget. She was also seeking ways to inspire the St. Helena community to carry a larger share of the burden, but the Beaufort Bank failure and the drop in the price of cotton hit the island just as the General Education

25. "Annual Report," 1928, p. 29, in PSP.
26. "How Penn School Serves Africa," 1926, in JMD.
27. T. J. Jones to Curtis, May 4, 1926, in PSP.

Board withdrew its support. Nevertheless, she could see the unmistakable improvement on the island—especially the tremendous strides taken by the people in the raising and preserving of their food—and she knew that the work of her school must go on.[28]

The vice-chairman of the Penn Board, the Reverend James Edgar Gregg of Pittsfield, Massachusetts, had followed Frissell as principal of Hampton. In that position he had developed a close relationship with several of the educational foundations, and he frequently used his influence on behalf of Penn as well as of Hampton. In the autumn of 1926 Dr. Gregg met with several officials of the General Education Board and induced them to consider a new appropriation for Penn on the basis of its demonstrated usefulness as an example to all who were interested in the education of undeveloped peoples. Under the leadership of Wickliffe Rose, the board had turned its attention toward the natural sciences, but apparently Dr. Gregg made such a forceful presentation that the distinguished gentlemen compromised, proposing that the board be ready at all times to consider new proposals based on new or special needs. The Penn trustees thus determined to appeal to the GEB for a special grant of $10,000 annually for five years for the purpose of "beginning" the distinctive work of the school to benefit persons interested in African native education.[29]

Appeals to the General Education Board always carried more weight when accompanied by the promise of a similar special contribution from other sources. Consequently, the Penn trustees decided to turn to Arthur Curtiss James, George Foster Peabody, and the Phelps-Stokes Fund to secure the annual ten-thousand-dollar matching fund. The affluent Mr. James amiably agreed to give $2,500 toward the sum total in addition to his regular annual contribution of the same amount. Peabody, however, was not so agreeable. He had given $5,000 toward the deficit when he re-

28. Trustees' minutes, June 18, 1924, Cooley to Cope, November 30, 1926, both in PSP.
29. James Edgar Gregg to Peabody, December 11, 1926, in PSP; Fosdick, *Adventure in Giving*, 229.

signed from the board two months before, and he had only that month given another $2,500. Now ill, he felt unappreciated and used, and he wrote with much irritation that he felt he had done his share.[30]

The response from the Phelps-Stokes Fund, whose interest in the maintenance of the school in its present mode of usefulness was vital, was equally disheartening. Dr. Gregg had written a masterful letter to Thomas Jesse Jones describing Penn's yearly expenditures of $48,000 as against its income of only $33,000. Of course, the school *could* be run for $30,000 a year, or even less, as an ordinary country high school with some elementary instruction of the conventional sort, eliminating the children's home acres, the care and health of the community, the organized encouragement of better homes, and all the other distinctive features that had made Penn School famous. But Gregg was confident that no friend of the institution who had firsthand knowledge of what it was doing would wish this done.[31]

His confidence, unfortunately, was misplaced. Within the week, Anson Phelps Stokes himself had written back to Gregg, graciously affirming the Fund's deep interest in Penn, but remarking that their limited resources prevented them from donating $25,000. Apparently the Phelps-Stokes Fund had an annual working income of about $30,000, and most of this had to go into a few large movements from which they hoped the cause of Negro education in Africa and America, and the interracial cause generally, would profit. Dr. Stokes did agree, however, to recommend to his board a payment of $5,000, to be distributed over the five-year period. In their haste to appeal to the General Education Board before the first of the new year, the Penn School trustees had rushed an ill-considered and ill-timed appeal to the Phelps-Stokes Board, which would not even meet again to consider such grants until the fall. Surely someone on the Penn School

30. Gregg to Peabody, December 11, 1926, Trustees' minutes, October 22, 1926, Curtis to Cooley, December, 1926, Gregg to Cooley, December 10, 1926, January 3, 1927, all in PSP.
31. Gregg to Peabody, December 11, 1926, Gregg to T. J. Jones, December 13, 1926, both in PSP.

Board, with all their connections and sophistication, should have had sufficient understanding of the possible to avoid such unreasonable requests.[32]

Despite the Phelps-Stokes Fund's refusal to shoulder Penn's burden, Thomas Jesse Jones wrote Miss Cooley of his unflagging admiration for the work she was doing, concluding with advice that they must all work together with a strong faith that they would succeed.[33] Miss Cooley clearly saw, however, that more than faith was needed.

So the African appeal had been a false hope, and Penn found itself facing the same old problems of staying afloat, now burdened with an ever-increasing stream of missionaries and visitors. Miss Cooley was pleased with this evidence of usefulness and service, and she basked in Penn's growing reputation as a unique community school; but the transporting and entertaining of guests put a heavy load on Miss Cooley and Miss House, as well as on the superintendent who had to greet them, the boys who drove them and thus missed time in the shops, and the girls who cooked and cleaned for them. The trustees finally directed the principals to expend less time "lavishing themselves" on the visitors, but the two ladies probably welcomed these opportunities to visit with others of their kind.[34]

Penn had not only missionary visitors, however. Dr. C. T. Loram had been so completely captivated by Penn that he arranged through the Phelps-Stokes Fund to send native African women for a year at a time to study the methods of Penn and adapt them for use in the training of community workers in South Africa.[35] So Penn now had this burden, however interesting, to add to its already-full curriculum.

Foiled in their attempts to beguile the foundations, the Penn trustees returned to their time-honored methods of approaching wealthy individuals, revealing again a lack of perspective and bal-

32. Anson Phelps Stokes to Gregg, December 18, 1926, Wood to General Education Board, January 12, 1927, Gregg to Peabody, December 11, 1926, all in PSP.
33. T. J. Jones to Cooley, December 22, 1926, in PSP.
34. "Annual Report," 1928, p. 29, "Superintendent's Report," 1927, pp. 2–3, Trustees' minutes, June 15, 1928, all in PSP.
35. James McCulloch to S. M. Colgate, December 2, 1927, in PSP.

ance. Dr. Gregg requested $50,000 from Edward S. Harkness and $25,000 from A. S. Frissell, Hollis Frissell's brother. Highly amused at such an enormous request, Frissell replied to Gregg, "Like the darkey who couldn't change the $10 bill I thank you for asking me," and he graciously declined to commit himself. As he wrote to Miss Cooley later, this naive request kept him from giving his modest bit to the fund, though he profoundly approved the work of the school and deeply appreciated Miss Cooley.[36]

Miss Curtis continued her awesome tasks—addressing and stamping appeals and reminders, two and three thousand at a time—and her methods remained the surest support of the school, though rather expensive in themselves. She sent copies of the annual report to fifteen hundred contributors (the report was a forty- to sixty-page affair, with pictures, on high quality paper). Her appeals were usually successful, though one, which she did not write, cost $250.00 and snared only twenty-five new contributors. In her delightfully frenetic way, she shot off an outraged appeal to Miss Cooley, demanding authority to print only what she approved: "Of course I am mentally and morally and nearly physically incompetent, and think that if I am to be responsible for money-raising I *MUST* have the appeals as seems good to me!"[37]

Miss Cooley continued her campaigns in the North, speaking to women's clubs, church circles, and luncheons. And as the rewards of her labors, she would receive letters such as the following: "The ladies of the Hospital Committee of the Madison Avenue Church have prepared a large package of supplies which we would like you to have as soon as possible." She spoke wherever her trustees could get her an audience, one week on the Philadelphia Main Line, the next in a Park Avenue apartment. She also visited the various Penn School Clubs, and she learned to improve her planning, gaining maximum benefit from her days in the North.[38]

36. [Gregg] to Edward S. Harkness, February 16, 1927, Gregg to Cooley, March 14, 1927, A. S. Frissell to Cooley, August 5, 1927, all in PSP.
37. Trustees' minutes, February 2, 1928, Curtis to "Girls," November 13, 1927, both in PSP.
38. Jeanie I. Harper to Cooley, June 20, 1927, Maule to McCulloch, December 29, 1927, Barbara Schieffelin to McCulloch, January 3, 1928, Cope to McCulloch, December 13, 1927, all in PSP.

Several cities had Penn School Clubs: Philadelphia, Germantown, Boston, and Poughkeepsie, as well as Hampton and St. Helena. The clubs usually met two times a year, once for business and once socially; and most of them had representatives on the Penn board of trustees. They collected money for the school and sent gifts at Christmas; and occasionally, when Miss Cooley could not be present, they had other speakers. The level of their understanding of racial problems in the South can be surmised from an article in the Poughkeepsie *Eagle*, reporting that at a meeting of the local Penn School Club Dr. Gregg had been asked, "Are negroes worth while?" Miss Cooley reported that she frequently was asked, "But what about the moral question?" and she tried to set the fearful at ease with explanations of the cultural inheritance from slavery that depressed black moral standards and with descriptions of improvements on St. Helena. Obviously Dr. Frissell had a point about educating the North.[39]

One Penn School Club that asked no such questions, and had no representative among the trustees, was the Penn School Club of New York City. Martin V. Washington, brother of Penn's farm manager, had organized this club among his Harlem neighbors in the mid-1920s. Clyde Vernon Kiser found several Penn School graduates in Harlem in 1928, and most of them belonged to Mr. Washington's club. They were an active and dedicated group that met once every month and sent money for scholarships every year.[40]

By the fall of 1928 Penn School had a deficit of $7,000 and Miss Cooley was writing to Julius Rosenwald for the money to build a new barn. The old one, built in 1905, had worn out, and Miss Cooley requested $5,000 to replace it. Typically, she requested the money immediately, but it was not until the following spring that the Rosenwald trustees appropriated $6,000 toward the work of Penn School, to be spread over a three-year period. Arthur Curtiss James had already paid for the new barn, and the

39. Alletta Platt Holden to Poughkeepsie Penn School Club, March 1927, "Miss Cooley's Work Praised," Poughkeepsie *Eagle*, March 14, 1927, clipping, "Annual Report," 1927, p. 24, all in PSP.

40. Kiser, *Sea Island to City*, 211–12, 253; McCulloch to T. J. Jones, November 8, 1927, in PSP.

Rosenwald money made Miss Colley feel she had a new grip on the work on St. Helena Island.[41]

In 1929 the General Education Board renewed its support of Penn School, much to the relief of all. "I have always felt that with the ever increasing difficulty of financing these institutions from the North," Mr. Cope wrote to George Foster Peabody, "it was vitally important to retain the support of some of the great educational foundations if the work was to go on as it ought to do." Cope felt that the ladies had built up such a remarkable school that it was unthinkable that it should fail because of inadequate financial backing. Apparently the General Education Board compromised slightly and contributed for current expenses instead of for a new project, though the following year that board did appropriate $15,000 for the specific purpose of building an addition to the classroom building.[42]

Despite this renewed support, however, Cope understood that the school still needed to have its income increased from $5,000 to $10,000 a year. Once again he brought up the question of an endowment, pointing out that an income from endowments of $25,000 a year would still leave a handsome margin to be raised by annual subscriptions. Peabody had long since resigned and now Cope's point of view prevailed, with the trustees finally voting in the fall of 1930 to raise $150,000 for invested funds. Of course, their financial awakening was too late, and the endowment fund never materialized.[43]

Despite the continuing financial crisis, the work being done at Penn School remained of superior quality, especially when compared with other educational opportunities, white or black, across the state of South Carolina. The trustees estimated that they spent $137 per pupil in 1928–1929, whereas in the same time period South Carolina public school funds gave $60.06 for

---

41. Cooley to Julius Rosenwald, October 29, 1928, W. B. Harrell to Cooley, May 13, 1929, Carman to Cooley, March 28, 1929, Cooley to Harrell, May 20, 1929, all in PSP.

42. Cooley to Jackson Davis, December 30, 1929, in PSP; Cope to Peabody, October 9, 1929, Cooley to Peabody, October 28, 1930, both in GFP.

43. Cope to Peabody, February 20, 1930, in GFP; Trustees' minutes, September 16, 1930, in PSP.

each white child enrollled and $7.89 for each black child. But the visitors to Penn were struck not so much by the quality of the instruction as by the peacefulness of the place, the religious aura that surrounded it, and the consequent disappearance of the fearful "Negro Problem." "Here," wrote one of Francis Cope's relatives in the Hampton House guest book, "they are making the world safe for democracy."[44]

---

44. Trustees' minutes, February 14, 1930, in PSP; Harlan, *Separate and Unequal*, 204. Woofter includes the following "Comparison of Educational Offerings on St. Helena Island with Average for Beaufort County, 1927–1928":

	St. Helena (Negro)	Average for Beaufort County	
		White	Negro
current expenditure per pupil enrolled*	$ 3.36	$ 56.00	$ 6.11
length of school session in days	100	178	117
average salary of teachers	$185	$1,004	$259
number of pupils per teacher	57	26	46

*Includes expenditures for teachers' salaries, fuel and incidentals, and transportation. Woofter, *Black Yeomanry*, 277; Joseph Paul Morris in Hampton House guest book, February 14–15, 1919, in JMD.

Rossa Belle Cooley and Grace Bigelow House on the steps of Hampton House.
Photograph by Margaret Noyes, 1937

Dr. Hollis Burke Frissell, president of Hampton Institute and chairman of the board of Penn School, at the dedication of the Cope Industrial Building, 1912.

Negro Civil War soldiers, the 1st South Carolina Volunteers, at the fiftieth anniversary of Penn School, 1912.

The laundry at Penn School.

Dedication of the Frissell Memorial Community House, 1925.

Trustees and guests at the dedication of the Frissell Memorial, 1925. Bottom step, seated on left: Francis R. Cope, Jr. Second row, seated, left to right: Charles Ware, Dr. James E. Gregg, Alfred Collins Maule, unidentified woman, unidentified man, George Foster Peabody, unidentified man. Top row, standing, left to right: two unidentified men, Dr. William H. Mills; seated, left to right: Henry Wilder Foote, James Hardy Dillard, Rossa Belle Cooley, Grace Bigelow House, four unidentified women.

Old South Pines School, 1933, showing overcrowded conditions.

New South Pines School, one of ten "better schools" on the island.

Bas-relief of Frissell, presented by George Foster Peabody to Hampton, Tuskegee, and Penn in 1928. The plaque depicts Frissell surrounded by an Indian, an island workman, Booker T. Washington, and a Penn School student, with the inscription: "The more abundant life prevails."

Ndulamo, the principals' retreat at the edge of the island, "a place of abounding joy."

10

Spreading the Gospel

In the winter of 1926 a sociologist from the University of North Carolina traveled to St. Helena Island to consider the possibilities of a comprehensive, interdisciplinary study of the history, culture, and economic arrangements of the island's people. Almost as soon as he saw the place, he realized, with mounting excitement, that St. Helena Island offered opportunities the social scientist rarely found; he believed that here he had found almost test tube conditions in which he could observe "the action of constructive forces on an isolated Negro group of as pure African descent as could be found in the country." The community had several peculiar conditions that made it so desirable: the homogeneity of the population and the consequent absence of racial friction, the history of severly limited contacts with whites, the isolation from the main avenues of commerce and travel, the existence of Penn School as almost the only extraneous influence on the group, and the fact of landownership. The professor returned to Chapel Hill and discussed his findings with Howard Odum and several others, and the Social Science Research Council decided to sponsor the project.[1]

The young professor, Thomas Jackson Woofter, was a south-

1. Woofter, "Preliminary Confidential Report for the Trustees of Penn School," 1; Woofter, *Black Yeomanry*, 6; Woofter Prospectus, 1927, pp. 1–4, Woofter to Cooley, August 22, 1927, both in PSP.

erner. As an undergraduate at the University of Georgia he had won a Phelps-Stokes Fellowship for the study of Negroes and had gone on to write a thesis on "The Negro of Athens, Georgia." This apparently had brought him to the attention of Thomas Jesse Jones, and after he graduated from Georgia, Woofter worked as Jones's assistant in compiling material for the older man's study of *Negro Education* (1916). Jones was an exceedingly zealous advocate of industrial education, and as his assistant, Woofter must have absorbed much of his commitment to the Hampton ideals of education. From the tone of Woofter's letters to Miss Cooley and from his book, it is clear that he shared the assumptions of the industrial education movement. As he described his intentions to Miss Cooley, his study would demonstrate the "improvability" of a group of people whose opportunities had been limited "in a very peculiar way." He pointed out that this would reflect credit on the work of Penn School and would lend encouragement to people in other sections of the country who were working with groups of Negroes who were "backward in assimilating American culture." These were precisely what the Penn School principals and trustees had declared their intentions to be—to prove black capabilities and to serve as an object lesson for other communities—and Miss Cooley jumped at the opportunity to have such a "scientific" study made of her efforts.[2]

Mr. Cope, however, had reservations. Always cautious and conservative, Mr. Cope thought first of the welfare of the school. This was at the peak of both the financial crisis and the missionary influx, and Mr. Cope admonished Miss Cooley that there was a limit to the amount of additional work and supervision that she and her teachers could give with justice to the efficiency of their regular work. As he also reminded her: "After all, the most vital work of every educational institution is the teaching and character development of the students and . . . this ought to have first place in every school program." Cope was overruled, however, and a team of researchers descended on St. Helena Island.[3]

2. Jones, *Negro Education*, xiii; Woofter to Cooley, May 4, 1927, in PSP.
3. Cope to Cooley, May 30, 1927, in PSP.

From January until June of 1928, the Woofter team lived at Ndulamo, and they, too, fell under the spell of the place. One of them, Guion Griffis Johnson, wrote to Miss Cooley later, "We shall long remember our sojourn at Ndulamo as three of the happiest months of our lives." The reserachers included Guion Johnson, who studied the social history of the Sea Islands; her husband, Guy Benton Johnson, who studied the language and folklore of the area; and Clyde Vernon Kiser, who studied population and migration patterns. The complete team included a director, historian, psychologist, physical anthropologist, cultural anthropologist, specialist in agricultural economics, specialists in crime study and taxation, and fourteen native enumerators. The researchers received another Penn School courtesy when George Foster Peabody and the Yaddo Corporation arranged for them to prepare their manuscripts at Triuna Island on Lake George.[4]

Peabody may have had hopes of his own for the study. In his incomparable incoherence he had written to Woofter earlier, trying to sell him his ideas on black music. "I should be glad for you to have in mind how important a factor such a research study may prove in connection with a proper relation of music to the slave life of the Negro and proper inquiry as to the advantage in a right and righteous civilization of music as a foundation stone, i.e., music of the people, not of the few skilled ones."[5] There is no evidence of Woofter's response, but it must have been bemused at best.

Woofter prepared a preliminary report for the Penn trustees in which he outlined his findings, concluding that "the social experiment of the building of a self-sufficient Negro community on the Island has not been completed." He supported the experiment wholeheartedly, however, appraising it as being well worth the effort and money expended by the patrons of Penn School.

4. "Annual Report of the Penn Normal, Industrial and Agricultural School," 1928, p. 28, Guy and Guion Johnson to Cooley, May 23, 1928, both in PSP; Guion Griffis Johnson, *A Social History of the Sea Islands with Special Reference to St. Helena Island. South Carolina* (Chapel Hill, N.C., 1930); Johnson, *Folk Culture on St. Helena Island*; Kiser, *Sea Island to City*; Woofter, "Preliminary Report," 2; Woofter, *Black Yeomanry*, viii.

5. Peabody to Woofter, May 16, 1927, in PSP.

In the book as it finally appeared, Woofter modified his conclusion considerably, hedging to the point that he seemed to declare Penn's efforts in community education almost a total success. This may be attributable to some advice he had received from Paul Underwood Kellogg about how to broaden his appeal. "The real lead," Kellogg had written, "lies in putting St. Helena forward as a sample of the southern countryside—one which has colorful distinction, but one which none the less lies close to the common problem there. There . . . lies the big lure of your book." And so Woofter repeatedly emphasized in his book that, if progress could be made with such a group, then similar methods might be relied upon to show even greater results when applied to people who had more advantages. In other words, the experiment on St. Helena Island suggested what could be accomplished with a group of pure-blooded, isolated Negroes when they were given the "stimulus of intelligent paternalism."[6]

Woofter dedicated his book, entitled *Black Yeomanry*, to Miss Cooley and Miss House—"whose devotion to the realities of education has given vital leadership to St. Helena and its people"— and he leapt almost immediately into praise of Penn School. "Education on such a broad community scale," he wrote, "applied to people whose other contacts with white culture have been limited, gives us a supreme test of the adaptability of the Negro." The accomplishments on St. Helena suggested what might be accomplished in other areas of the South and shed much light on the practical aspects of race betterment.[7]

Woofter found that the health conditions on St. Helena were far superior to those found elsewhere in the rural South, and he claimed this improvement for Penn School. He declared the island homes far superior to the tenements occupied by so many migrants in the city, and he dwelt at length on the remarkable improvements of the island homes. He learned from the county tax collector that no other group of people in Beaufort County were so regular in paying their yearly taxes, and he found that migra-

---

6. Woofter, "Preliminary Report," 15, 16; Kellogg to Woofter, August 31, 1929, in PSP; Woofter, *Black Yeomanry*, 244.
7. Woofter, *Black Yeomanry*.

tion from St. Helena was small when compared to the movement from some of the other southern rural areas. Clyde Vernon Kiser modified the force of this statement considerably when he claimed that St. Helena had been unable to hold its young people. The older people remained, but the younger ones revolted against the mode of life on St. Helena and struck out for the cities to get jobs as stevedores, porters, cobblers, carpenters, masons, domestic workers, hair dressers, and factory workers.[8]

Woofter declared Penn's program a success in all areas except farming, and here Penn had been unable to reverse the sweeping economic forces that had depressed agriculture since the boll weevil's arrival. Out of 1200 farmers on the island, he concluded that only 85 could be termed successful; 600 derived half of their income from outside wages, 450 placed major dependence on outside wages, and 50 old people barely subsisted on odd jobs and gifts from their children. Of the successful farmers, about half were in the Cooperative Society. Woofter reported that most farmers had not adopted the new habits necessary to grow cotton successfully, such as using fertilizer or poison. Kiser later extended this critique of farming: "The average farms are too small to have any land for pasturage or for growing a sufficient amount of feed for the animals. . . . Farm implements are generally poor and methods of work are consequently inefficient." Despite these limitations, however, Woofter referred to the relative self-sufficiency of the island farmers as contrasted with the black belt tenants, and he thought this was evidenced by the widespread ownership of farm animals. Nearly every farm had a cow and calf and either an ox or a horse; each farm also had several pigs and a flock of poultry. During the hard times of the boll weevil crisis many people had sold off this farm capital, but by the time of the Woofter study in 1928, these animal losses were being replaced.[9]

In addition to the disastrous effects of the boll weevil, Woofter found several handicaps to farming. The land had been sub-

8. *Ibid.*, 1–3, 89, 125; Kiser, *Sea Island to City*, 76, 83, 142.
9. Woofter, *Black Yeomanry*, 11, 116, 141, 143–44, 152; Kiser, *Sea Island to City*, 70.

divided by equal inheritance into plots entirely too small; much other land had been entailed and was shared among a number of heirs, making individual initiative difficult; the periodic hurricanes and storms wiped out crops and salted the land; the pre-bridge isolation had caused marketing difficulties that prohibited the selling of anything but staple crops; the loss of savings in the recent bank failure only aggravated the widespread thriftlessness of the people. All of these factors, in addition to the boll weevil, arrayed themselves against "the natural advantage of soil and climate, the traditional love of the land, and the educational forces of the school." Woofter concluded, nonetheless, that a larger proportion of farmers was making a living on St. Helena than in other Negro agricultural communities and that the people had had more success in holding on to their land.[10]

There were three major areas in which the islanders had not adapted themselves to American standards. The most fundamental of these was their easy-going attitude toward life and a contentment with less than would satisfy the average American. Woofter found that the average income on St. Helena was $420 per year, though this included much food produced at home and the use of an owned house. This yeoman standard of living did not satisfy all, for many drifted to the cities; but for the majority who remained, life was the "Oriental pursuit of a calm, unhurried destiny, rather than a drive under the spur of ambition."[11]

Associated with this relative lack of ambition was the failure of most of the families to accumulate that surplus which is essential to progress. The third major deviation from American standards was "the relative laxity of sex morals," evidenced by the high illegitimacy rate and the ease with which migration disrupted the family, leaving the women to bear the brunt of rearing the family.[12]

Despite these aberrations from the American norm, Woofter described a relatively high standard of living, and he believed the island to be important as a demonstration of what a Negro landowning community could become. He found the explanation for

10. Woofter, *Black Yeomanry*, 146, 150.
11. *Ibid.*, 249, 251.
12. *Ibid.*, 251.

Spreading the Gospel 187

this success in Penn School as well as in landownership. Not only did Penn orchestrate a variety of community activities and lead in agricultural development, it also provided a process of training and character building that had unmistakable, though intangible, results. The genius of its work lay in the relationship of the teaching to the realities of life in many subtle ways. Thus the classroom work and the industrial subjects were continually adapted to community needs, and education became a living, vital process. The Hampton philosophy of character building flourished: "Pupils participate in industrial work not only to become skilled, but also to cultivate the fundamental habits of thoroughness and morality which are best formed by doing tasks well." And as Woofter concluded, "It is in character as well as in knowledge and skill that the results of this program show."[13]

Woofter concluded that Penn's demonstration of the improvability of health, home life, farm life, and religion had been so convincing that other southern counties could well afford to assume as government functions some of the semiprivate activities of Penn School. "One can hardly fail to speculate," he mused, "on the probable improvement in the Southern racial situation if the whole area had been dotted with Penn Schools."[14]

The Penn School reaction to Woofter's book was strong and quite naturally positive. Paul Kellogg thought it would be very valuable as a detached appraisal and interpretation, and he praised Woofter's efforts. One of Penn's admirers praised the book as "a measure of Penn School's influence made in as scientific a way as such things can be made," and all thought it would be wonderful publicity for the school. Miss House expressed a widespread hope when she remarked to the trustees that Woofter's study would show the state officials the need for Negro schools. Written by a distinguished southern author, published by a respected southern press, the book may well have had such an impact on southern school officials.[15]

One who responded less favorably to Woofter's book was

13. *Ibid.*, 126, 157, 187, 196, 199.
14. *Ibid.*, 247.
15. Kellog to Woofter, August 31, 1929, J. L. B. Buck to Cooley, September 12, 1930, Trustees' minutes, June 15, 1928, all in PSP.

Booker T. Washington's old foe, W. E. B. Du Bois. Reviewing *Black Yeomanry* in *The Crisis*, Du Bois criticized the book as being another result of the recent school of white southern investigations into the situation of the southern Negro. He deprecated the $16,500 spent on research, the beautifully manufactured volume, and the study itself, which he claimed was mostly copied from other works. More to the point, he claimed that "on the main subject of what life means to these black folk, of the real difficulties of their economic and social development, of the way in which emancipation has developed into the modern color line, there is not a single word of really illuminating information." This was nonsense, dictated by Du Bois's consuming desire to catalog white America's failure to deal justly with black people. In fact, Woofter had described thoroughly St. Helena's social and economic development in terms that befitted a social scientist and not a novelist, and he explained very carefully that one of the key attractions of St. Helena was the absence of a color line on the island. Wherever white political domination intruded, which was rare, as in the issue of the bridge, Woofter documented it fully, and with obvious though restrained disgust.

Du Bois wrote disparagingly of Woofter's various chapters, accusing the southern author of insensitivity to the blacks' political and economic depression. In fact, however, the book displayed much concern and subdued irony, though Woofter usually confined himself to describing rather than judging. Du Bois wanted the judgment. "It would . . . have been possible," he wrote, "for a black man making this study to have gone off into bitter complaint and righteous indignation and to have showed how slavery in the sea islands of Carolina simply transformed itself into economic and political exploitation." As a social scientist himself, Du Bois knew that what he was suggesting was untenable, yet in a fit of ill-logic he continued, "If this kind of study might not be regarded as scientific, on the other hand, Woofter's study is little less than a calamity." Du Bois claimed that Woofter had glossed over obvious facts and was seeking to say that on the Sea Islands of South Carolina there was a simple development in agricultural depression much like that elsewhere in the world and not particularly complicated by political disfranchisement, race prejudice, and enforced ignorance. Of course, on St. Helena Island there was very little race prejudice or enforced ignorance, and political disfranchisement bore very lightly on the people, given their isolation and the protective shield of Penn School. But Du Bois ranted on, lamenting that the boards and funds which supported this kind of "so-called sociological research" would continue to do so, while brave and honest black scholars like Carter Woodson and E. Franklin Frazier went begging. The primary difficulty with reports such as Woofter's, Du Bois concluded, was that they were "propaganda, pure and simple, and attempt to say to the world that whatever is wrong in the South is not due to the race question but to ordinary social difficulties which can be found everywhere."[16] Of course, Woofter said nothing of the sort. His motivating thought, though cautiously presented, was that the things that were wrong with the South *were* attributable to race, and he hoped to discover a solution. Du Bois had completely missed the point, and his rantings were all misdirected. Had he read Woofter's book carefully enough to perceive and follow the argument, he doubtless would have been apoplectic, for he would have seen that Woofter was looking for proof of black improvability and for a source of hope to all the doubters who thought of blacks as hopeless.

Curiously, Du Bois never sank his teeth into this inner core of the Hampton philosophy. Though he battled it all his life, he never grasped the argument of character building, dismissing "uplift" as a sentimental cover for exploitation. His outlook was always conspiratorial. In 1918 he had attacked Thomas Jesse Jones's report on *Negro Education* for recommending white control and industrial education. In 1930 he gave full elaboration to the industrial education conspiracy, laying down an interpretation that has persisted, unchanged, through the years. "The truth of the matter was," he claimed, "that Robert Ogden, Wallace Buttrick, and the Southern Education Board surrendered entirely to the white South on the matter of Negro education." In concen-

16. W. E. B. Du Bois, "The Browsing Reader," *Crisis*, XXXVIII (November, 1930), 378.

trating on the Hampton-Tuskegee industrial plan, "they proposed to fill the South with nonunion black artisans warranted never to vote nor strike and always to be happy." Here again, the South was the villain, the North was the patsy, and the Negro was the loser. It was all a great plot, hatched for the purpose of keeping the black man down. Especially absurd was old Seaman Knapp in this scheme of things, who "proposed to revolutionize the rural South, failed, and has been suitably forgotten."[17]

Du Bois never saw the threads that tied all of this to Hampton. Yet, even had he understood the central argument of uplift, or race adjustment, or race betterment, or whatever other euphemisms the Hamptonians had used to keep from offending blacks (and thus, consequently, making infinitely more difficult the task of uncovering their meanings), Du Bois would have opposed them. For Du Bois represented a new departure in American race relations—he demanded respect. Even had he understood what they were about, he would have scoffed, or raged, at the Hamptonians' experiments to prove what the Negro could accomplish. He would have blasted the fine sensibilities of these abolitionists' descendants, who wanted proof before they opened their society to black people.

Du Bois had had enough. In painful rage he lashed out at what he thought he saw. He mistook his enemy, but he had a victory nonetheless; for through his labors, and those of men like him, a new Negro began to emerge, a Negro who had been trained at Hampton and Tuskegee and Fisk, as well as at Atlanta and Howard, a Negro who had fought in America's great war for democracy and who now had a new conception of himself and his place in America's social order. As August Meier described him, he was "resourceful, independent, race-proud, economically advancing, and ready to tackle political and cultural ambitions." Though he denied any interest in social equality, he denounced the inequities of American racism and insisted upon his citizenship rights. The term *New Negro* symbolized the idea that "large

17. W. E. B. Du Bois, "Negro Education," *Crisis*, XV (February, 1918), 173–78; *Crisis*, XXXIV (July, 1930), 230; see especially Harlan, *Separate and Unequal*; and more recently Kirby, *Darkness at the Dawning*.

numbers of ex-slaves and their descendants were becoming proud of their race and self-dependence, and yet were assimilating to American middle-class standards and were anxious to partake of all the rights of American citizens."[18]

Black campuses across the nation felt the impact of the New Negro's arrival, and Hampton was not spared the turmoil. As principal, James E. Gregg had established a conventional college curriculum alongside the older vocational program, and he strove to come to grips with the new demands. "The War, the changed economic conditions which it has brought, and other factors," he informed his trustees, "have given to Negro Americans a new self-consciousness, a new skill, culture, wealth, and all else that is suggested by the word 'progress.'" But despite Dr. Gregg's struggle to understand and accept, the Hampton students went on strike in 1927, preceding the withdrawal of almost two hundred of their number. Hampton was in a crisis of the first magnitude, and the supporters of the old Hampton ideal now saw all they had worked for threatened. As Dr. Gregg explained to his trustees: "Sound character is over and over again declared to be the chief object of education and the indispensable element in all true success." And yet, now that the older Hampton methods were in question, how could the vital characteristics of the older Hampton training be preserved? The New Negro now scoffed at the need for proof and uplift, and the old Hampton slowly died. Whereas the Hamptonians had thought of the problem in terms of black deficiencies, the New Negro now refused to carry that burden, righteously blaming his problems on an unjust society and refusing to submit to white experimentation any longer. Eventually Dr. Gregg resigned, and he left the Hampton board to men who had different visions for black Americans.[19]

Penn School was not immune to these developments, though it was somewhat isolated from them. An alarmed Miss Cooley wrote to Dr. Gregg in 1929 before he resigned, demanding an

18. Meier, *Negro Thought In America*, 227–59.
19. Tindall, *Emergence of the New South*, 275; Dabney, *Universal Education in the South*, I, 473; James Edgar Gregg, "Report of the Principal," *Southern Workman*, LVII (June, 1928), 210, 211; Peabody to Dillard, March 29, 1930, in PSP.

explanation for an editorial in the *Southern Workman*. "I can't believe that it expressed Hampton," she wrote with deep concern. "I have heard this note struck during my visits at Hampton in recent years but have believed the view was held by a few who would be gradually weeded out, so that the ideals of Hampton Institute would not be lost. The Editorial," she correctly concluded, "expressing as the policy and principles of Hampton a spirit to be deplored seems to bring out into the open the question as to whether all that Frissell and Armstrong worked for is to be done away with." And what did this seditious bit of literature say to create such a flurry? For one thing, it said that with the adoption of more courses that conformed to the standards of the modern college, Hampton was becoming less different from other schools. More to the point, it said that Hampton teachers were becoming more like teachers elsewhere; their presence as teachers was "not due to consecration to a given missionary task involving the notion of personal sacrifice to a worthy cause." But what Miss Cooley found deplorable, what she would never accept, was the statement that "the 'missionary spirit,' which somehow always carried with it the idea of superior going out to help uplift inferior, has departed, although the color of educational adventure still attaches. . . . In securing its teachers, Hampton must now compete on the open market and not rely on consecration."[20]

Miss Cooley never understood the New Negro. She fought him with all the weapons at her command (and they were considerable), and she kept him (she believed) from the shores of St. Helena. She felt, understandably, that sentiments such as those in the *Southern Workman* editorial threatened all that she had believed, all that had made life for her a noble adventure. She was a missionary, and she would have no scoffing at that; and because her island was so isolated, she was able to maintain her Utopia.

20. Cooley to Gregg, March 15, 1929, in HBF; "The New Because of the Old," *Southern Workman*, LVIII (March, 1929), 111, 112. As Kelly Miller had written just a few years earlier, the northern teachers in the South's small black schools had been "indoctrinated in the Puritan cult which believed that character could be inspired only through religious consecration. . . . As they began to withdraw, this influence began to wane. The Negro colleges were shifted from a Puritan to a pagan basis." Miller, "The Higher Education of the Negro Is at the Crossroads," *Educational Review*, LXXXII (1926), 273–74, as quoted in McPherson, *The Abolitionist Legacy*, 200.

Spreading the Gospel 193

That was the point where Penn School stopped dealing with realities.

Though Penn School had become something of a showpiece by 1930, Miss Cooley and Miss House were not content to sit back and stop growing. They knew that Penn could touch directly the lives of only about two hundred and fifty children each year, usually the better prepared and more ambitious children from the public schools, and they dreamed of spreading the Penn School methods and gospel to all of the school children on the island.[21] To this end they had always worked to prepare teachers for the little county schools—St. Helena had nine of them—and they encouraged their graduates to believe that teaching in those little schools was the highest form of service to their people.

Despite all of Penn's efforts, however, no amount of higher dedication or missionary zeal could overcome the deplorable conditions in the county schools—the inadequacies of space and equipment and the burdens of overcrowding. Although the county authorities taxed St. Helena at the same rate as the other county districts, they apparently felt no obligation to equalize educational opportunities. Prior to 1927 they had not made a single expenditure for school buildings in sixty years. Consequently, five of the county schools met in rented society halls—unceiled buildings with backless benches and no desks or blackboards—that had replaced buildings claimed by storms, fire, and general decay over the years.[22]

The average enrollment was fifty-two, and three of the schools had an enrollment of more than seventy-five per teacher. Many times a school became so overcrowded that the teacher packed in students from wall to wall and from teacher to doorstep, and then she simply closed the door, telling the late arrivals they would have to go home. The schools had a term of five months, although three of the schools had two half-day sessions, which meant that these children received only ten weeks of schooling each year. As if all this were not enough, the county furnished no equip-

21. Woofter, *Black Yeomanry*, 195–96.
22. *Ibid.*, 183, 188; "Report on Rosenwald Schools on St. Helena Island," 1930, in PSP.

ment, and the teachers' salaries were only $35 or $40 a month.[23]

Very little teaching must have gone on in these classrooms. One of Miss Cooley's guests, having visited some of these schools, described his impressions of "rooms full of small black children, very solemn, but at the same time absurdly and delightfully merry." As Miss Cooley correctly perceived, teachers of a rural school who chose their profession with "a determination to change these conditions and to serve their people are missionaries of a high caliber." She added with typical confidence and self-assurance, "It is not too much to expect from a Penn School graduate." Nevertheless, very few Penn School graduates wanted to undertake the awesome tasks of the county school teacher.[24]

Penn School had, however, raised appreciably the desires and expectations of the island parents, and more of them every year realized the benefits of the Penn influence and wanted them for their children. Miss Cooley and Miss House also began to see the advantages of an improved county school system as they ran into serious financial difficulties and began to dream of shifting some of their educational burden to the state. They realized that if the state and county authorities would assume Penn's program of primary education, funds and energies thereby released could be used to extend Penn's other work. Penn could then concentrate its energies on serving as a laboratory for working out the problems of backward rural communities everywhere, thus rendering incomparable service to the South and to missionaries in other parts of the world.[25]

As early as 1920 Miss Cooley had initiated correspondence with the county school superintendent in hopes of persuading him to build two Rosenwald Schools on the island. The Sears, Roebuck magnate, Julius Rosenwald, had established a fund to stimulate the building of improved schoolhouses across the rural South, and Miss Cooley saw this as her opportunity to quicken

23. Kiser, *Sea Island to City*, 75; Woofter, *Black Yeomanry*, 187, 189; "Description of St. Helena School District for 1932–1933," "Annual Report," 1927, p. 9, both in PSP.
24. Description of Penn School by unidentified visitor, n.d., "Annual Report," 1927, p. 9, both in PSP.
25. Unsigned "Memorandum," 1925, in PSP.

Spreading the Gospel 195

southern interest in her rural school experiment. Initially, the county superintendent seemed interested in the plan to build the Rosenwald Schools; but as an elected official, he opposed any form of taxation for this purpose (he said it would be impossible to get a delegation to put it through the legislature), and the early negotiations came to naught.[26]

At length Penn School's Community Council took upon itself the responsibility for providing every child on St. Helena with an improved schoolhouse. They formed a Rosenwald Committee composed of ministers, island teachers, leading citizens, and county school trustees; and they initiated a program to canvass the community and to decide where the need was greatest. The council decided to work on the Coffins Point School first, and through relentless effort and diligence they raised $500. They needed $922 in order to qualify for the Rosenwald grant of $461, and this, of course, seemed like an astronomical sum in an economy where cash was scarce in the best of times. Mr. Rosenwald heartily approved the work of Penn School; and upon hearing of the islanders' struggle, he generously wrote out a personal check for the remaining $422, stipulating that this was to be presented as a gift from a friend of Penn School. The Coffins Point School was built amid great expressions of community pride, and the Community Council began to plan consolidated schools for South Pines and Ladies Island.[27]

While the Woofter survey team had been on St. Helena, they had made a careful survey of the island's educational needs. On the basis of this survey, the committee drew up a ten-year building program to replace inadequate school buildings with Rosenwald Schools in every section of the island.[28]

Unfortunately, Mr. Rosenwald's death put an end to the formal Rosenwald school building program, and the depression eliminated any hope that the state or county might help build the

26. J. Davis to Cooley, November 12, 1920, J. B. Felton to Cooley, November 11, 1920, both in PSP.
27. House, "Roads of Learning on St. Helena Island," 13; Alfred K. Stern to Cooley, September 1, 1927, "Report on Rosenwald Schools on St. Helena Island," 1930, both in PSP.
28. "Report on Rosenwald Schools on St. Helena Island," 1930, in PSP.

remaining new schools. The state of South Carolina was reportedly near bankruptcy, and in 1932 a state legislator had even presented a bill proposing that all South Carolina schools be closed for a year to save money. But the depression also brought cheaper materials and relief labor, and Miss House led the way in securing federal aid for the remaining schools in the Rosenwald Committee's ten-year program. The committee pushed through three more schoolhouses, and in 1934 the Civil Works Administration made grants assuring the building of the last four schools on the island.[29]

One day in 1934 Miss Cooley, Miss House, the Rosenwald Committee members, and legions of happy islanders traversed the island the whole day long attending the Schoolhouse Blessings for the last four county schools. Now a new schoolhouse graced every section of the island, all of them monuments to the parents' pluck and detertimation. The parents had raised $3,279.15 among themselves, in addition to paying $2,000 in taxes. They had also bought thirty acres of land so that each school could have its playground and its school acre. And all of this had been done by a people reeling from the effects of the boll weevil's arrival, the loss of a cash crop, and a nationwide economic depression. Now that the schools had blackboards and other equipment, now that the children had elbowroom instead of being crammed together on benches, Miss Cooley believed that she could look forward to the "saving" of a larger group.[30]

In time the new county schools began to cause a decrease in Penn School's enrollment, though they never assumed completely the burden of primary teaching on the island, as Miss Cooley had hoped they would. They did have the effect, however, of bringing the Penn School venture to the attention of the county and state officials, for Miss Cooley had shrewdly invited some of these southern gentlemen to attend the various Schoolhouse Blessings. The state superintendent of education especially was

29. Trustees' minutes, February 2, 1932, January 31, 1933, January 30, June 18, 1934, House to Allen Paul, September 19, 1933, [House?] to Brantley Harvey 1934, all in PSP.
30. Cooley to contributors, November 15, 1934, in PSP.

moved by the work being done at Penn and its influence on the community, and all of the officials spoke most appreciatively of Penn's accomplishments. Such affirmation was of more than passing significance, for cooperation with the state and county authorities was to become an ever more coveted goal as the depression drove Penn School finances to the wall.[31]

The thirties saw a great awakening of interest in the problems and inadequacies of black education. Carter Woodson, Ambrose Caliver, Charles Spurgeon Johnson, Dwight Oliver Wendell Holmes, Doxey Wilkerson, Lance G. E. Jones, and many others documented the plight of black Americans, especially southern rural blacks. The thirties also witnessed an increasing alarm over the disintegration of America's rural communities and a number of studies that sought the secret of rural regeneration.[32]

Penn School seemed to many people to have discovered that secret. In a remarkably creative way it had taken the traditions and conditions of the people and built on them from the ground up. In every sense of the word, it had become a community center, sponsoring over thirty committees that touched the community at every point. Athletics, Better Homes Campaigns, Corn Club, Homemakers Clubs, Folk Lore Society, Midwives' Class, Progressive Young Farmers Club, Rosenwald Committee, St. Helena Cooperative-Credit Union—all of these and more were within the range of interest of the Penn School program. And none of these activities had sprung up suddenly; all of them had evolved gradually as conditions had changed to make them possible.[33]

It was this linking of school and community, this conception

31. Trustee's minutes, November 3, 1938, Cooley to trustees, April 7, 1933, both in PSP.

32. Woodson, *The Mis-Education of the Negro;* Ambrose Caliver, *Fundamentals in the Education of Negroes* (Washington, D.C., 1935); Ambrose Caliver, *Availability of Education to Negroes in Rural Communities* (Washington, D.C., 1936); Charles Spurgeon Johnson. *The Negro in American Civilization* (New York, 1930); Dwight Oliver Wendell Holmes, *The Evolution of the Negro College* (Concord, N.H., 1934); Doxy A. Wilkerson, *Special Problems of Negro Education* (Washington, D.C., 1939); Lance G. E. Jones, *Negro Schools in the Southern States* (Oxford, 1928); Orrin L. L. Keener, *Struggle for Equal Opportunity: Dirt Farmers and the American Country Life Association* (New York, 1961).

33. W. H. Seaton, "Schools in Travail," Carnegie Corporation Report, 1932, p. 38, in PSP.

of the school as an agent of community betterment, that caused educators and rural reconstructionists to flock to Penn School in the thirties. Jackson Davis of the General Education Board might be content to proclaim simply that Penn was the best rural school he had ever seen, but other educators saw Penn as far more than a school. "Here," wrote one of them, "education as a progressive force is in its beginnings."[34]

The flexibility they gained from the absence of a clearly articulated philosophy had allowed Miss Cooley and Miss House to modify their appeal from time to time. Now they began to couch their work in terms of its usefulness to the South, developing this appeal to win financial support from the state of South Carolina. As early as 1928 Miss Cooley had initiated correspondence with the South Carolina Department of Agriculture, seeking state aid for some of the agricultural work being done on St. Helena. Plans for a Smith-Hughes agriculture teacher for the island, however, did not begin to materialize until 1934. As Miss House wrote to the state supervisor of agriculture, making her case for such assistance, "With the eight improved county schools available and Penn School ready to cooperate in every way possible, it seems a wonderful opportunity to work out a demonstration in Smith-Hughes agricultural instruction that might be helpful for other agricultural communities." Repeating her newly-discovered refrain, Miss House concluded, "We hope Penn School can be of constantly increasing service to the State and County."[35]

Ultimately, a Penn School and Hampton graduate, Philip Seabrook, received the appointment as vocational agriculture teacher for Penn School and the county schools, and he was able to create considerable enthusiasm for agricultural education on the island. Penn School paid half his salary, and the county paid the other half. In this way Miss Cooley was able to further her own ambitions for the island in the name of cooperation with the state.[36]

34. Mrs. Jackson Davis to Cooley and House, January 27, 1932, Seaton, "Schools in Travail," 38, both in PSP.
35. Verd Peterson to Cooley, March 14, 1928, House to Peterson, February 7, 1934, both in PSP.
36. Trustees' minutes, January 29, 1935, in PSP.

In its teacher-training program, also, Penn was able to forge an alliance with the state. In 1929 Penn had added the twelfth grade to its curriculum, primarily to provide a "teacher-training" course with practice teaching. In 1932, however, the state of South Carolina had raised its standards for accreditation, requiring that all teachers have at least two years of college training. This not only threatened Penn's relationship to the county schools, it also jeopardized Penn School's own accreditation, for several of Penn's workers had not had college training. Miss Cooley now found herself confronting a difficult decision. Should Penn add the necessary courses to satisfy the state requirements—at considerable expense and to fulfill a program that Miss Cooley deemed arbitrary and unsuited to St. Helena's needs—or should she confine herself to the secondary work and the community program already developed, allowing graduates interested in teaching to go away to Hampton or the state college for Negroes at Orangeburg? If Miss Cooley could not count on staffing the county schools with Penn School graduates, she would run the risk of seeing the wrong kind of influence introduced into the St. Helena environment. "The important thing," she informed her trustees, "is not to be swept away in the whirl for collegiate training for those not fitted for it, nor to lose the chance of fitting a group to do the missionary service require[d] in these remote rural schools. The college graduates are all too apt to be city girls with little love for the country and her problems." Miss Cooley must have feared that potential rural school teachers, increasingly difficult to interest in her work, would go away to Hampton or Tuskegee and decide, as many had done before them, not to return to the island.[37]

In time, Jackson Davis of the General Education Board conceived a creative solution to Penn's problem. He suggested that Penn cooperate with the state college for Negroes at Orangeburg in a program to train rural teachers. Situated as it was in a rural community, with easy access to several county schools, and having confronted and solved many of the problems facing the rural

---

37. Cooley to J. H. Hope, March 16, 1932, Trustees' minutes, October 28, 1932, J. Davis to Carney, February 8, 1935, Cooley, "Report of Penn School, 1931–1932," p. 5, all in PSP.

teacher, Penn would offer an unparalleled opportunity for the potential teacher to see a successful rural program in operation; it would also present rural teaching as an inspiration and a challenge rather than as a burden. First priority in the program would be given to Penn School graduates, and in this way Miss Cooley could be somewhat assured that her protégés would not stray. Eventually the teacher-training program would become a reality, with Penn School and the state college for Negroes cooperating under the aegis of the state board of education and with the General Education Board providing the funds for the endeavor. Penn also won accreditation from the state of South Carolina, with permission as well to retain the freedom it had always enjoyed in developing its curriculum.[38]

The experience of the teacher-training program reflects two of Miss Cooley's continuing strategies and explains a large part of her success. She always described the Penn effort in terms that would appeal to the available sources of support, and she couched her appeal in terms of usefulness to others. In this instance she managed to retain control of her own program while assuring the kind of teacher training she desired, and at the same time she was able to extend the Penn School influence to a much larger group of young girls. While maintaining her autonomy, she was able to establish herself as an important ally of the county and the state and to further her own objectives of influencing southern educational development. And she accomplished all of this without incurring additional expense for herself or her trustees, convincing the General Education Board to finance the whole project. She was a skillful woman, with a lot of ambition and a lot of brass, and through it all she remained as charming and as genuinely gracious as it was possible for a lady to be.

In the twenties Miss Cooley had believed that Penn's influence was felt more fully in Africa and other foreign lands than in her own country. Visitors from India, China, Japan, the East and West Indies, South America, New Zealand, and Africa had found in Penn a solution to the educational problems of a backward

38. Cooley to Leo Favrot, June 4, 1935, Felton to Cooley, September 26, 1935, Trustees' minutes, February 5, 1931, "Annual Report," 1936, p. 1, all in PSP.

people.³⁹ The experiences of the thirties convinced Miss Cooley that Penn could serve a greater purpose as an example, and as a guide, in the South's struggles to educate her black citizens and to preserve her rural communities.

By the end of the thirties Miss Cooley could write to a contributor of her conviction that "South Carolina and the South generally is closely allied with Penn and needs this school and community to help in the larger educational program which we can see being worked out in the southern states."⁴⁰ Rossa Cooley was in her finest hour, and she never perceived that the tides of fortune had washed away the substance of her pride, leaving her poised on a foundation of ideas and assumptions that was deceptively attractive but that could no longer bear the weight of St. Helena's ponderous economic problems.

39. Cooley to Ralph Rounds, December 4, 1940, in PSP.
40. *Ibid.*

11

The Outside Presses In

In the twenties Miss Cooley had often relaxed at Ndulamo, surrounded by serene tidal rivers and marshes, completely removed from the riot of activity that was Penn School. In this atmosphere of calm and peace, she was able to reflect on the work she was doing, to put it in perspective and examine its larger meanings and possibilities. She did not deceive herself; she knew that despite the lavish praise her work had received, many years would have to pass before lasting results could be measured.[1]

There was much promise in all that she had accomplished. Everywhere she looked she could see evidence of improved standards of living and nobler conceptions of life. But the larger questions could not yet be answered, and these were the questions on which the success or failure of the Penn School experiment ultimately rested: "Will the homes of the free continue in their own hands? Will the children of this generation continue the struggle that means real freedom?"[2]

The passage of time held a cruel fate for Miss Cooley and her aspirations for the people of the island. The arrival of the bridge and the emergence of the New Negro had already conspired to undermine her cultural influence on St. Helena Island. The boll weevil had obliterated the economic basis of the islanders' lives,

1. Cooley, *School Acres*, 90.
2. Cooley, *Homes of the Freed*, 158.

and the disastrous failure of the white potato crop had overcome those farmers who had been courageous and resourceful enough to follow the leadership of the credit union. By the end of the twenties, St. Helena Island had already been suffering from a severe agricultural depression for ten years, and the efforts to find a new cash crop had been entirely without success. Weather conditions and natural disasters continued to plague the island; and with the collapse of the national economic structure, St. Helena plunged into an economic chaos from which it has never recovered.

In 1931 a drought hit the island; yielding only four showers from May to October, it continued well into 1932, only to be followed by torrential rains. Predictably, the crops were very poor in those years, rendering the island farmers even more vulnerable to the nation's deepening economic distress. In 1932 Macdonald, Wilkins and Company closed, and one of the banks in Beaufort failed. Soon thereafter, the one major industry on the island—the oyster canning factories—collapsed, throwing 37 percent of all island families into the relief class and seriously threatening an additional 50 percent of the people who had used factory wages to supplement their income from farming. Thus, 87 percent of the island families found themselves with insufficient food and no money at all to buy clothes or pay taxes.[3]

In 1930 thirty-four people in St. Helena Township had forfeited their land because of inability to pay the taxes, and in 1931 forty-six more followed suit. Many had traditionally relied on relatives in the cities to send them money for taxes, and now, of course, this source of support had vanished. In all, the people lost 268 acres in these two years. (Fortunately, one of Penn's old friends, Dr. Arthur Elting of Albany, New York, bought much of the forfeited land because he maintained a vacation home and a hunting preserve on the island; thus, the land did not fall into the hands of any "down-and-out poor whites," which was Miss Cooley's greatest fear.) People who had left the island and were doing badly in the cities were also ready to listen to offers for their land,

---

3. Cooley to trustees, October 10, 1931, Trustees' minutes, October 28, 1932, "Journal of the Rural School Exploration," 9, all in PSP.

and the basis of Miss Cooley's whole economic program seemed to be disintegrating fairly rapidly. Miss Cooley despaired to think that the islanders might lose their birthright of land, for she feared that if the land were lost "the upward trend will be that much the more retarded."[4]

In 1932 the money crop had failed completely, though the corn and potato yields were good and there was no fear of starvation. A bitterly cold winter caused more suffering and distress than the island had seen since the great storm of 1911, and many people had to ask for help who had never asked for it before. The county made Miss Cooley chairman of the relief committee for St. Helena Township, so she was able to provide food for the hungry and work for the able; but of course she could not give them all the help they needed. Penn School also served as the Red Cross center for the island for the distribution of flour and clothing, as well as the center for all state and county relief agencies.[5]

Completely apolitical, the islanders looked to Penn instead of to the government for relief. Though they must have been aware of the larger world around them, there is no indication that they identified themselves with one political party or the other or that they even grasped the significance of the major issues concerning the rest of the country. While the rest of the nation's desperate and downtrodden were looking to Franklin D. Roosevelt as a father figure and savior, the island blacks still thought in terms of Uncle Sam. As one of the old women said to a relief worker, who was trying to organize a recreation project and despairing because she could find none but matriarchs on the relief rolls, "We *'blong* to Uncle Sam, Miss Crisenten, if he want us for jump, praise God, we can jump til we drop."[6]

Miss Cooley retained her boundless faith and optimism even through a disastrous failure in the marketing of turkeys and a fairly severe hurricane that led to a serious outbreak of malaria

---

4. Report of the Beaufort County Legislative Delegation, April 11, 1933, Cooley to trustees, October 10, 1931, January 22, 1936, Cooley to James, January 9, 1933, all in PSP; Cooley, "Education in the Soil," 5.

5. Cooley to Mrs. Lent, November 15, 1932, Cooley to Jane [?], November 15, 1932, Cooley to James, January 9, 1933, Trustees' minutes, January 31, 1933, all in PSP.

6. Helen [Christensen?] to Cooley, August 5, 1935, in PSP.

and that destroyed the greater part of the crops following a hopeful planting and growing season. She wrote to one of her large contributors that she believed new strength would come to many people as a result of their struggle, and that "the going through makes our days full of excitement and planning." Her good spirits may have been bolstered by the fact that few of the islanders were migrating to the cities in the face of the continuing depression. As Benjamin Barnwell explained, "Before the depression, with high wages in the North and the boll weevil in the South, there was every temptation to leave the farms"; but the reduction, if not curtailment, of wages in the cities had reversed the tide of migration, returning men to their farms where at least they would not starve.[7]

Doubtless, Miss Cooley was also encouraged by the enthusiastic response her work now began to receive from state and federal officials who visited the island investigating relief activities. Most of the relief work on the island took the form of ditching, an endeavor to assure proper drainage that had never received the kind of attention it should have had. As chairman of the local relief committee, Miss Cooley put many island men to work in this important area, thus accomplishing one of her long-sought goals. Then reports began to circulate in Beaufort that the island farmers had abandoned their farming, choosing to live instead on the beneficence of the government. The farm demonstration agent, Benjamin Barnwell, disclaimed this idea vigorously, explaining that the extended drought had forced the farmers to accept relief employment in order to earn something on which to farm the next year. "To give food and clothing to strong and healthy people is distasteful, encourages laziness and is a challenge to our self-respect," he wrote to the Beaufort *Gazette*, revealing his thorough absorption of the values and ideals Penn School had worked to instill.[8]

The investigators from the South Carolina Emergency Relief

---

7. Cooley to Peabody, October 21, 1935, in GFP; "Superintendent's Report, 1934–1935," Cooley to W. C. Dougall, October 16, 1935, Barnwell to E. O. Wilson, January 3, 1933, all in PSP.

8. Beaufort *Gazette*, November 15, 1934, clipping, in PSP.

Administration supported Barnwell's claims of a self-respecting citizenry on St. Helena, and they laid all the credit at the door of Penn School. They chose ten of the island families, all Penn School graduates, to participate in a program of rural rehabilitation, claiming that no finer field for rehabilitation could be found than on St. Helena Island. As the district supervisor of the rural rehabilitation program wrote to Miss Cooley, "Whatever success we achieve, I hope all concerned will feel as I do that Penn School 'killed the Bear' and all we did was make it a fine 'pelt.' "[9]

The rural rehabilitation program sought contented, thrifty, honest men with experience in agriculture, proposing to make an example of them by helping them get back on their feet. St. Helena Island seemed to be ideally suited for these purposes, and the Emergency Relief Administration had no trouble finding qualified men to seize the new opportunity. The administrators were particularly impressed with the islanders' desire to get off the relief rolls and become self-sustaining once again. Some of them attended one of the annual Farmers' Fairs, and they were flabbergasted to find such a sincere and earnest interest in enlightened agriculture among Negroes. One administrator wrote, "Miss Cooley and Miss House have done a remarkable work, and their services are reflected in the educational and agricultural background that has been instilled in the negroes who once were considered as farm hands not hardly capable of being educated." On the whole, the rural rehabilitation officials approved the simplicity and dignity of St. Helena's blacks, as well as their contentment in remaining on the island; and they concluded that the St. Helena blacks were ideal clients for their program.[10]

As gratifying as this must have been to Miss Cooley and as reassuring that her educational program was bearing fruit, the rehabilitation of ten families hardly affected the desperate conditions on the island. Slowly, Miss Cooley began to perceive that farming and education would no longer suffice for the people of

9. Louis Le Conte, supervisor of rural relief, to R. E. Sims, state director, October 18, 1934, "ERA Aiding the Negro Farmers St. Helena Island," 1934, clipping, Le Conte to Cooley, October 18, 1934, all in PSP.

10. "Rural Rehabilitation on St. Helena Island," Columbia *State*, November 28, 1934, "ERA Aiding the Negro Farmers St. Helena Island," clipping, both in PSP.

St. Helena, that what they needed was work, and work of a permanent character. In the days before the boll weevil, cotton had assured taxes, clothes, and other things that money can buy. But the boll weevil ate up that sense of security as well as the cotton, and now the school as well as the people faced "an economic situation that may dwarf or even destroy the future of the boys and girls."[11]

Upon realizing the inadequacies of small-scale farming on St. Helena Island, Miss Cooley and Miss House began to develop a long-range rehabilitation project for the island that they could present to a state or federal relief agency. This project would involve a comprehensive attack on all aspects of the community's problems, including farming, home life, health and sanitation, and the languishing cooperative organizations. Under each of these headings the ladies listed numerous activities that could profitably engage the labor of the island's men, and they must have trembled with excitement as they contemplated the possibility of the government's assuming responsibility for all these community activities that Penn School had traditionally sponsored.

They presented their plan first to the South Carolina Federal Emergency Relief Administration. Mr. William Keyserling, formerly of Macdonald, Wilkins and Company, also attended, opening the meeting by expressing his appreciation of the island's dependable and worthy black people. Miss Cooley explained the long-continued beneficent influences of the school as well as the present status of rehabilitation work on the island. Apparently, however, the officials had already decided against the St. Helena rehabilitation project, one of them declaring his opposition to a federal project taking the project from county and state administration and indicating that he would bitterly resent the adoption of St. Helena for such a special program.[12]

The South Carolina Penn School trustee, Dr. W. H. Mills of Clemson College, urged Miss Cooley not to expect any assistance from this group: "Not one of them knows anything about the sub-

11. Trustees' minutes, January 29, 1934, "Annual Report of the Penn Normal, Industrial and Agricultural School," 1934, both in PSP.
12. Cooley to W. H. Mills, April 7, 1935, in PSP.

ject, and every one is a political appointee." Soon word came from the regional director of the Emergency Relief Administration advising the ladies that their proposal had been rejected. Dr. Mills, however, continued to work on the situation through some of his friends at Columbia, hoping to secure a reversal of the decision.[13]

In the meantime a tropical storm struck the Sea Islands, rendering the relief situation more critical than ever. Beaufort County's meager relief roll had been sharply pared just prior to the hurricane's arrival, with the thought that these subsistence farmers could survive on the little patches of cotton, corn, and potatoes around their cabins. Now those were gone. Furthermore, the only relief work available in the county was at the marine base at Parris Island, and transportation to the island cost $1.20 a week. Any man who declined the work at Parris Island found himself ineligible for further relief projects; and since the Parris Island project was thus unable to secure its quota of workers, no new relief projects could be started in the county. It was an enormous bureaucratic mess, and in the meantime Beaufort County's blacks suffered.[14]

William Keyserling's son, Leon, had grown up on the island, and he had developed a high regard for the Penn School endeavor. By 1935 he had become one of President Roosevelt's leading economic advisors and a close friend of Rexford Guy Tugwell, director of the Resettlement Administration. In March of 1932 young Keyserling had taken Tugwell with him to St. Helena Island, and they had visited the school. Now Miss Cooley drew on this association to place the island's case before the federal government. She also drew on her acquaintance with Will W. Alexander, assistant director of the Resettlement Administration. Alexander had had at least a passing acquaintance with L. Hollingsworth Wood in the twenties, and George Foster Peabody had been one of the original sponsors of Alexander's Interracial Commission. Furthermore, Thomas Jackson Woofter, a new Penn School trustee, was now working in Washington as a coordinator

13. W. H. Mills to Cooley, April 8, June 28, 1935, Cooley to W. A. Hartman, May 27, 1935, all in PSP.
14. Harvey to Senator James F. Byrnes, September 7, 1935, in PSP.

of rural research for the Works Progress Administration, and he used his influence to win for the Penn School program a hearing with the government.[15]

In the immediate crisis caused by the hurricane, Miss Cooley ignored the bureaucratic hierarchy and went directly to Alexander to secure some relief work for the island. Alexander called the field representative of the Works Progress Administration, who called the state director of the WPA, who called the director of Projects and Planning, who called the Public Health Service engineer who was in charge of the statewide malarial control project; and within a week, a small number of men had been put to work digging ditches on St. Helena Island.[16]

Will Alexander assured Miss Cooley that she should let him know if he could be of any further help to her; and since he could, she did. She sent him a copy of the rehabilitation program she and Miss House had drawn up, suggesting that his office should accept responsibility for the plight of the landowners on St. Helena. She knew that her program would take years to develop, but she felt that a beginning should be made; and with the leadership and backing of Penn School, she felt that "an experiment could be worked out that would be of permanent value to all of rural America." It was the same old appeal, but it was new to the government, and it intrigued them. Furthermore, Miss Cooley sent a copy of her most recent annual report, which included a lengthy description of Abraham Lincoln's interest in the Negroes at Port Royal and his feeling about the necessity of federal aid for this group of islands. As Miss Cooley pointedly concluded her letter to Alexander: "That hoped-for experiment did not go through, but isn't it possible now for the backing so sorely needed to be given?"[17]

15. Arthur Meier Schlesinger, Jr., *The Coming of the New Deal* (Boston, 1958), 96–97; Ware, *George Foster Peabody*, 188–90; Wood to Cooley, April 30, 1924, Trustees' minutes, October 15, 1931, Woofter to Cooley, March 6, 1937, all in PSP.

16. Lawrence M. Pinckney to Alan Johnstone, November 19, 1935, Johnstone to Will W. Alexander, November 19, 1935, Alexander to House, November 22, 1935, Cooley to Alexander, November 29, 1935, all in PSP.

17. Alexander to House, November 22, 1935, Cooley to Alexander, November 28, 1935, both in PSP.

One of Alexander's subordinates soon wrote to Miss Cooley asking for more specific information about the landowners in danger of losing their lands because of delinquent taxes. Miss Cooley responded that 356 persons stood to lose $7,561.48 worth of land at the next tax sale, to be held within a month. Apparently she expected Alexander's organization to step into the breach and provide loans for these landowners ("I advise loans to be made to all who are worthy," she wrote Alexander, "and direct help to be given to old people and those physically handicapped"), but her letter reached his office along with an appeal for several thousand people on the mainland in the same situation. Learning that an owner had a year in which to redeem his property, Alexander decided that his office should try to deal with the situation as a whole to determine whether they could find a program that might bring some degree of help. Alexander, therefore, referred the matter to the new regional director of the Resettlement Administration, R. W. Hudgens, encouraging him to develop a comprehensive program for the area and suggesting pointedly (he sent a copy of these instructions to Miss Cooley) that Hudgens get in touch with the two ladies "because they have been pressing our office here on this matter which is really a regional function."[18]

In the meantime William Keyserling also submitted a proposal to the Resettlement Administration outlining his ideas on the course the government ought to pursue in rehabilitating the coastal regions. He prefaced his report with a protestation of his belief that once again emancipation must come from without, that any relief measures designed to help black people through the state machinery "would be thwarted and dwarfed by prejudice and politics," and that unless the federal government managed to help the Negroes through local agencies, they were lost.[19]

Basically, his proposal called for a plan of cooperation or collective-individualistic farming based on farm centers provided by the government. Each center would be divided into areas for

18. James C. Derieux to Cooley, November 13, 1935, Cooley to Alexander, January 22, 1936, Alexander to Cooley, February 10, 1936, Alexander to R. W. Hudgens, February 10, 1936, all in PSP.
19. William Keyserling to Hudgens, April 6, 1936, in PSP.

community pastures, reforestation plots, housing of machinery, and homesteads. The state extension service would formulate all farming operations with an eye to cash returns, as well as sustenance. The homes on the homesteads would be built according to the needs of the homesteaders and could be bought over a period of years with the proceeds of farming operations. The operations of these centers would be carried on under the supervision of practical farmers on a cooperative or collective basis with regard to items that could not as easily or profitably be handled by the individual farmer; all other items would be handled on an individual basis with regard to responsibility and benefits. Keyserling also included provisions for a form of tenantry for those whose home acres had become exhausted but could be rebuilt through cover cropping, and also for repatriates from industrial centers.[20]

In a benedictional conclusion that revealed his complete surrender to New Deal assumptions, Keyserling declared, "Our people, inured to hardships, would be satisfied with reasonable comforts of the pioneer; they would be happy in the thought of better days and greater comforts ahead, assured by the guidance of the Administration, the Extension Service and sympathetic local Committees."[21]

Miss Cooley and Miss House had been in close touch with Keyserling in the formulation of his ideas, and they heartily approved the letter he sent to Hudgens, since every day showed more clearly that something needed to be done.[22] The Keyserling program was doomed to fail, however, because of a number of distressing realities.

First, Keyserling was unable to secure enough land for his program on St. Helena Island because Dr. Elting refused to sacrifice his shooting rights, and he owned the best land on the island. Dr. Elting had been a good friend of Penn School—always giving tractors, mules, or school buses whenever Miss Cooley presented him with a special appeal. He frequently brought friends to the school to hear the spirituals when he was on the island, and

20. *Ibid.*
21. *Ibid.*
22. Cooley to Woofter, April 30, 1936, in PSP.

he often conferred with Miss Cooley about various problems, offering advice and encouragement. But his reason for coming to the island was to shoot the game that abounded on his preserve—since long before the Civil War the rights over quail, deer, and duck had been reserved to the white owners of the island's hunting preserves—and he did not feel that his duty to Penn School extended to relinquishing the land he had been able to add to his holdings during the depression.[23]

William Keyserling knew that representatives of the Resettlement Administration planned to visit St. Helena in the near future, and he feared that they would report unfavorably on the project if he did not present them with an alternative. Consequently, he located three thousand acres on Ladies Island, reasonably priced and separated from St. Helena only by a tidal river. Unfortunately, however, Benjamin Barnwell felt that it would be very difficult to find industrious and desirable farmers on Ladies Island. "They are not real farmers now," he had written Miss House, "and are not doing as well as they could on the land they do have." Barnwell felt that the project would be a failure if it had to depend on getting fifty or a hundred families from Ladies Island, and he doubted that St. Helena people would go over there. He even felt doubtful about such a project on St. Helena, although he thought an educational campaign would increase the likelihood of success.[24]

The representative from the Resettlement Administration spent four days on St. Helena and then submitted a report very similar to Keyserling's proposal. He suggested that the government buy 100,000 acres of potential farmland in the coastal regions, on which they would develop corporation farms to be worked by area blacks. He stressed the necessity of education and

---

23. House to Cooley, November 6, 1936, Trustees' minutes, January 30, 1934, "Report of Penn School, 1931–1932," Cooley to contributor, February 9, 1938, Cooley to trustees, January 22, 1936, all in PSP; Woofter, *Black Yeomanry*, 222. One of Dr. Elting's close friends has explained that the Albany physician wanted to do whatever was expected of a man of his station and that he wanted to be "in the spirit of things" at Penn School but that he had no great commitment to Penn's educational or cultural objectives. Interview with John Davis Hatch, Jr., June 17, 1971, Lenox, Mass.

24. House to Cooley, November 6, 1936, in PSP.

supervision, as well as a long-run health program, but he believed that potentially the area offered a good opportunity for doing some very profitable work.[25]

Regional Director Hudgens forwarded all these proposals to Penn School's Dr. Mills, asking for his comments and evaluation. Dr. Mills had given considerable thought to St. Helena's problems, and he had concluded that the greatest needs were pastures and wages. (He had thought at one time that truck farming was the answer to the ravages of the boll weevil, but experience had taught him that trucking was quite risky for small farmers unless they diversified.) Since the livestock ran at large on the island at certain seasons, year-round gardens were exceedingly difficult to maintain, and this accounted for the inadequate diets of the majority of the people. Only if the people developed sodded, year-round pastures would they be able to acquire better gardens, milk, and meat, Dr. Mills believed, but he realized that such pastures could not be developed and maintained by individuals. So he suggested that government-sponsored pasturage should be the first order of business on St. Helena.[26]

Dr. Mills supported the idea of a corporation farm, if by this the government meant a large farm on which the people could work for wages and not be responsible for any deficit that might occur. He vehemently opposed the idea of cooperative farming, however, suggesting that such enterprises generally lasted through only one generation and succeeded only insofar as the cooperators were bound together by some powerful motive, such as a common religious interest. He concluded that neither he nor the state extension service had been able to find anything permanent to take the place of Sea Island cotton and that community pastures and corporation farms were the enterprises the government could most profitably develop on St. Helena Island.[27]

Apparently the senior Keyserling had more than a humanitarian interest in the blacks of the coastal regions. He had suf-

25. Frate Bull to Hudgens, November 19, 1936, in PSP.
26. W. H. Mills to Hudgens, December 4, 1936, in PSP.
27. W. H. Mills to House, December 4, 1936, W. H. Mills to Hudgens, December 4, 1936, both in PSP.

fered heavy losses when Macdonald, Wilkins and Company fell victim to the depression, and now he hoped to recoup those losses by developing a new cotton empire on the island, for which he would be sole agent. He became extremely impatient with Penn School, and especially with Benjamin Barnwell, for refusing to support his campaign to return the people to a one-crop economy, even going so far as to initiate a movement to oust Barnwell from his post as demonstration agent. All such decisions had to pass through Clemson College, however, and Dr. Mills protected Barnwell's interests against the onslaughts of Keyserling and his political friends.[28]

Keyserling did manage, however, to block Miss Cooley's efforts toward rehabilitation on the island. His proposals had taken precedence over hers with the authorities at the Resettlement Administration; and when she became aware of Keyserling's manipulations, Miss Cooley tried once again to place her rehabilitation project before the government. This time she used methods more to her taste and liking than the dry, written proposal. Through Woofter, she invited Will W. Alexander, now head of the Resettlement Administration, and M. L. Wilson, undersecretary of agriculture, to come to Penn School for the celebration of its seventy-fifth anniversary. This was a glorious occasion full of speeches and appreciations, and it showed Penn School to good advantage. Alexander and Wilson received a grand tour of the island, seeing both farmers who were prospering and those who needed help, and then Miss Cooley laid her plan before them once again. Despite all her considerable efforts, however, the two gentlemen concluded that the St. Helena situation, while impressive, was not typical of the coastal regions, and they rejected her proposals. In an unusual moment of discouragement Miss Cooley wrote to Jackson Davis, "I begin to think that everything connected with the government is inelastic and can't be made to fit so simple a community as our Sea Island group." But it was not long before she was submitting another proposal for federal aid for the Sea Islands.[29]

28. W. H. Mills to House, December 4, 1936, Woofter to Cooley, March 6, 1937, Barnwell to Cooley, August 4, 1937, all in PSP.

29. Woofter to Cooley, March 6, 1937, Cooley to J. Davis, May 9, 1939, both in PSP.

In 1936 the National Youth Administration had chosen Penn School as one of the eight schools in South Carolina to be an NYA work center, thereby providing jobs and wages for a number of young men who had been unable to find work. This eased the unemployment situation on the island somewhat, but as the depression lengthened, more and more young boys and girls set their sights on the cities as centers of fun and employment, Penn School graduates among them. The young people usually finished high school without any money to begin farming, and their parents were unable to get them started in the farming business. With only education as capital, and unable to borrow as the white boys could, they drifted off to the cities, hoping to return to the farm when they had secured adequate capital. Enthusiasm for the rural life evaporated in the cities; as the young people got settled there, they feared to give up their jobs and face an uncertain future.[30]

Miss Cooley began to realize that her best graduates, those who should have been the backbone of the St. Helena community, were being forced off the land and into the cities; and she turned to the government once again to help her hold her young. She met Mary McLeod Bethune, director of the Division of Negro Affairs of the National Youth Administration, in Washington and discussed with her the problems of her rural community. The NYA had already developed programs to help young people go on to college, and Mrs. Bethune suggested that perhaps her agency could sponsor a similar scholarship program to help young farmers set themselves up in farming. Miss Cooley enthusiastically drew up a plan for Farm Home Scholarships and sent it to Mrs. Bethune, reminding her that it was a pity for such young men and women to lose themselves when their parents owned land and when the training at Penn had enabled them to make a living. Miss Cooley's plan did not fit anything that was already being done, but she hoped that the government would realize that there were hundreds of young people in rural communities across the country who were in a similar situation. As Miss Cooley wrote to the state director of the NYA, "I believe that many high schools

---

30. Cooley to trustees, January 22, 1936, Cooley to contributors, April 19, 1939, Cooley to Roger L. Coe, October 17, 1938, all in PSP.

in our rural state of South Carolina would be glad to modify their more academic training to the kind of education which would fit their young people to meet the problems of rural life enthusiastically," if only they could be as assured of future assistance in such an undertaking as they were for the college-bound group. "It seems to me," Miss Cooley concluded, "that our rural sections would be able to hold the best in a group that is now being lost in the cities."[31]

Miss Cooley turned once again to Will Alexander for assistance, and also to Aubrey Williams, hoping that perhaps a program could be worked out in conjunction with the Farm Security Administration. The Farm Home Loan plan came to naught, however, and a few months later Miss Cooley gave up all hope of receiving government aid. She had lost valuable time, though she had gained some important contacts for the school and the island, but now she turned her attention once again to solving St. Helena's problems through private philanthropy.[32]

As Miss Cooley took stock of the island's problems, she realized that St. Helena and Penn School had finally reached the situation they knew they must face when the bridge was built. The young people must now either take hold of the land or lose it. The whole economic basis of the experiment was at stake. "And I am sure we shall have to do more than give guidance," she wrote to Dr. Mills; "practical help in the way of loans to high school graduates is vital." But the school had fallen on hard times financially, and securing a loan fund without interfering with the regular contributions was a problem. Dr. Mills even suggested using the school's own principal to make loans to students or to buy land on the island, and Miss Cooley considered the suggestion carefully, which gives some indication of the critical nature of the situation.[33]

Miraculously it seemed, and in the best Penn School tradi-

31. Cooley to W. H. Mills, September 19, 1938, Cooley to Coe, October 17, 1938, Cooley to Mary McLeod Bethune, September 30, 1938, Cooley to Coe, October 17, 1938, all in PSP.
32. Karl Borders to Cooley, November 1, 1938, Cooley to W. H. Mills, May 31, 1939, both in PSP.
33. Cooley to W. H. Mills, May 31, 1939, in PSP.

tion, the money for a Student Farm Loan Fund came unexpectedly. Mr. and Mrs. W. W. Smith II of Smith Brothers Cough Drops fame sent Miss Cooley a check to establish such a fund. Breathlessly, Miss Cooley wrote to the Smiths of her elation, "What *fun* it all is, and I am dreadfully excited and wondrously happy—and now we must do it all exactly right and I'll be keeping you both in close touch."[34]

Immediately she posted the news of the fund at strategic points around the island, instructing graduates and former students of high school rank to get in touch with members of the Loan Fund Committee for details. "These loans depend on good character," she wrote, "and it is our hope that all those who wish to stay in the community and establish their own home will be able to do so." Miss Cooley also wrote letters to former students who had left the island, encouraging them to return now that funds were available to set them up in farming. There is little evidence of the response to this program, or the effects it had on the island, although there is one rather discouraging letter from the school bookkeeper to Solomon Hamilton, Jr.: "Miss Cooley would be very much disappointed to learn that you had sold the cattle without advising the school, and left the State without turning in the cash, especially when you have a chattel mortgage recorded in the Court House."[35]

The St. Helena Cooperative Society and Credit Union had suffered throughout the depression, but at the end of the thirties they received a new breath of life when the General Education Board sponsored a trip to Nova Scotia for four of the Penn School men to study cooperative endeavors there. Another group of men also took an extended tour through the American West to study cooperatives, and they returned to St. Helena filled with a new enthusiasm and the knowledge to give it substance. The men reorganized their program and doubled their membership, but St. Helena needed far more than enthusiasm and a will to succeed.

34. Cooley to Mr. and Mrs. W. W. Smith, February 14, 1940, in PSP.
35. "Report of the Farm Loan Fund," February 20, 1940, Henry M. Jenkins to Cooley, February 19, 1940, H. M. Rollins to Solomon P. Hamilton, Jr., July 29, 1941, all in PSP.

As Dr. Mills wrote to Miss Cooley shortly before his death: "The future of the Negro farmers on St. Helena concerns me more than their present. What are they going to do? What is the School going to plan for them? . . . As I see it, the pattern of life must be radically changed."[36]

Penn School was never able to change that pattern of life. Ultimately, as was to happen in communities across the country, World War II put an end to the depression on St. Helena, but the war also disrupted farm life so completely that women, children, and old men were left to carry on the work. Penn School had found no solution to the complex agricultural problems introduced by the boll weevil, and it certainly had no control over the adverse conditions that continued to plague the island in the thirties. In 1938 an epidemic had struck the island killing horses and mules, and this was followed by a year-long drought. The Penn School farm manager planted his 1939 crops early in the fall of 1938 to offset the shortage caused by the drought, and through constant watering he managed to secure a good stand of vegetables. And then the weather changed again. "The season had been very warm till about the first of January," he wrote to Miss Cooley, "when a double frost which happened overnight hurt most severely all crops." The next year brought another hurricane, this one as severe as the great storm of 1911; and only the extra cash brought in from the defense work at Parris Island kept many of the families from destitution. Again in 1941 the island suffered another drought, and even the indomitable Miss Cooley admitted the discouragement of the small farmer's life. "The sand seems to come up to one's ankles," she wrote to Francis Cope, "and all the gardens are 'through making the struggle.' The worst of it is the discouragement in trying to make a go of agriculture, but a go without stopping is essential!" As Miss House had written just a few years before, she and Miss Cooley had come to the conclusion that the farmer's life is the biggest gamble there is, and

---

36. "Superintendent's Report," 1934–35, Trustees' minutes, January 29, 1935, St. Helena Cooperative and Credit Union minutes, March 8, 1940, Cooley to trustees, January 25, 1943, "Report of Committee on Resolutions, Cooperative Credit Union," January 25, 1940, W. H. Mills to Cooley, November 30, 1940, all in PSP.

yet they had been unable to fashion an economic life free from the ravages of weather and natural disaster.[37]

In an earlier time, in the halcyon days of cotton and easy living from the sea, when St. Helena was a world unto itself and Penn School was the source of all things noble and good, the island could afford an experiment in Negro education, an object-lesson, a laboratory, and an outlet for Yankee charity, service, and guilt. The world had changed, however, and the assumptions of the old experiment no longer sufficed. The ideal of a happy yeomanry had been a white ideal; and as the Negro found his strength and his voice, he rejected the white man's solution to the "Negro Problem." Rossa Belle Cooley was not equipped to deal with the complex agricultural problems the boll weevil brought in its wake; she had no solutions to the yearnings of a rural people for the stimulation and excitement of the city; and despite her protestations of usefulness and service, she was unable to maintain on St. Helena a viable, self-sustaining community. The fault was not all hers. Economic conditions and natural disasters were quite beyond her control, but her emphasis on character-building and proof of the Negro's ability grew out of the assumptions of an earlier age. The twentieth century arrived on St. Helena sometime in the thirties; and though Miss Cooley would never understand what had happened, Penn School had become an anachronism.

37. Rollins to Paul Brown, June 2, 1941, W. H. Mills to Cope, November 29, 1941, Cooley to Miss Jessie Nunnally, September 8, 1943, Trustees' minutes, October 27, 1943, Cooley to W. H. Mills, September 19, 1938, Benjamin Washington, "Annual Report of the Farm, 1938–1939," May 15, 1939, Cooley to Cope, June 3, 1941, all in PSP; House, "Roads of Learning on St. Helena Island," 8.

12

Years of Struggle

"Stir us to desperate faith; drive us to the undertaking of impossible tasks"—such was Miss Cooley's frequent prayer as she lay awake in the early morning hours, contemplating the unfinished business still before her.[1] As the Great Depression settled down on the American countryside, many believed desperate faith to be the only solution to the problems that swirled about their lives. For a school such as Penn, however, dependent as it was on private beneficence, much more than faith was needed to deal with the impossible tasks they would face during the depression years.

The collapse of the national economic structure simply increased and prolonged the economic depression St. Helena Islanders had been suffering since the arrival of the boll weevil in 1919. The loss of a cash crop and the failure to find a suitable substitute coupled with the bad weather conditions of the 1920s had played havoc with the islanders' desire to hold on to their land and to make a success of farming; Miss Cooley was determined, however, that these adverse conditions would not frustrate the people's desire to educate their children, thus jeopardizing even further her experiment and her dreams for the blacks of St. Helena Island. Consequently, in 1931 she agreed to accept labor and produce from the parents in lieu of cash for

1. "A Day's Work at Penn School," n.d., in JMD.

Years of Struggle   221

the school fees. While making it possible for many parents to keep their children in school, this action reduced the amount of cash available for operating expenses just at the time that large numbers of former contributors discontinued their subscriptions to the Penn effort. Penn had gone into the year of 1931 with an indebtedness of $13,000, and by the end of the year that figure had increased to $20,000. As they became increasingly aware that funds would be severely diminished because of the depression, Miss Cooley and Miss House began to curtail expenses at every possible point.[2]

In the summer of 1931 the two ladies had reluctantly discontinued the summer term. The All-Year School had caused a deficit in Penn's financing every year since it began in 1917, and now it had to be abandoned, although Miss Cooley was sorely disappointed to have to end her most celebrated innovation. Miss Cooley and Miss House also eliminated all expenditures for repairs and equipment. Originally, of course, this was intended as a temporary expedient; but as the depression lengthened, the school plant fell increasingly into a state of disrepair, and the equipment depreciated severely. Although foundation grants eventually repaired or replaced the most glaring inadequacies, the school never recovered its predepression level of efficiency.[3]

At Miss Cooley's recommendation, the trustees also voted to turn over the basketry shop and the cobbling and harness-making shop to the community, hoping that the two instructors for these shops might be able to supplement their half-time pay by doing community and farm work in their free time. Unfortunately, the demand for baskets and shoes declined drastically under depression conditions, and these instructors found it difficult to find either work or cash, thus causing them serious personal problems.[4]

The one economy measure that saved the school a consider-

2. Cooley to trustees, October 10, 1931, in PSP; "Two Women on an Atlantic Island," 5.
3. Trustees' minutes, February 5, June 4, 1931, Cooley to Edwin Embree, January 4, 1934, PSP.
4. Trustees' minutes, February 2, 1932, Cooley to trustees, January 22, 1936, both in PSP.

able amount of money during each of the next few years also revealed the extent of Penn's hold on the imagination and loyalty of its teachers. In a Sunday night chapel service in the fall of 1931, Miss Cooley called all the Penn School workers together to discuss the school's financial crisis. After considering the seriousness of the situation, the workers resolved to subscribe 5 percent of their salaries to help the trustees raise the budget for 1931–1932. The resolution to the trustees read in part, "We want you to feel that we would hearten you in your efforts during this critical year, for we realize that new subscribers will be hard to find, and that old subscribers will find it more difficult to carry on." In a spirit of genuine selflessness and sacrifice, the teachers wrote to Miss Cooley confirming their decision. "I am glad for the privilege of giving 5% of my salary toward the Penn School budget," wrote Benjamin Barnwell. "We have always been happy and felt it an honor to be able in a small way to help shoulder the heavy load," wrote Fred and Salome Fripp; and from Aurelius J. Brown came a sentiment apparently shared by all: "With my honest prayer for all schools and institutions which point the way to a higher and better life. My only regret is that I cannot give more." The elimination of the All-Year School had reduced the salaries of most of the workers; even so, the following year some of them voluntarily reduced their salaries an additional 10 to 15 percent. For these men and women whose income was small in the best of times, this was dedication and commitment of the highest order, and it reflected these workers' conception of their roles as participants in a lofty and ennobling enterprise.[5]

The annual report for 1932 expressed the need for a radical reduction in operating expenses without seriously crippling the usefulness of the school. Throughout the thirties this was the common aim of Miss Cooley, the workers, and the trustees; but with the severe loss of income, the school also lost the flexibility it needed to adjust to the needs and demands of the community.

---

5. Cooley to trustees, October 26, 1931, Barnwell to Cooley, October 26, 1931, Fred and Salome Fripp to Cooley, October 26, 1931, A. J. Brown to Cooley, October 26, 1931, all in PSP; "Faith Versus Depression and Encouragement Versus Drought," n.d., 3, in JMD.

Under depression conditions nearly all private institutions suffered a reduction of income and a stabilization of growth, but Penn's failure to secure adequate funds in these years must ultimately be explained as a failure of resourcefulness and initiative on the part of the trustees.

In the early years of the depression, the trustees continued their uninspired attempts to raise funds. At the trustees' meeting in October, 1933, the new publicity chairman, A. C. Maule, again urged the board members to find new contributors. In a telling commentary on his committee's resourcefulness, he acknowledged that appeals such as Penn School's flooded the mails and were not the best possible way to raise money, but he suggested no alternative solution to Penn's continuing financial difficulties. Before long, as she had done so many times in the past, Miss Cooley found herself writing to Arthur Curtiss James once again, explaining that income had decreased $5,500 while expenditures had decreased only $4,000 during 1932. Within a few days, James responded with his now-customary check for $2,500.[6]

In the spring of 1934 an auspicious visitor to the island felt intrigued and deeply moved by the work being done at St. Helena. Lady Elizabeth Lindsay, wife of the British ambassador, and Mrs. August Belmont had heard of Penn School from Paul Underwood Kellogg, editor of the *Survey* and member of Penn's advisory board, and they had taken an excursion to the island while vacationing in the South. Lady Lindsay's father had owned a large plantation on St. Helena Island where she had spent every summer during her girlhood, and this visit was the first time she had returned in twenty-five years. She marveled to see a great conception so well executed, and she determined on her return to Washington to endow a scholarship at the school. Even more important, in terms of spreading the Penn appeal, Lady Lindsay invited the St. Helena Quartette to come to Washington and perform at the embassy for a gathering of her friends. After a flurry of excited activity the four men—Mr King, Mr. Wildy, Mr. Benjamin Washington, and Mr. Aurelius Brown—boarded the

---

6. Trustees' minutes, October 27, 1933, Talbot Lewis to Cooley, December 18, 1933, both PSP.

train for their visit to the nation's capital. They were undoubtedly four impressed men as they stood in the exquisite reception room of the British Embassy one April evening singing for over two hours such spirituals as "Swing Low, Sweet Chariot" and "Go Down, Moses" in their rich Negro voices. Among the guests in the audience were Mr. and Mrs. Dean Acheson, W. Averill Harriman, Mrs. Alice Longworth, Sir Wilmott Lewis, and the Canadian Minister and Mrs. Herridge. All responded enthusiastically to the quartet's performance. As Lady Lindsay reported, the men "covered themselves with glory," and they returned to the island full of exciting tales about their journey. Before many days had passed to cloud the memory of those haunting melodies, Miss Cooley began to write all of Lady Lindsay's guests, placing Penn's story before them in the hope of capturing their interest and loyalty for the school.[7]

Another group of visitors in the spring of 1934 typified a more customary demand on Miss Cooley's time and energy. Charles T. Loram, former representative of the Carnegie Corporation and the Phelps-Stokes Fund in Africa, and now chairman and director of graduate studies in the Department of Race Relations at Yale, conducted a group of twelve students to St. Helena Island to observe the operation of what he thought to be the best example of industrial education in the country. For two days Miss Cooley gave her full attention to the Loram group, guiding them through farm, shops, classrooms, better homes, and home acres, as well as chapel and Community Council, and even turning them over to Benjamin Barnwell for a trip with the demonstration agent. The visit ended with an oyster roast at Ndulamo with several of the Penn workers, and Miss Cooley's expert public relations technique created the desired effect. "Our critically minded group can find nothing but praise and appreciation for Penn," Dr. Loram wrote to Miss Cooley. "All are agreed that from the pedagogic point of view Penn meets their ideals more than any school they have ever seen." Such appreciation heart-

7. Kellogg to Mrs. August Belmont, February 10, 1934, Belmont to Kellogg, March 8, 1934, Charleston *News and Courier*, February 3, 1935, clipping, Lady Elizabeth Lindsay to Cooley, March 4, April 13, 1934, Cooley to Lindsay, March 26, 1934, Martha Blair, "These Charming People," Washington *Herald*, April 15, 1934, clipping, Cooley to Hon. William D. Herridge, May 23, 1934, all in PSP.

ened Miss Cooley in her work and sustained her conviction that her efforts had genuine educational significance; but the drain on her energy as well as on her staff was enormous, and the disruption of normal school operations was considerable. And, of course, the expense of entertaining a steady stream of visitors was not negligible, especially when these visitors' enthusiasm for Penn rarely found significant monetary expression.[8]

Despite Mr. James's personal generosity and his regular biannual checks for $2,500, Miss Cooley's financial woes did not diminish. By April of 1935 she was writing to him of the depressingly familiar deficits. "Our income from all sources has shrunk by $7,044," she wrote him, "so you can imagine how I feel—part of the time as if I were in a dark wood—and yet when I see the Islanders and their struggle to keep the children in school and to raise the crop in the fields, I realize that there can be no letting go nor letting down." The General Education Board had appropriated $11,600 for a new waterworks system—an absolute necessity—but their emergency grants were no longer forthcoming, and the deficit had begun once again to grow. By June the deficit had reached $6,000, and Miss Cooley learned with dismay that the Carnegie Corporation would not be able to provide the $8,000 for teachers' salaries that she had expected. Frantically, she dashed off an appeal to the Rosenwald Fund, explaining that seventy-three people from all parts of the world had visited St. Helena to study Penn School that year and that the struggle to secure sufficient income had become a very great strain. Describing herself as "living on top of a volcano," she vowed that in the future she would endeavor to secure some pledges for the next fiscal year, "so as not to be forced to face our present situation, which seems like a catastrophe, so hard have we worked to keep up our standards, to secure funds—and to run within our reduced budget." The Rosenwald Fund regretfully declined the contribution.[9]

At the same time that Miss Cooley was struggling to secure

8. Loram to Cooley, October 6, 1933, March 29, 1934, "Program for Yale Party," March 27–28, 1934, all in PSP.
9. Cooley to James, April 18, 1935, Cooley to W. W. Brierley, April 17, 1935, Cooley to Embree, June 3, 1935, Robert M. Lester to Cooley, May 29, 1935, Cooley to F. P. Keppel, February 11, 1935, Embree to Cooley, June 20, 1935, all in PSP.

sufficient income, she was also engaged in developing plans for the rural teacher-training program, securing accreditation for Penn under South Carolina's new educational requirements, orchestrating the completion of the Rosenwald school-building program, soliciting federal funds for a nurse's salary, directing the county relief work on the island, soliciting a federal rural rehabilitation program for St. Helena, developing a long-range rehabilitation program, serving as hostess at meetings with Federal Relief Administration and Resettlement Administration officials, securing aid for the farmers most severely damaged by the 1935 hurricane, encouraging farmers who had lost all their venture capital in the collapse of the turkey market, visiting the islanders in their homes, speaking to the students in chapel services, inviting important guests to attend the Farmers' Fair and other school functions, entertaining a steady stream of visitors, and overseeing the general operation of Penn School. Miss House coordinated the day-to-day activities of the school, but Miss Cooley clearly had too many demands on her time to have to worry about fund raising. Unfortunately, in the absence of a financial secretary or a committee of dedicated trustees, Miss Cooley spent valuable hours writing appeals and traveling in the North, calling on wealthy matrons and speaking to fashionable gatherings of socially-conscious patricians. Despite her heroic efforts, Penn School's finances remained chronically depressed.

By the summer of 1940 the Penn School endeavor clearly needed some dramatic rallying cry to rekindle interest that had sagged or been diverted to the more urgent needs of the war-torn European countries. Such a cry came that summer in the winds of a devastating hurricane that swept the coastal region and caused heavy damage to the homes and fields of St. Helena Island's people. Immediately, Penn School launched a fervent campaign for emergency aid in the crisis. Miss Cooley dashed off an appeal to her contributors asking the obvious question: "How can these trusting, stricken people be cheered to clean up and start over unless a generous public puts funds in the hands of . . . the School heads, to help where help is needed in the most intelligent way?" Although she had recently informed her trustees that only $2,000 would be needed to make repairs at the school, Miss Cooley now appealed to the public for $10,000, "to keep the School at its helpful job." She had learned over the years to modify her appeal to suit whatever sources of support might be available, and she revealed her expertise in this field in one final reminder to her contributors: "No tangles of red tape prevent our sending aid to these loyal, stricken islanders as in the cases of need in stricken Europe, and we will be helping make America a safer place for the democratic spirit." Before long, almost $12,000 in private and foundation contributions had been received at the school. Some of this money was transferred from the hurricane fund to the current expenses budget, and eventually the trustees voted to merge the hurricane fund with general income with the understanding that records be kept at the school to show that the hurricane fund was used for the purposes for which it was raised. Most of the money eventually found its way into repairs at the school (many of which had been needed before the hurricane ever appeared), and by the end of the year Miss Cooley could write to Dr. Mills that if he could see the people in their churches or the children at school he would hardly realize there had been a hurricane. By the spring of the following year, Miss Cooley was reporting to her trustees that the school plant never looked better, and a budget estimate bearing a later date revealed that she had spent over $6,000 on repairs and renewals in the fiscal year 1940–1941. Surely few people have ever been more adept at building advantage out of adversity than was Rossa Belle Cooley.[10]

At length the trustees perceived that the school's continued existence demanded much more generous financing. In 1937 they had added to their number a young Philadelphian, John Silver of the F. J. Stokes Machine Company. John Silver found in the Penn School history and tradition a romance and purpose he could heartily affirm, and he threw himself unsparingly into Penn's flagging publicity effort.[11]

After a year or so of disappointing return on his investment,

10. King to Cooley, August 12, 1940, Philip Seabrook to Cooley, August 13, 1940, Trustees' minutes, August 22, 1940, Cooley, "In the Path of the Hurricane!" August 29, 1940, Cooley to P. Brown, October 29, 1940, Trustees' minutes, November 14, 1940, Cooley to W. H. Mills, December 10, 1940, Cooley to trustees, May 31, 1941, "Budget Estimate, 1942–1943," all in PSP.
11. Cooley to James, November 19, 1937, in PSP.

Silver concluded that the school's publicity procedure left much to be desired and that the school would have to appeal to a wider audience if it was to survive financially. Thus, he conceived the idea of a Penn School film which would enable the various clubs, colleges, churches, and prospective friends to be moved to support the school, thereby relieving some of Miss Cooley's arduous publicity efforts. When he first suggested his idea to the trustees, they dismissed it with little discussion; but Silver would not be dissuaded, and by December of 1941 the trustees had succumbed to his youthful assurance and their own critical need, authorizing the expenditure of $1,500 to produce a publicity film.[12]

As Silver explained his idea to Miss Cooley: "The future is in small contributions from a wider group of friends rather than from the comparatively few wealthy individuals who were available to us in the past for appeals." Francis Cope had stated his belief on a number of occasions that popular interest in black education had declined radically and that schools such as Penn could no longer hope to receive adequate support from smaller contributors; but he either did not consider the implications of John Silver's project, or he acquiesced in desperation. Whatever the explanation, the trustees approved the film project; and soon cameramen, sound trucks, and all manner of equipment appeared along the oyster shell roads and the placid tidal rivers which interlaced the island of St. Helena. At the summer board meeting in July, the trustees listened with interest and delight to recordings of the spirituals and plans for the film; and when Silver informed them that the film would cost more than $1,500 and maybe even $3,000, they quickly authorized up to $5,000 for completion of the project.[13]

Francis Cope, at least, was not blind to the financial difficulties the trustees were so freely claiming for themselves. As he had written a month earlier: "I hope John Silver and his Committee will somehow have been able to raise enough additional money

12. John Silver to Curtis, March 20, 1942, Silver to Cooley and House, June 2, 1939, Silver to Cooley, December 3, 1941, Trustees' minutes, December 2, 1931, June 6, 1939, all in PSP.

13. Silver to Cooley, December 3, 1941, Trustees' minutes, July 6, 1942, both in PSP.

to complete the new sound movie picture . . . but personally I do not see where the money is coming from." As chairman of the board, Cope had directed Penn's depressing financial campaigns for several years, and he must have known that John Silver's hopes of creating a vast new audience for the Penn enterprise were illusory. As he explained his point of view to John Silver at the very time the film was being produced: "We must do all we can, of course, to keep up the interest of our present subscribers and add as many new ones as possible, but most of us who have been active in the educational world feel that this form of support for private institutions will inevitably become more and more precarious."[14]

Cope understood that widespread changes in attitudes toward charitable giving had diminished traditional sources of support and that schools like Penn would have to depend increasingly on help from the great educational foundations as well as from state and federal aid. This conviction and Penn's present financial crisis notwithstanding, Cope allowed the Silver film project to become the primary focus of Penn's publicity effort.[15]

Late in the summer Hollingsworth Wood and John Silver read the script of the film and found it to be well suited to their needs. Within a month Silver had authorized a fourth reel since he believed that it was impossible to cut the film to less than three and one-half reels without losing an important part of the script. Since he was exceeding his appropriation, Silver agreed to underwrite the difference, for he believed that the extra reel would improve the final result. By November the uncompleted film had cost $5,600, and the trustees submitted an appeal to the General Education Board to cover the total cost, including advertising.[16]

Eventually the General Education Board informed the Penn trustees that it could not contribute to the publicity film. The trustees managed to raise $3,900 from special contributors, and the remainder was taken from the school's productive funds—a dangerous practice justified as "a long-time investment [that

14. Cope to Curtis, May 29, 1942, Cope to Silver, December 15, 1942, both in PSP.
15. Cope to Silver, December 15, 1942, in PSP.
16. Silver to Cope, August 24, 1942, Silver to Cooley, September 24, 1942, Trustees' minutes, November 20, 1942, all in PSP.

would] eventually give the publicity needed to make the new friends needed to finance the work."[17]

According to the letter of invitation to its showing, the Penn School movie, *To Live As Free Men*, was the story of the last slaves smuggled into the United States, their struggle, and the struggle of their children to join in the army of progress. It was also the story of a program of community education that had made Penn School a leader in the advancement of the Negro race.[18]

"This is the story of an investment in Humanity," began the film, leading into a thoroughly romanticized account of Penn's eighty-year history and revealing at every point the assumptions of an earlier age. "Penn School has demonstrated the power of the school as a social dynamo.... It is making good citizens—intelligent, self-supporting families. For at Penn School, education is literally preparation for life.... These are the people of the sea islands—deeply religious, happy, industrious, good citizens—who look upon Penn School as having brought to them the first true emancipation of the Negro race." Miss Cooley's "kindly advice shows these people how to solve their own problems and to feel the real satisfaction of standing on their own feet as self-sufficient individuals.... Their love of laughter, their native, rhythmic musical talent, their worship of the only gods they knew—gave them a resilience of disposition characteristic of their people everywhere."[19]

"Things of the mind and hand," the film continued, "are those activities to which their native talents are best suited. The first of these is the 'soil.'" Then after a discussion of the school's emphasis

---

17. Silver to Cope, December 11, 1942, Trustees' minutes (Executive and Finance Committees), May 26, 1943, Cooley to J. Herbert Johnson, March 10, 1943, all in PSP. Ultimately the film did increase contributions to the school somewhat, but it never had the kind of impact its promoters envisioned for it. Doubtless this was a function of the changing public attitude toward philanthropy and the rise in wartime taxes, but it was also a reflection of a popular shift away from the attitudes and assumptions of the Penn endeavor. As a future Penn fund raiser has reported, the students in a Yale University classroom actually laughed when he presented the film to them as a chronicle of Negro life in the South—or as a solution to the dilemmas of contemporary race relations. After its completion in 1943, the film was shown for only one or two years and then retired. Interview with Howard Kester, July, 1971, Black Mountain, N.C.

18. Invitation to Penn School film, January 25, 1943, in PSP.

19. Script, "To Live as Free Men," August 20, 1942, in PSP.

on agriculture and the uplifting aspects of the industrial program, the film rose to a crescendo of feeling and prophecy. "Over this backdrop of a simple, genuine people going their various ways to useful moral and mind-elevating endeavors on this out-of-the-way island off South Carolina," the film modestly suggested, "can be seen the beginnings of a great educational and racial revolution. A movement that is all too late in coming. That must stem the growing tide in many localities throughout the world." For there was no color discrimination on St. Helena. "Here we judge an individual by his character—and there is no doubt in your mind when that character shines in his eyes and permeates his entire person. When you meet one of these island folk and talk to him, you are gripped by his inner-self—color of skin soon becomes less important than color of personality. . . . Oh, Lord," the film concluded, with strains of an island spiritual sounding in the background, "bless the friends of the School. . . . We pray that their help will continue and the number of our friends increase for there is so much yet to be done. Our progress has been slow for we are not merely learning lessons. We are learning a new life—a better life—a more useful life, learning things of the spirit as well as of the mind and hands." Dr. Frissell would have applauded the film, and clearly his spirit was very much alive on St. Helena Island.[20]

Between 1938 and 1941 Penn School lost two of its oldest and most generous supporters; the deaths of George Foster Peabody and Arthur Curtiss James heralded the end of a spirited but declining effort. Everything about the Penn School program had grown old. Very few changes had been made in the program or the personnel since the earliest hopeful years. Miss Cooley and Miss House had arrived on St. Helena in their mature youth and had willingly spent their lives in the service of the island blacks; the same nucleus of dedicated teachers had overseen classrooms and home acres for at least twenty years; the same nucleus of trustees and essentially the same band of supporters had sus-

20. *Ibid.*

tained Penn financially since the earliest years of the experiment in industrial education; and the same goals of character development, community building, landownership, and proof of what the Negro could accomplish had guided the principals' efforts and sustained the contributors' enthusiasm since the days of Hollis Burke Frissell's first endorsement of Penn. But the years had begun to take their toll on the Penn School endeavor; and as the new publicity film now suggested, the rigidity of old age had settled on the enterprise just as the demands for creative youth and vitality seemed most urgent.

World War II caused an unmistakable drain on Penn School revenues; an unexpected boon of the war situation, however, was an increase of cash among blacks on the island. The Marine installation at Parris Island was just across the river, and many St. Helenians secured part- or full-time jobs there, or on road or airplane projects, increasing their income dramatically. As a result, many of them began to bring their cars and tools into the Penn shops for long-overdue repairs, and revenue from this source increased significantly.[21]

An unfortunate by-product, from the trustees' point of view, of the appealing defense jobs so near by was that many teachers and workers were enticed away from their jobs at Penn School. Only an eleventh-hour effort to raise salaries forestalled a general exodus of teachers from the island. Even so, many who had not been drafted left of their own accord, leaving the older workers responsible for a greatly increased teaching load.[22]

As a result of the war, the school farm was in real danger, as was the agricultural production of the whole island. But as in World War I, the government emphasized food production in the agricultural areas, and Penn School led the way in encouraging high standards of production on the island. The school organized evening classes in iron work, auto mechanics, and carpentry to prepare the young men for work on Parris Island; and many secured employment at the Marine base as a result. Also, one of the Penn School teachers visited two hundred island homes, explain-

21. Rollins to P. Brown, June 2, 1941, Trustees' minutes, June 6, 1941, Cooley to Carman, March 18, 1942, Cooley to trustees, October 23, 1943, all in PSP.

22. Cooley to trustees, January 25, 1943, in PSP.

ing the need for increased production and preparing lists of available workers for the farms. As a consequence of the expanded acreage, intensified farming, and heightened efforts of the children, St. Helena's food production soared remarkably in the war years.[23]

In her own inimitable way, Miss Cooley turned every exigency of the war situation into an advantage for her school, even incorporating the nationalistic mood in her appeals for funds: "To fit the Negro for his share in our country's great responsibilities in this world crisis," she wrote in a Penn School newsletter in 1942, "will do much to strengthen our democratic frontiers and save democracy for the world." And as she explained the situation to another potential contributor: "Again we face a year of crisis when the Negro morale should be strengthened for their own sake and for the sake of our country. If Penn School is crippled then education work among the Negroes in the South will be crippled."[24]

Miss Cooley also used the war situation to demonstrate that Penn's program of uplift and advancement was working. "Our men in the service are scattered to the four winds," she wrote to a generous contributor, "and good records are being made. On the foundations made here, they are showing that they can build in character and achievement." Indeed, the reports from Penn School soldiers did suggest that Penn's training had prepared the young men for positions of usefulness and responsibility. As Corporal Fred Moran, Quartermaster Department, Seattle, Washington, described his life in the Army: "I'm up before five a.m. to blow the bugle and I learned that from Mr. King in the Penn School Band. I go to the Carpenter Shop, and I use what I learned from Mr. Boyd. I have landscaping work and I learned that from Mr. Seabrook. Yes, Penn School goes right along with me."[25]

Despite all the hopeful reports, however, and despite Miss

23. Cooley to Nunnally, September 8, 1943, Peterson to [?]Elloree, South Carolina Draft Board, February 23, 1943, Cooley to J. H. Johnson, March 10, 1943, Cooley to trustees, October 23, 1943, all in PSP.
24. "Penn School News, Volume 1, 80th Year," 1942, p. 1, Cooley to Mary J. Jordan, September 19, 1942, both in PSP.
25. Cooley to J. H. Johnson, March 10, 1943, Cooley, "Report to Trustees," January 25, 1943, both in PSP.

Cooley's valiant attempts to sustain her good cheer and optimism in the face of staggering obstacles, there could be little doubt that the impact of the war, following close upon the drain of the depression and the devastation of the boll weevil, placed crushing burdens on the school's already-precarious existence. By mid-1943 Miss Cooley had to acknowledge that the old Penn School spirit had declined and she sent an urgent letter to her trustees requesting a blanket increase in salaries. The high salaries nearby presented strong temptations to her workers to leave the school, and even some of the old-timers seemed to have lost their enthusiasm for continuing to work as "missionaries." When such old-timers as Mrs. Bailey, B. H. Washington, the Browns, and the Fripps began to express dissatisfaction, the whole basis of the Penn School experiment became jeopardized. And yet no one seemed to have a solution for the deterioration in program and spirit so clearly taking place on St. Helena Island.[26]

Aside from the competition of higher wages in Beaufort or at Parris Island, a large part of Miss Cooley's inability to resolve her problems of staff unrest stemmed from a division of command that had developed in the early 1940s. The trustees had always allowed Miss Cooley and Miss House a maximum of freedom in developing and directing the programs and policies of the school. With the deepening financial crisis, however, and with the prospect of the two ladies' retirement looming on the horizon, the trustees were no longer willing to grant the principals a free rein in conducting the affairs of the school. After a ten-day visit to the school early in 1940, Francis Cope became genuinely alarmed about the situation on St. Helena, and he began to exercise a much greater degree of control over the decisions and expenditures made by the two ladies.[27]

Over the years, Francis Cope had developed warm relationships with various members of the Penn School staff, going out with the men to hunt the prized drum fish, leading any who wished

---

26. Trustees' minutes (Executive and Finance Committees), May 26, 1943, Cope to P. Brown, August 17, 1943, both in PSP.

27. In 1939 the trustees selected a Committee on Successors to the Principals; see Trustees' minutes, June 6, 1939, in PSP.

to follow on nature hikes across the island, attending meetings of the island societies, and visiting the workers in their homes. On occasion he also invited various Penn School workers to spend parts of their summer vacations at his guesthouse in Dimock, Pennsylvania. He was a welcomed and respected guest on the island, and through his close personal contacts he believed that he kept himself informed about the workers' reactions to developments at the school.[28]

During his annual visit to the school in the winter of 1940, Cope formed a number of distressing impressions of the work being done at St. Helena. Not only was the school not leading the way in solving the island's agricultural problems, but Penn was apparently failing to give most of the students thorough instruction in agriculture and the shop trades. Many of the workers were either weak teachers or they were carrying too heavy a load, and Mr. Cope felt uneasy about paying high salaries to the shop teachers unless the school could find a way to give more thorough instruction to vocational students. Cope was especially concerned about Penn's tendency to undertake too many different activities and spread itself too thin.[29]

With an attention to detail bordering on tedium, Cope now cited a host of major and minor changes he felt were needed at the school. His concern for the fine points of Penn's operation was new, and it signified a loss of confidence in the ladies. Miss Cooley and Miss House, he now believed, were no longer physically able to oversee properly the functioning of the school. Furthermore, Miss Cooley was more unable than before to listen even to the most friendly criticism; even Mr. King and the most trusted members of the staff were afraid to tell her what she needed to know. In short, the situation at St. Helena called for a complete overhaul, but Cope feared that the two principals had neither the strength nor the knowledge to reorganize the school program.[30]

28. Cope to Mr. and Mrs. J. P. King, May 7, 1941, King to Cope, May 23, 1941, both in PSP.
29. Cope, "Impressions and Suggestions During Visit to Penn School, February 24–March 4, 1940," March 8, 1940, in PSP.
30. Cope, "Impressions and Suggestions," in PSP; Cope to Curtis, March 19, 1940, in JMD.

Meanwhile, Miss Cooley pressed her demands for improved equipment because changes were coming rapidly and she did not want to cling to old methods of work. In the manner to which she had grown accustomed, she went out and bought an unauthorized truck for the farm, much to the chagrin of Francis Cope and a few of the other trustees he had alerted. As one of them replied to Cope, "I agree with thee that a strong hand should be used in deterring Rossa and Grace from further unathorized [sic] expense." Miss Cooley also requested a variety of new machines—apparently with little regard for efficiency or future usefulness. She wanted to spend $1,000 for a planer, a piece of machinery that did only a small amount of work in the Penn shops. She had spent over $1,000 on a woodworking shop a few years before, and yet this shop and the machines in it were used infrequently. She now requested $600 worth of equipment for the cobbling shop, just at the time the trustees were considering abandoning that shop altogether. Mr. Cope countered these requests with a long letter warning Miss Cooley that they would have to go slowly in this period of financial crisis and that no new shop equipment could be purchased unless it was considered absolutely essential by the executive committee. Cope was alarmed to have Miss Cooley make what he considered to be such blithe requests and also to realize how woefully out of touch she was with the realities of her own program. As he had learned from his visit the previous winter, the ladies believed that their industrial program was reasonably up-to-date and efficient, but the shop instructors reported that they were giving little practical instruction in their departments.[31]

Under all these distressing considerations lay Penn's worsening financial condition. The hurricane fund had helped for a while, but Mr. James's death followed by the Second World War played havoc with Penn's dwindling income. Contributions continued to decline while expenses continued to rise; the treasurer

---

31. Cooley to trustees, May 31, 1941, Cope to William E. Cadbury, June 27, 1941, Cadbury to Cope, July 3, 1941, Silver to Cope, July 10, 1941, Cope to Silver, July 8, 1941, all in PSP; Cope to Curtis, March 19, 1940, in JMD.

was forced to draw heavily on the school's productive funds, and all were pinning their hopes on Penn's publicity film.[32]

In short, when Miss Cooley and Miss House stepped down from their forty-year rein as St. Helena's undisputed rulers, the Penn School trustees turned over to their successors an impossible situation. The school's productive funds had been seriously eroded and its income-generating power had become ineffective. The staff was feeling disillusioned and abused, and most of the younger recruits had abandoned their posts at St. Helena for more lucrative positions elsewhere. The program was not only out of touch with the demands of the modern world, it no longer satisfied the needs of the not-so-modern island of St. Helena. And probably most important, the community-wide feeling of pride in Penn School—and the heady feeling of participating in a significant educational experiment—had been lost. Penn School would never be the same again, and the future would hold only pain for those who sought to sustain what might have died with dignity.

32. Brown to Cope, September 21, 1943, in PSP.

13

Years of Decline

Rossa Belle Cooley and Grace House created at St. Helena an extension of themselves. In a sense, Penn School was their child—the product of their vision and devotion, a reflection of their ideals. Through forty years they remained constant in their dedication to the teachings of Hollis Burke Frissell and John Dewey. Against all odds they fought to encourage landownership and to build character; despite boll weevils, depression, and war they held on to their vision of community. As Progressives long after progressivism had died, their goal was nothing less than the total regeneration of the life and culture of St. Helena Island; and though their goal was clearly too broad, they clung with the unreasonableness of parents to the belief that their child could do it all. Inevitably, perhaps, the two ladies increasingly expressed themselves in maternal terms, referring to the Penn School "family" and pouring into their work all the devotion and affection normally reserved for children. The gentle amusement with which they reported various incidents from around the island leaves little doubt that they viewed the Negroes as children, and it is equally clear that they exulted in the work they had chosen to do. As Miss Cooley described one of the school chapel services: "It's a relaxation, for who could see all those children, some in overalls, some in aprons, some ragged, some very well dressed, all sizes, all ages from 6 to 23, all singing spirituals . . . without being glad to be one with them."[1]

The satisfactions in the work were boundless: the day-to-day pleasures of living among a gentle and grateful people, the knowledge of having changed and uplifted lives, the exhilaration of being pioneers in a celebrated educational experiment, and the deeply reassuring sense of purpose that comes with doing good. Though they never had a clearly articulated philosophy, Miss Cooley and Miss House never wavered in the conviction that they were building a better world on St. Helena Island.[2]

Undoubtedly, the two white ladies were Penn School's greatest strength and its greatest attraction. Consistently through the years, visitors to the island praised the noble inspiration of the lady missionaries. Set against the calming, languorous background of the island and the startling self-direction and self-respect of the blacks, the ladies projected a powerful image—dedicated, high-minded, consecrated, selfless. Increasingly over the years, their nobility and their gentle conception of Penn as their family blinded all comers to the realities of the situation on St. Helena. But as a perceptive observer described what he found at St. Helena just four short years after Miss Cooley and Miss House had stepped down from their lofty posts: "There are at least two St. Helena Islands. One is part memory and part myth. The other is a stern reality."[3]

In the waning years of the Cooley-House leadership, while

---

1. "A Day's Work at Penn School." Howard Kester, who followed Miss Cooley as principal of Penn School, claims that every Monday she would go into each classroom and write on the board: "I love you." Interview with Howard Kester, June 28, 1971, Chapel Hill, N.C.

2. Loram to Cooley, February 20, 1934, in PSP.

3. Ira DeAugustine Reid, "An Evaluation of the Facilities, Program, and Objectives of the Penn Normal, Industrial and Agricultural School," February 19, 1948, in PSP.

Penn School fought unsuccessfully against agricultural depression, wartime inflation, and the escalating attractions of life beyond St. Helena Island, the trustees abandoned themselves to a wholehearted belief in Penn's enduring success. When L. Hollingsworth Wood called it "the Island of Enchantment," he expressed better than he knew an assessment of the endeavor that ultimately would explain its demise.[4] For in the minds of those who controlled its fate, Penn School had become a fairy tale, detached from reality, Utopian and sacred.

Miss Cooley and Miss House could write with utter sincerity in 1942 that it was their aim to meet the growing and changing needs of that rural community, but by 1942 the needs of their community had moved far beyond the limits of their capabilities or assumptions. As Lawrence Cremin has said in another context, but in terms that apply to Penn School, by the 1940s "the enthusiasm, the vitality, and the drive were gone; all that remained were the slogans."[5]

The ladies were now nearing seventy, and Miss Cooley's continuing poor health in the late 1930s had caused her trustees to turn their thoughts to the question of her successor. In 1939 the trustees had appointed a search committee, and they had suggested that the two ladies retire in 1942. Cope was chariman of the committee on successors; and after becoming aware of the conditions on the island, he began to press the search vigorously, causing the volatile Miss Curtis to protest on behalf of "the girls" that he was trying to "throw 'em out." In assuring Miss Curtis that this was not the case, Cope explained his point of view: "The problem of how long they will really be able to carry on is the thing that now worries me the most, and I fear they cannot do so much longer unless they have some promising assistant (or assistants) to help carry some of the details of administration."[6]

For the next two years the trustees conducted an extended search for possible successors, sending out an impressive number

    4. Wood to Cooley and House, November 28, 1937, in PSP.
    5. "Penn School News," n.d., 1, in PSP; Cremin, *The Transformation of the School*, 181.
    6. Trustees' minutes, June 6, 1939, in PSP; Cope to Curtis, March 19, 1940, in JMD.

of inquiries and pursuing the search on many fronts. Their efforts were frustrated, however, by a lack of unanimity concerning what they were hoping to find and by a set of qualifications that excluded all but the most exceptional. Mr. Cope wanted a male successor to follow the two ladies, but Mr. Wood felt that a man with enough youth and energy to do a really good job would only use Penn School as a stepping stone to some larger service. Wood claimed that a woman principal would be far better, for she would "lavish upon the school and its interests the energies and affections and instincts which are generally associated with maternity in a woman's life." Miss Cooley emphasized the centrality of religion as a primary qualification, claiming that "to have some one to whom religious life were not the most vital thing in the world come to Penn as Principal would, to my mind, be a disaster." Miss House called for the Christian spirit of service, and Cope endorsed the need for the missionary spirit.[7]

At length the trustees came upon the names of a young couple who had long been active in interracial and church work in the South. Howard Anderson Kester had become close friends with Ethel Paine Moors through membership in the Fellowship of Reconciliation, an organization founded after World War I to promote lasting peace and brotherhood throughout the world; and Mrs. Moors now recommended him for the leadership of Penn School. As an ordained Congregational minister and a white southern male with a wide range of contacts among interracial organizations in the North and in the South, Howard Kester met many of the qualifications the trustees had specified as being desirable in the new administrator.[8]

"Buck" Kester, as he was called by his friends, had been involved in a variety of radical and reform activities throughout the

---

7. The voluminous correspondence surrounding the search for successors is in the possession of Mrs. James McBride Dabbs, Rip Raps Plantation, Mayesville, S C [Wood] to Celestine Smith, September 5, 1941, in PSP; Cooley to Cope, April 16, 1940, Cope to Wood, December 30, 1941, House to Cope, January 8, 1942, Cope to Curtis, March 18, 1940, all in JMD.

8. Interview with Howard Kester, July, 1971, Black Mountain, N.C.; E. M. Wayland, "Howard Anderson Kester," brochure announcing Kester's Papers for Microfilm Corporation of America, February, 1974, p. 2; Kester Biography, n.d., Box 12, Folder 116, in PSP.

South—from investigating lynchings for the NAACP to aiding striking miners in the West Virginia coalfields to organizing Arkansas sharecroppers in the Southern Tenant Farmers' Union. Most recently he had been involved in a movement to revolutionize the rural church. He believed that the organized church had played an "evil" role in the life of the southern people, thus creating "the need for a movement of Christian men and women who would combine prophetic insight with courage and skill." This belief had led him to accept the full-time leadership of a small group of southern ministers who called themselves the Fellowship of Southern Churchmen.[9]

As a man committed to bringing the world into harmony with the teachings of Jesus Christ, Kester was impatient with the slow pace of change in a South that seemingly tolerated so much oppression and injustice. He had always been a man in a hurry, and his lack of a clearly articulated philosophy impeded him from finishing his projects once he had broken through the barriers of conservatism and tradition. His forte was his ability to dramatize the injustices of a situation, but he had little patience with the tedium of detail that was necessary to consolidate his gains. As a result, he had moved from one activity to another, time and again drawn to new fields of endeavor, while the wounds he had made in the walls of injustice slowly mended themselves.

As a student at Princeton Theological Seminary, Kester had studied with the liberal theologian, Reinhold Niebuhr; and he had come to believe that the church must lead the attack on such social evils as racism, tenancy, and industrial oppression. As a student at Vanderbilt University in the late 1920s, he had absorbed the philosophy of the Nashville Agrarians; and he had developed a mystical reverence for the soil as the source of all spiritual sustenance. At a time when the southern economy was moving away from a rural and agricultural base, Kester called for a return to the land as a corrective for man's spiritual starvation. "If we fail to build a healthy rural civilization," he wrote to a colleague in the Southern Tenant Farmers' Union, "all else fails for we are essen-

9. John Egerton, *A Mind to Stay Here: Profiles from the South* (New York, 1970), 70–91; Kester Biography, in PSP.

tially a rural civilization." The twin themes of the Social Gospel and a love of the soil characterized all his later work; both were servants of his deeper commitment to the realization of the promise of New Testament truths.[10]

The Kesters' response to what they found at St. Helena was strong and unreserved. "Here we were privileged to see," Kester wrote in the Fellowship of Southern Churchmen newsletter, "one of the most inspiring educational experiments, anywhere in the entire country.... Here is education for life, not just preparation for it." In a phrase that was undoubtedly genuine but that was also superb public relations, Kester concluded: "Here indeed is a laboratory and a workshop which has already yielded immensely rich rewards and which more than ever stands as a light house for those who want enlightenment and understanding in the academies of darkness." In February of 1943 Ethel Moors formally placed the Kesters' names before the board; and by the end of the year, the Penn School endeavor had entered a new phase of its history.[11]

Kester approached his inauguration as Penn's new principal in January of 1944 believing that he could master the situation on St. Helena within a year or so, and that he would then be able to rechannel his energies into battling the problems of racism and the rural church. As he expressed his anticipation soon after his election: "the opportunities are almost endless and we hope that

---

10. Wayland, "Kester," 2. Kester claimed that he was not influenced by the Agrarians, but he apparently absorbed their ideas. Undoubtedly it would have been difficult to be in Nashville in the late 1920s and fail to be infected with the spirit of the Agrarian movement. Interview with Kester, July, 1971, Black Mountain, N.C. Kester's ability to combine the various elements of his social philosophy is reflected in the following excerpt from the closing prayer of his "Ceremony of the Soil": "Speed now the day when the plains, the hills, and all the wealth thereof shall be the people's own and free men shall not live as tenants of men on the earth which Thou has given to all. Enable us humbly and reverently, with clean hands and hearts to prepare ourselves for the day when we shall be Thy tenant alone and help us become faithful keepers of one another and of Thy good earth—our home." "The Making of a Southern Radical," brochure announcing the Kester Papers for the Microfilm Corporation of America, February, 1974; Howard Kester to J. B. Butler, January 28, 1941, University of North Carolina, Southern Historical Collection, Southern Tenant Farmers' Union Papers. (I am indebted to Daniel Singal for bringing this letter to my attention.)

11. Kester to Cooley, May 31, 1943, Trustees' minutes, February 2, 1943, both in PSP.

at St. Helena we may be able to make some further contribution to the manifold problems besetting our world today, and which will continue into tomorrow's tomorrow." As the school's old liberty bell rang out to mark the change in leadership, Kester pledged himself to use his new position at Penn School to build a more just and harmonious world. "We shall labor to affirm the integrity of those principles which have made Penn School justly famous," he promised his listeners. "We shall labor—all of us—to have an increasing share in the rebirth of that knowledge of God, man and nature and that freedom and dignity of man himself without which our world will perish."[12]

In the next few weeks Kester reorganized the farm program and tackled the school plant, and he established a cordial correspondence with Francis Cope. Cope was thrilled with Kester's analysis of the island situation and with the tone of their developing relationship. "Your spirit and understanding are a great comfort and assurance in tackling the many problems that undoubtedly lie ahead of Penn School," he wrote to Kester, but he had no intention of relinquishing control of the school to the new administrator. "As you know," he pointed out in characteristic tones, "we have always to bear in mind our all too limited financial resources and especially the need for proceeding slowly in changing from the old order to the new." Soon Kester was to realize that he had assumed a greater burden than he had anticipated. The situation was not as he had expected, and he withdrew from the office of secretary of the Fellowship of Southern Churchmen. Before long he would conclude that someone had misled him in his evaluation of Penn; but for awhile, at least, his ideals and vision sustained his enthusiasm for the cause he had adopted as his own.[13]

12. Kester to Pickens Johnson, July 28, 1943, "Southerner Made Penn School Head," New York *Times*, January 10, 1944, clipping, both in HKP; Kester to Earle Hitch, January 18, 1944, Kester inaugural address, January 9, 1944, both in PSP. For a full discussion of the Kesters' four years at Penn School, see Betsy Jacoway Burns, "Penn School" (M.A. thesis, University of North Carolina, 1968).

13. Kester to Barnwell, January 13, 1944, Eugene Smathers to Kester, January 18, 1944, Kester to Cope, January 24, 1944, Kester to Silver, January 24, 1944, Cope to Kester, January 28, 1944, Kester to Walter Sykes, January 28, 1944, all in PSP; Cope to Mr. and Mrs. Kester, January 25, 1944, in HKP; interview with Howard Kester, July, 1971, Black Mountain, N.C.

There is a certain irony in Howard Kester's being chosen to go to Penn School. A radical and something of a socialist, he was completely outside the Penn School tradition. The ultraconservative patricians who had sustained the Penn School endeavor over the years had a world view and an understanding of social processes at least 180 degrees away from Kester's. Their view of society was hierarchical; his was egalitarian. They believed in gradual, organic changes; he sought instant amelioration of the world's ills. They revered tradition and the time-honored truths; he wanted a new heaven and a new earth. There is irony also in Kester's choosing to go to Penn School. As a champion of the underdog, he had always fought to undermine the capitalist oppressors; now he eagerly locked arms with his new patrician comrades, perfectly willing to march into tomorrow's tomorrow by their sides.

Of course, there were important areas of agreement: the Kesters spoke the language of the consecrated Christian, and they shared the moralistic outlook of their predecessors; they also thought in terms of spreading the gospel of human love and dignity throughout the earth. Probably, however, the most cogent explanation of the improbable marriage is the simple element of timing. The Penn trustees had invested three years and incalculable amounts of energy in securing successors for Miss Cooley and Miss House. Howard Kester had just lost his primary source of income when Reinhold Niebuhr discontinued the financing for his work with the rural churches.[14] Each needed the other; and though neither was completely happy, both were relieved to have the uncertainty terminated.

The Kesters' early weeks and months at Penn School were filled with much activity and promise, but the couple realized very quickly that the situation there was not what they had anticipated. Almost immediately the relationship with Francis Cope began to deteriorate, leading ultimately to Cope's resignation from the chairmanship of the Penn board. Kester's sweeping changes and his abrasive manner also alienated many of the island people, including such important members of the Penn establishment as Joshua Blanton, Benjamin Barnwell, J. P. King,

14. Wayland, "Kester," 7

Dr. and Mrs. Bailey, and Mr. and Mrs. Boyd. The presence of Miss Cooley and Miss House on the island served to make Ndulamo a center of irritation and discontent, and Penn's continuing financial difficulties aggravated an already deteriorating situation.[15]

The Penn School trustees finally realized that they had reached an operational stalemate. Though the Kesters had outlined many plans for the future, these plans met with continuing opposition, both from the members of the board and from the island community. Repeated failures to cover their current operating deficit, without even considering money for expansion, forced the board to call for a reevaluation of its program and policies. In November of 1947 the trustees resolved to take immediate steps to evaluate and validate their objectives "through consultation with authorities whose judgments were valued with respect to the educational needs of the South."[16]

At Kester's suggestion, the board decided to invite Dr. Ira DeAugustine Reid, editor of *Phylon* and chairman of the Department of Sociology at Atlanta University, to make an evaluation of their plans for the school and to prepare for them a program that would fit the educational needs of the region. Dr. Reid readily accepted the invitation and then chose a distinguished team of experts to work with him. During a three-day visit to St. Helena, this group studied the school's records and observed the actual situation on the island. As Dr. Reid stated in his report, "We sought always to move ahead in our thinking from what *was* to what we saw *is*, and into what *might become* at Penn School." The survey staff made their study with the intention of helping the trustees "develop Penn School to a point where it effectively can serve its region in the conservation, development and utilization of its human and natural resources."[17]

---

15. Once when Kester preached in one of the island churches, the minister praised his sermon in terms that must have expressed the general contempt for all the Kesters were trying to do; he declared that Kester's sermon was "just like snake oil—so penetrating." Interview with Howard Kester, June 29, 1971, Chapel Hill, N.C.

16. Resolution passed by the Penn School Board of Trustees, November 13, 1947, in PSP.

17. Interview with Howard Kester, June 29, 1971, Chapel Hill, N.C.; Trustees'

All the interested parties had high hopes for the outcome of this investigation, and few were prepared for the shattering report that Dr. Ried delivered in February, 1948, recommending "the transfer of the formal educational program of Penn School to public authorities under conditions consonant with the Penn School ideals and the public interest."[18] This recommendation called for a radical shift in emphasis and left the trustees wondering, "What then will be Penn School?" In essence, Dr. Reid had told them that Penn had outlived its usefulness.

During their investigation, the survey committee had discovered some basic educational and social problems in the Penn School situation. Specifically, they were concerned about the economic and social changes of the St. Helena community, the quality and quantity of education offered at Penn School, the volume of financial support, the quality of personnel, the quality and extent of community cooperation, and the role of public education in the community.[19]

Dr. Reid pointed out the great changes that continued to take place in the South, the St. Helena community, Penn School, and all of their interrelationships. Not only had the external features of St. Helena changed but the community itself had developed new attitudes; and with these internal changes came an altered attitude toward Penn School. Formerly, community life had been centered around the community affairs at Penn School or at one of the churches; by 1948 a more urban type of social life had begun to develop, with jukeboxes in beer parlors, social clubs, and people who talked about political action.

In the past all good things on St. Helena had come from the

---

minutes, November 13, 1947, in PSP. The members of Reid's survey team were as follows: J. Curtis Dixon, vice-president and executive director of the Southern Education Foundation and formerly director of Negro education for the state of Georgia; Alfonso Elder, president of North Carolina College; Timothy W. Jones, acting dean of the Department of Mechanical Industries at Tuskegee Institute; Jane Ellen McAllister, professor of education at Miner Teachers College and a member of the Penn Board of Trustees; and Fred G. Wale, associate director of the Bureau for Inter-cultural Education and formerly director of the Rural Education Program, Julius Rosenwald Fund; Reid, "Evaluation," 2, in PSP.

18. Reid, "Evaluation," 48.
19. Reid to Henry W. Pope, January 26, 1948, in PSP.

North and white northerners, private philanthropy, and Hampton. St. Helena residents and Penn School students were taught to respect these symbols, along with the fundamental virtues of the simple, rural life.[20] With the coming of the depression and the war, however, private philanthropy was not enough, and the government began supplying relief; as the outside world moved in, it voided many of the values heretofore held constant. As new schools opened on the island and across the bridge, Penn School became *another* school rather than *the* school on St. Helena.

After having set the stage for his analysis, Dr. Reid turned to an evaluation of Penn's specific problems. Academically, Reid felt that the school was respectable enough, though it had many deficiencies of staff and equipment. The teachers were inadequately trained and the library was grossly understocked in comparison with the other schools in the county. The trades and mechanics department was reported to be overcrowded, poorly managed, and inadequately supplied. Reid noted that the farm program was inefficient and mismanaged, though it did provide a service to the community and a valuable supply of produce to the school. In the areas of food, clothing, and laundering, Dr. Reid reported that the emphasis was on training future homemakers and that the vocational training of the program was practically worthless.

Reid felt that in comparison to the public schools in the community, Penn's costs were extremely high. Although Penn's academic program had been improved, it did not seem to warrant per capita expenses of $403 per year. The cost appeared particularly high when compared with the same per capita costs for the public education program in Beaufort County, which was $136 for white children and $38 for black children. Dr. Reid concluded that Penn's service to the community, measured in dollars and cents, was not that much better. Not only did Penn fail to provide superior opportunities, in many respects the school's program was pathetically inferior to that offered by the county. This situation was doubtless the result of South Carolina's increased financial

---

20. Reid, "Evaluation," 7.

support to black schools in an attempt to forestall desegregation, for during the 1940s the southern states had become increasingly aware of the inferior quality of black education and had come to see the disparities in allocations and services as threats to the dual systems.[21]

The survey committee felt that the public school system could provide training that was at least as good as that provided at Penn at much lower cost.[22] To turn the academic program over to the state would mean a more equitable distribution of public funds and would then permit a more definitely oriented social program under private auspices. Under this plan the Penn board could devote itself more fully to developing much-needed community programs such as guidance, library services, recreation, social welfare, and adult education. And this would cut Penn's annual expenses by almost half. Dr. Reid's committee saw almost unlimited possibilities for development once the Penn board had divested itself of its superfluous educational functions. As a sociologist and a sophisticated urban black, Ira Reid had little patience with the paternalism of the old Penn School and little appreciation of the educational philosophy of its leadership. He was the expert, however, and the board had little choice but to accept his expert advice.

Although the Reid report had devastated the very foundations of their operations at St. Helena, the trustees began immediately to lay the groundwork for a new program. After considerable deliberation, they decided to relinquish their academic program to the state of South Carolina, to abandon their farming operation, and to concentrate their efforts on providing

---

21. *Ibid.*, 10; Carroll L. Miller, "Educational Opportunities and the Negro Child in the South," *Harvard Educational Review*, XXX (Summer, 1960), 197.

22. In a letter to Penn's publicity secretary, Howard Kester clarified the Reid statement: "With regard to the letter to the contributors, the sentence, 'The Survey findings indicated that the great advances in public education in South Carolina have made adequate public schools available to the Negro children on St. Helena Island' is again not in keeping with the facts. Adequate public schools are not available to the children of St. Helena. The Survey indicated that there is a growing sense of responsibility and in time the state would be able to furnish adequate education. To say that the facilities are now adequate is to invite resentment on the part of the people of St. Helena especially." Kester to Lennie Schley, n.d., in PSP.

community planning and improvement, sanitation and health, recreation and sport, and mental and spiritual hygiene. On May 6, 1948, Penn Normal, Industrial and Agricultural School became Penn Community Services, Inc. At a March meeting of the board of trustees, Howard Kester resigned as principal, and he soon thereafter resumed his duties as executive secretary of the Fellowship of Southern Churchmen, consoling himself with a favorite quotation from Erasmus: "In great things, it is enough to have tried."[23]

Francis Cope was deeply wounded and dismayed by the Reid report. He felt that it did not give enough credit to the past accomplishments of the school, and he was bitter that it did not heap calumny upon the heads of Howard and Alice Kester. Cope's annotated copy of Reid's report was replete with comments such as, "Doubtful, but definitely not true before the Kesters arrived." Perhaps the most pathetic statement came from Miss Cooley, who wondered how the trustees accounted for the many guests to the school—educators, social workers, and government officials, some of whom had returned to the island for further study.[24]

On January 25, 1940, Courtney Siceloff, another southerner, became the director of Penn Community Services. For several years after his appointment, Mr. and Mrs. Siceloff were all that there was of Penn. The Siceloffs spent most of their time among the people, and they gradually evolved a program of community development. They described the new Penn program as a down-to-earth, grass-roots approach. They might be working on a water supply for one community, helping a fisherman get a loan for a boat in another, or helping the residents of an isolated island get regular transportation. The key to the whole program was to create initiative from within the communities.[25]

23. Cadbury to Penn School contributors, 1948, press release, May 1, 1948, both in PSP; interview with Howard Kester, June 29, 1971, Chapel Hill, N.C.
24. Cope's copy of the Reid Report is included in the Penn School Papers; Cooley to Cadbury, February 2, 1948, in PSP. In April Ira Reid commented to Wood: "In a way it grieved me to have to talk as I did about what had happened at St. Helena while Miss Cooley was in the room. I do not like to hurt people, and while I am certain that she did a tremendous job as she saw it, in her time, the effects of the pampering have been so disastrous and have caused so much concern that it was our duty to say it." Ira Reid to Wood, April 6, 1948, in PSP.
25. News release from Penn Community Services, 1967.

Under Siceloff, Penn often hosted interracial conferences, most notably serving as an isolated retreat for Martin Luther King and his Southern Christian Leadership Conference. Until after the passage of the 1964 Civil Rights Act, Penn was one of the few facilities available in the South for such biracial meetings.[26]

In 1969 Penn turned over its leadership to a young black man, John W. Gadson, a native of Orangeburg County in South Carolina and a former high school science teacher. Gadson encouraged economic development on the island, and his emphasis on landownership and self-help, cooperative marketing, and participation in the St. Helena Credit Union bore a remarkable resemblance to the economic solutions Rossa Belle Cooley pursued in trying to guarantee genuine freedom to her beloved "children."[27]

The board of trustees also underwent a marked transformation beginning in 1961 when a native South Carolinian, Marion Wright, became chairman of the board. Wright led the Penn trustees in endorsing the civil rights revolution in South Carolina; and this tradition continued after Wright stepped down in 1965 to be followed by the eminent southern liberal, James McBride Dabbs, and then in 1971 by the black sociologist, Herman Blake. The northern trustees disappeared from the board one by one, until today Penn Community Services, Inc., has become almost exclusively a southern biracial phenomeon.

26. "Negro Will Head Carolina Center," New York *Times*, October 5, 1969.
27. *Ibid.*; interview with John Gadson, March 19, 1972, St. Helena Island, S.C. Roy Reed, "Blacks in South Struggle to Keep the Little Land They Have Left," New York *Times*, December 7, 1962.

14

The Penn School Experiment

For more than forty years the tides of time and fortune swirled their changes about the island of St. Helena, now bringing in refreshing conceptions of life and work, now washing away a faulty economic system, now adding dependency and passivity, now taking a precious cultural inheritance. The tides came in slowly, quietly, creeping into the marshes so gently that their ebb and flow were barely perceptible—bringing their changes so softly, so deceptively, that the workers on the shore did not notice the reshaping of their island, did not stop to reckon their losses and their gains. Even had they watched, had they laid down their tools and stood for a moment at the water's edge, they could not have said which way the tide was moving; for though the thousands of tiny ripples across the surface of the water suggested stronger currents beneath, the ripples themselves were all that the eye could see, and they danced unceasingly in all directions at once.

The participants in the unfolding Penn School drama could not see, did not have time to note, the patterns of the changes they were to bring to St. Helena. Only with the perspective of time and distance can those patterns be discerned; only through the dispassion of the nonparticipant can they be understood. And yet, even now the tides protect their mysteries, gently washing the island in an incomparable serenity and calm, yielding only the remains of a once vital endeavor. But the remains themselves reveal the currents that produced them; and though they cannot be expected to yield all of the secrets of the unseen deep beneath the surface, they can suggest, at least, which way the tide is running.

Beneath all the change and activity so apparent on the surface at St. Helena, some themes and characteristics remained constant through the years. For a full understanding of the nature of the Penn School experience, identification of these constant elements is as important as familiarity with the day-to-day story of change and vitality the records reflect; and it is the currents beneath, not the ripples, that offer the surest passage into the minds of the white participants.

Among those features of the Penn School phenomenon that remained constant over time, the most prominent is the fact that Penn was a product of northern efforts. From Laura Towne to Hollis Frissell to Rossa Cooley, from wealthy matrons to large foundations to ill-conceived films—it was all the work of northern minds and hands, and it was all designed to appeal to northern sensibilities; what is more, it all grew out of northern needs and assumptions, and from the first it sought to dispel northern fears. Southerners were hardly aware of the existence of the little island school, and southern contributions were a very small part of its growth. Southern white desires and problems, in fact, were only of the remotest concern to the builders and supporters of this school, which was celebrated as a model of industrial education.

The character of that northern support is as revealing as its source. Never very generous, it always left the principals scrambling for funds, exhausting themselves in endless appeals and crisis measures, and reining in their imaginations—and their compassion—to fit the available funds. Although praise for the Penn School program of uplift could always be found in abundance, actual support for that program was meager, and even the trustees seemed unwilling to commit themselves to an all-out effort on behalf of the southern black. Perhaps this is because the Penn endeavor was not perceived as an effort on behalf of the southern black. Perhaps the desire for proof of black improvability suggests instead that the interest in Penn School reflected the existence of persistent northern fears—fears about black immorality and ignorance, fears about black corruption of the democracy, fears about a black exodus to the North. If so, when these fears had been laid to rest by Penn's apparent success—when the Penn "demonstration" had proved that blacks could become contented, useful, and safe—then the school's mission had been accomplished; and a polite participation in sustaining this proof was all that was necessary or appropriate. Such a thesis is suggested and strengthened by other important elements in the Penn School experience.

A second major element that remained constant through the years was the set of goals the Penn principals and trustees sought. Penn School lacked, however, a consistent, articulated philosophy. As a Yale educator once wrote to Miss Cooley after visiting the island with his students: "Only a few minutes ago in our Seminar in Education your school was under discussion and it was most interesting to see the efforts of the students to discover the so-called philosophy underlying your work. I cannot be sufficiently appreciative of your statement that you had no philosophy in mind when you undertook the school other than common sense."[1] Miss Cooley and her trustees never encumbered themselves with a rigid, preconceived philosophy; thus, they could remain flexible and adaptable to the needs—and the sources of support—that they perceived. They did, however, share a common understanding of the goals they were seeking.

The overriding goal of the white participants in the Penn School experiment was to prove to white America (and to themselves) that blacks could be uplifted and thereby rendered nonthreatening—and that in the meantime, blacks could find a place in the American system that would allow them a measure of dignity. Penn School's whole program—of keeping blacks in the country until they had developed character—was designed to prove this point. Although caste distinctions were freely accepted, temporarily at least, the Penn School program did not seek, and was not designed, to impose them. And although self-sufficiency and productivity were primary goals, the Penn School program was

---

1. Loram to Cooley, February 20, 1934, in PSP.

in no way designed to exploit black labor. It was designed instead to provide a demonstration to the nation of black worth—primarily moral and spiritual—and of the value of industrial education in increasing that worth. Furthermore, although the skills being taught were often outmoded even as they were introduced, this was not thought to be important, for the goal was not preparation for work in the modern factory; the goal most often stressed was the development of character, which the Hampton plan of industrial education promised to develop.[2]

All of these goals were reflected in the Penn School program, the third major element of the Penn experience that remained constant. On the surface the Penn School program seemed to be directed toward economic ends with its emphasis on agriculture, industrial skills, and cooperative ventures among the farmers; the economic program, however, was important only as a basis for the larger experiment in uplift. As Miss Cooley once wrote, "A school like ours is a factory; its ultimate product, homes."[3] Miss Cooley saw the island home as her ultimate target—and the ultimate test of her program—for she believed the home to be the basis of all civilized living; only if she reached into those homes and improved the moral and spiritual lives of their occupants could she hope for real success. And only if she created a viable economic program, one that would hold the youngsters on the island, would she be able to reach into those homes and change those lives in any meaningful way. Thus Penn School remained a laboratory, in which solutions were sought for the problems of rural living and in which methods were tested daily for uplifting a "backward" people.

In one of her first years at Penn School, Miss Cooley had written, "The tendency to go to the cities can be checked only by substituting a new interest, and it is the aim of the school to give to the pupils a training which shall make them see their opportunities at home." Thirty-five years later, in one of her last years as principal of Penn School, Miss Cooley informed her trustees that the blacks were still drifting to the cities and that methods

2. Grace Bigelow House, "The Need and Purpose of Industrial Education," 92.
3. Cooley, *Homes of the Freed*, 192–93.

would have to be found to hold them in their rural communities where they were needed.[4] At first glance this would seem to be evidence of a callous and pernicious program to hold the black man down—to keep him in the country where he would not be a threat or where he could be easily exploited—but such an analysis would be only partially correct.

The Penn School emphasis on landownership, country living, and regeneration of the community reflected the belief that, although blacks lacked the fundamental attitudes and values of civilized living, they could develop those characteristics if they could be kept away from the dangers and temptations of the city. Avid proponents of what Richard Hofstadter has called the agrarian myth, the Penn School supporters believed that industrial education could instill in blacks the values and the ethical understanding of the truly civilized man, as well as prepare them for the economic independence that would allow them to grow. But the whole program depended on protecting blacks from the dangers that surrounded them: the vicious and prejudiced attitudes of unenlightened, fearful whites; an economic competition for which they were not prepared; and the temptations to sloth that would hinder them from taking up the challenge of self-development. In sum, the Penn School program was designed to improve life in the country, so the black would see his opportunity there for advancement and work to lift himself up.

The white participants in the Penn School endeavor believed that they had found the solution to a great national problem. They believed that they had found the means of ameliorating a great threat to the American experiment in democracy and that this knowledge, this helpful program, legitimized their stewardship over the lives of the blacks on St. Helena Island. This certainty led them into an attitude that became the fourth major characteristic of the Penn School experience, an acceptance of white control.

From the beginning of the Cooley-House leadership, the Penn School principals endeavored to adapt their school to the

---

4. "Annual Report of the Penn Normal, Industrial and Agricultural School," 1905–1906, Trustees' minutes, January 31, 1939, both in PSP.

needs of the island community. As a result of their Hampton training and their schooling in the principles of the new progressive education, the two ladies had an abhorrence of an education that involved "isolated facts learned not because they fitted into life but because they fitted into the examinations."[5] One of the first goals of the new principals had been to venture out into the community and identify the needs of the people. Their forays into the homes and their helpful missions of ministering to the aged and the sick had given them abundant reason to believe that they could bring much-needed help to this community. And especially in the early years, the Penn School attention to basic problems of health and sanitation, diet, farming, and homemaking went far toward raising the standards and ameliorating the distress of this isolated rural community.

The early years of the Penn School venture saw a marked improvement in the quality of island living, but woven into the fabric of white beneficence was a basic flaw of the missionary endeavor: outsiders were defining the needs of the island people. Whereas one of the strengths of the new progressive education was supposedly its responsiveness to the needs of the community, the identification of those needs had to remain in the hands of the community itself if initiative and self-respect were to be preserved. This was not the case at St. Helena.

Although the Community Council played an active role in directing the expenditure of islander energies, the Community Council always reflected the desires and the control of the two white ladies at Hampton House. And although the two ladies had only the best of intentions and the purest of motives, their increasing control over the shape of island lives bred resentment in some and passivity in others. Dependence was inescapable, because for all the members of this isolated community, Penn School was the only real link with the outside world, the only ameliorative institution on the island, and the only hope of rising above the difficulties and limitations of a yeoman economy. Thus, Penn gathered to itself a measure of authority and control that stifled much

5. Cooley, *School Acres*, 36.

native talent and initiative and that poisoned the Penn School endeavor at its base.[6]

The paternalism at Penn School grew out of the assumptions of the whites who conceived and supported the endeavor. Seeking a solution to the "Negro Problem" that would lay their own fears to rest, Penn's white participants perceived the problem at St. Helena to be one of culture rather than of economics. Thus, their primary effort was directed at what they took to be the moral and spiritual needs of the islanders. They were responding, therefore, to "needs" the blacks themselves could not have perceived.

Although the program at Penn School clearly did not involve the economic exploitation usually associated with paternalism, it did involve a form of exploitation nonetheless. Forcing black development along lines dictated by white fears, Penn School asked the blacks of the Sea Islands to participate in an experiment, ostensibly for their own good, but actually designed to aid their white benefactors through a difficult and frightening period in the American national experience. Thus the truly significant needs in the Penn School endeavor were those of the whites, and the blacks found once again that white promises of freedom and dignity carried hidden clauses in the fine print. Paralyzed by paternalism, Penn School held out a false promise to the blacks of St. Helena Island.

Penn School had a significant impact on the lives of the Sea Island blacks who came under its influence and control. That impact could be seen in improved standards of living and in expanded conceptions of life, and in a hundred different ways St. Helena Island reflected the beneficial effects of Penn School's presence. The school never fulfilled its promise, however, of providing a demonstration for white America of the worth of industrial education or of proving to the Sea Island blacks that life in the country could be rewarding and fulfilling. Aside from the fact

---

6. As educational historian Buell Gallagher has suggested, there was more of the grandmother than of the father in this paternalism. The students and islanders were controlled as effectively as if they had been subjects of an authoritarian state, and yet the method used was that of "wheedling, cajoling, pampering, coaxing, indulging the student's whims in order to get his aquiescence." Buell G. Gallagher, *American Caste and the Negro College* (New York, 1938), 267.

that it was working against the major trends of the times—stressing agrarianism and community building at a time when the forces of mechanization and urbanization were depressing farming operations and disintegrating communities across the country—Penn's failure was largely the result of insufficient financing. Penn's failure also reflected the principals' excess of enthusiasm. Endeavoring to perform all the functions that the family, the church, the local government, and the school had performed in an earlier America, Miss Cooley and Miss House were increasingly overwhelmed by their task.

The truth of Penn's limited effectiveness was never clear to the principals for a number of reasons: their indisputable success in bringing better homes, better farms, and better health to large parts of the island fostered an exaggerated sense of accomplishment; Penn's widespread fame and the never-ending praise for their school reassured the women that their program was appropriate and effective; the frantic pace of their activities and the enormity of their task kept their attention focused on present problems and crises and left little time for either reflection or evaluation; and their increasing identification with Penn as their "family" caused a distortion of perception that precluded objective analysis. In fact, however, Penn School reached directly only about 250 students each year (out of an island student population of about 2,000), though its influence was felt in a myriad of community activities. Added to the fact that the Penn endeavor consumed about $40,000 a year for forty years, there seems to be ample reason for asking, along with a disgruntled Penn School teacher who asked in 1926: "Are we hitting the mark? . . . Are the results commensurate to the amount of money and labor being invested?"[7] This teacher did not last long at Penn School, but he had raised some important questions that were rarely asked on St. Helena. And his questions deserve an answer.

Just how successful was the Penn School endeavor? Did the white principals and trustees achieve the goals they had set for themselves? Can their efforts be termed a success, or a failure, in

7. "Aims of Penn School," 1926, in PSP.

any wider sense? An expertise beyond the scope of this endeavor would be required to answer these questions completely—for the tools of the sociologist and the anthropologist, at least, would be needed to determine the full extent of Penn's impact on the economy and the value systems of St. Helena Island. But enough evidence can be gleaned from the records of the experience, from interviews with participants, and from impressionistic observation to paint in broad strokes the outlines of success or failure for the goals and the programs of Penn School.

At the foundation of the Penn experiment lay the hope of economic development. Through agricultural instruction for increased productivity, shop training for self-sufficiency, experience in cooperative techniques, and regeneration of the life of the community, Penn sought to foster landownership and an acceptance of rural living, or in other words, to create a contented, self-respecting yeomanry. In all these areas, Penn School fell short of its goals.

The development of Penn's agricultural program involved starting from scratch: purchasing the land for a school farm and making it produce; convincing students and parents of the propriety of agricultural instruction in the schools; identifying and overcoming such basic problems as clogged ditches; demonstrating the effectiveness of the new methods; and convincing the conservative islanders to abandon ancient techniques. Miss Cooley's efforts in behalf of such new gospels as diversification were truly heroic, and her enthusiasm never flagged despite intense islander skepticism and resistance; but Miss Cooley had neither the knowledge nor the technical expertise to effect the kind of agricultural revolution she envisioned for her island. And because her primary interest lay with the cultural development of the blacks, she never concentrated her energies on the agricultural program with sufficient intensity to guarantee success.

In the early years, Miss Cooley made great headway toward convincing many islanders to adopt the new techniques. By bringing the farms into the school, by making the school farm produce, by enlisting the energies of the demonstration agent, and then by taking the school out to the farms with the addition of school acres to the classroom equipment, Miss Cooley and Penn School seemed to be wearing down islander resistance and assuring themselves of eventual success in transforming all phases of life on St. Helena Island. But the arrival of the boll weevil upset the economic life of the island so completely that the basis of the school's program was destroyed. Miss Cooley never found the answer to an economic problem that plagued the whole southern region. This, coupled with Miss Cooley's expenditure of her energies elsewhere and her trustees' failure to step into the breach, meant that the school was never able to provide the basis for islander self-sufficiency.

Penn's industrial program was similarly ineffective. Growing out of a desire to provide the blacks with all the basic skills a rural community needed, and thus to make the island truly self-sufficient, the industrial program never received the emphasis or the financing to assure success. Though the trades such as blacksmithing and wheelwrighting were outmoded even as they were taught, they were responsive initially to the needs of the island. But as Miss Cooley's agricultural utopia failed to materialize, the shop equipment simply wore out and was not replaced. Especially after the boll weevil devastation and the national economic collapse, the industrial program became daily less useful and effective.

The Penn School venture into cooperative buying and selling also failed to achieve its ends. Designed to give training and experience in modern business techniques, as well as to rationalize the farming and business operations on the island, the Cooperative Society went the way of the agricultural and industrial programs when the boll weevil invaded the island. Resting on a shaky foundation, the Cooperative Society could not withstand the successive years of bad luck that culminated in the white potato fiasco, and thus that program also slipped quietly into oblivion.

The program to regenerate the life of the community found its fullest expression in the development of the All-Year School, which also fell a victim to economic crisis and inadequate financing. The myriad of community activities, nonetheless, from corn clubs to Rosenwald committees to mystery plays, reflected Miss

Cooley's magnetic dynamism and her ability to capture imaginations on the island. The community program was probably the capstone of the entire Penn School venture, and yet, St. Helena was unable to hold its young people.

Consistently through the years, St. Helena lost its young people to the cities. Though Penn School might battle such a trend with words and dire predictions, it was never able to create either an economic program or a community program that could compete with the opportunities or the excitement of the cities. By the time of the arrival of the Second World War, even the teachers—the dedicated Christian missionaries—had tightened their belts too often; and they, too, abandoned the failing enterprise.

Despite the loss of the young, the blacks who remained on St. Helena continued to value landownership over the years, and there was much evidence across the island of a self-respecting yeomanry. But it is possible that Penn cannot claim these as a victory: the valuing of landownership may have been the birthright of these unusual blacks who had bought land from the government after the Civil War, and their oft-remarked dignity and self-respect may have stemmed from their landownership and their isolation from white racism. But surely Penn School contributed to the development and preservation of these characteristics. This having been said, however, on the most basic level Penn's economic program must be considered a failure.

The failure of the economic program precluded the full development of the cultural program Miss Cooley had envisioned for St. Helena Island. The emphasis on better homes and better health never wavered, however, and Miss Cooley held fast to her belief that the girls held the key to her program of uplift. She poured herself unsparingly into improving the lot of the women, and she expected that investment to yield a rich return in increased morality and heightened spiritual understanding. The extent of her success, however, is difficult to determine.[8]

It is clear that the Penn School message reached some, and that some of the islanders internalized the values the two ladies

---

8. See Miss Cooley's *Homes of the Freed* for a moving description of her commitment to solving the problems of St. Helena's women.

sought to instill. One former trustee remembered his visits at Penn to have been especially enjoyable—and even ennobling—because of the unusual qualities of the black people he met there. He found them to be intelligent, articulate, and sensitive; and he felt humbled by their philosophy and their way of life. He did believe, however, that Penn School was an island within an island—an oasis of sophistication—that did not extend beyond the campus.[9]

Judging from the large numbers of Penn School students who left St. Helena, Miss Cooley and Miss House must have failed in their mission to instill in the blacks a spirit of service to the island, for this was at the heart of the Penn School message.[10] And judging from surface appearances—St. Helena is not vastly different in appearance from other Sea Islands that did not have Penn Schools—the program would not seem to have altered significantly the course of the island's development. But there are other kinds of evidence, more subtle, perhaps, but more revealing, that suggest that Penn School made a lasting impression.

Even today, thirty years later, Penn School graduates are socially dominant on St. Helena Island, which may indicate a widespread respect for the kind of person Penn School produced. Their homes, their personal demeanor, their conception of their responsibility to the community—all reflect a set of values that would stand them in good stead in any middle-class community in America. What is more, they have led the opposition to the development of black militancy on the island—which would seem to suggest a rejection of the techniques, if not the ends, of that movement—and they have struggled to maintain the symbols of the old Penn School. But the graduates are a fairly small group, and their influence is limited.

Perhaps more indicative of Penn School's lasting influence on the values of the people is the affection it continues to inspire from the people it served. The York W. Bailey Museum on St. Helena Island bears eloquent testimony to the living respect to Penn School. Housed in the old Founders' Hall, its walls and

9. Interview with Paul Brown, July 23, 1974, Philadelphia, Pa.
10. Interview with Edith Fields Sumpter, March, 1975, St. Helena Island, S.C.

shelves are lined with pictures and records of an experience that set this island apart, that brought it worldwide acclaim and made its people special. There is also a certain reverence for Penn School that is clearly in evidence at Frissell Memorial Hall every third Sunday in the month when the islanders gather for their community sing. Here there is a certain sense of the old excitement and the old purpose that has since gone out of the lives of these Sea Island blacks. Here amid the haunting spirituals, the lively games of call and response, the solemn coming-forth for the offering, and the gospel singing of one of the plantation church choirs, one can almost feel Miss Cooley's presence, and one knows she would be welcome.

Penn School brought many special joys to the blacks of St. Helena Island. There was the indefinable, unmeasurable excitement of having embarked on an ennobling adventure, one that would lead the way into a better world. Blacks and whites together were on a common quest, and they believed that they served as a torch that could light the way for others. The excitement of that adventure was very real, and it must not be discounted in any effort to assess Penn School's contribution or to measure its effect.

Equally real, however, was the deadening force of paternalism at Penn School. Psychologists have suggested that people often come to see themselves as they are seen by significant others, and Miss Cooley clearly regarded the blacks on her island as children. In all of her writings she romanticized them, though she may have designed her pleasant, nonthreatening images to counter more fearful stereotypes. Nonetheless, her benevolent guidance and her iron will undoubtedly silenced opposition, and the rewards of accepting her guidance and control were unmistakable. In return for accepting white guidance, the blacks received approval and status; and no tradition of leadership or initiative ever developed on St. Helena Island.

John Mercer Langston identified the core of the problem of paternalism when he resigned his post as dean of the Law School at Howard University. Giving full vent to his frustration and bitterness with white paternalism, Langston suggested that such enterprises "relieve the object of their sympathy of the pressure of responsibility and the honor due its effective discharge, and thus weaken him, as an over affectionate and indulgent father does his son."[11] The blacks became dependent on Penn School to direct their lives and to solve their problems, and the school was not up to the task. When the two ladies retired, the truth of Penn's failure became apparent. With no tradition of leadership and paralyzed by paternalism, the blacks of St. Helena Island fell into a chaos from which they have not yet emerged.

Penn School also failed in its attempt to prove to white America that industrial education could remove the threat of black degradation and ignorance. It proved to many concerned citizens, such as Albert Bushnell Hart, that such a "School of Civilization" could demonstrate "the effect that can be produced by civilizing influences upon members of the colored race, providing there is no discouragement or interference on the part of other white people."[12] But though it demonstrated black "improvability," it never provided a convincing solution to the "Negro Problem." In part, this failure sprang from inadequate trustee commitment and the consequent failure to provide the needed funds for such a test. In part, it may have sprung from black resistance—whether because of islander conservatism or because the independent blacks of St. Helena Island refused to accept the Penn School analysis of their deficiencies. It is possible that these Sea Island blacks were unmoved by the white desire to experiment with them; they lived an idyllic life from the sea, and they may well have had no desire to be "civilized." They certainly would not have been moved by any imperative of cultural unity, and they hardly could have seen themselves as a "threat" to a world they had never known.

The larger explanation of Penn's failure, and the one that goes to the heart of the matter, is that the whole enterprise grew out of fallacious assumptions. Refusing to accept the validity of a culture and a world view different from their own, the white par-

---

11. John Mercer Langston, *Emancipation and Citizenship: The Work of the Republican Party, Addresses at Chillicothe, Ohio* (Washington, 1875), 7–8; as quoted in McPherson, "White Liberals and Black Power in Negro Education, 1865–1915," 1364.
12. Albert Bushnell Hart to Cooley, November 14, 1933, in PSP.

ticipants in the Penn School venture invested their energies in removing the threat they perceived to their world. They could not prove that blacks were worthy because they could not make blacks white, and their efforts to do so were thus doomed from the beginning.

Penn School held out a false hope to the blacks of St. Helena Island and to the whites who labored in their behalf. Many of the blacks were willing to accept the need for uplift, for an escape from the limitations of their condition, and Penn School seemed to promise a way up. Although never stated, the implication of the Penn School message must have been that some day blacks would be accepted and that they could hope for an end to racism through self-help. Miss House certainly believed this, and Dr. Frissell may have believed it, too; but they were radical Christian idealists and visionaries as well. Probably more widespread were the assumptions of Miss Cooley. In the conclusion to her little book about St. Helena Island's women, Miss Cooley revealed a hope that must have sustained her in her work: "Great tide rivers seem to typify the separation of the young people of the two races. There can be mutual respect only through knowledge. Many of the oncoming generations of the white race are coming across the rivers. When they understand the conditions, the struggles, the successes of the oncoming generation of the black race, then we can hope that the great experiment in democracy has a chance of winning out."[13]

Here were the commitment and the faith in man's disposition to right the wrongs he sees of the genuine Progressive. Here also were the sympathy, intelligence, practicality, and idealism that could make even such a critic as Mary White Ovington praise the efforts of Penn School.[14] It must be accounted a tragedy that black and white dreams and lives were bound up together in a false hope—in the belief that the deep-seated evils of racism and prejudice would yield their hold as a result of an educational experiment on an out-of-the-way island in the Atlantic.

13. Cooley, *Homes of the Freed*, 199.
14. Mary White Ovington, review of *Homes of the Freed*, Norfolk *Journal and Guide*, April 2, 1927, clipping, in PSP.

The Penn School venture grew out of the same impulse that had motivated those earlier northern missionaries in the midst of the Civil War, causing them to undertake the Port Royal experiment. The desire to inculcate morality, or traditional New England values, reflected these northerners' doubts about black people's preparation for citizenship and the wisdom of including them in the great experiment in democracy. These doubts had had a long tradition; the controversy over Afro-American character had preceded the American Revolution, and it did not end with emancipation.[15] The political acts of conferring freedom and citizenship had done nothing to dispel white doubts and fears, and though questions about black worth were clearly inconsistent with the choices the nation had made—and clearly unfair to the freedmen—the old questions persisted. Thus Penn School had been struggling for forty years, before Hollis Frissell ever conceived his new experiment, to dispel northern fears by proving the black man's worth. And the new Penn School was simply a continuation of that old impulse. Though the modern observer might regret the need for proof, the need was nonetheless there; Penn School was an effort to deal with that reality and to lay old fears to rest.

As Edwin Hoffman concluded over twenty years ago: "An experiment is always a test of the observer as well as the subject under examination. If the nation might sit in judgment on these freedmen, so it must be judged by what it learned from the experiment and what it did about its lesson."[16] The nation learned very little from the Penn School experiment. Though Miss Cooley and Miss House and their band of dedicated workers struggled forty years to provide a demonstration for the nation, white America was not watching. Satisfied with the solution of segregation, white Americans lost interest in questions of black worth; and Penn School became an irrelevant reminder of a promise unfulfilled.

15. Rose, *Rehearsal for Reconstruction*; Winthrop Jordan, *White over Black: American Attitudes Toward the Negro, 1550–1812* (Chapel Hill: University of North Carolina Press, 1968); Fredrickson, *The Black Image in The White Mind*; Lawrence J. Freidman, *The White Savage: Racial Fantasies in the Postbellum South* (Englewood Cliffs, N.J. 1970).

16. Hoffman, "From Slavery to Self-Reliance," 41.

APPENDIX A

Penn School Trustees

Aull, Dr. George Hubert, Clemson, South Carolina, November, 1942–November, 1948.
Bailey, Mrs. York, St. Helena Island, S.C., January, 1945–November, 1948.
Batchelder, Mr. Mark D., St. Helena Island, S.C., January, 1918–November, 1939.
Bemis, Mrs. A. Farwell, January, 1929–June, 1929.
Blanton, Joshua Enoch, Denmark, S.C., January, 1945–June, 1947.
Bradford, Mrs. Amory H., Jr., N.Y., N.Y., June, 1940–February, 1944.
Brown, Paul, Philadelphia, Pa., January 31, 1939–November, 1948.
Cadbury, William Edward, Philadelphia, Pa., November, 1935–November, 1948.
Coker, Mr. David Robert, Hartsville, S.C., April, 1915–January, 1916.
Cooley, Rossa Belle, St. Helena Island, S.C., March, 1907–November, 1948.
Cope, Francis Reeve, Jr., Dimock, Pa., October, 1902–November, 1948.
Cope, Thomas P., Philadelphia, Pa., February, 1909–April, 1912.
Cornish, Mrs. Louis Craig, Boston, Mass., June, 1904–January, 1913.
Curtis, Miss Isabella, Boston, Mass., October, 1916–November, 1948.
Davis, Miss Lucy, Philadelphia, Pa., April, 1901–November, 1948.
Eliot, Mrs. Thomas, Boston, Mass., November, 1938–November, 1948.
Emlen, Mr. John Thompson, Philadelphia, Pa., July, 1905–January, 1920.
Eustis, Mr. Frederick A., Readville, Mass., April, 1912–April, 1925.
Evans, Mr. Harold, Philadelphia, Pa., April, 1927–November, 1948.
Foote, Henry Wilder (Rev.), Boston, Mass., December, 1902–June, 1947.
Frierson, Mr. J. Nelson, Columbia, S.C., September, 1924–November, 1948.
Frissell, Dr. Hollis Burke, Hampton, Va., December, 1900–September, 1917 (died).
Goodwin, Mrs. W. W., Boston, Mass., December, 1905–?
Gregg, Dr. James Edgar (Rev.), Pittsfield, Mass., January, 1918–June, 1946.
Holden, Mrs. Benjamin D., Poughkeepsie, N.Y., June, 1931–January, 1935.

Hopkinson, Miss Joan, Manchester, Mass., November, 1935–November, 1948.
House, Miss Grace Bigelow, St. Helena Island, S.C., October, 1931–November, 1948.
Howe, Mrs. Arthur, Hampton, Va., October, 1931–November, 1939.
Howell, Mr. Lardner, Philadelphia, Pa., February, 1914–October, 1926.
James, Arthur Curtiss, New York, N.Y., April, 1901–February, 1909.
Jeffries, Mrs. John A., Boston, Mass., March, 1908–?
Jenks, Mrs. Horace, Haverford, Pa., May, 1936–November, 1948.
Jenks, Dr. Horace C., Haverford, Pa., March, 1926–October, 1931.
Jenks, Mrs. William F., Philadelphia, Pa., December, 1900–October, 1926 (died).
Kellogg, Paul Underwood, New York, N.Y., September, 1919–November, 1948.
Kirkbridge, Miss Elizabeth Butler, Philadelphia, Pa., January, 1903–January, 1905.
Lamb, Mrs. Horace, Washington, D.C., September, 1929–January 1935.
McAllister, Dr. Jane, Washington, D.C., November, 1942–November, 1948.
Macdonald, Mr. James Ross, St. Helena Island, S.C., December, 1900–January, 1919 (died).
Mathews, Miss Alberta, Poughkeepsie, N.Y., January, 1935–February, 1938.
Maule, Alfred Collins, Philadelphia, Pa., July, 1903–April, 1937.
Maule, Miss Margaret C., Philadelphia, Pa., February, 1931–October, 1932.
Maule, Mr. Samuel George Morton, Philadelphia, Pa., June, 1912–February, 1914.
Mays, Dr. Benjamin, Atlanta, Ga., January, 1945–November, 1948.
Mills, Dr. W. H., Clemson, S.C., June, 1924–February, 1942 (died).
Moors, Mrs. John, Boston, Mass., March, 1908–November, 1948.
Morris, Miss Ellen, Philadelphia, Pa., October, 1916–May, 1936.
Moton, Robert Russa, Tuskegee, Ala., June, 1939–June, 1940 (died).
Murray, Miss Ellen, St. Helena Island, S.C., December, 1900–March, 1908.
Myers, Mr. Louis G., New York, N.Y., June, 1904–April, 1910.
Niebuhr, Mrs. Reinhold, Princton, N.J., March, 1945–November, 1948.
Osborne, Lithgow, New York, N.Y., 1947–November, 1948.
Peabody, George Foster, New York, N.Y., April, 1901–October, 1926.
Pope, Henry W., November, 1946–November, 1948.
Purves, Mrs. Alexander, Hampton, Va., February, 1914–January, 1946.
Russell, Mr. William Channing, Philadelphia, Pa., 1901–1903.
Sachs, Miss Elizabeth, February, 1928–June, 1931.
Sachs, Mrs. Paul J., January, 1913–February, 1928.
Scattergood, Mr. Henry, Philadelphia, Pa., October, 1926–February, 1942.
Schieffelin, Miss Barbara, New York, N.Y., April, 1927–February, 1931.
Sharpless, Isaac, Haverford, Pa., April, 1901–March, 1920.
Silver, John, Philadelphia, Pa., 1937–1946.
Smith, Mrs. W. W., Poughkeepsie, N.Y., 1938–1948.
Smith, Miss Alice Fitch, New York, N.Y., January, 1935–November, 1937.
Smith, Mrs. Wilson Fitch, New York, N.Y., June, 1931–January, 1935.
Stimson, Mrs. Henry Lewis, June, 1911–April, 1912.
Storer, Miss Edith, Boston, Mass., 1932–1935.
Tate, Professor William Knox, Columbia, S.C., 1912–1914.
Thorp, Miss Erica, January, 1913–January, 1916.

Towne, Miss Laura, St. Helena Island, S.C., December, 1900–April, 1901.
Valentine, William R., Bordentown, N.J., 1940–1948.
Van Sinderen, Mr. Henry B., New York, N.Y., February, 1921–March, 1926.
Ware, Miss Harriet, Milton, Mass., December, 1905–September, 1920.
Walker, Mr. W. R., Union, S.C., December, 1900–April, 1912.
Wood, L. Hollingsworth, New York, N.Y., March, 1908–November, 1948.
Wright, Mr. Marion, 1947–1948.

Appendix **B**

Calendar of the All-Year School

Autumn Term	Winter Term	Spring Term	Summer Term
School opens with Parents' Day	Regular classroom schedule	"Planting Week" Picnic	Spring schedule continued on farms
Classes reorganized	Home Acres reported on and charts kept in classrooms	"Planting Week" All pupil above fourth grade and teachers go out to the Home Acres	
Reports on summer holidays	Parents' Day		
	Arbor Day		
Reports on Home Acres	Christmas Entertainments and Mystery Play	Parents' Day	Canning at homes and schools
Farmers' Fair		Temperance Rally	
"Potato Week" All pupils stay home All classroom teachers visit the homes according to advertised routes		Teachers above fourth grade go to Home Acres every Friday	Community Sings Watermelon Picnic Holidays
Pupils above fourth grade select their home acres and projects			
Community Sings	Week of Prayer	Community Sings	
Community Council	Week of Song	Clean-up Week	
Games	Negro History Week	Mother's Day	
	Games	Better Homes Week Baby Day Penn School Sunday Exhibition Games	

APPENDIX C

Contributors to Penn Normal, Industrial, and Agricultural School June 1, 1917–May 31, 1918*

Agassiz, Mr. George R.	$ 50.00
Allen, Mrs. Wm. N.	2.00
Allison, Miss Caroline	1.00
American Unitarian Ass'n., Boston, Mass.	118.03
Ames, Mrs. Jas. B.	25.00
Anderson, Miss Agnes	5.00
Anonymous	50.00
Anonymous	1.00
Arnold, Miss Katharine	25.00
Atkinson, Mrs. E. W.	25.00
Auryansen, Mr. G. W.	5.00
Bacon, Miss E. S.	5.00
Baker, Mr. Ray Stannard	10.00
Balch, Mrs. F. G.	3.00
Barbour, Mr. E. D.	5.00
Bartlett, Miss Mary F.	20.00
Bartol, Miss Elizabeth H.	100.00
Barton, Mrs. F. O.	25.00
Batchelder, Mrs. Chas. F.	25.00
Batchelder, Mr. M. D.	25.00
Beers, Mr. Henry	5.00
Belfield, Mr. T. Broom	10.00
Bennett, Mr. S. W.	3.00
Bigelow, Mrs. Albert F.	15.00
Binney, Mrs. Charles C.	5.00
Blair, Mrs. A. A.	10.00
Blake, Miss M. L.	10.00
Blakeston, Miss Mary	10.00
Blanchard, Miss Harriet	500.00
Blue Mountain Lodge of St. Helena	10.00
Borton, Mr. C. Walter	10.00
Bowditch, Miss Olivia Y.	20.00
Bowers, Mr. Henry L.	25.00
Bowne, Miss Fannie	1.00
Bowne, Miss Sarah	5.00
Bradley, Mrs. Leverett	3.00
Bradshaw Missionary Ass'n, Arlington, Mass.	15.00
Brazier, Mrs. J. H.	25.00
Bremer, Miss Sarah F.	100.00
Brookline, Mass., First Parish of	20.00
Brookline, Mass., First Parish Sewing Circle of	15.00
Brooks, Mrs. Chas. S.	5.00
Brooks, Mrs. Shepherd	30.00
Brown Bros. & Co.	10.00
Buckley, Miss Mary S.	2.00
Bulkley, Mr. Edwin M.	25.00
Bullard, Miss Ellen	10.00
Bullard, Miss Katherine	40.00
Bunce, Mr. James H.	15.00
Burnham, Mrs. George, Jr.	25.00
Burr, Mr. and Mrs. Allston	25.00
Butterfield, Mr. K. S.	5.00
Caldwell, Miss F. F.	15.00
Card, Mr. Geo.	5.00
Carter, Mr. John E.	10.00
Carter, Mrs. John W.	10.00
Carter, Miss Mary P.	1.00

*Annual Report of Penn Normal, Industrial and Agricultural School, 1918, in University of North Carolina Southern Historical Collection, Penn School Papers.

Case, Mrs. James B.	50.00	Denniston, Mrs. W.	5.00
Chace, Mrs. Arnold C., Jr.	5.00	Devers, Mr. A. H.	10.00
Chalfant, Miss Isabella C.	25.00	De Yarmett, Mr. and Mrs. H. J.	5.00
Chambers, Mr. Frank R.	150.00	Dixey, Mr. R. C.	10.00
Chandler, Miss Alice G.	5.00	Dodge, Mr. Cleveland H.	100.00
Chapman, Mr. John Jay	10.00	Dorchester, Mass., Village Church Sunday School	10.00
Cheever, Mrs. David W.	10.00		
Chew, Mrs. Samuel	25.00	Douglas, Mr. James	50.00
Christian Endeavor Society, First Presbyterian Church, Poughkeepsie, N.Y.	25.00	Douw, Mr. Chas. G.	10.00
		Dresel, Miss Louise L.	10.00
		Dreyfuss, Mrs. Ludwig	100.00
Christian Endeavor Society, First Presbyterian Church, Poughkeepsie, N.Y.	15.00	Dudley, Mr. Guilford	10.00
		Duryee, Miss Amy	5.00
		Duryee, Miss A. B.	10.00
Christmas Service Collection on St. Helena	12.48	Ebenezer Church, St. Helena Sunday School	5.25
Clark, Mr. C. M.	100.00		
Clark, Mrs. Harold T.	10.00	Eliot, Mrs. Chas. W.	10.00
Class in Lincoln School, N.Y. City	5.00	Eliot, Miss Edith	2.00
		Elliott, Mrs. J. W.	10.00
Cobb, Mrs. Henry E.	10.00	Emlen, Mr. John T.	50.00
Collins, Mr. H. H.	20.00	Emmons, Mrs. R. W., 2d	10.00
Converse, Miss Mary E.	25.00	Estlack, Mr. Chas. E.	5.00
Cooley, Miss Mary Elizabeth	10.00	Eustis, Mr. Augustus H.	250.00
Coolidge, Mrs. Algernon	10.00	Eustis, Mr. F. A.	250.00
Coolidge, Miss Ellen W.	10.00	Eustis, Mr. W. E. C.	200.00
Coolidge, Mrs. J. Randolph	50.00	Evans, Mr. and Mrs. F. Algernon	5.00
Coonley, Mrs. Avery	25.00	Evans, Mrs. E. W.	5.00
Cope, Mrs. Alexis T.	100.00	Evans, Mrs. Jonathan	10.00
Cope, Miss Caroline E.	250.00	Everett, Mrs. W. B.	10.00
Cope, Mr. Francis R., Jr.	50.00		
Cope, Mr. Francis R., Jr.	100.00	Farnsworth, Miss Alice	25.00
Cope, Mr. Francis R., Jr.	150.00	Fitz, Mrs. W. Scott	25.00
Cope, Mrs. F. R. and Miss Theodora M.	10.00	Flinn, Mr. and Mrs. Alfred D.	10.00
		Ford, Mr. Fred	10.00
Crary, Mrs. Geo.	30.00	Fox, Miss Hannah	10.00
Cummings, Mrs. C. K.	100.00	Friedman, Mrs. J.	5.00
Curtis, Miss Frances G.	50.00	Friend, A	50.00
Curtis, Mr. and Mrs. Greely S.	75.00	Friend, A	5.00
Curtis, Miss Isabella	100.00	Friend, A	25.00
Curtis, Isabella, Collected by	205.00	Frothingham, Mrs. Louis A.	100.00
Curtis, Mr. Jas. F.	20.00	Fuller, Mrs. Gardner	10.00
Cushing, Estate of Emmeline	50.00		
Cushing, Mrs. W. E.	10.00	Gannett, Mr. W. C.	10.00
Cutler, Miss Anna W.	5.00	Garrett, Mr. John B.	50.00
		Garrett, Mrs. Mary M.	200.00 0
Darrah Hall Entertainment on St. Helena	10.55	Garrett, Mrs. William	5.00
		General Education Board	5,000.00
Davids, Mr. Richard W.	5.00	Gest, Mr. William P.	25.00
Davis, Mr. Andrew McF.	100.00	Gibson, Miss Mary K.	25.00
Davis, Miss Katharine Bement	5.00	Glenn, Dr. John M.	25.00
Davis, Miss Lucy	30.00	Goff, Mrs. Frances M.	20.00
Day, Miss Katharine S.	10.00	Goldman, Mr. Henry	100.00

Appendix C

Goldman, Mrs. Julius	150.00	Lathers, Miss Agnes	10.00
Gray, Miss Hope	50.00	Lathers, Miss Julia	50.00
Gregg, Mr. Jas. E.	5.00	Lawrence, Mrs. William	10.00
Griscom, Miss Frances C.	5.00	Lea, Miss Nina	30.00
Guild, Mrs. Chas. E.	5.00	Lee, Mrs. Francis H.	50.00
Guild, Miss Sarah L.	15.00	Lee, Mrs. Joseph	10.00
		Lincoln, Mrs. Roland C.	25.00
Hague, Miss Eleanor	25.00	Lincoln Society, The, St. Helena Island, S.C.	5.00
Haines, Mrs. Jansen	10.00		
Hall, Mrs. Charles Cuthbert	5.00	Lippincott, Miss Mary W.	25.00
Hall, Mrs. Frederick G.	15.00	Little, Mrs. D. M.	10.00
Hallowell, Miss Susan M.	10.00	Lobenstine, Mrs. W. C.	10.00
Hampton Friends	5.00	Longstreth, Mrs. C. A.	5.00
Hampton Institute Jeanes Fund	200.00	Low, Mr. Wm. G.	25.00
Hartshorne, Miss Cornelia	10.00	Lyman, Mrs. R. T.	10.00
Haskell, Miss Margaret	10.00		
Helping Hand, The, Haverford, Pa.	10.00	McCaleb, Miss Ella	10.00
		McElwain, Mrs. Wm. M.	10.00
Hill, Dr. and Mrs. Wm. Bancroft	100.00	McGraw, Mrs. Thomas S.	5.00
Higginson, Mrs. H. L.	10.00	McMurtrie, Miss Ellen	25.00
Hinchman, Mrs. L. S.	25.00	MacBride, Mrs. Malcolm L.	10.00
Hinchman, Mr. Walter	10.00	Macdonald, Miss Elizabeth	5.00
Holmes, Miss Mary M.	5.00	Maderia, Mrs. Louis C.	20.00
Homans, Mrs. John	25.00	Markoe, Mrs. Jno.	50.00
Hooker, Mrs. E. H.	15.00	Mason, Mrs. Caroline R.	10.00
Hopkinson, Mrs. Charles	10.00	Mason, Mrs. Chas. E.	50.00
House, Mrs. Chas. F.	25.00	Mason, Miss Ellen F.	50.00
Household of Ruth of St. Helena Island, S.C.	2.00	Mason, Miss Mary Taylor	10.00
		Maule, Mrs. S. G. Morton	25.00
Houston, Mr. J. W.	5.00	May, Miss Mary C.	10.00
Hoyt, Miss G. L.	10.00	Means, Mr. Charles J.	10.00
Hubbard, Mrs. Chas. W.	75.00	Means, Mrs. Jas.	10.00
Huntington, Mr. Ellsworth	5.00	Meigs, Mrs. Ferris J.	25.00
Huston, Mr. Chas. Q.	10.00	Mellor, Miss Margaret	1.00
		Merriman, Mrs. Daniel	10.00
James, Mr. Arthur Curtiss	4,000.00	Milton Branch, Women's Alliance, Milton, Mass.	20.00
Jeanes Rural School Fund	450.00		
Jenks, Mrs. Wm. E.	400.00	Monroe, Mrs. Elbert B.	150.00
Johnston, Miss Edith	5.00	Moodey, Mrs. Robert	10.00
Jones, Miss Amelia H.	10.00	Moore, Mrs. Edward C.	5.00
Joseph, Mrs. Fred	5.00	Moore, Mrs. Eliza Coe	5.00
Junior Auxiliary Christ Church, Poughkeepsie, N.Y.	2.00	Moors, Mrs. John F.	211.16
		Moors, Mrs. John F.	105.00
		Moors, Mrs. John F.	20.00
Kelsey, Mr. C. H.	50.00	Morris, Miss Anna	15.00
Keyserling, Mr. Wm.	25.00	Morris, Mr. C. C.	25.00
Kimball, Mrs. David	100.00	Morris, Miss and Mr. Christopher	10.00
King, Mrs. Henry P.	50.00		
King, Mrs. Iola Cooley	5.00	Morris, Miss Ellen	50.00
Kirkbridge, Miss E. B.	5.00	Morris, Mrs. F. W.	5.00
		Morris, Rev. Jos. Paul	10.00
Ladd, Mrs. William Sargent	50.00	Morris, Mrs. Wm. H.	5.00
Lane, Mr. Wm. T.	25.00	Morris, Mrs. Wistar	5.00

Morse, Dr. Henry Lee	5.00	Riley, Mr. Chas. E.	25.00
Morse, Mr. John T.	10.00	Roberts, Miss Frances A.	10.00
Mosenthal, Mr. Philip J.	5.00	Robinson, Miss Mary P.	2.00
Munro, Mr. M. H.	2.00	Roe, Miss Mary W.	5.00
		Rogers, Miss Harriet B.	1.00
Newlin, Miss Sarah	150.00	Rosenwald, Mr. Julius	500.00
Newlin, Miss Mary S.	10.00	Ruggles, Mrs. T. E.	5.00
Newlin, Miss Katherine	75.00	Russell, Miss Marian	20.00
Nicholson, Dr. and Mrs. Percival	2.00		
		Sachs, Mrs. Paul J.	150.00
Paine, Mr. Geo. L.	50.00	Sachs, Mrs. Samuel	400.00
Paine Association, Robert Treat	50.00	St. Helena Quintette	10.00
Parents League of Penn School	20.73	St. Helena Women's Union	5.00
Parkman, Mrs. S.	15.00	Schiff, Mr. Jacob H.	100.00
Peabody, Rev. Francis G.	25.00	Scott, Mr. Donald	100.00
Peabody, Mr. George Foster	30.00	Scoville, Mrs. Wm. B.	10.00
Peabody, Mrs. M. E.	1.00	Sears, Miss Mary P.	15.00
Pell, Rev. Alfred Duane	20.00	Seligman, Mrs. Isaac N.	25.00
Pelton, Mr. Henry V.	10.00	Semple, Mrs. Matthew	10.00
Penn School Club of Boston	1,300.00	Shaw, Mrs. Robert Gould	100.00
Penn School Club of		Sheppard, Miss Louise	5.00
Germantown	50.00	Sherwin, Miss Belle	25.00
Penn School Club of		Sherwin, Mrs. H. A.	25.00
Germantown	30.00	Sherwin, Miss Prudence	25.00
Penn School Club of		Sibley, Miss Florence	50.00
Germantown	200.00	Silsbee, Miss E. W.	5.00
Penn School Club of Hampton	5.00	Slater Fund, Jno. F.	600.00
Penn School Club of Hampton	2.05	Smith, Mrs. Wm. W.	100.00
Penn School Club of		Spingarn, Major J. E.	10.00
Philadelphia	424.50	Sprague, Dr. F. P.	10.00
Penn School Club of		Star-Spangled Banner Society,	
Poughkeepsie	350.00	St. Helena Island, S.C.	1.00
Penn School Club of St. Helena		Smith-Lever Fund	100.00
Island	30.00	Stephenson, Mrs. Walter B.	5.00
Perot, Miss Mary W.	6.00	Stevenson, Mrs. R. H.	10.00
Phelps, Mrs. George	2.00	Strauss, Mr. Frederick	20.00
Phelps-Stokes Fund	100.00	Strobell, Mrs. Caroline Lloyd	3.00
Philbrick, Mrs. E. S.	10.00	Strong, Miss Carol	5.00
Philbrick, Mrs. E. S.	10.00	Sturgis, Mr. S. W.	5.00
Pickman, Mr. Dudley L.	10.00	Sutphin, Miss Josephine H.	1.00
Pickman, Mrs. D. L.	20.00	Swann, Mrs. Roger D.	5.00
Pillsbury, Mr. Albert E.	10.00		
Platt, Mr. J. O.	10.00	Tapley, Miss Alice P.	50.00
Poteat, Mrs. Edwin M.	2.00	Tappan, Miss Mary A.	10.00
Poughkeepsie, N.Y., First Pres-		Taylor, Mrs. James M.	10.00
byterian Sunday School	35.00	Taylor, Mrs. Wm. O.	10.00
Powell Knitting Co.	5.00	Thayer, Mrs. E. R.	10.00
Purves, Mrs. Alexander	200.00	Thelberg, Dr. Elizabeth B.	5.00
		Thomas, Mrs. Geo. C.	10.00
Ramborger, Mr. Wm. K.	5.00	Thomas, Mrs. Washington B.	10.00
Randolph, Mrs. E.	175.00	Thorn, Miss Mary	205.00
Rhoads, Mrs. Charles James	25.00	Tileston, Mrs. John B.	5.00
Rich, Mr. Wm. T.	10.00	Tileston, Mrs. Mary W.	5.00

Appendix C   277

Towne, Mr. Henry R.	350.00	Waterhouse, Mr. George	10.00
Townsend, Mrs. Harriet M.	5.00	Warton, Mr. Jos. S. Lovering	5.00
Townshend, Vt., Congregational Sunday School	10.00	Wheeler, Miss E. T.	10.00
		Whittemore, Mr. Chas.	5.00
Tutt, Miss Myra R.	30.00	Wilkins, Mr. G. W.	25.00
Titus, Mr. Henry	5.00	Willcox, Mrs. Wm. G.	25.00
		Wing, Mr. and Mrs. Asa S.	10.00
Upham, Mrs. E. K.	15.00	Winslow, Mrs. Harriet W.	75.00
		Winsor, Mrs. Frederick	25.00
Van Wagenen, Mr. Bleecker	10.00	Wister, Mrs. Wm. Rotch	115.00
Vassar College Christian Ass'n	75.00	Woodall, Mrs. John	2.00
Vickery, Mrs. H. F.	25.00	Wood, Mr. George	100.00
Vickery, Miss Margaret	10.00	Wood, Miss Juliana	25.00
		Wood, Mrs. L. Hollingsworth	2.80
Walcott, Mrs. Chas. D.	10.00	Wood, Mr. Walter	10.00
Warburg, Mr. Felix M.	50.00	Wright, Mr. T. Houard	10.00
Warburg, Mr. Paul	50.00		
Ware, Mr. Charles P.	5.00	Yeatman, Mrs. Pope	10.00
Ware, Miss Harriet	5.00	Young, Miss Fanny	5.00
Warren, Miss Katharine	5.00		

BIBLIOGRAPHY

PRIMARY SOURCES

Manuscripts

Hampton Normal and Agricultural Institute. Hampton, Va.
   Hollis Burke Frissell Papers (HBF)
High Top Colony. Black Mountain, N.C.
   Howard Anderson Kester Papers (HKP)
Library of Congress. Washington, D.C.
   George Foster Peabody Papers(GFP)
Rip Raps Plantation. Mayesville, S.C.
   (Mrs. James McBride Dabbs, JMD)
   Grace Bigelow House Papers
   James Plato King Papers
   Penn School Papers
Southern Historical Collection. University of North Carolina. Chapel Hill, N.C.
   Penn School Papers (PSP)
      Francis Reeve Cope, Jr., Manuscripts
      Marion Wright Papers
   Southern Tenant Farmers' Union Papers
Vassar College. Poughkeepsie, N.Y.
   Rossa Belle Cooley Papers
York W. Bailey Museum. St. Helena Island, S.C.
   Penn School Papers

Interviews

Boyd, Mr. and Mrs. Benjamin F. St. Helena Island, S.C., March, 1972.
Brown, Aurelius J. St. Helena Island, S.C., April 1, 1975.
Brown, Paul. Philadelphia, Pa., July 23, 1974.
Capers, Tecumseh. St. Helena Island, S.C., March, 1972.
Cope, Mrs. Francis R. Dimock, Pa., August 5–6, 1974.
Dabbs, Mrs. James McBride. Chapel Hill, N.C., June, 1971; St Helena Island, S.C., March, 1972; Mayesville, S.C., March, 1972, June, 1974, June, 1975, July, 1976, July, 1977, August, 1978.
Englehardt, William. St. Helena Island, S.C., September, 1967.
Evans, Harold. Westerly, R.I., July 27, 1974.
Foote, Arthur. Southwest Harbor, Maine, August 21,1975.
Gadson, John. St. Helena Island, S.C., March, 1972.
Hatch, John Davis, Jr., Lenox, Mass., June, 1971.

Hatch, Olivia Stokes. Lenox, Mass., June, 1971.
Johnson, Guion and Guy B. St. Helena Island, S.C., January, 1975., Chapel Hill, N.C., June, 1976.
Kester, Howard Anderson. Chapel Hill, N.C., June, 1971; Black Mountain, N.C., July, 1971.
McChesney, Mrs. Donald. St. Helena Island, S.C., February 23, 1974.
Middleton, Mrs. Bessie Banks. St. Helena Island, S.C., March, 1972.
Passmore, Robert. St. Helena Island, S.C., September, 1967.
Ragsdale, Mrs. Jett. Beaufort, S.C., March, 1972.
Sanders, Mrs. Edd. St. Helena Island, S.C., September, 1967.
Sapp, Mrs. Jane. St. Helena Island, S.C., March, 1972.
Sherman, Mrs. Agnes C. St. Helena Island, S.C., March, 1972.
Siceloff, Mrs. Courtney. St. Helena Island, S.C., September, 1967.
Silver, John. By telephone to Pipersville, Pa., August 6, 1974.
Sumpter, Edith Fields. St. Helena Island, S.C., March, 1975.

General Works

Adams, Henry. *The Education of Henry Adams.* Boston: Houghton Mifflin, 1918. .
Baker, Ray Stannard. *Following the Color Line: American Negro Citizenship in the Progressive Era.* New York: Doubleday, Page, 1908.
Burlin, Natalie Curtis. *Negro Folk Songs.* Hampton Series Numbers 6716, 6726, 6756, 6766. New York & Boston: G. Schirmer, 1918–19.
Carney, Mabel. *Country Life and the Country School: A Study of the Country Community.* Chicago: Row, Peterson, 1912.
Cooley, Rossa Belle. *Homes of the Freed.* New York: New Republic, 1926.
———.*School Acres: An Adventure in Rural Education.* New Haven, Conn.: Yale University Press, 1930.
Dabney, Charles William. *Universal Education in the South.* 2 vols. Chapel Hill: University of North Carolina Press, 1936.
De Garmo, Charles. *Principles of Secondary Education.* Vol. III: *Ethical Training.* New York: Macmillan, 1910.
Dewey, John. *Democracy and Education.* New York: Macmillan, 1916.
Du Bois, William Edward Burghardt. *Souls of Black Folk.* Chicago: McClurg, 1904.
Foote, Arthur. "The Life and Times of Henry Wilder Foote, 1838–1889." Ph.D. dissertation Meadville Theological School, 1936.
From Servitude to Service: Being the Old South Lectures on the History and Work of Southern Institutions for the Education of the Negro. Boston: American Unitarian Association, 1905.
Hampton Normal and Agricultural Institute. *Armstrong's Ideas on Education for Life.* Hampton, Va.: Hampton Press, 1926.
Herbart, John Frederick. *Outlines of Educational Doctrine.* Translated by Alexis F. Lange; annotated by Charles De Garmo. New York: Macmillan, 1901.
Higginson, Thomas Wentworth. *Army Life in a Black Regiment.* Boston: Lee & Shepard, 1890; reprinted, Boston: Beacon Press, 1962.
Holland, Rupert Sargent, ed. *Letters and Diary of Laura M. Towne: Written from the*

Sea Islands of South Carolina, 1862–1884. Cambridge, Mass.: Riverside Press, 1912.
Jones, Lance G. E. *Negro Schools in the Southern States*. Oxford: Clarendon Press, 1928.
Jones, Thomas Jesse, ed. *Negro Education: A Study of the Private and Higher Schools for Colored People in the United States*. 2 vols. Washington, D.C.: Government Printing Office, 1917.
Kester, Howard Anderson. *Revolt Among the Sharecroppers.* New York: Covici, Friede, 1936.
Krishnayaja, Stephen G. *The Rural Community and the School: The Message of Negro and Other American Schools for India*. Calcutta: Association Press, 1934.
Loram, Charles Templeman. *Adaptation of the Penn School Methods to Education in South Africa*. New York: Phelps-Stokes Fund, 1927.
———.*Education of the South African Native*. London: Longmans, Green, 1917; reprinted, New York: Negro Universities Press, 1969.
———.*The School as Social Centre*. New York: Phelps-Stokes Fund, 1927.
McCulloch, James E., ed. *The Human Way: Addresses on Race Problems at the Southern Sociological Congress, Atlanta, 1913*. Nashville, Tenn.: Southern Sociological Congress, 1913.
Moton, Robert Russa. *What the Negro Thinks*. Garden City, N.Y.: Doubleday, 1929.
The Negro Problem: A Series of Articles by Representative American Negroes of To-Day. New York: James Pott, 1903.
Peabody, Francis Greenwood. *Education for Life: The Story of Hampton Institute; Told in Connection with the Fiftieth Anniversary of the School*. New York: Doubleday, Page, 1919.
Pearson, Elizabeth Ware, ed. *Letters from Port Royal, 1862–1868*. Boston: W. B. Clarke, 1906.
Seaton, William H. *Schools in Travail: A Short Study of the One-Teacher Negro Rural School of the Southern States with Some Applications to African Conditions*. New York: Published for the Carnegie Corporation Visitors' Grants Committee, 1932.
Washington, Booker Taliaferro. *Character Building: Being Addresses Delivered on Sunday Evenings to the Students of Tuskegee Institute*. New York: Doubleday, Page, 1902.
———.*Up From Slavery*. New York: Doubleday, Page, 1901; rev. ed., Garden City, N.Y.: Doubleday, 1947.
Weatherford, Willis Duke. *Negro Life in the South, Present Conditions and Needs*. New York: YMCA, 1910.
Woofter, Thomas Jackson. *Black Yeomanry: Life on St. Helena Island*. New York: Henry Holt, 1930.

Articles

SOUTHERN WORKMAN
Aery, William Anthony. "Negro Progress and the Phelps-Stokes Fund." LXI (October, 1932), 391–97.

"Biography of Dr. Peabody, by Certain Contemporary Newspapers." LXVII (May, 1938), 154–60.

Blanton, Joshua Enoch. "One Man's Life Story." LII (August, 1923), 405–408.

Brawley, Benjamin. "'Ironsides': The Bordentown School." LX(October 1931), 410–16.

Christensen, Niels, Jr. "The Negroes of Beaufort County, S.C." XXXII (October, 1903), 481–85.

Cooley, Rossa Belle. "Service to Penn School" XLVI (October, 1917), 605–606.

———."Tribute to a Faithful Nurse." LXIV (March, 1935), 70–71.

Cope, Francis Reeve, Jr. "Service to Penn School." XLVI (October, 1917), 603–605.

Dabney, Charles William. "Penn School, St. Helena Island." LX (June, 1931), 277–81.

Davis, Jackson E. "Hampton at Penn." XLVI (February, 1917), 81–89.

———."The Negro in Country Life." XLI (January, 1912), 15–26.

———."New Head of Jeanes and Slater Fund." LX (October, 1931), 404–406.

———."A Unique People's School." XLIII (April, 1914), 217–28.

"Editorials." XLI (March, 1912), 134; XLII (December, 1913), 643–45; XLIV (February, 1915), 69; XLVI (May, 1917), 260–61; XLVI (June, 1917), 329–30; XLVI (October, 1917), 515–17; LVIII (March, 1929), 111–12.

Editorials: "Interesting Meetings in April." XLI (April, 1912), 196.

———."Report on the Negro Migration Conference." XLVI (March, 1917), 133–35.

———."Work on the Sea Islands." XXX (July, 1901), 381.

Eliot, Charles William. "The Hampton Idea of Education." XXXIX (January, 1910), 12–14.

"Ellen Murray." XXXVII (February, 1908), 71–73.

Emerson, Rev. Chester B. "'He Who A Dream Hath Possessed'—Samuel Chapman Armstrong." LXII (March, 1933), 99–107.

Foote, Henry Wilder. "The Penn School on St. Helena Island." XXXI (May, 1902), 263–70.

"Founders Day at the Penn School." XXXVII (May, 1908), 263–64.

Frissell, Hollis Burke. "Annual Report of the Principal of Hampton Institute." XXVIII (July, 1899), 249–64; XXIX (May, 1900), 289–301; XXX (May, 1901), 279–93; XXXI (May, 1902), 279–91; XXXII (May, 1903), 225–48; XXXIII (May, 1904) 290–305; XXXIV (May, 1905), 291–306; XXXV (May, 1906), 292–305; XXXVI (May, 1907), 289–301; XXXVII (May, 1908), 291–305; XXXVIII (May, 1909), 294–305; XXXIX (May, 1910), 295–316; XL (June, 1911), 354–76; XLI (May, 1912), 294–316; XLII (May, 1913), 289–308; XLIII (May, 1914), 281–312; XLIV (May, 1915), 273–304; XLV (June, 1916), 343–78; XLVI (May, 1917), 273–300.

Bibliography 283

———."The Biography of Dr. Curry." XLI (January, 1912), 4-5.
———."European Impressions." XXXI (November, 1902), 585-88.
———."Rural Segregation." XLIV (March, 1915), 137-38.
———."The Training of Negro Teachers." XXIX (November, 1900), 612-15.
Gibson, Carleton B. "Industrial Education for the South." XXX (November, 1911), 591-94.
Gregg, James Edgar, "Facts: Not Feelings." LVI (February, 1927), 60-61.
———."Fifty-Eighth Annual Report of the Principal." LV (June, 1928), 209-12.
———."Sixtieth Annual Report of the Principal." LVII (June, 1928), 209-12.
———."Sixty-First Annual Report of the Principal." LVIII (June, 1929), 257-78.
Hammond, Mrs. L. H. "The White Man's Debt to the Negro." XLIII (January, 1914), 45-50.
"Hampton Incidents." XXXVII (July, 1908), 414-15.
House, Grace Bigelow. "The Fiftieth Anniversary of Penn School." XLI (May, 1912), 316-20.
———."How Freedom Came to Big Pa." XLV (April, 1916), 217-26.
———."The Little Foe of All the World." XXXV (November, 1906), 598-614.
———."Penn School and the Farmers' Conference." XXXVI (January, 1907), 58-60.
———."The Promise of Better Days." XXXVII (October, 1908), 547-57.
———."Stormy." XXXIX (April, 1910), 221-33.
Houston, D. F. "The Rural School: A National Failure." XLI (November, 1912), 635-42.
Howe, Arthur. "Hollis Burke Frissell—Christian Statesman." LX (October, 1931), 507-12.
———."President Howe's Address at Chapel." LXV (November, 1936), 341-44.
———."President Howe's Boston Address Before the NAACP." LXV (May, 1936), 141-48.
———."Report of the President." LXIV (June, 1935), 174-88.
James, Helen Lou. "Why Penn School Is Needed on St. Helena Island." XXXVII (February, 1908), 90-94.
Jones, Thomas Jesse. "Frissell of Hampton." LX (January, 1931), 11-16.
———."Industrial Education and Industrial Progress." XXXVIII (March, 1909), 139-44.
Kuyper, George A. "The Powerful Influence of a Notable School." LX (January, 1931), 29-32.
Mitchell, Samuel Chiles. "Industrial Education in the South." XXXIX (June, 1910), 326-34.

———."My Neighbor, the Negro." XL (March, 1911), 134–42.
———."Proposed Solutions of the Negro Problem." XXXII (November, 1903), 545–50.
Moton, Robert Russa. "Editorial." LX (October, 1931), 452–53.
———."The Negro and the South's Industrial Life." XLIII (July, 1914), 411–18.
———."Race Pride." XLV (January, 1916), 48–49.
———."Signs of Growing Cooperation." XLIII (October, 1914), 552–59.
———."Some Elements Necessary to Race Development." XLI (July, 1912), 399–408.
Murphy, Edgar Gardner. "Industrial Education and Industrial Friction." XXXII (March, 1903), 175–79.
"Negro Education." XLIV (June, 1915), 324–25.
Peabody, Francis Greenwood. "Education for Life." LV (June, 1926), 248–56.
———."Hampton's Builder." XLVI (October, 1917), 568.
Peabody, George Foster. "The Negro in Education." LXII (December, 1934), 373–75.
———. "Presentation of the Memorial Bas-Relief of Dr. Frissell." LX (January, 1931), 8–9.
Peterson, A. Everett. "Hollis Burke Frissell." LX (October, 1931), 408–10.
Plunkett, Sir Horace. "The Improvement of Rural Conditions." XXXVII (February, 1908), 78–80.
"The Real Aim of Industrial Schools." XXXVII (January, 1908), 374–75.
"Report of the Third Annual Negro Conference." XXVIII (September, 1899), 326–41.
"Resolutions Re Services of Dr. House." LXVI (January, 1937), 25–27.
Rowe, George C. "The Negroes of the Sea Islands." XXIX (December, 1900), 709–15.
"St. Helena's Needs." XL (October, 1911), 553.
Seaton, William H. "Linking School and Community in Southern Rhodesia." LX (January, 1931), 32–37.
Stokes, Anson Phelps. "The International Influence of General Armstrong." LVII (July, 1928), 249–54.
Tate, William Knox. "Editorials: Southern Superintendents on Negro Education." XL (February, 1911), 69.
Thomas, William I. "Education and Racial Traits." XLI (June, 1912), 378–86.
Towne, Laura Matilda. "Pioneer Work on the Sea Islands." XXX (July, 1901), 397–401.
Vawter, C. E. "The Need of Industrial and Technical Education in the South." XXX (February, 1901), 117–20.

Washburn, Henry Bradford. "Samuel Chapman Armstrong's Larger Self." LXI (March, 1932), 98–110.
Weatherford, Willis Duke. "The Basis of Understanding Between the Races." XLVI (December, 1916), 655–61.
———."First Steps in Solving the Race Problem." XXXIX (November, 1910), 589–92.
———."Negro Training in the South." XLI (October, 1912), 550–58.
Williams, W. T. B. "The Outlook in Negro Education." XL (November, 1911), 638–52.
———."The Yankee School Ma'am in Negro Education." XLIV (February, 1915), 73–80.
Wilson, James Harrison. "The Negro's Progress in Fifty Years of Freedom." XLIII (February, 1914), 71–79.
Winston, George T. "Industrial Education for White and Black in the South." XXX (February, 1909), 58–66.

OTHERS
Baker, Ray Stannard. "Problems of Citizenship." *Annals of the American Academy of Political and Social Science*, XLIX (September, 1913), 92–104.
Blair, Martha. "These Charming People." Washington *Herald*, April 16, 1934.
Bruce, Roscoe Conkling. "Tuskegee Institute." *From Servitude to Service*. Boston: American Unitarian Association, 1905.
Caldwell, I. S. "A School That Teaches a Community." *Survey*, March 15, 1928, pp. 764–65.
Carney, Mabel. "Desirable Rural Adaptations in the Education of Negroes." *Journal of Negro Education*, V (July, 1936), 448–54.
Christensen, Niels. "Fifty Years of Freedom: Conditions in the Sea Coast Regions." *Annals of the American Academy of Political and Social Science*, XLIX (September, 1913), 58–66.
Clarana, Jose. "The Schooling of the Negro." *Crisis*, VI (July, 1913), 132–36.
Cooley, Rossa Belle. "America's Sea Islands." *Outlook*, April 30, 1919, pp. 739–41.
———."Education in the Soil." *Progressive Education*, X (December, 1933), 448–55.
———."History of the Penn Normal." *Southern Ploughman*, April 11, 1911.
———."IS There an Explanation?" *Survey*, September 13, 1919, p. 858.
———."The Negro in His Own Environment." *Vassar Quarterly*, May, 1920, pp. 177–81.
———."Penn Normal, Industrial, and Agricultural School." *Encyclopedia of Africana* (1944).
Crum, Mason. "The Good Samaritan of St. Helena Island." *South Atlantic Quarterly*, XXXIV (April, 1935), 145–49.
Davis, Jackson E. "Recent Developments in Negro Schools and Colleges." *Bulletin of the National Association of Teachers in Colored Schools*, VIII (April–May, 1928), 5–12.
[Du Bois, William Edward Burghardt.] "Advice." *Crisis*, XV (March, 1918), 215.
Du Bois, W. E. B. "Atlanta University." *From Servitude to Service*. Boston: American Unitarian Association, 1905.

[Du Bois, W. E. B.] "The Browsing Reader." *Crisis*, XXXVII (November, 1930), 378.
[Du Bois, W. E. B.] "Hampton." *Crisis*, XV (November, 1917), 10–12.
Du Bois, W. E. B. "Negro Education." *Crisis*, XV (February, 1918), 173–78.
———."Of Mr. Booker T. Washington and Others." *Souls of Black Folk*. Chicago: McClurg, 1904.
———."Opinion." *Crisis*, XXIX (February, 1925), 151–52.
———."A Protest." *Crisis*, XVI (May, 1918), 10–11.
———."The Talented Tenth." *The Negro Problem: A Series of Articles by Representative American Negroes of Today*. New York: James Pott, 1903.
———."Thomas Jesse Jones." *Crisis*, XXII (October, 1921), 252–56.
Dudley, T. V. "How Shall We Help the Negro?" *Century Magazine*, June, 1885, pp. 273–80.
Emlen, John Thompson. "The Movement for the Betterment of the Negro in Philadelphia." *Annals of the American Academy of Political and Social Science*, XLIX (September, 1913), 81–92.
Favrot, Leo M. "How the Small Rural School Can More Adequately Serve Its Community." *Journal of Negro Education*, V (July, 1936), 430–38.
———."Schools for Negro Children: Past Practices and Present Hopes." *Nation's Schools*, X (October, 1932), 59–65.
Foote, Frances Eliot. "A Pioneer in the New South." Boston Evening *Transcript*. November 12, 1904.
Frissell, Hollis Burke. "Hampton Institute." *From Servitude to Service*. Boston: American Unitarian Association, 1905.
———."Popular Education in the South: An Address Before the Southern Society for the Promotion of the Study of the Race Conditions and Problems in the South." *Race Problems in the South*. New York: Negro Universities Press, 1909.
"The General Education Board." *Crisis*, XXXVII (July, 1930), 229–30.
Grant, Frances R. "Negro Patriotism and Negro Music." *Outlook*, February 26, 1919, pp. 343–47.
Gray, Lewis Cecil. "Southern Agriculture, Plantation System, and the Negro Problem." *Annals of the American Academy of Political and Social Science*, XL (March, 1912), 90–99.
Hart, Joseph K. "A School Somewhere." *Survey-Graphic*, September, 1925.
———."The Waste Land." *Survey*, April 15, 1923, pp. 78–79.
Haynes, George Edmund. "Conditions Among Negroes in the Cities." *Annals of the American Academy of Political and Social Science*, XLIX (September, 1913), 105–19.
House, Grace Bigelow. "The Long Look." *Christian Endeavor World*, December 31, 1944, pp. 246–55.
———."Roads of Learning on St. Helena Island." *Progressive Education*, XIV (April, 1937), 246–55.
———."The Need and Purpose of Industrial Education." James E. McCulloch, ed. *The Human Way: Addresses on Race Problems at the Southern Sociological Congress, Atlanta, 1913*. Nashville, Tenn.: Southern Sociological Congress, 1913.
Jones, Thomas Jesse. "Negro Population in the United States." *Annals of the American Academy of Political and Social Science*, XLIX (September, 1913), 1–9.

Langford-Smith, N. "Mass Education and Rural Africa." *International Review of Missions*, April, 1945.
Lichtenberger, J. P., ed. "The Negro's Progress in Fifty Years." *Annals of the American Academy of Political and Social Science*, XLIX (September, 1913).
Ludlow, Helen W. "Hampton Normal and Agricultural Institute." *Harper's Magazine*, October, 1873, pp. 672–85.
Morgan, Joy Elmer. "South Carolina Takes the Lead." *Journal of the National Education Association*, May, 1938).
"Negro Education." *Outlook*, August 15, 1903, pp. 937–39.
Packard, Winthrop. "The Oldest Negro School in America Among the Best Behaved Negroes." Boston Evening *Transcript*. April 12, 1922.
Washington, Booker Taliaferro. "Industrial Education for Negroes." *The Negro Problem*. New York: James Pott, 1903.
Weatherford, Willis Duke. "Race Relationship in the South." *Annals of the American Academy of Political and Social Science*, XLIX (September, 1913), 164–71.
Wood, L. Hollingsworth. "A Negro Island Community." New York *Evening Post*, May 8, 1910.
———."The Urban League Movement." *Journal of Negro History*, IX (January, 1924), 117–26.
Wooten, Jack. "Rural Rehabilitation on St. Helena Island." Columbia, S.C. *State*, November 28, 1934.

Pamphlets

Armstrong League of Hampton Workers. *Memories of Old Hampton*. Hampton, Va.: Institute Press, 1909.
Armstrong, Samuel Chapman. *22 Years Work at Hampton*. Hampton, Va.: Normal School Press, 1893.
Bull, Oswin Boys. "A Report on a Visit to North America, Under the Auspices of the Carnegie Corporation." Masern, Basutoland, February, 1934. (Mimeographed)
Carter, Franklin. *General Armstrong's Life and Work*. Hampton, Va.: Normal School Press, 1902.
Dabney, Charles William. *The Problem in the South*. New York: General Education Board, 1903.
Davis, Jackson E. *The Jeanes Visiting Teachers: An Address Given at the Inter-Territorial Jeanes Conference, Salisbury, Southern Rhodesia, May 27, 1935*. New York: Carnegie Corp., 1936.
Education of the Negro. Southern Education Board Publication Number 20, December 21, 1903.
Favrot, Leo M. *County Training Schools for Negroes in the South*. John F. Slater Fund Occasional Papers Number 23. Charlottesville, Virginia: John F. Slater Fund, 1923.
Gilman, Daniel Coit. *A Study in Black and White: An Address at the Opening of the Armstrong-Slater Trade School Building, November 18, 1896*. John F. Slater Fund Occasional Papers Number 10. Baltimore: John F. Slater Fund, 1896.
Horton, McDavid. *St. Helena Island: A Negro Community*. Columbia, S.C.: State Company, 1924.

House, Grace Bigelow. *Soldiers of Freedom*. N.p., n.d.
Johnson, G. B. "Report by Mr. and Mrs. G. B. Johnson on a Visit to the U.S.A. to Study the Organization, Aims, and Methods of Rural Schools for Negroes." Zanzibar, 1934. (Mimeographed)
Julius Rosenwald Fund. "Penn School on St. Helena Island: Journal of the Rural School Exploration, Number 7." Chicago, July, 1936. (Mimeographed)
Loram, Charles Templeman. *Address by Charles T. Loram, of the Native Affairs Commission, Union of South Africa, on the Occasion of a Dinner in His Honor by the Phelps-Stokes Fund at 101 Park Avenue, New York, October 25, 1926*. New York: Phelps-Stokes Fund, 1926.
Robert D. Jenks, 1875-1917: A Memorial and a Tribute from His Friends. Philadelphia: Franklin Printing Co., 1917.

SECONDARY WORKS

General Works

Bailey, Hugh C. *Liberalism in the New South: Social Reformers and the Progressive Movement*. Coral Gables, Fla.: University of Miami Press, 1969.
Baker, Paul Ernest. *Negro-White Adjustment: An Investigation and Analysis of Methods in the Interracial Movement in the United States*. New York: Association Press, 1934.
Bond, Horace Mann. *The Education of the Negro in the American Social Order*. New York: Prentice-Hall, 1934.
Bontemps, Arna *100 Years of Negro Freedom*. New York: Dodd, Mead, 1966.
Broom, Leonard, and Norval D. Glenn. *Transformation of the Negro American*. New York: Harper, 1965.
Bullock, Henry Allen. *A History of Negro Education in the South from 1619 to the Present*. Cambridge, Mass.: Harvard University Press, 1967.
Butts, R. Freeman, and Lawrence Arthur Cremin. *History of Education in American Culture*. New York: Henry Holt, 1953.
Cash, Wilbur J. *The Mind of the South*. New York: Knopf, 1941; reprinted, New York: Doubleday Anchor Books, 1954.
Chamberlain, John. *Farewell to Reform: The Rise, Life and Decay of the Progressive Mind in America*. New York: Liveright, 1932.
Clift, Virgil A., Archibald W. Anderson, and H. Gordon Hullfish. *Negro Education in America: Its Adequacy, Problems and Needs*, New York: Harper, 1962.
Cremin, Lawrence Arthur. *American Education: The Colonial Experience, 1607-1783*. New York: Harper and Row, 1970.
―――.*The Transformation of the School: Progressivism in American Education, 1876-1957*. New York: Alfred A. Knopf, 1961.
Curti, Merle. *Social Ideas of American Educators*. New York: Charles Scribner's Sons, 1935.
Dabney, Virginius. *Liberalism in the South*. Chapel Hill: University of North Carolina Press, 1932.
Du Bose, Rene. *So Human an Animal*. New York: Charles Scribner's Sons, 1968.
Egerton, John. *A Mind to Stay Here: Profiles from the South*. New York: Macmillan, 1970.

Elkins, Stanley M. *Slavery: A Problem in American Institutional and Intellectual Life.* Chicago: University of Chicago Press, 1959; reprinted, New York: Universal Library, 1963.
Ellison, Ralph. *Invisible Man.* New York: Random House, 1947.
Franklin, John Hope. *From Slavery to Freedom: A History of American Negroes.* New York: Alfred A. Knopf, 1947; 2nd ed., 1956.
Frazier, E. Franklin. *The Negro in the United States.* New York: Macmillan, 1949; rev. ed., 1957.
Frederickson, George M. *The Black Image in the White Mind: The Debate on Afro-American Character and Destiny, 1817–1914.* New York: Harper and Row, 1971.
Gallagher, Buell G. *American Caste and the Negro College.* New York: Columbia University Press, 1938.
Ginzberg, Eli, and Alfred S. Eichner. *The Troublesome Presence: American Democracy and the Negro.* New York: Free Press, 1964.
Goldman, Eric F. *Rendezvous with Destiny: A History of Modern American Reform.* New York: Alfred A. Knopf, 1952; revised, abridged edition, New York: Vintage Books, 1958.
Gossett, Thomas F. *Race: The History of an Idea in America.* New York: Schocken Books, 1963.
Harper, Manly H. *Social Beliefs and Attitudes of American Educators.* New York: Teachers College Press, Columbia University, 1927.
Hays, Samuel P. *The Response to Industrialism, 1885–1914.* Chicago: University of Chicago Press, 1957.
Herberg, Will. *Protestant, Catholic, Jew: An Essay in American Religious Sociology.* 1st rev. ed. Garden City, N.Y.: Doubleday, 1955.
Herskovits, Melville Jean. *The Myth of the Negro Past.* New York: Harper, 1941.
Highsaw, Robert Baker, ed. *The Deep South in Transformation.* University, Ala.: University of Alabama Press, 1964.
Hofstadter, Richard C. *The Age of Reform: From Bryan to F.D.R.* New York: Alfred A. Knopf, 1955.
———. *Anti-intellectualism in American Life.* New York: Alfred A. Knopf, 1963.
———. *Social Darwinism in American Thought.* Rev. ed. Boston: Beacon Press, 1955.
Holmes, Dwight Oliver Wendell. *The Evolution of the Negro College.* Concord, N.H.: Rumford Press, 1934.
Hughes, William Hardin, and Frederick D. Patterson, eds. *Robert Russa Moton of Hampton and Tuskegee.* Chapel Hill: University of North Carolina Press, 1956.
Johnson, Charles Spurgeon. *Growing Up in the Black Belt.* Washington, D.C.: American Council on Education, 1941.
———. *Into the Mainstream: Best Practices in Race Relations.* Chapel Hill: University of North Carolina Press, 1947.
———. *The Negro in American Civilization.* New York: Henry Holt, 1930.
Kirby, Jack Temple. *Darkness at the Dawning: Race and Reform in the Progressive South.* Philadelphia: J. B. Lippincott, 1972.
Kolko, Gabriel. *Triumph of Conservatism: A Re-Interpretation of American History, 1900–1916.* Chicago: Quadrangle Books, 1963.
Leopold, Richard William. *Elihu Root and the Conservative Tradition.* Boston: Little, Brown, 1954.

Leuchtenberg, William E. *Franklin D. Roosevelt and the New Deal, 1932–1940.* New York: Harper and Row, 1963.
———.*The Perils of Prosperity.* Chicago: University of Chicago Press, 1958.
Lewinson, Paul. *Race, Class, and Party: A History of Negro Suffrage and White Politics in the South.* London: Oxford University Press, 1932; reprinted, New York: Russell and Russell, 1963.
Logan, Rayford Whittingham. *The Negro in American Life and Thought: The Nadir, 1877–1901.* New York: Dial, 1954.
———. *The Negro in the United States: A Brief Review.* Princeton, N.J.: Van Nostrand, 1957.
———, ed. *What the Negro Wants.* Chapel Hill: University of North Carolina Press, 1944.
McConnell, Grant. *The Decline of Agrarian Democracy.* Berkeley and Los Angeles: University of California Press, 1953.
McKean, Keith F. *Cross Currents in the South.* Denver, Colorado: Swallow Paperbacks, 1960.
May, Henry. *The End of American Innocence: A Study of the First Years of Our Own Time, 1912–1917.* New York: Alfred A. Knopf, 1959; Chicago: Quadrangle Books, 1959.
Meier, August. *Negro Thought in America, 1880–1915: Racial Ideologies in the Age of Booker T. Washington.* Ann Arbor: University of Michigan Press, 1963.
Mowry, George E. *The Era of Theodore Roosevelt and the Birth of Modern America.* New York: Harper, 1958.
———.*The Urban Nation, 1920–1960.* New York: Hill and Wang, 1965.
Myrdal, Gunnar. *An American Dilemma: The Negro Problem and Modern Democracy.* 2 vols. New York: McGraw-Hill, 1944.
Newby, Idus A. *Jim Crow's Defense: Anti-Negro Thought in America 1900–1930.* Baton Rouge: Louisiana State University Press, 1965.
Nolen, Claude. *The Negro's Image in the South: The Anatomy of White Supremacy.* Lexington: University of Kentucky Press, 1967.
Reuter, E. B. *The American Race Problem.* New York: Thomas Y. Crowell, 1927.
Roche, John Pearson. *The Quest for the Dream: The Development of Civil Rights and Human Relations in Modern America.* New York: Macmillan, 1963.
Rose, Arnold Marshall. *The Negro in America.* New York: Harper, 1948.
Rugg, Harold. *Foundations of American Education.* Yonkers-On-Hudson, N.Y.: World Book Co., 1947.
Schlesinger, Arthur Meier, Jr. *The Crisis of the Old Order.* Boston: Houghton Mifflin, 1957.
Silberman, Charles E. *Crisis in Black and White.* New York: Colonial Press, 1964.
Smith, Lillian. *Killers of the Dream.* New York: W. W. Norton, 1949.
Taylor, William R. *Cavalier and Yankee: The Old South and American National Character.* New York: George Braziller, 1961.
Tindall, George Brown. *The Emergence of the New South, 1913–1945.* Baton Rouge: Louisiana State University Press, 1967.
Welter, Rush. *Popular Education and Democratic Thought in America.* New York: Columbia University Press, 1962.
Wiebe, Robert H. *The Search for Order, 1877–1920.* New York: Hill and Wang, 1967.

Wiley, Bell Irwin. *Southern Negroes*. New Haven: Yale University Press, 1938.
Woodson, Carter Godwin. *The Mis-Education of the Negro*. Washington, D.C.: Associated Press, 1933.
———.*The Rural Negro*. Washington, D.C.: Association for the Study of Negro Life and History, 1930.
———.*The Story of the Negro Retold*. Washington, D.C.: Associated Publishers, 1935.
Woodson, Carter Godwin, and Charles H. Wesley. *The Negro in Our History*. Washington, D.C.: Associated Publishers, 1922.
Woodward, C. Vann. *The Burden of Southern History*. Baton Rouge: Louisiana State University Press, 1960.
———.*Origins of the New South, 1877–1913*. Baton Rouge: Louisiana State University Press, 1951.
———.*The Strange Career of Jim Crow*. New York: Oxford University Press, 1955.
Woofter, Thomas Jackson, *Southern Race Progress: The Wavering Color Line*. Washington, D.C.: Public Affairs Press, 1957.
Works, George Alan, and Simon O. Lesser *Rural America Today*. Chicago: University of Chicago Press, 1942.

Monographs and Dissertations

Augustus, Amelia. "Penn School at Home and Overseas: A Study of a Unique American Educational Institution and Model for Foreign Visitors." Ed.D. dissertation, Columbia University, 1970.
Availability of Public School Education in Rural Communities. Washington, D.C.: Government Printing Office, 1931.
Bailey, Joseph Cannon. *Seaman A. Knapp: Schoolmaster of American Agriculture*. New York: Columbia University Press, 1945.
Baxter, Madeline E. "Negro Education as Viewed in *The Outlook* (1893–1935)." Master's thesis, University of North Carolina, 1951.
Berman, Edward Henry. "Education in Africa and America: A History of the Phelps-Stokes Fund, 1911–1945." Ed.D. dissertation, Columbia University, 1970.
Bleser, Carol K. Rothrock. *The Promised Land: The History of the South Carolina Land Commission, 1869–1890*. Columbia: University of South Carolina Press, 1969.
Caliver, Ambrose. *Availability of Education to Negroes in Rural Communities*. Washington, D.C.: Government Printing Office, 1936.
———, ed. *Fundamentals in the Education of Negroes*. Washington, D.C.: Government Printing Office, 1935.
———.*Secondary Education for Negroes*. Washington, D.C.: Government Printing Office, 1930.
Clarke, Charles Morgan. "Philanthropic Foundations and Teacher Education in the South, 1867–1948." Ph.D. dissertation, University of North Carolina, 1948.
Crum, Mason. *Gullah: Negro Life in the Carolina Sea Islands*. Durham: Duke University Press, 1965.
Davies, John D. *Phrenology: Fad and Science*. New Haven: Yale University Press, 1955.

Dykeman, Wilma, and James Stokely. *Seeds of Southern Change: Biography of Will Alexander*. Chicago: University of Chicago Press, 1962.
Fosdick, Raymond Blaine. *Adventure in Giving: The Story of the General Education Board*. New York: Harper and Row, 1962.
———.*A Philosophy for a Foundation: On the Fiftieth Anniversary of the Rockefeller Foundation, 1913–1963*. New York: Rockefeller Foundation, 1963.
Grubbs, Donald H. *Cry from the Cotton: The Southern Tenant Farmers' Union and the New Deal*. Chapel Hill: University of North Carolina Press, 1971.
Gusfield, Joseph R. *Symbolic Crusade: Status Politics and the American Temperance Movement*. Urbana: University of Illinois Press, 1963.
Harlan, Louis R. *Booker T. Washington: The Making of a Black Leader, 1856–1901*. New York: Oxford University Press, 1972.
———.*Separate and Unequal: Public School Campaigns and Racism in the Southern Seaboard States, 1901–1915.*. Chapel Hill: University of North Carolina Press, 1958.
Hoogenboom, Ari. *Outlawing the Spoils: A History of the Civil Service Reform Movement, 1865–1883*. Urbana: University of Illinois Press, 1961.
Johnson, Guion Griffis. *A Social History of the Sea Islands with Special Reference to St. Helena Island, South Carolina*. Chapel Hill: University of North Carolina Press, 1930.
Johnson, Guy Benton. *Folk Culture on St. Helena Island, South Carolina*. Chapel Hill: University of North Carolina Press, 1930.
King, Kenneth James. *Pan-Africanism and Education: A Study of Race Philanthropy and Education in the Southern States of America and East Africa*. London, 1971.
Kiser, Clyde Vernon. *Sea Island to City: A Study of St. Helena Islanders in Harlem and Other Urban Centers*. New York: Columbia University Press, 1932.
Lawton, Samuel Miller. *The Religious Life of South Carolina Coastal and Sea Island Negroes*. Nashville, Tenn.: George Peabody College for Teachers, 1939.
Leavell, Ullin Whitney. *Philanthropy in Negro Education*. Nashville, Tenn.: George Peabody College for Teachers, 1930.
Luker, Ralph. "The Northern Social Gospel Prophets and the Negro: 1890–1917." Master's thesis, University of North Carolina, 1969.
McPherson, James M. *The Abolitionist Legacy: From Reconstruction to the NAACP*. Princeton, N.J.: Princeton University Press, 1976.
———.*The Struggle for Equality: Abolitionists and the Negro in the Civil War and Reconstruction*. Princeton, N.J.: Princeton University Press, 1964.
Mann, Arthur. *Yankee Reformers in the Urban Age: Social Reform in Boston, 1880–1900*. Cambridge: Belknap Press, 1954.
Milne, Gordon. *George William Curtis and the Genteel Tradition*. Bloomington: Indiana University Press, 1956.
Mott, Frank Luther. *A History of American Magazines*. Cambridge: Harvard University Press, 1957.
Nankivell, Joice M. *A Life for the Balkans*. London: Fleming H. Revell, 1939.
Newby, Idus A. *Black Carolinians: A History of Blacks in South Carolina from 1865–1968*. Columbia: University of South Carolina Press, 1973.
Redclay, Edward E. *County Training Schools and Public Secondary Education for Negroes in the South*. Washington, D.C.: John F. Slater Fund, 1935.

Rose, Willie Lee. *Rehearsal for Reconstruction: The Port Royal Experiment*. New York: Bobbs-Merrill, 1964.
Smedley, Katherine. "The Northern Teacher on the South Carolina Sea Islands." Master's thesis, University of North Carolina, 1932.
Spencer, Samuel R. *Booker T. Washington and the Negro's Place in American Life*. Boston: Little, Brown, 1955.
Sproat, John G. *"The Best Men": Liberal Reformers in the Gilded Age*. New York: Oxford University Press, 1968.
Swint, Henry Lee. *The Northern Teacher in the South, 1862–1870*. Nashville, Tenn.: Vanderbilt University Press, 1941.
Thomason, John Furman. *The Foundations of the Public Schools of South Carolina*. Columbia, S.C.: The State, 1925.
Thompson, Henry Tazewell. The Establishment of the Public School System of South Carolina. Columbia, S.C.: R. L. Bryan, 1927.
Thrasher, Max Bennett. *Tuskegee: Its Story and Its Work*. Boston: Small, Maynard, 1901.
Tindall, George Brown. *South Carolina Negroes: 1877–1900*. Columbia: University of South Carolina Press, 1952.
Turner, Lorenzo Dow. *Africanisms in the Gullah Dialect*. Chicago: University of Chicago Press, 1949.
Ware, Louise. *George Foster Peabody: Banker, Philanthropist, Publicist*. Athens: University of Georgia Press, 1951.
Wilkerson, Doxey A. *Special Problems of Negro Education*. Washington, D.C.: Government Printing Office, 1939.
Williamson, Joel. *After Slavery: The Negro in South Carolina During Reconstruction, 1861–1877*. Chapel Hill: University of North Carolina Press, 1965.
Woofter, Thomas Jackson. *Teaching in Rural Schools*. Cambridge: Riverside Press,
Yavenditti, Michael John. "The Muckrakers and the Negro." Master's thesis, University of North Carolina, 1963.

Articles

Baldwin, James. "A Letter to My Nephew." *Progressive*, December, 1962, pp. 19–20.
Bascom, William R. "Acculturation Among the Gullah Negroes." *American Anthropologist*, XLIII (January, 1941), 43–50.
Caliver, Ambrose. "Segregation in American Education: An Overview." *Annals of the American Academy of Political and Social Science*, CCCIV (March, 1956), 17–25.
Dabbs, James McBride. "A New Southerner." *Progressive*, December, 1962, pp. 39–42.
Davis, David Brion. "Abolitionists and the Freedmen: An Essay Review." *Journal of Southern History*, XXXVI (May, 1965), 164–70.
Donald, David. "Toward a Reconsideration of Abolitionists." *Lincoln Reconsidered*. New York: Alfred A. Knopf, 1959.

Evans, Edward. "Isaac Sharpless." *Quaker Biographies*. Series II. Philadelphia: Philadelphia Yearly Meeting of Friends, n.d.
Funke, Loretta. "The Negro in Education." *Journal of Negro History*, V (January, 1920), 1–21.
Gannett, William Channing. "The Freedmen at Port Royal." *North American Review*, CI (July, 1865), 1–28.
Harlan, Louis R. "Booker T. Washington and the White Man's Burden." *American Historical Review*, LXXI (January, 1966), 441–67.
———."The Southern Education Board and the Race Issue in Public Education." *Journal of Southern History*, XXIII (May, 1957), 189–202.
Heyman, Richard D. "C. T. Loram: A South African Liberal in Race Relations." *International Journal of African Historical Studies*, V (January, 1972), 41–50.
Hoffman, Edwin D. "From Slavery to Self-Reliance." *Journal of Negro History*, XXI (January, 1956), 8–42.
Hoogenboom, Ari. "Spoilsmen and Reformers: Civil Service Reform and Public Morality." *The Gilded Age: A Reappraisal*. Edited by H. Wayne Morgan. Syracuse: Syracuse University Press, 1963.
Jackson, Luther Porter. "The Educational Efforts of the Freedmen's Bureau and Freedmen's Aid Societies in South Carolina, 1862–1872." *Journal of Negro History*, VIII (January, 1923), 1–40.
———."The Origin of Hampton Institute.' *Journal of Negro History*, X (April, 1925), 131–49.
Johnson, Charles Spurgeon. "A Southern Negro's View of the South." *Journal of Negro Education*, XXVI (Winter, 1957), 4–9.
Johnson, Guion Griffis. "The Ideology of White Supremacy, 1876–1910." *James Sprunt Series in History and Political Science*, XXXI (1949), 124–56.
———."Southern Paternalism Toward Negroes after Emancipation." *Journal of Southern History*, XXIII (November, 1957), 483–509.
King, Andrew A. "Booker T. Washington and the Myth of Heroic Materialism." *Quarterly Journal of Speech*, LX (October, 1974), 323–27.
Leavell, Ullin Whitney. "Trends of Philanthropy in Negro Education: A Survey." *Journal of Negro Education*, II (January, 1933), 38–52.
Locke, Alain. "The Unfinished Business of Democracy." *Survey-Graphic*, November, 1942, pp. 455–59.
McNeil, Bertha. Review of *Homes of the Freed*, by Rossa Belle Cooley. *Opportunity*, March, 1927, p. 89.
McPherson, James. "White Liberals and Black Power in Negro Education, 1865–1915." *American Historical Review*, LXXV (June, 1970), 1357–85.
Meier, August. "The Beginning of Industrial Education in Negro Schools." *Midwest Journal*, VII (Spring, 1955), 23–44.
Melish, J. Howard. "George Foster Peabody." *Religion in Life* (Winter, 1938), 85–96.
Miller, Carroll L. "Educational Opportunities and the Negro Child in the South." *Harvard Educational Review*, XXX (Summer, 1960), 195–208.
Miller, Richmond P. "What Is a Quaker?" *A Guide to the Religions of America*. Edited by Leo Rosten. New York: Simon and Schuster, 1955.

Morsell, John A. "Schools, Courts, and the Negro's Future." *Harvard Educational Review*, XXX (Summer, 1960), 179-94.
Ovington, Mary White. Review of *Homes of the Freed*, by Rossa Belle Cooley, Norfolk *Journal and Guide*, April 2, 1927.
Pease, William H. "Three Years Among the Freedmen: William Channing Gannett and the Port Royal Experiment." *Journal of Negro History*, XLII (April, 1957), 98-117.
Pierce, Edward L. "The Freedmen of Port Royal." *The Atlantic Monthly*, September, 1863, pp. 291-95.
Reed, Roy. "Blacks in South Struggle to Keep the Little Land They Have Left." New York *Times*, December 7, 1962.
Robbins, Gerald. "Laura Towne: White Pioneer in Negro Education, 1862-1901." *Journal of Education*, CXLIII (April, 1961), 40-54.
———. "Rossa B. Cooley and Penn School: Social Dynamo in a Negro Rural Subculture, 1901-1930." *Journal of Negro Education*, XXXIII (Winter, 1964), 43-51.
Smith, Timothy L. "Progressivism in American Education, 1880-1900." *Harvard Educational Review*, XXXI (Spring, 1961), 168-93.
Smuts, Robert W. "The Negro Community and the Development of Negro Potential." *Journal of Negro Education*, XXVI (Fall, 1957), 456-65.
Szwed, John F. "Africa Lies Just off Georgia: Sea Islands Preserve Origins of Afro-American Culture." *Africa Report*, XV (October, 1970), 29-31.
Thompson, Charles H. "The Negro College: In Retrospect and in Prospect." *Journal of Negro Education*, XXVII (Spring, 1958), 127-31.
Wish, Harvey. "Negro Education and the Progressive Movement." *Journal of Negro History*, XLIX (July, 1964), 184-200.
Woodson, Carter Godwin. "The Mis-education of the Negro." *Crisis*, XL (August, 1931), 266-67.
Woodward, Comer Vann. "The South in Perspective." *Progressive*, December, 1962, pp. 12-17.

Pamphlets

Brinton, Howard H. *Quaker Education in Theory and Practice*. Pendle Hill Pamphlet Number Nine. Wallingford, Pennsylvania, 1940.
Brawley, Benjamin. *Early Effort for Industrial Education*. Slater Fund Occasional Papers Number 22. Baltimore: John F. Slater Fund, 1923.
Dabbs, Edith Mitchell. *Walking Tall*. Frogmore, S.C.: Penn Community Services, 1964.
Embree, Edwin Rogers. *Every Tenth Pupil: The Story of Negro Schools in the South*. Chicago: Julius Rosenwald Fund, n.d.
Fant, Cora O. *Tuskegee Institute Bulletin*. Tuskegee, Alabama: Tuskegee Institute Press, 1939.
McCuiston, Fred. *The South's Negro Teaching Force*. Nashville, Tenn.: Julius Rosenwald Fund, 1931.
Museum of Modern Art *The Hampton Album*. Garden City, N.Y.: Doubleday, 1966.

School Money in Black and White. Chicago: Julius Rosenwald Fund, 1934.
Wayland, Edward M. *Howard Anderson Kester, 1923–1972.* Announcement of Kester papers for Microfilming Corporation of America, 1974. (Mimeographed)

Bibliographies, Dictionaries, and Encyclopedias

Crawford, Mary C. *Famous Families of Massachusetts.* 2 vols. Boston: Little, Brown, 1930.
Miller, Elizabeth W. *The Negro in America: A Bibliography.* Cambridge: Harvard University Press, 1966.
The National Cyclopedia of American Biography. New York: James T. White, 1930.
Virkus, Frederick A., ed. *The Abridged Compendium of American Genealogy: First Families of America.* Chicago: F. A. Virkus, 1925.
Who's Who In America: A Biographical Dictionary of Notable Men and Women. 32 vols. Chicago: A. N. Marquis, 1899–1962.
Who Was Who In America: A Companion Biographical Work to "Who's Who in America," 1897–1960. 3 vols. Chicago: A. N. Marquis, 1942–1960.

Reports and Proceedings

America's Race Problems: Addresses at the Annual Meeting of the American Academy of Political and Social Science, Philadelphia, April 12–13, 1901. Philadelphia: 1901.
General Education Board. Annual Report, 1915–1932. New York: GEB, 1932.
―――. *The General Education Board: An Account of Its Activities from 1902–1914.* New York: GEB, 1914.
Phelps-Stokes Fund. *The Twenty-Year Report of the Phelps-Stokes Fund, 1911–1931.* New York: Phelps-Stokes Fund, 1932.
Proceedings of the Trustees of the John F. Slater Fund for the Education of Freedmen, 1888–1936. Washington, D.C.: John F. Slater Fund, 1936.
Recent Social Trends in the United States: Report of the President's Research Committee on Social Trends. Vol. I. New York: McGraw-Hill, 1933.
Southern Society for the Promotion of the Study of Race Conditions and Problems of the South. *Race Problems of the South: Proceedings of the First Annual Conference.* Richmond, Va.: Southern Society, 1900.

Index

Abolitionists, 9*n*, 25, 28, 45
African education, 170–74, 200
Agriculture: training program, 2, 49–52, 67–71, 77–81, 85, 198, 255; demonstration farms, 51, 68, 69, 77–81; new methods, 51, 69–70, 79–80; traditional methods, 69–70, 93–94, 144–46; problems, 78–79, 138–40, 185–86, 202–205, 218–19; loans, 84–86, 94, 141, 143–46, 185, 216–17, 251, 261; importance of, 112, 115; cooperative farming, 210–13; training program critiqued, 235, 248, 260–61. *See also* Cotton production
Alexander, Will W., 208–210, 214, 216
All-year school, 132, 134–36, 272
Armstrong, Samuel Chapman, 6, 8, 9, 11, 12, 40, 42, 132–33, 161

Baby Day, 152–53
Bailey, Ethel, 115, 116, 234, 246
Bailey, Liberty Hyde, 44
Bailey, York, 76, 92, 246
Baker, Newton, 128
Baker, Ray Stannard, 91
Ballanta, Nicholas Julius, 124
Barnwell, Benjamin, 115, 126, 129, 131, 145, 164, 205, 212, 214, 222, 224, 245
Barnwell, Grace, 115
Belmont, Mrs. August, 223
Bethune, Mary McLeod, 215
Better Homes Program. *See* Home Improvements

Black education, xi–xiii, 9, 10, 25–27, 33–34, 99
Black migration, 44–45, 71–72, 139, 184–85, 215, 255–56, 262
Black music, 124–28, 165–66, 183
Black Yeomanry (Woofter), 181–89
Blake, Herman, 251
Blanton, Joshua Enoch: agricultural improvements, 68–70, 77, 92; as demonstration agent, 78, 79, 80, 81; St. Helena Cooperative Society, 84–85; special projects, 89, 90, 92, 128, 130, 164; leaves Penn School, 145; and Kester, 245
Boll weevil, 77, 138–40, 163, 185, 261
Boyd, Benjamin F., 115, 129, 154, 246
Boyd, Catherine Gregory, 115, 116, 246
Brown, Aurelius, 115, 222, 234
Brown, George, 115
Building program: Penn School, 62, 88–90, 179, 221, 225; community hall, 153–55; county schools 194–97
Burlin, Natalie Curtis-, 123–24, 127
Burwell, W. Harris, 154
Butler, Frances Cora, 54–55, 57
Buttrick, Wallace, 47, 52–53, 65, 78, 84, 96

Caliver, Ambrose, 197
Carnegie Corporation, 225
Carney, Mabel, 98, 171
Character-building: as rationale for industrial education, xii–xiii, 9*n*, 12–22

passim, 53, 118; as formulated at Hampton Institute, 2–3, 5, 6, 8–9, 11, 12–13, 33, 191–92; as basis for northern support of Penn School, 4–5, 10, 99–100; as implemented at Penn School, 6–7, 10, 39, 43, 46, 49–51, 160–61, 187, 219, 233, 254–56, 262–63, 265
Chase, Salmon P., 25
Child care. *See* Baby Day
Christensen, Niels, Jr., 52
Churches, 105–107. *See also* Religious practices
Civil War, 24–28
Community Council, Penn School, 114–15, 195, 257
Community development, 64–65, 92–94, 114–15, 153–55, 197, 250–51, 256, 261–62
Community education, 52, 68, 74–77, 81, 99, 136, 147–50, 197
Community hall, 153–55
Community Sings, 125, 126*n*
Cooley, Rossa Belle: educational goals, 15, 63, 159–61; appointed to Penn School, 53–55; and Frissell, 55, 57–58, 67, 73, 88, 96, 169; relation to former principals, 55, 65–66; arrival at Penn School, 56–58; criticisms of Penn School, 62–63; description, 63–64; workload, 91, 155–56, 226; tribute to Frissell, 95–96; concept of religion, 101–104, 107–11, 118–19; view of blacks, 118, 159–61, 192, 264; and World War I, 128–30; life on St. Helena Island, 155–59; fund raising, 177–78, 226–27, 233; management strategies, 200–201; depression programs, 206–17; leadership declines, 235–36; feelings about Penn School, 238–40; replaced, 240–41; reaction to Reid report, 250
Cooperative spirit, 84–86, 114–15, 255
Cooperative Society, St. Helena, 84–86, 94, 141, 143–44, 185, 217, 261
Cope, Francis: description, 40–41; decisions about Penn School, 51, 53, 56, 78, 128, 142, 169; tribute to Frissell, 96; and school finances, 163–65, 173, 179, 228–29; as chairman of the board, 167, 168; and Woofter study, 182; replaced Cooley, 234–36, 240–41; and Kester, 244, 245, 250; mentioned, 88, 89, 218

Cotton production, 25, 48, 69, 77, 79, 80, 93, 138–40, 213, 214
Country Life Movement, 98
County schools, 193–97, 248–49. *See also* Public school system
Credit Union, St. Helena, 144–46, 217, 251
Curtis, George William, 123
Curtis, Isabella, 169–70, 177, 240
Curtis-Burlin, Natalie, 123–24, 127

Dabbs, James McBride, 251
Davis, Jackson, 98, 198, 199, 214
Dawkins, P. W., 47–55, 67–68
Demonstration programs: farm demonstration, 51, 68, 69, 77–81; home demonstration, 52, 73, 81
Depression, 202–17
Dewey, John, 58, 132–33, 136, 238
Diet, 48, 49, 51, 52, 69, 70, 77, 81, 146, 147, 148, 213, 257
Dillard, James Hardy, 96, 151
Du Bois, W. E. B., 2, 3*n*, 188–90
Dudley, Moses, 71
DuPont, Samuel Francis, 24

"Education for life," 6, 11, 18–20, 63
Eliot, Charles W., 11, 40
Elting, Arthur, 203, 211
Emergency Relief Administration, 205–208

Farmers' conferences, 49–52, 68, 70
Farming. *See* Agriculture
Farm loans, 84–86, 94, 141, 143–46, 185, 216–17, 251, 261
Fiftieth anniversary of Penn School, 86–88, 90–91
Financial difficulties, 162–64, 166–67, 178–79, 220–23, 225, 236–37, 259. *See also* Fund raising
Flynt, C. B., 115
Flynt, William, 115
Foote, Frances Eliot, 57
Foote, Henry Wilder, 40
Ford, Henry, 166
Foundations. *See* Fund raising
Frazier, E. Franklin, 189
Fripp, Fred, 115, 222, 234
Frissell, A. Sidney, 155, 177
Frissell, Hollis Burke: goals for Hampton Institute, 11, 12–13, 33–34, 90; description, 32–33; interest in Penn School, 32, 34, 37–38, 232; and first

Penn School Board of Trustees, 39–45 *passim*; appointed Cooley, 53–54; supported Cooley, 55, 57–58, 67, 73, 88, 96, 169; and improved farming methods, 77–79; and cooperative activities, 84, 94, 153; tributes to, 95–96, 153–55; and school finances, 162, 165, 169; mentioned, 47, 168, 177, 178, 238, 253
Frissell Memorial Community House, 153–55
Fund raising: buildings, 89, 153–54, 179, 221, 225; operating expenses, 98–100, 164–66, 170, 173–79, 223–27, 229, 233; foundations, 98–100, 170, 174–76, 221, 225, 227, 229; endowment, 165, 179; private donors, 163, 174–75, 223, 225, 227, 229; state assistance, 196–200, 205–208; federal assistance, 208–11, 214–16; farm loans, 216–17; publicity film, 228–31. *See also* General Education Board
Furness, William, 28, 38

Gadson, John W., 251
General Education Board: evaluation of Penn School, 49, 52–53; building funds, 89, 179; funds for Penn School, 98–99, 134, 164–65, 167, 170, 173–75, 179, 225; special programs, 200, 217, 229; mentioned, 78, 91, 122, 198, 199
Goals of Penn School, xi–xiii, 31, 71–72, 116, 118, 160–61, 254–55
Gregg, James Edgar, 44, 174, 175, 177, 178, 191
Gullah dialect, 35, 35n–36n

Hamilton, Solomon, Jr., 217
Hampton Institute: goals, xii–xiii, 2, 5, 84, 189, 190, 255; program, 11–12, 14, 33; as model for Penn School, xi, xii, 10; difficulties, 191–92; trustees, 41, 42; mentioned, 32, 37, 38, 112, 115, 166, 174, 248
Harkness, Edward S., 177
Hart, Albert Bushnell, 97, 265
Health care, 29, 75–76, 81, 91–94, 150–53, 184
Higginson, Thomas Wentworth, 87
Homans, Marian, 90
Home improvements, 52, 73–74, 81, 146–50, 184, 248, 255, 262
Hookworm, 92–93
House, Grace Bigelow: educational goals, 14, 118; description, 58–60, 63–64,
156–59; school activities, 91, 108, 111, 226; feelings about school, 238–40; retirement, 246
House Blessing, 106–107
Hudgens, R. W., 210, 211, 213
Hurricanes, 82–83, 208, 218, 226

Industrial education: aims, xi–xiii, 2, 5–6, 10, 18–21, 133, 255; criticisms, 2–3, 9, 21, 22, 189–90; versus vocational education, 5–6, 133; underlying assumptions, 7–9, 33–34; based on service ideal, 14, 17, 40, 41, 59, 86, 110; fostered service ideal in students, 65, 86, 110–12, 118, 131; northern support, 4–5, 7–10, 15–17, 43–46; as missionary effort, 17, 20, 43, 54, 58, 60, 67, 102, 112, 117–19, 192, 257. *See also* Character-building
Industrial training, 88–89, 235–36, 248, 255, 261

James, Arthur Curtiss: description, 41–42; financial contributions, 70, 89, 158, 163, 174, 178, 223, 225; death, 231
Jeanes Fund, 98, 151
Jenks, Helen Carnan Towne, 38
Jenks, Robert Darrah, 39–40, 41, 53, 54, 56, 67
Jenks, Mrs. William Furness, 37, 38, 39
Johnson, Guion Griffis, 183
Johnson, Guy Benton, 125, 183
Jones, Thomas Jesse: as proponent of industrial education and Negro education, 6, 99–100, 182; and Woofter, 189; mentioned, 12, 96, 130, 170–76 *passim*

Kellogg, Paul Underwood, 143, 184, 187, 223
Kester, Howard Anderson, 241–46, 250
Keyserling, Leon, 208
Keyserling, William, 86, 94, 207–14 *passim*
King, James Plato, 113, 115, 117, 129, 130, 145, 235, 245
Kiser, Clyde Vernon, 178, 183, 185
Knapp, Bradford, 81
Knapp, Seaman, 78–80, 84, 190

Landownership: importance, 27, 256, 260; problems, 140–44, 203–204, 210; loans for, 216–17
Langston, John Mercer, 264
Lathrop, Miss Alice, 48, 53, 54, 55, 65–67

Lindsay, Lady Elizabeth, 223
Loram, Charles Templeman, 170, 172, 176, 224
Lumpkins, Linnie, 68, 113

Macdonald, James Ross, 42, 88
Macdonald, Wilkins, and Company, 42
Mason, Rosetta, 73, 113, 115
Maule, Alfred Collins, 41, 95, 223
Medical care. *See* Health care
Midwives, 151–52
Migration to cities, 44–45, 71–72, 139, 184–85, 215, 255–56, 262
Mills, W. H., 144, 207–208, 213, 214, 216, 218, 227
Mitchell, Samuel Chiles, 87, 98
Moors, Ethel Paine, 43, 241
Moral development. *See* Character-building
Morehouse, Henry L., 20n
Moton, Robert Russa, 68, 116–17, 155, 159–60
Murray, Ellen, 29–31, 38, 42, 48, 49, 53–55, 65–67, 74, 103, 110
Mystery play, 108–110

National Urban League, 41
Ndulamo, 158, 183, 246
Northern fears of black degradation, 15–17, 20, 27n, 97, 253–54, 267
Northern support for Penn School, 90–91, 98–100, 177–78, 248, 253–54

Ogden, Robert, 59

Paternalism, 10, 95, 249, 256–58, 264–65
Patriotism, 125–31
Peabody, Francis Greenwood, 17–20, 40
Peabody, George Foster: description, 42, 120–23; Negro music, 124–26, 165–66; and World War I, 126–28, 130; Frissell memorial, 155; and Cooley, 158; chairman of board, 163, 165–67, 168; financial donor, 174–75; death, 231; mentioned, 47, 154, 179, 183, 208
Penn Community Services, Inc., 250
Penn School Quartette, 126, 166, 223–24
Phelps-Stokes Fund, 98, 99, 170, 173–76, 182
Pierce, Edward L., 25
Plunkett, Horace, 84, 85
Port Royal Experiment, xi, 25–28, 267
Praise houses, 104–105, 107

Price, Mabel, 115
Progressive education, 10–14, 15, 18, 58–60, 132–33, 257
Public health. *See* Health care
Public school system, 52, 74, 193–97, 248–49
Puritan work ethic, 8–9, 12

Quaker beliefs, 40–41
Reorganizations of Penn School, 32–34, 37–38, 53, 62–63, 240–41, 248–51
Reid, Ira DeAugustine, 246
Reid Report, 246–50
Religious practices on St. Helena, 101–11
Resettlement Administration, 208–14
Rockefeller, John D., 166
Rockefeller Sanitary Commission, 92
Roosevelt, Theodore, 44
Rose, Wickliffe, 174
Rosenwald, Julius, 99, 178, 194–95
Rosenwald Fund, 225
Routh, F. M., 92
Rural rehabilitation program, 206–16
Russell, James Earl, 59
Russell, William Channing, 39

St. Helena Island: description, 34–36, 101; isolation, 34, 73–74; primitive conditions, 48, 72–73, 147–48; isolation threatened, 142; Woofter study, 183–87; economic crises, 202–205, 208, 210
Saxton, Rufus, 26n
Seabrook, Philip, 198
Sharpless, Isaac, 39
Shout, the, 106
Siceloff, Courtney, 250–51
Silver, John, 227–29
Slater Fund, 98, 151, 170
Smalls, Robert, 87
Smith, W. W., 217
Smith-Hughes Act, 81
Smith-Lever Act, 81
Southern Education Board, 122
Southerners: and Negro education, 9, 10; and Penn School, 98, 201; as trustees, 42, 251
Spencer, Herbert, 63
Stimson, Mrs. Henry L., 43
Stokes, Anson Phelps, 96, 175
Strieby, Michael, 9n

Taft, William Howard, 32

Tate William Knox, 43, 91–92
Taylor, G. L., 124
Teachers at Penn School, 112–17, 129–30, 222, 232, 234, 248, 262
Teacher training, 74, 199–200
Thorne, Charlotte, 37
Towne, Henry Robinson, 28
Towne, John Henry, 28*n*
Towne, Laura, 23, 28–32, 37, 38, 40, 42, 48, 74, 102, 103, 110, 147–48
Trask, Katrina, 120–21, 123, 156
Trask, Spencer, 120–21, 123
Trustees: first board, 38–43; motivations, 43–46; lack of leadership, 168–69; successor to Cooley, 240–41; and Kester, 245–46; Penn Community Services, Inc., 251
Tugwell, Rexford Guy, 208
Tuskegee Institute, xi–xiii, 2, 14, 37, 49, 155, 164, 166
Typhoid, 91–93

Visitors to Penn School, 90, 156, 172, 176, 200, 223–25
Vocational education, 5–6. *See also* Industrial training

Washington, Benjamin H., 115, 234
Washington, Booker T., 1–2, 6, 9, 18, 47, 49, 155
Washington, D. C., 150
Washington, Martin V., 178
Weatherford, Willis Duke, 98
Wildy, Maurice, 115, 116
Williams, Aubrey, 216
Wilson, M. L. 214
Women, programs for, 72–75, 81, 152–53, 262
Wood, L. Hollingsworth, 41, 166–68, 208, 229, 241
Woofter, Thomas Jackson, 181–89, 208, 214
Works Progress Administration, 209
World War I, 125–31
World War II, 218, 232–33, 262
Wright, Lottye, 115
Wright, Marion, 251

Youth activities at Penn School, 80, 108–11, 130, 134–36, 149–50, 215–17